THE HUMAN ECONOMY

THE HUMAN ECONOMY

A CITIZEN'S GUIDE

EDITED BY
KEITH HART, JEAN-LOUIS LAVILLE AND
ANTONIO DAVID CATTANI

polity

The chapters by Anne Salmon, Alfonso Cotera Fretell and Humberto Ortiz Roca, Alain Caillé, Philip S. Golub and Jean-Paul Maréchal, François-Xavier Merrien and Angèle Flora Mendy, Jean-Michel Servet, Jean-Louis Laville, Jacques Defourny, Jérôme Blanc, and Adalbert Evers appeared originally in French in *Dictionnaire de l'autre économie* edited by Jean-Louis Laville and Antonio David Cattani © Desclée de Brouwer, 2006

First published in 2010 by Polity Press

Polity Press
65 Bridge Street
Cambridge CB2 1UR, UK

Polity Press
350 Main Street
Malden, MA 02148, USA

ISBN-13: 978-0-7456-4979-5 (hardback)
ISBN-13: 978-0-7456-4980-1 (paperback)

A catalogue record for this book is available from the British Library.

Typeset in 10.5 on 12 pt Garamond MT Pro
by Servis Filmsetting Ltd, Stockport, Cheshire

The publisher has used its best endeavours to ensure that the URLs for external websites referred to in this book are correct and active at the time of going to press. However, the publisher has no responsibility for the websites and can make no guarantee that a site will remain live or that the content is or will remain appropriate.

Every effort has been made to trace all copyright holders, but if any have been inadvertently overlooked the publishers will be pleased to include any necessary credits in any subsequent reprint or edition.

For further information on Polity, visit our website: www.politybooks.com

CONTENTS

NOTES ON CONTRIBUTORS

Catherine Alexander is a Reader in Anthropology at Goldsmiths, University of London. After voluntary work and then working for central government in Britain and Turkey, she was trained in anthropology. An economic and political anthropologist, her interests are in property relations, urban anthropology, waste and the third sector. She has worked in Turkey, Britain and Kazakhstan. Her books include *Personal States: Making Connections between People and Bureaucracy in Turkey* (2002).

Jérôme Blanc is Associate Professor of Economics at University Lumière Lyon 2 and a member of the LEFI research centre. His works deal with money, through its uses and the history of monetary ideas. He works on plural money forms, especially community and complementary currencies. His books include *Les Monnaies parallèles: Unité et diversité du fait monétaire* (2000) and (editor) *Monnaies sociales: Exclusion et liens financiers, rapport 2005–06* (2006).

John M. Bryden is a Research Professor with the Norwegian Agricultural Economics Research Institute (NILF) in Oslo and President of the International Rural Network. He is Emeritus Professor at the University of Aberdeen, where he co-directed the Arkleton Centre for Rural Development Research. He has published on tourism, agrarian change, land reform and community development. Trained in political economy, he has been a development economist, human geographer and farmer.

Alain Caillé is Professor of Sociology at the University of Paris X, Nanterre, and co-director of SOPHIAPOL (Laboratoire de sociologie, philosophie, anthropologie, politiques). He is a leading member of MAUSS (The Anti-Utilitarian Movement in the Social Sciences) and editor of its journal, *La Revue du MAUSS*. His books include *Anthropologie du don. Le Tiers paradigme* (2000), *Théorie anti-utilitariste de l'action* (2009) and with Jacques Gobout *The World of the Gift* (2000).

Antonio David Cattani is Professor of Sociology and member of the Postgraduate Sociology Institute Board at the Universidade Federal do Rio Grande do Sul (Porto Alegre, Brazil); also a 1A grade researcher for the Brazilian National Science and Technology Research Centre. His books include *Dicionário de trabalho e Tecnologia* (2009), *Dicionário Internacional da Outra Economia* (2009) and *Diccionario de la otra Economía* (2009). His current research is on the sociology of inequality and wealth, social class and power (http://antoniodavid-cattani.net).

José Luis Coraggio is Research Professor and Academic Director of a Master's in Social Economy at the National University of General Sarmiento, Argentina. He co-ordinates the Network of Latin American Researchers on Social and Solidarity Economy (RILESS www.riless.org). His research is on popular economy, the economics of work, local development and social policy. He has written and edited twenty-five books including *Política social y economía del trabajo* (1999), *La Economía Social desde la Periferia* (2007) and *¿Qué es lo económico?* (2009). He is a co-editor of *Diccionario de la otra Economía* (2009).

Alfonso Cotera Fretel is a social activist and consultant for local development, solidarity economy, fair trade, social finance, social tourism and alternative communications. He has a number of publications in all these areas. He currently serves as Executive Director of the Solidarity Economy Network of Peru (GRESP), the Peruvian Network of Fair Trade and Ethical Consumption (RPCJyCE) and the Latin American Office of Co-ordination for Fair Trade.

Jacques Defourny is Professor of Economics and a director of the Centre for Social Economy (www.ces-ulg.be) at the University of Liège, Belgium. He was a founding co-ordinator and president of the EMES European Research Network (2002–10) which co-ordinates eleven university research centres specialized in social enterprise and third-sector studies (www.emes.net). He is the author or editor of twelve books including, as co-editor, *The Emergence of Social Enterprise* (2001). His current work focuses on emerging forms of social enterprise in third-sector development across the world.

Thomas Hylland Eriksen is a social anthropologist at the University of Oslo, where he was research manager of the interdisciplinary project 'Cultural Complexity in the New Norway' and is now directing a project on place and identity in a multi-ethnic Oslo suburb. He has written extensively on globalization and identity politics. His books include *Engaging Anthropology* (2005), *Globalization: The Key Issues* (2007) and (co-editor) *A World of Insecurity* (2010). Eriksen's website, since 1996, is http://folk.uio.no/geirthe.

Adalbert Evers is Professor of Politics at the Justus-Liebig University of Giessen in Germany. He is co-editor of the series 'Sociology and Social Policy' published by Verlag für Sozialwissenschaften and has written a number of works including as co-author *Balancing Pluralism* (1993), *Developing Quality in Personal Social Services: Concepts, Cases and Comments* (1997) and *The Third Sector in Europe* (with Jean-Louis Laville, 2004).

Philip S. Golub, an American author living in Paris, teaches International Relations and International Political Economy at the Institute of European Studies, University of Paris 8 and at the American University of Paris. He is a contributing editor of *Le monde diplomatique*. His research is mainly on the historical sociology of international relations, especially the construction of hierarchy and inequality in the late modern world system. He is the author of *Power, Profit and Prestige: A History of American Imperial Expansion* (2010).

David Graeber is Reader in Social Anthropology at Goldsmiths, University of London. He has written on value, debt, direct action, magic, violence, Malagasy mortuary ritual, and many other topics.

Over the years he has worked with a number of groups dedicated to developing direct democracy and getting rid of capitalism. These range from People's Global Action to Industrial Workers of the World.

Chris Hann is a Director of the Max Planck Institute for Social Anthropology in Halle, Eastern Germany. He is an economic anthropologist with a special interest in property relations. He has carried out fieldwork in Hungary and Poland during both socialist and post-socialist periods, in rural Turkey and in China. His books include *'Not the Horse We Wanted!': Postsocialism, Neoliberalism and Eurasia* (2006).

Keith Hart lives in Paris, where he collaborates with several French intellectuals, and is currently Honorary Research Professor at the University of Kwazulu-Natal, Durban. He is an economic anthropologist who contributed the concept of the informal economy to development studies. His books include *The Memory Bank: Money in an Unequal World* (2000). He recently founded an online association, the Open Anthropology Co-operative, and has an active blog at http://thememorybank.co.uk.

Lars Hulgård is a Professor at Roskilde University, Denmark who founded the Centre for Social Entrepreneurship in 2007 http://www.ruc.dk/paes/cse/. He also founded the CINEFOGO-Network of Excellence, an international cross-disciplinary network on civil society and new forms of governance. He was co-founder of the European EMES Network and is now president http://www.emes.net). He has been a member of the executive committee of the National Association on Social Policy and president of the Danish Sociological Association. Research interests include social enterprise, social economy and solidarity economy.

Jean-Louis Laville is a Professor of Sociology and Economics at the Conservatoire national des arts et métiers, Paris (http://relations-service.cnam.fr), researcher in Lise (CNRS.Cnam) and European co-ordinator of the Karl Polanyi Institute of Political Economy (http://polanyi.concordia.ca/). He was a founding member of the EMES European Research Network and is a member of the board (http://www.emes.net). He is also a founding member of the Riless (www.riless.org). His numerous books include *L'économie solidair* (2007), *Politique de l'association* (2010), *The Third Sector in Europe* (2004, co-author), *Tackling Social Exclusion in Europe* (2001, co-editor). He is co-editor of *Dicionário da Outra Economia* (2009) and of *Diccionario de la otra Economía* (2009).

David Lewis is an anthropologist working on international development policy and practice with organizations such as Oxfam GB, BRAC Bangladesh and Concern Worldwide. He is Professor of Social Policy and Development at the London School of Economics and Political Science, where his research includes the ethnography of policy processes, the non-governmental sector and the political economy of Bangladesh. He is co-author of *Anthropology, Development and the Postmodern Challenge* (1996) and *Nongovernmental Organizations and Development* (2008). See www.personal.lse.ac.uk/lewisd/.

Desmond McNeill is a Professor at SUM (Centre for Development and the Environment), University of Oslo. He was a lecturer at University College London, where he wrote his PhD, 'Fetishism and the Value-Form: Towards a General Theory of Value'. He is co-author of *Global Institutions and Development: Framing the World?* (2004), *Development Issues in Global Governance: Public–Private Partnerships and Market Multilateralism* (2007) and *Global Poverty, Ethics and Human Rights: The Role of Multilateral Organizations* (2009). See http://www.sum.uio.no/staff/mcneill-desmond.html.

Jean-Paul Maréchal is Associate Professor of Economics at the University of Rennes 2. He is a researcher at the Institute for Applied Mathematics and Economics and a member of Political and Ethical Knowledge on Economic activities. His research is on economic ethics, environmental economics, sustainable development and epistemology. He has published over one hundred articles and five books including *Humaniser l'économie* (prize of the French Academy of Moral and Political Sciences in 2001).

Paulo Henrique Martins lives in Recife, Brazil. He is Professor of Sociology at the Federal Universtiy of Pernambuco (UFPE) and a 1C grade researcher for the Brazilian National Science and Technology Research Centre (CNPq). He is an associate member of the Mouvement Anti-Utilitariste en Sciences Sociales (MAUSS). He is currently vice-president of the Latin American Sociological Asociation (ALAS) and chair of the commitee that is organizing the ALAS meeting to be held in Recife in September 2011.

Angèle Flora Mendy is a PhD student at the University of Lausanne and Research Assistant at IHEID, Geneva, Switzerland. She holds a master's degree in sociology (University of Saint-Louis, Senegal) and a master's degree in globalization studies (University of Lausanne). Her current research interests include international migration of health workers and gender and development. (angeleflora.mendy@ unil.ch).

François-Xavier Merrien is Professor at the Faculty of Social and Political Science at Lausanne University, Switzerland and an international expert. His current research interests include social protection, poverty reduction strategies, developing countries, donors and the New World Order. (francoisxavier.merrien@unil.ch).

Julie A. Nelson is a feminist economist, a founding member of the International Association for Feminist Economics (www. iaffe.org) and a Professor in the Department of Economics at the University of Massachusetts Boston. She is also a Senior Research Fellow at the Global Development and Environment Institute (www.gdae.org) and participates in groups working on climate change and economics education. One of her books is *Economics for Humans* (2006).

Marthe Nyssens is a Professor at the Catholic University of Louvain, Belgium, where, as a social economist, she co-ordinates a research team in the Centre for Interdisciplinary Research on Work-State-Society (CIRTES). She works on conceptual approaches to the third sector, in developed and developing countries, and on links between third-sector organizations and public policy. Among her books is *Social Enterprise at the Crossroads of Market, Public Policies and Civil Society* (2006). She teaches on non-profit organizations, social policy and development theory and is a founding member of the EMES European Research Network (www.emes.net).

Sabine U. O'Hara is President of the US Society for Ecological Economics. She serves in Washington DC as executive director of the Council for International Exchange of Scholars and vice president of the Institute of International Education. She is a past president of Roanoke College and is well known for her expertise in sustainable economic development and global education.

Humberto Ortiz Roca is a Peruvian economist who organizes a course on development projects for the German Foundation for International Development (DSE) and several programmes promoting popular economy. He is responsible for several projects concerned with solidarity economy, is a member of several international networks, was on the organizing committee of the Third International Meeting for Solidarity Economy (held in Dakar, 2005) and is President of the Solidarity Economy Network of Peru.

Vishnu Padayachee is Senior Professor and Head of the School of Development Studies at the University of KwaZulu-Natal, Durban. He is an Associate of Cambridge University's African Studies Centre, has served as non-executive director of the South African Reserve Bank and co-owns Ike's Books and Collectables. A political economist, his research interests include macroeconomic policy; finance, banking and monetary policy; and the politics of race and sport. He is editor of *The Political Economy of Africa* (2010).

Geoffrey Pleyers teaches global studies and the sociology of social movements at the University of Louvain and the École des Hautes Études en Sciences Sociales. He is a research fellow of the Belgian Foundation for Scientific Research at Louvain and a visiting fellow at LSE's Global Governance. His fieldwork includes seven World Social Forums and alter-globalization networks in Western Europe and Latin America. His latest book is *Alter-Globalization: Becoming Actor in the Global Age* (2010). He is now researching grassroots movements for sustainable and convivial food.

Leandro Raizer is a researcher in the sociology of development and environment, science and technology and alternative energy sources. He currently works on renewable and alternative energies at the international level, with an emphasis on energy production of renewable in Brazil and Canada. This research is conducted with the support of the Federal University of Rio Grande do Sul, Brazil and the University of Montreal, Canada.

Arnaud Sales is Emeritus Professor of Sociology at the Université de Montréal (Canada). He is an economic sociologist, focusing on private–public relations. Among his books are *The International Handbook of Sociology* (with Stella Quah, 2000) and *Knowledge, Communication and Creativity* (with Marcel Fournier, 2007). He is currently working on a book for Sage Publications entitled *Social Transformations in a Globalizing World*.

Anne Salmon is a Professor of Sociology at the Paul Verlaine University, Metz. Her current research interests are in ethics and economics. Her publications include: *Ethique et ordre économique. Une entreprise de séduction* (2002), (co-editor) *Responsabilité sociale et environnementale de l'entreprise* (2005), (co-author) 'Ethique, économie et société – Une affaire de politique?', *European Journal of Economic and Social Systems* (2006) and *Moraliser le capitalisme?* (2009).

Jean-Michel Servet is a Professor in the Graduate Institute of International and Development Studies, for whom he teaches in Geneva and Peru. He collaborates in interdisciplinary research, especially with the Institute for Development Research in Paris. He has published widely on the history of economic thought and on the social economics of money and finance. His books include *Banquiers aux pieds nus: La Microfinance* (2006), *Le Grand Renversement: De la crise au renouveau solidaire* (2010).

Felix Stalder lives in Vienna and is a lecturer in theories of media and society at the Zurich University of the Arts. He is a researcher and activist focusing on new forms of cultural production, surveillance, control and subjectivity, and new patterns of spatial organization. He has been a moderator of the nettime mailing list since 1998 and has organized numerous international conferences in Europe and beyond. See felix.openflows.com for publications.

Marilyn Taylor lives in Bristol, UK and has long researched and written about community participation. She is Emeritus Professor at the University of the West of England and Visiting Research Fellow at the Institute for Voluntary Action Research. She is a Trustee of the British Association of Settlements and Social Action Centres, a member of the Advisory Council for the National Council for Voluntary Organizations in England and on the editorial boards of *Voluntas* and *Community Development Journal*. She is writing a second edition of *Public Policy in the Community*.

John Urry is Distinguished Professor of Sociology, Lancaster University. He was educated in economics and sociology at Cambridge; is Founding Academician, Academy of Social Sciences and Editor, International Library of Sociology. He has published around forty books including *Mobilities* (2007), *After the Car* (2009), *Aeromobilities* (2009), *Mobile Lives* (2010), *Mobile Methods* (2010), *Climate Change and Society* (in preparation). His current research is on the implications of climate change and peak oil for social life.

1

Building the Human Economy Together

Keith Hart, Jean-Louis Laville and Antonio Cattani

We have just been through a prolonged social experiment in which markets and money were left to find their own way around the world without much political interference. This experiment has been called 'neoliberalism', at one time 'the Washington consensus'. The freedom of these markets was mainly for those with lots of money. The rest of us had to adjust; and society became much more unequal as a result. One victim of neoliberalism was certainly democracy in any meaningful sense. Then came the financial crisis of 2008, which provoked massive intervention by the most vulnerable governments, using taxpayers' money to save the banking system from collapse. No one knows whether capitalism, the winning side in the Cold War, will recover without fundamental change or if a major shift is taking place in its prime location, to China and other 'emerging markets' like India and Brazil. Neoliberalism has been wounded, but it is not yet defeated. In the meantime, what can we, the people, do about it? Surely the time is ripe to consider other possible ways forward?

Neoliberalism was and is at its core an Anglophone phenomenon. The Italian finance minister was only half joking when he said that his country's banks were in reasonable shape because their managers didn't speak English! (They are not, by the way.) The United States and Britain gained most from the credit boom and lost most when it went bust. The rest of the world had been told to join the neoliberal revolution or get used to life in the dustbin of history. The 'French social model' epitomized the lingering failure of post-war social democracy when strong states built up their economies by investing heavily in public services and enterprises. The relative attractiveness of the two models looks rather different now. But we are not here just to celebrate another swing of the pendulum from state to market and back again. It is time for the people to have their say in economic matters.

We want to bring to the attention of English readers some currents of economic theory and practice that have flourished in non-Anglophone countries over the last two decades, particularly in France, Brazil, Hispanic America and Scandinavia. To these we have added significant work by English-speaking authors that was sidelined during neoliberalism's heyday and deserves to find a wider audience now. We have brought these strands of new thinking together under the umbrella concept of 'the human economy' which refers to an emphasis both on what people do for themselves and on the need to find ways forward that must involve all of humanity somehow.

In the second half of the twentieth century, we formed a world society – a single interactive social network – for the first time. It was symbolized by several moments, such as when the 1960s space race allowed us to see the earth from the outside, or when the internet went public in the 1990s. This world is massively unequal and voices for human unity are often drowned. But now at last we have means of communication adequate to expressing universal ideas. Anthropologists and sociologists have shown that *Homo economicus* – the idea of an economy based on narrow self-interest, typified as the practice of buying cheap and selling dear – is absent from many societies and does not even reflect what is best about ourselves. We ought to be able to do better than that by now. But ideas alone are insufficient. Emergent world society *is* the new human universal – not an idea, but the fact of our shared occupation of the planet crying out for new principles of association. The essays assembled in this volume are intended as a contribution to that urgent project for our species.

Economics after the crash

The failure in September 2008 of the New York investment bank Lehman Brothers triggered a financial collapse whose ramifications are still with us. Predictions of the outcome of the ensuing global economic crisis vary widely. Following a sustained equities rally in 2009, some commentators argued that the recession that followed Lehman's demise is already over and the free market ready to assume its inexorable rise, while others talk of a double-dip recession, a sovereign debt crisis and a recovery that could take twenty-five years. After the fall of the Berlin Wall, it was claimed that the world had entered a new stage of economic evolution to which all countries would eventually have to conform, where money flowed without political restriction and the market penetrated everywhere. There were a few doubters, of course, who identified the shaky foundations of the boom long before it crashed. But it took courage then to go against the prevailing orthodoxy that all was best in the best of all worlds. What happened next did change a lot, if not everything.

Economic growth can now be seen to have been sustained by a regime of cheap consumer credit, especially in the United States; many banks and other financial houses, notably the insurance giant AIG, exposed themselves to unacceptable levels of risk, particularly in the new market for credit derivatives; these became 'toxic assets' which were bought by taxpayers at huge cost in order to preserve the banking system as a whole; access to loans dried up overnight, despite these government subsidies; the leading exporters of manufactures, such as China, Germany and Japan, suffered massive reductions in demand for their products; the newly 'liberated' Eastern Europeans went into free fall, as did countries like Ireland (hitherto a 'Celtic tiger') and Spain, not to mention little Iceland; despite governments printing money like there was no tomorrow, the threat of deflation was real; business bankruptcies and rising unemployment contributed to the economic malaise in rich and poor countries alike.

The economy, which had been represented as an eternally benevolent machine for growth, was suddenly pitch-forked into the turmoil of history. The chattering classes rediscovered the 1930s. The market was now seen to require massive state intervention if it were to have any chance of surviving. The financial 'masters of the universe' quickly brought out the begging bowl and in some cases had to suffer nationalization. Anglophone governments who once claimed to be leading the world to a free-market future desperately embraced remedies they called 'Keynesian', incurring the risk of hyperinflation if the bond market collapsed. The global shift of economic power from the West to Asia has probably been accelerated by these events. It is all rather murky, but even at the best of times the present is like that.

Whatever place the financial crisis eventually finds in economic history, one certain victim has been free-market economics. It is impossible any more to hold that economies will prosper only if markets are freed from political bondage. Attacks on the economists by politicians and journalists have become commonplace. Even Queen Elizabeth asked publicly why none of them saw it all coming. The ideological hegemony of mainstream economics, especially since the 1980s, has been holed below the water. This is not to say that the free marketers have been silenced, but public acceptance of the notion that the economy is social, institutional and in need of political guidance is now commonplace. And Karl Marx, after being sidelined for decades, is once again a best-seller. All of this suggests to us that the crisis has opened up a new terrain for thinking about the economy.

For millennia, economy was conceived of in domestic terms as 'household management', usually a manorial estate with its slaves, livestock, fields and orchards. Then, when markets, money and machines began their modern rise to social dominance, a new discipline of political economy was born, concerned with the public consequences of economic actions. For well over a century now, this discipline has called itself economics and its subject matter has been the economic decisions made by individuals as participants in markets of many kinds. People as such play almost no part in the calculations of economists and they find no particular reflection of themselves in the quantities published by the media. The economy is rather conceived of as an impersonal machine, remote from the everyday experience of most people. The idea that we put forward here of a 'human economy' is intended to remind readers that the economy is made and remade by people in their everyday lives. We hope to identify some of its principles and to provide instances of how it works. So what is it?

Why a human economy?

There are two prerequisites for being human: we must each learn to be self-reliant to a high degree and to belong to others, merging our identities in a bewildering variety of social relations. Much of modern ideology emphasizes how problematic it is to be both self-interested and mutual, to be economic as well as social, we might say. When culture is set up to expect a conflict between the two, it is hard to be both. Yet the two sides are often inseparable in practice and some societies, by encouraging private and public interests to coincide, have managed to integrate them more effectively than ours. One premise of the new human universal will thus be the unity of self and society. If learning to be two-sided is the means of becoming human, then this lesson is apparently hard for some to learn, and economics as we know it makes it impossible to do so.

The project of economics needs to be rescued from the economists. The mask of neoliberal ideology has been half-ripped from the politics of world economy. It is up to us to propose an effective replacement. In order to be human, the economy must be at least four things:

1. It is made and remade by people; economics should be of practical use to us all in our daily lives.
2. It should address a great variety of particular situations in all their institutional complexity.
3. It must be based on a more holistic conception of everyone's needs and interests.
4. It has to address humanity as a whole and the world society we are making.

You may well ask where this human economy is and how it might be created. The human economy is already everywhere. People always insert themselves practically into economic life on their own account. What they do there is often obscured, marginalized or repressed by dominant economic institutions and ideologies. Thus in the twentieth century, society was supposed to be impersonal: life was organized by state bureaucracy, capitalist markets and scientific experts. Not surprisingly most people felt estranged and powerless in the face of all this. But they did not sit on their hands: they expressed themselves in domestic life and organized informally in the cracks of the economic system; they made associations for their own protection, betterment and recreation. Whenever we speak of 'capitalism' or 'socialism', we are referring to just part of what goes on in an economy, perhaps to the part that makes it historically distinctive. But there is a lot more going on than is highlighted in this way and economies in practice are more like each other than superficial contrasts might suggest.

Any programme to make an economy more human is thus not in itself a revolutionary exercise. It builds on what is there already and seeks only to gain recognition and legitimacy for what people do for themselves. In this book we try to show how a new direction and emphasis for the economy can be based on many initiatives that are already established, but which could do with more room to grow. This means that our approach is 'bottom up' and 'gradualist' initially. We want to encourage readers to try things out for themselves in a piecemeal way. There is a tension between any movement's aspiration to universalism and its appeal to specifically local interests. Our emphasis is mainly on the second of these and what we offer here is very much 'work in progress'. At the same time, the potential of all that we propose, when taken together, *is* a revolution. There is no knowing how far we could go if the principles outlined here took off. In the end our human predicament is global and requires global solutions. If we imagine taking many small steps now rather than waiting for one great transformation later, this is not for lack of ambition. It is more an acknowledgement of what we have achieved so far. Once more people engage with the economy in a different way, who knows what they will conclude about the need for broader systemic change?

The object of an economy was always the reproduction of human life and beyond that the preservation of everything that sustains life. In the modern era, it is supposed to serve the common good and in that respect has shifted from a preoccupation with material survival to meeting a wide range of cultural needs. But for some time now the object of economy has been to make money through producing and selling things, with human life secondary, a means to that end. Economics, which ought to be a science for human emancipation, has become a dehumanized expert ideology remote from people's practical concerns and from their ability to understand what to do.

Traditional African societies supported economies whose object was the production of life embodied in human beings. Hence for many of them money took the form of cattle used to secure the reproduction of kin groups through marriage. Modern capitalist economies have as their object the accumulation of money through the production of inanimate things for sale. But in recent decades, the fastest-growing sector of world trade has been in cultural commodities, services such as entertainment, education, media, software and information, along with explosive growth in financial and transport services. These trends make the economy more about what people do for each other than the physical objects that go into making up their material livelihood. It may be that, after the early phase of industrialization, the predominant focus of the world economy will revert to the production of human beings. There is no limit to the stories we can tell each other or to the pleasure we can derive from watching performers excel at what they do. The world's largest television audiences are for sporting events like football's World Cup and the Olympic Games men's 100 metres final.

Humanity is a collective noun – all the people who have ever lived, live now and will live in future; it is a quality of kindness, of treating all people as if they were like ourselves; and it is a historical project for our species to assume stewardship of life on this planet, since we are the part of life that can think, the frontal lobes of the biomass. Any such project must find its own social forms, but it is likely that these will include installing democracy as a universal political principle and valuing science as a means of acquiring the knowledge needed for that task. The idea of economy is likewise central to the project of installing truth and justice in the world. It took its modern form from the eighteenth-century Enlightenment that gave birth to the modern democratic revolutions. This classical liberalism culminated in the late work of Immanuel Kant on moral judgement, cosmopolitics and anthropology. We must renew that revolutionary project for our own times.

Our world is much more socially integrated than it was two centuries ago and its economy is palpably unequal. The task of building a global civil society for the twenty-first century should be compelling. One source for such a project may be found in the work of the great intellectuals of the twentieth century's anti-colonial revolution, such as the Caribbean writer-activists Frantz Fanon and C. L. R. James and, above all, Mohandas K. Gandhi. This movement was driven by peoples forced into world society by Western imperialism a century earlier who aspired to make their own independent relationship to it. They did not repudiate the legacy of the Enlightenment, only its perversion by Empire as a system of racial exclusion. In the process they made the original project more inclusive, more human. And we take our lead from them.

What we propose here is a new 'new institutional economics' to be formed out of anthropology, sociology, political economy, economic philosophy and world history. Marcel Mauss and Karl Polanyi, who pioneered such a synthesis, argued that we must rely on practical experience for information and analysis; in other words, start from the 'real economic movement'. This is a concept of social change as self-expression, of change which is, in Mauss's words, 'by no means committed to revolutionary or radical alternatives, to brutal choices between two contradictory forms of society' but which 'is and will be made by a process of building new groups and institutions alongside and on top of the old ones'. Rather than make an abstract appeal to an alternative economy, Mauss and Polanyi showed us a concrete road to 'other economies' based on the field of possibilities already open to us.

One of Mauss's key modifications to Durkheim's legacy was to conceive of society as a historical project of humanity whose limits were extended to become ever more inclusive. The point of his famous essay on *The Gift* is that society cannot be taken for granted as a pre-existent form. It must be made and remade, sometimes from scratch. How do we behave on a first date or on a diplomatic mission? We make gifts. Heroic gift-exchange is designed to push the limits of society outwards. It is liberal in a similar sense to the 'free market', except that generosity powers the exchange, self-interested for sure, but not in the way associated with *Homo economicus*. No society is ever economically self-sufficient, least of all small Pacific islands. So to the need for establishing local limits on social action must always be added the means of extending a community's reach abroad. This is why markets and money in some form are universal, and why any attempt to abolish them must end in catastrophe.

Polanyi drew attention to how economic institutions organize and are in turn organized by a plurality of distribution mechanisms that, in the modern world, affect the lives of millions of people who participate in them, without being granted any measure of control. This led him to highlight the inequality created by these institutions, as they swing between the poles of market and state, of society's external and internal relations. In the current crisis, the immediate reaction is to turn to a variety of government institutions, flipping the coin from tails to heads as it were, instead of insisting that states and the markets have to work together in less one-sided ways than before. To this end, Polanyi's call for a return to social solidarity, drawing especially on the voluntary reciprocity of associations, reminds us that people in general must be mobilized to contribute their energies to the renewal of society. It is not enough to rely on impersonal states and markets.

The human economy is an elastic idea, a vision more than a social recipe, or rather many social recipes articulated by a unifying vision. It embraces at once what each of us does in daily life and what all of us might become as a species. Some might find that indeterminacy less compelling than a sharper alternative vision. We embrace it because there is an intrinsic connection between these poles and economy ought to be capable of spanning them in a fluid way. Even so, it is reasonable to ask what a political programme with the human economy in mind might look like.

Some political principles

Two great lessons may be drawn from the history of the twentieth century. First, market society sustained by a concern for individual freedom generated huge inequalities; then submission of the economy to political will on the pretext of equality led to the suppression of freedom. These two solutions called democracy itself into question, whether in the form of totalitarian systems or, with a similar result, through the subordination of political power to that of money. If we reject both of these options, it is then a question of developing institutions capable of guaranteeing a plural economy within a democratic framework, exactly what is compromised when the rationale of material gain without limit has a monopoly. To answer this question, we must seek out new institutional forms anchored in social practice; these will point the way towards the reinsertion of democratic norms in economic life. Any return to the old compromises is doomed to failure and any reflection on how to reconcile freedom and equality, which remains the goal of democracy in a complex society, can only make progress by taking into account the reactions of people in society.

Another way of putting our case is to express it, in Jürgen Habermas's words, as the need to resolve 'an irreducible tension between capitalism and democracy'. Far from guaranteeing prosperity for all, the deregulated economy unleashed by neoliberal policies threatened to dissolve the social fabric to a point where it might pave the way for authoritarian regimes, as market failure did in the 1930s. While the market economy is legitimate, a market that knows no limits poses a threat to democracy. This book examines the essential question of what form the post-crisis economy might take and of the preconditions for the emergence of a truly human economy. We base our approach on three principles.

The idea of reason has animated economics from the beginning.

Who could argue with the aim of putting our common affairs on a rational footing? What was originally conceived of as a specifically human capacity for discernment has gradually been reduced by the modern discipline to a purely formal concept: in order to be rational, choice is nothing more than the maximization of individual utility. This anthropological definition of human beings as calculating machines has the effect, among other things, of over-estimating the market's ability to allocate resources. We can all now see its consequences: while wealth when measured in terms of commodities increases, natural resources are wasted at an ever-increasing rate and there is a dizzying increase in inequality. This is not sustainable in either ecological or social terms.

Our second principle is thus the need for solidarity within and between generations. We might call this horizontal and vertical solidarity. We must reduce inequality for those who are alive now and protect the living conditions of future generations. The hardest question is whether a new importance may be granted to solidarity while adapting to the existing system. Our authors differ quite widely in how they might answer that question. We will say here only that, if rationality consists in the means replacing the ends of economic actions, the answer must be no. But we reject an over-determined view of our societies as being merely 'capitalist' in nature.

People everywhere pursue ends of a very different nature, be they political, cultural, environmental or whatever. We look to their initiatives for democratic ways of building solidarity in the human economy. So our third principle is methodological. Theoretical and practical work must be closely articulated. This was acknowledged at the 2009 World Social Forum in Belém, Brazil, where activists and researchers came together to discuss how the goals of democracy and science might be combined more effectively.

An institutional approach to the economy is one where economic activities are defined by rules of various kinds (not just state-made laws) that are debated and enforced by political means. The recent attempt to 'naturalize' the market was a species of 'utopian capitalism' that inevitably provoked a many-sided social movement in response. This experiment was reductive in at least two senses: the market was withdrawn from the domain of political action (even as public life was invaded by the market); and the modern economy came to be confused with capitalism. While modern society has been shaped by modes of reasoning (notably economics) that are indeed an expression of capitalist economy, it is not reducible to it. We hold that contemporary politics also sustains economic inventiveness based on a premise of democratic solidarity. The present volume is an exploration of that premise.

We know now that society will not become democratic unless we can find ways of democratizing the economy. This will not happen just by developing a new model for the ideal society. Rather we must look at actual experiments that have been made around the world. If we are to advance further in the direction of a human economy, we must recognize activities that have non-economic ends. We should also try to avoid the two major pitfalls of progressive politics. The centre-left, having swallowed claims that the market is the only source of wealth-creation, has adopted neoliberal economic policies, moderated only by less restrictive social policies. The far left wants to break with capitalism, but has no definite programme for the transition. A revolution in that sense is an illusion.

Building a human economy presupposes renewed public engagement. Regulation by the political authorities must be balanced by the public expressions of a civil society focused on attaining the common good. The social rights of citizens must be made consistent with encouraging forms of self-organization where solidarity has a greater economic role. Market contracts and citizenship are not the only way of delivering freedom and equality. These also come from people living together, from the mutuality and egalitarianism of everyday life. At the other extreme, there is no getting round the need to curb the power of the capitalist corporations. This requires a new alliance of grassroots movements, harnessing the voluntary reciprocity of self-organized groups, and public policy aimed at regulating capitalism and co-ordinating redistributive institutions. One challenge of course is to identify the appropriate levels of political association in a world that can no longer assume a national monopoly of politics. Above all, whatever principles we identify here must have demonstrable consequences for action.

About this book

Each of the chapters that follow provides an account of ideas and practices that our authors have been personally involved in developing; this is combined with their guide to the most important and accessible literature in that field. The editors have not tried to impose a standard theory or style on them, beyond some limited formalities. Each author is responsible for their own chapter. Taken together, this volume is the product of an extended international collaboration, remarkable in itself for the unusual range of those who have taken part. *The Human Economy* is the first expression in English of a project that began a decade ago at the first World Social Forum in Porto Alegre, Brazil, as part of a strong counter-movement that took root in Latin America and Europe. Much of this theoretical and practical work is unknown in the English-speaking world. But the economic crisis has surely generated political conditions ripe for its adoption there.

A series of publications before this one involved a creative mix of academic researchers, political activists and social networks (both national and international) who supported the project in various ways. *A outra economia* was published in Brazil in 2003 and edited by Antonio David Cattani with the support of an inter-university network, Unitrabalho. It was soon translated into Spanish through the RILESS network and published in Argentina. Some of these Latin American entries along with new Francophone contributions were used for a volume, *Dictionnaire de l'autre économie*, edited by Jean-Louis Laville and Cattani, published in Paris and aided by the EMES and CRISES networks, based in Belgium and Quebec respectively. An abridged version was published in Italian as *Dizionario dell'altra economia*.

Another version in Spanish, *Diccionario de la otra economia,* was edited by Cattani, Laville and José Luis Coraggio; and a Portuguese edition, *Dicionário internacional da outra economia*, edited by Cattani, Laville, L. Gaiger and P. Hespanha, was published in 2009. An expanded French paperback edition was published in 2006 and sold 6,000 copies in its first year. Keith Hart wrote an enthusiastic review essay about the *Dictionnaire* which led to our present collaboration. Our authors are drawn from Argentina, Austria, Belgium, Brazil, Britain, Canada, Denmark, France, Germany, Norway, Peru, South Africa, Switzerland and the United States. This is impressive enough, but the absence of Asia suggests where this roadshow ought to be heading next.

This English edition draws on updated translations of several entries from earlier books and on newly commissioned pieces by Anglophone authors. It differs from the others in content, in its thematic organization and perhaps in placing less emphasis on a search for alternatives. But the enterprise rests squarely on its predecessors' achievements. The human economy is not a dream. It exists theoretically and practically, but this existence has been obscured by the economic models and approaches that dominate both the media and the universities. We hope to make our knowledge of these phenomena more widely available, so that a new audience, with English as its first or second language, might use what we have discovered to build a better world.

There are five parts. We start with 'World Society' since thinking concretely about our common humanity is both urgently necessary and difficult for us, given our habit of thinking in national terms. This is followed by 'Economics with a Human Face', where we explore several approaches to the economy with people more in mind than the mainstream discipline allows for. Politics has been ideologically excluded from the market economy (but not in reality) and this goes with a similar exclusion of morality. Yet people want to be good, to pursue the good life, so we next examine their integration as 'Moral Politics'. The longest part, 'Beyond Market and State', brings together a number of distinct but overlapping attempts to articulate ways of making the economy explicitly social. Here, terms that are often debated individually come together as an incipient language for building the human economy. Finally, we address 'New Directions' in some strikingly different ways. The movement of the book is therefore from our common predicament in today's world, through thinking about the human economy as a moral and political project, to attempts to build a new institutional synthesis in practice, while always being open to imagining a better world in future.

Part I starts from 'globalization', the current expression for the making of world society, primarily by means of finance, information technology and transport. The idea of 'public goods' has been in retreat recently; yet concern for the planet's wellbeing brings them sharply into focus at the global level. World governance is strikingly defective, but we next examine the record of the 'international organizations', especially those like the IMF, World Bank and WTO who claim responsibility for managing the world economy. This world is desperately unequal and 'development' has been the name for evolving relations between rich and poor countries. The picture is not pretty, especially over the last three decades. A remarkably successful network of social movements has arisen to challenge the prevailing global (dis-)order. This now goes by the name of 'alter-globalization', not *against* one world but *for* a different way of organizing it.

Part II provides a vision of the 'plural economy' taken from institutional economics, one that cannot be imagined as either 'the market' or 'capitalism' alone. This chapter develops several ideas already expressed here in this introductory essay to the volume. 'Ecological economics', while aiming for an environmental synthesis at the planetary level, is inspired by a 'small is beautiful' philosophy that keeps people very prominently in mind. Economics is a strongly male-centred discipline, but, as throughout the social sciences and humanities, feminists have made an important contribution to opening this field up to the interests of men, women *and* children or, in Julie A. Nelson's terms, to an *Economics for Humans*. 'Fair trade' is an idea with limited resonance in the rich countries, a minor ethical gloss on shopping, but here two Latin American authors show how it might be expanded to become a principle of regional development with implications for global economic justice. In a departure from the gradualist perspective generally adopted here, we next consider what a 'labour economy' might look like, conceived of as the antithesis of the 'capital economy' that is currently dominant. For many people, economics with a human face is epitomized by 'microcredit' schemes such as Bangladesh's Grameen Bank. Here we take a critical look at microfinance in general. Finally, the idea of an 'informal economy' has run for the last forty years as a popular counterpart to the world of governments and corporations whose principles are addressed by macroeconomics. Whatever it lacks in theoretical rigour is compensated for by its focus on what people really do.

An impersonal approach to politics is often justified in terms of the higher interests of society. In Part III we revive Kant's programme of seeking to ground world politics in the moral judgements that each of us brings to living in society. The most powerful of these is 'citizenship', a term which is made more complex by persisting inequality in our world and by growing confusion over where political association might be most effectively located. This is reflected in the idea of 'corporate social responsibility', which seeks to redraw the lines of governance between states and corporations and reveals the latter as super-citizens capable of eclipsing the rest of us. The welfare state underpinned post-war social democracy not least through its redistributive policies; it has been radically undermined by the recent drive to privatize the public sector. Against this statist perspective, we then consider three bottom-up approaches. The gift offers a rich imaginative field for building alternatives to conventional politics, one that has inspired an active cluster of engaged intellectuals in France. 'Moral economy' has become a diffuse expression for popular conceptions of the good life coming out of the experience of early industrialism, peasant society and indeed market economy at all times. 'Communism' is of course closely associated with state socialism in the twentieth century and with utopian alternatives throughout history. Here we explore 'everyday communism', a common human propensity for sociability that, with some redirection of emphasis, might serve as grounds for non-capitalist economic organization.

Part IV takes off from a review of the 'third sector', the attempt to find a middle ground between public responsibility and private gain in the voluntary or non-profit activities of a wide variety of organizations around the world. The idea of an economy built on solidarity is already well entrenched in Brazil and France as *économie solidaire*, but it is gaining ground in the Anglophone countries where it is known, somewhat awkwardly, as 'solidarity economy'. A third way between market and state often invokes the notion of community and especially the active connotations of 'community participation'. This is sometimes linked to privileging 'local development', where people may be expected to participate on the basis of occupying a given place. It can also open up a space for non-governmental organizations (NGOs) over a wide range of locations, but here we focus on NGOs in the field of international development. The idea of 'social capital' has enjoyed a vogue of late, not least at the World Bank. We trace the history of the concept in policymaking circles and the popular imagination. Finally, 'social enterprise' or 'social entrepreneurs' have become important designations for many attempts to combine economic and 'non-economic' approaches to the provision of public and private goods. We offer two complementary readings of this phenomenon. Throughout there is a tension between the attempt to develop genuinely solidary approaches to markets and politics and the suspicion that this only reinforces neoliberalism's program for dismantling social democracy. This section underlines the systemic nature of that contradiction.

In Part V, we relax our focus on what exists to imagine some future possibilities, but still with our eyes firmly fixed on the past and present. Given the importance of money for our world, it is unsurprising that 'community and complementary currencies' (the less cumbersome term in some languages is 'social money') have seen some potentially far-reaching experiments in making alternatives to national money. The internet is a site of rapid and radical innovation at all levels of economy and society. Here we explore three approaches to the formation of a 'digital commons' against the forces of corporate privatization. The contemporary world is marked by hypermobility. We examine the history of this movement and consider various scenarios when the cheap oil on which it is based runs out. Climate change, when combined with a prospective shortage of fossil fuels, gives added impetus to the search for 'alternative energy', here reviewed with considerable attention to science and technology. But where would we be without dreams of utopia? In 'worlds of emancipation' we trace the history of an active hope of a better world. Humanity is and always will be inspired by visions of a future fit for us all to live in. For all our emphasis on practical solutions to economic problems, we end with this affirmation of our human potential.

If sceptical readers doubt what concrete difference our documentation of 'the human economy' might make to the world, we invite them to consider the chapters assembled in this last section, each of which addresses a theme of huge significance for our economic future: new approaches to money, digital democracy, mobility after cheap oil, renewable energy and the struggle for emancipation from inequality and repression. *The Human Economy* is a work of reference that has come out of a dialogue between successful social experiments in many parts of the world and theoretical reflections on them. The resulting synthesis is an invitation to advance knowledge along the lines we have begun and to dare to build a better world.

Further reading

Allard, J., Davidson, C. and Matthaei, J. (2008) *Solidarity Economy: Building Alternatives for People and Planet.* US Solidarity Economy Network, Amherst, MA.

Amin, A. (2009) *The Social Economy.* Zed Books, London.

Cattani, A. D. and Holzmann, L. (eds) *Dicionário de trabalho e tecnologia.* Editora da UFRGS, Porto Alegre.

Cattani, A. D., Laville, J-L., Gaiger, L. and Hespanha, P. (eds) (2009) *Dicionário internacional da outra economia.* Almedina, Coimbra.

Evers, A. and Laville, J-L. (2004) *The Third Sector in Europe*. Edward Elgar, Cheltenham.

Gibson-Graham, J. K. (1996) *The End of Capitalism (As We Knew It): A Feminist Critique of Political Economy*. Blackwell, Oxford.

Hann, C. and Hart, K. (eds) (2009) *Market and Society: The Great Transformation Today*. Cambridge University Press, Cambridge.

Hann, C. and Hart, K. (2010) *Economic Anthropology: History, Ethnography, Critique*. Polity, Cambridge.

Hart, K. (2007) Towards an alternative economics: the view from France, *Social Anthropology* 15 (3), 369–74.

Hart, K. (2007) Marcel Mauss: in pursuit of the whole, *Comparative Studies in Society and History* 49 (2), 473–85.

Hart, K. (2008) The human economy, *ASAOnline*, http://www.theasa.org/publications/asaonline/articles/asaonline_0101.htm .

Laville, J-L. and Cattani, A. D. (eds) (2006) *Dictionnaire de l'autre économie*. Gallimard, Paris.

Laville, J-L. (2010) *Politique de l'association*. Seuil, Paris.

Mauss, M. (1990 [1925]) *The Gift: Form and Reason of Exchange in Archaic Societies*. Routledge, London.

Nelson, J. A. (2006) *Economics for Humans*. University of Chicago Press, Chicago.

Polanyi, K. (2001 [1944]) *The Great Transformation: The Political and Economic Origins of our Times*. Beacon, Boston, MA.

Sachs, W. (ed.) (2009) *The Development Dictionary: A Guide to Knowledge as Power*. Zed Books, London.

Part I

World Society

2

Globalization

Thomas Hylland Eriksen

Globalization, a term that became fashionable around 1990, generally refers to processes of increased density, speed and reach of transnational connections associated with the global spread of capitalism and new information and communications technologies. Globalization can be studied in its economic, political, ecological or cultural aspects, and there is a rich scholarly literature on the subject. Moreover, it can be studied as a macro phenomenon, with a focus on the global economy, transnational companies etc.; or as a micro phenomenon, focusing instead on relationships between persons and small groups. The current economic crisis has led some commentators and analysts to conclude that globalization has suffered a severe setback. While this may be true for finance capitalism, other processes of economic globalization continue in the realms of investment, migration and remittances, commodity trade and so on, although the growth rate has slowed down in many parts of the world since 2008.

Although the term globalization is recent, the phenomena to which it refers are older. Ancient empires in Eurasia, Africa and the Americas engaged in transcontinental trade and created vital connections between local economies. However, if by globalization we mean both increased interconnectedness on a global scale *and* the widespread awareness of such connectedness, it is reasonable to date the first era of globalization to the nineteenth century. This was a period of European colonial expansion, scientific discovery and industrialization, and accompanying these processes were new forms of thought, new models of the world. Hegel's concept of the world-spirit (*die Weltgeist*) indicated an awareness of heightened global interconnectedness, as did Kant's cosmopolitan philosophy. Marx's political philosophy was definitely global in its ambitions and continues to inspire new generations. Thanks to industrial development, colonial expansion and technological innovations, the growth in international trade was formidable at this time. The current era of globalization is fuelled by transnational capitalism and trade as well as by the new information and communications technologies enabling the development of global financial systems operating in real time.

A question often raised in the debates over globalization concerns its relationship to neoliberal economic ideology, that is the view that free trade will eventually lead to prosperity everywhere, and that states should encumber the economy as little as possible. Severely criticized for not delivering the goods – many countries that complied with measures imposed by international agencies like the World Bank and the International Monetary Fund have experienced a decline in standards of living – neoliberalism is often associated with, indeed sometimes treated as a synonym for, globalization. After 2008, neoliberal triumphalism has fewer supporters, and many aspects of the contemporary world economy have dimensions not reducible to neoliberalism.

Another debate concerns the relationship between poor and rich countries – do the poor become poorer and the rich richer as a result of economic globalization? Again, there can be no simple answer. Some countries mired in poverty, notably in Africa, are among the least globalized in terms of integration into the world economy, and might therefore be less affected by the 2008 turndown. The small elites in these countries, integrated into global capitalism by virtue of monopolizing foreign trade and investments, at any rate are more strongly affected by global crises than the majorities, from whom they have detached themselves. On the other hand, some rich countries are exposed to competition from countries such as China, India and Brazil. In other cases, it can be argued that the trade regime supervised by the World Trade Organization helps rich countries to continue exploiting poor ones by buying cheap unprocessed goods from them and selling them expensive industrial products back. However, this describes an older neocolonial pattern better than the current one, where Chinese companies are making inroads into markets with their inexpensive industrial goods and willingness to invest in infrastructure and industrial enterprises. Under these circumstances, the poorest countries are not so much exploited as neglected by transnational investors.

The significance of communications technologies

A useful concept for understanding the scope of globalization is 'time–space compression', coined by David Harvey. You may envision it as the 'squeezing together' of time and space. The history of the last two hundred years could be seen as a process of acceleration. Strangely, this is rarely emphasized in the literature on globalization, even though it reduces the importance of distance, frequently obliterating it altogether. In an era of wireless communications, duration and distance are no longer tied together. In 1903, Theodore Roosevelt sent a round-the-world telegram to himself, and it reached him in nine minutes. This demonstrated how much the world had become a shrunken place: the space–time continuum had been compressed enormously compared with the situation half a century earlier. Today an email message travels the world in seconds.

Technological change is a necessary condition for time–space compression. The jet plane and the satellite dish automatically speed up communication, but their mere invention says nothing about their social importance. Who has access to these technologies, how are they are being used, how do they transform economies and everyday lives worldwide? These changes, therefore, must always be placed in their social context. Interdisciplinary research on information and communications technologies reveals that they have hugely different social and cultural implications in different societies.

Yet the speed-up is being felt all over the world. Harvey indicates the dramatic acceleration of transport (see *Mobility*) by comparing four historical moments in European modernity.

1. 1500–1840: best average speed of horse-drawn coaches and sailing ships was 10 mph – the same as the Romans!
2. 1850–1930: steam locomotives averaged – in theory – 65 mph and steam ships 36 mph.
3. 1950s: propeller aircraft, 300–400 mph.
4. 1960s: jet passenger aircraft, 500–700 mph.

A table showing the acceleration in the transmission of messages would be no less striking. For thousands of years, the fastest means of communication was a written document transported by horse. Intercontinental communication could take place no faster than a sailing ship. With the coming of the train and steamship, the speed of communication increased as much as the speed of ground communication. Long before steam had fully replaced sail, however, the telegraph saw the light of day, being first demonstrated in 1838. A transatlantic cable was opened between New York and London in 1866; the first cable from London to Bombay in 1870. It revolutionized how people experienced time and space. The telephone (invented in 1877) similarly contributed to changing the time–space continuum. As from the late nineteenth century, one could no longer assume a direct connection between distance and delay. Some towns and cities were connected by fast ground transportation and instantaneously through the telegraph and telephone. In the world of finance, the telegraph (and later, electronic communications) enabled investors in stock markets to draw on instant information transmitted eventually from all corners of the world.

Towards a more abstract world

Modernization, of which globalization is a part, can be described as a gradual movement from the concrete and tangible to the abstract and virtual. The example of money illustrates this point. The concepts of language and time exist in traditional societies, but not writing and clocks. Similarly, money-like instruments exist in many kinds of societies, but our kind of money, 'all-purpose money', is recent and culture-bound. It does roughly the same thing for payment, value measurement and exchange as clocks and writing do for time and language, respectively. All make transactions more abstract and impose a standard, ultimately taking in the whole world. They place individual, mundane transactions under the one invisible umbrella.

Shell money, gold coins and other valuables are known in a wide range of traditional societies. They are sometimes used as a standard, making different goods comparable – a bag of grain equals half a gold coin; a goat equals half a gold coin; thus, a sack of grain can be bartered with a goat. They may be used as means of exchange; I can buy two goats with a gold coin. They may even be used as means of payment – if you kill your neighbour, you have to pay his widow and children three gold coins in compensation. But modern money is a much more powerful technology than anything comparable in traditional societies. Above all, it is *universal* in its field of applicability. In many cases, one kind of money functions as a universal means of payment and exchange, and as a standard of value. West African cowries had no value outside a limited area; and even there, only certain commodities and services could be purchased with them. All-purpose money is legal tender in a state with millions of inhabitants, and it can usually be converted into other currencies worldwide. Regarded as information technology, money has truly contributed to the creation of one world, albeit a world into which only people of means are integrated. Money makes wages and purchasing-power all over the world comparable, allows a ton of yams from New Guinea to be exchanged with electronics from Taiwan. Without it as a medium, the world economy would be impossible. Whereas trade in many societies often depended on personal relations of trust between seller and buyer, the abstract universal money with which we are familiar permits economic transactions to be externalized. As long as there is agreement over the economic value of the coloured paper or increasingly of the numbers on a screen, I need not know my debtors or my creditors personally. The recent move into cyberspace, allowing the same plastic card to be used for economic transactions nearly anywhere in the world, has made money more virtual than ever.

A networked global economy?

Manuel Castells has written about 'the network enterprise' as a new kind of company. It is loosely organized, there is little job security, it has assets in several locations, and it stands in a complex relationship to other businesses. Recent changes in capitalism have often been described as a transition from mass production to flexible production (and accumulation), or from Fordism to post-Fordism. This means a shift away from large, stable enterprises, often involving assembly lines and mechanized production of large quantities of standardized goods. Such a system became too rigid and was replaced by a more adaptable system of production that was more responsive to global market trends. Castells also refers to the 'crisis of the large organization'; much of contemporary job-creation and innovation comes from middle-sized and small enterprises functioning in a larger network of complementary and competing businesses.

On the other side, some huge corporations have benefited from increased globalization. By 2004, Unilever had more than five hundred subsidiaries located in one hundred countries; and the mass media conglomerate Bertelsmann had more than six hundred affiliates in fifty countries. Production sites are more easily moved overseas than ever before, and markets are more easily accessible than they used to be. Certain services can easily be outsourced overseas, American call centres in India being the most commonly cited example. Some thirty transnational companies have a higher turnover than the GDP of all but eight countries. The annual total sales of transnational corporations increased in two decades (1982–2002) from $3 trillion to $18 trillion. These figures would suggest a tighter integration of global economic networks from the 1980s.

The same technologies that make networking possible have moved to the core of the global economy. Some of the fastest-growing companies in the world deliver hardware, software or services associated with computing. Nokia, which produced rubber boots and a few TV sets in the 1980s, now sells more than three hundred million mobile phones a year. The United States' leading exports are of movies, music and software. Internet-related infrastructure and commodities are the fastest-growing and most profitable sectors of the world market.

The universality of capitalism as a system of production, distribution and consumption is underpinned by the breadth of economic involvement by major enterprises. The networked structure of the global economy – with subsidiaries, joint ventures, a worldwide distribution of assets – led Michael Hardt and Antonio Negri, in their much discussed book *Empire*, to depict the world as being ruled by a web of transnational corporations and organizations – an empire with no geographical centre or government or executive committee. But they exaggerated the reach of the global network society.

Governments still regulate trade and organize incentives at home, often with significant results. Environmental problems, usually blamed on globalization, may equally be traced to national government policies, such as subsidies to extractive industries from Alaska to the Amazon. There is nothing even resembling a global labour market, given the severe restrictions placed on immigration by rich countries. Citizens are endowed with particular rights and obligations in territorial states, some of whom still maintain universal welfare programmes. As Joseph Stiglitz quips, the Americans favour free trade, but are against imports. So the global network society could hardly be said to be omnipresent and omnipotent. Yet figures indicate a strong tendency towards wider and denser transnational networks, leading to new forms of capital accumulation and increased concentration of economic power. It remains to be seen whether this pattern will survive the global economic downturn.

Networks do not preclude centralization. Writing about transnational business, Saskia Sassen points towards the emergence of an inter-urban geography that joins major international financial and business centres: New York, London, Tokyo, Paris, Frankfurt, Zurich, Amsterdam, Los Angeles, Sydney, Hong Kong, more recently incorporating cities like São Paolo, Buenos Aires, Mumbai and Bangkok. As these intercity links have become denser owing to growth in transnational finance, the distance between each city and the rest of its own country has increased. Networks may be deterritorialized, but their boundaries can be as rigid as those of a closed structure.

Globalization from below

Global capitalism produces losers and winners, poverty and wealth. Even when increased material wealth is measurable, one effect may be poverty at the cultural or spiritual level. Counter-movements against the standardization and homogenization resulting from globalization can thus be founded in a variety of motivations, but all of them are related to autonomy at the personal or community level (see *Alter-Globalization*). Even when globalization is met with little or no resistance, it can usually be described as *glocalization* (a term coined by Roland Robertson). The pre-existing local is fused with global influences; the particular merges with the universal to create something true to the universal grammar of global modernity, but at the same time is locally embedded.

Transnational connections involving migrants are economically important. A study of Senegalese Wolof in Emilia Romagna demonstrates several important features of transnational entrepreneurship. The Wolof are traditionally associated with trade in West Africa, and they have successfully adapted their skills to span Senegalese and European markets in their business flows. Migrant traders in Italy are morally and socially bound by their allegiance to a Sufi brotherhood in Senegal (the *Mourides*), but without a strong organization of Wolof wholesalers based in Italy offering not only goods but also training, individual peddlers would have no chance of success. The Wolof traders live in Italy part of the year and in Senegal for the other part, offering goods for sale in Senegalese markets that range from hi-fi equipment and other electronic goods to the trader's own second-hand clothes. The Mourides transnational network also imports a lot of shoes into the United States through its base in Harlem, New York; and when they recently switched supplies from Italy to China, the impact on the Italian shoe industry was drastic.

Transnational micro-economies have become widespread during the last decades; and migration must be seen as a transnational venture rather than as a one-way process resulting in segregation, assimilation or integration in the receiving society. The economics of transnationalism can be observed among Congolese *sapeurs* (members of SAPE, *Société des Ambianceurs et des Personnes Élegantes*, founded in 1922) flaunting their wealth in Brazzaville following a frugal period of hard work in Paris; in the informal *hawala* banking system whereby Somali refugees send remittances to their relatives; in the flow of goods into and out of immigrant-owned shops in any European city; and most certainly in thousands of local communities, from Kerala to Jamaica, which benefit from the work of locals working overseas. Seen from a global perspective, this kind of transnational economy could be seen as an ethnic division of labour continuing the exploitative systems of colonialism; but seen from the perspective of the local community and indeed from that of many national economies, it is a much-needed source of wealth. In many countries, the remittances and bank savings of citizens living abroad have come to represent a huge factor in the economy. Remittances received in Morocco represent twice the value of direct foreign investment and a third of the total value of Moroccan exports; more than 20 per cent of Malawian households depend on remittances; and one could go on. There is considerable variation between countries in the size of remittances and how they are spent. As a rule, they are more important the poorer a country is, representing a quarter of GDP in Haiti, a sixth in Guyana and an eighth in Jamaica, falling to a negligible amount in prosperous Trinidad and Tobago. No matter how poor the recipients are, a proportion is invested in land, livestock, education or small enterprises. Every dollar sent back to the Philippines, it is claimed, leads to a further three dollars in local growth, either through investment or through boosting local demand. This 'multiplier effect' is offset against increased dependence, brain drain and the loss of incentives to generate jobs locally.

The dialectics of globalization

Globalization is two-sided and operates through dialectical negation. It *shrinks* the world by facilitating fast contact across former boundaries and it *expands* the world by creating an awareness of difference. It *homogenizes* human lives by imposing a set of common denominators (state organization, labour markets, consumption etc.), but it also leads to *heterogenization* through the new forms of diversity emerging from the intensified contact. Globalization is *centripetal* in that it connects people worldwide; and it is *centrifugal* in that it inspires a heightened awareness of, and indeed (re-)construction of local uniqueness. It centralizes power and prompts movements, among indigenous peoples, small nations and others, fighting for local autonomy and self-determination. Finally, globalization makes a universalist *cosmopolitanism* possible in political thought and action because it reminds us that we are all in the same boat and have to live together in spite of our mutual differences; but it also encourages *fundamentalism* and various forms of missionary universalism as well as parochial localism, because global integration leads to a sense of alienation threatening identities and notions of political sovereignty.

Working out these tensions generates a variety of third ways or alternatives. This is, among other things, where the term *glocalization* comes into its own, but also terms like *alter-globalization* (see below), that is alternative forms of globalization or 'the globalization of the Other', NGO-based or grassroots initiatives aiming to use the technology and networks enabled by globalization for the benefit of the disenfranchised. Modernization and increasing scale in social organization are marked by a complex process of simultaneous homogenization and differentiation. Some differences vanish, whereas others emerge.

Truly global processes affect the conditions of people living in particular localities, creating new opportunities and forms of vulnerability. Risks are globally shared in the era of nuclear weapons, transnational terrorism and potential ecological disasters. On the same note, the economic conditions in particular localities frequently (some would say always) depend on events taking place elsewhere in the global system. If there is an industrial boom in Taiwan, towns in the English Midlands will be affected. If oil prices rise, this is a boon for the oil-exporting Trinidadian economy and a disaster for its oil-importing neighbour, Barbados.

Patterns of consumption also merge in certain respects; people everywhere seem to desire similar goods, from cell phones to ready-made garments. A precondition for this to happen is the more or less successful implementation of dimensions of modernity, notably a money economy – even if wage employment and literacy are less evenly distributed. The rising transnational flow of commodities, be they material or immaterial, creates a set of common cultural denominators that seem to eradicate local distinctions. The hot-dog, the pizza and the hamburger (or, in India, the lambburger) are truly parts of world cuisine; identical pop songs are played in discotheques in Costa Rica and Thailand; the same Coca-Cola commercials are shown with minimal local variations at cinemas all over the world, Dan Brown's novels are found wherever books are sold, and so on. Investment capital, military power and world literature are being disembedded from the constraints of space; they no longer belong to a particular locality. With the development of the jet plane, the satellite dish and more recently, the internet, distance no longer imposes limits on the flow of influence, investments and cultural meaning.

Yet, disembedding is never total; it is always counteracted by *re-embedding*. Sometimes, re-embedding is not even necessary – if one cares to look, the social world where most of humanity lives remains embedded in important respects, notwithstanding decades of intensive, technology-driven globalization. The impact of globalization – or, rather, its significance for the lives we lead – is considerable, but any one-sided account is ultimately false. Warning against the view of globalization as somehow 'the outcome' or the 'end product' of modernity, Mittelman writes that if 'globalization is a contested and political phenomenon, then it cannot have a predetermined outcome. A political agenda of inevitability overlooks the fact that globalization was made by humans, and, if so, can be unmade or remade by humankind.' It is far-reaching and consequential, but globalizing processes are always full of contradictions that are not likely to go away soon. Some people are globalizing, some are just being globalized, and many might be said to be scarcely affected directly by globalization.

Transnational capitalism creates both wealth and poverty. Millions of people – indeed hundreds of millions – will never have access to this wealth, not chiefly because they are actively exploited, but because they are ignored and squeezed into marginal areas of the modern world, like hunter-gatherers escaping from armed, well-organized farmers in an earlier period. The suffering of slum dwellers, dispossessed peasants, unemployed men and women everywhere, victims of war and of economic exploitation – and their occasionally well-orchestrated rebellions or projects seeking autonomy from globalized capitalism – are as much the results of globalization as the cellphone and the internet, international NGOs, cheap tropical holidays and transnational football fans. This means that any attempt to create a more just and equitable world inevitably has to use the tools provided by globalization with the aim of creating a different kind of globally interconnected world rather than dreaming of a return to a pre-globalized world. As Hegel and Marx foresaw, global interconnectedness need not be a tool of oppression; it can be the servant of human aspirations for liberation.

Further reading

Castells, M. (1996) *The Rise of the Network Society*. Blackwell, Oxford.

Cohen, D. (2006) *Globalization and its Enemies*. MIT Press, Boston, MA.

Eriksen, T. H. (2007) *Globalization: The Key Concepts*. Berg, Oxford.

Gilpin, R. (2002) *The Challenge of Global Capitalism: The World Economy in the 21st Century*. Princeton University Press, Princeton, NJ.

Hardt, M. and Negri, A. (2000) *Empire*. Harvard University Press, Cambridge, MA.

Hart, K. (2000) *The Memory Bank: Money in an Unequal World*. Profile, London.

Harvey, D. (1989) *The Condition of Postmodernity*. Blackwell, Oxford.

Held, D. and McGrew, A. (2000) The great globalization debate: an introduction. In Held, D. and McGrew, A. (eds) *The Global Transformations Reader*. Polity, Cambridge, pp. 1–50.

Mittelman, J. (2001) Globalization: captors and captives. In Mittelman, J. H. and Othman, N. (eds) *Capturing Globalization*. Routledge, London, pp. 1–17.

Robertson, R. (1992) *Globalization: Social Theory and Global Culture*. Sage, London.

Sassen, S. (2003) Spatialities and temporalities of the global: elements for a theorization. In Appadurai, A. (ed.) *Globalization*. Duke University Press, Durham, NC, pp. 260–78.

Scholte, J. (2005) *Globalization: A Critical Introduction*, 2nd edn. Palgrave, London.

Stiglitz, J. (2002) *Globalization and its Discontents*. Allen Lane, London.

3

Global Public Goods

Philip S. Golub and Jean-Paul Maréchal

Neoliberal globalization is producing deleterious outcomes at both the social and environmental levels. As Joseph Stiglitz points out, 'Globalization today is not working for many of the world's poor. It is not working for much of the environment. It is not working for the stability of the global economy.' This problem reflects an insufficient production of public goods, in particular of global public goods.

History and definition

The notion of public goods goes back at the very least to the classical British school of political economy founded by Adam Smith in the 1770s. Smith assigned public authorities with the triple task and duty to ensure the defence of society, administer justice and provide for 'works and institutions . . . facilitating the commerce of the society . . . and the instruction of the people'. The idea that there is a specific set of goods that must be provided by the state was subsequently reprised and deepened by economic theory and analysis.

Today, following Paul Samuelson, we commonly distinguish between two categories of goods: 'private consumption goods' and 'collective consumption goods'. The first are goods 'which can be parcelled out among different individuals' while the second are goods 'which all enjoy in common in the sense that each individual's consumption of such a good leads to no subtraction from any other individual's consumption of that good'. Put otherwise, contrary to what one observes for private goods of all kinds, the consumption of a public good by an economic agent, such as public lighting or a high-quality environment, does not reduce the available quantity of that same good for other economic agents. A public or collective good is considered 'pure' if it has two properties: 'non-excludability' and 'non-rivalry'. Non-excludability signifies that no economic agent can be excluded from the benefit of production of the good. Non-rivalry signifies that the consumption of that good by a person in no way diminishes the possibility for others to consume it.

National defence constitutes a perfect example of a pure public good insofar as each new citizen benefits from it (non-excludability) without reducing the level of protection benefiting all other citizens (non-rivalry). Besides national defence the most frequently discussed public goods are: domestic security, fundamental research (in contrast to applied research that can be privatized through patents), anti-poverty programmes, economic and financial stabilization policies, regulatory frameworks, redistributive public policies, and norms and conventions that reduce transaction costs (including language and units of measurement).

There is a large spectrum of goods between purely private and purely public goods. These in-between cases – sometimes called 'impure' public goods – belong either to the category of 'club goods' if they are exclusive but non-rival (coded TV broadcasts) or to the category of 'common resources' (or simply 'commons') if they are non-exclusive but rival (fish stocks). The climate may be considered a pure natural public good or, to be more precise, it was a pure natural global public good prior to the ability of human beings to modify it. Since the industrial revolution it has gradually became a global public good that has, in part, to be created by human beings. Of course, what has to be created is not the earth climate *per se* but earth climate stability. Put differently, climate stability is no longer a 'pure natural public good' nor a 'pure artificial public good'. It is both in part. It is a 'global common' or, to be more precise, 'carbon sinks' are global common resources. The increase in earth temperatures – which could be defined as a 'public bad'– is the result of an overuse by some economic agents (states, producers, consumers . . .) of the carbon absorbing capacities of the planet.

Being non-rival and non-excludable, public goods cannot be produced through capitalist market mechanisms. This constitutes their essential specificity. Indeed, a rational consumer will not spontaneously pay for a good that s/he can profit from freely (free-riding). Consequently, no firm will readily take on its production. This failure of the market to furnish goods and services that are collectively useful makes intervention by the public authorities indispensable. The state is the only economic agent in a position to constrain citizens to finance public goods through taxation.

The notion of public goods, initially conceived in the context of the national economy, has in recent decades been transposed to the international and global levels, hence the increasing use of expressions such as 'international public goods', 'world public goods' or 'global public goods'. These may be defined according to various criteria such as their intrinsic characteristics (natural goods such as water, artificial goods such as pharmaceutical products, or immaterial goods, such as knowledge), their spatial dimension (local, international or planetary), or their inter-temporal dimension (that is to say their greater or lesser irreversibility). The primary and most important international public good is of course peace.

The production of collective international or global public goods is made problematic by the absence of recognized and empowered transnational regulatory authorities. In addition to market failures, which justify government intervention, there is the problem, as far as international or global public goods are concerned, of state failures. The problem of opportunistic behaviour in interstate relations is analogous to the problem of opportunistic behaviour by economic agents in the national economy context.

Hegemonic stability and international regimes

Market failures and state failures imply the need to elaborate binding sets of rules and regulations at international and global levels. These rules and regulations are themselves an international public good. In the face of this series of failures, it is necessary to identify sources of authority allowing for global governance guaranteeing the production of international and world public goods. To do so, we have to turn to international relations theory. According to the dominant neorealist paradigm in international relations, international public goods are produced by dominant states that take on the responsibility of system management. Following Charles Kindleberger, neorealist authors such as Robert Gilpin developed the 'theory of hegemonic stability', which assumes that the stability of the international system depends on a *hegemon* having the capacity and the will to set up and maintain international order.

Basing themselves on the British and American cycles of predominance in the nineteenth and twentieth centuries and the breakdown of the interwar period, they argue that the *hegemon* (or 'benevolent despot' in Kindleberger's words) produces international public goods insofar as it ensures peace and security as well as an open liberal international economic system. Since the concentration of power generates order, it follows that de-concentration flowing from the decline of the hegemonic state generates systemic disorder and favours conflict, for instance through the constitution of rival trade blocks. The implicit and sometimes explicit corollary is that perpetuation of hegemony is in the universal interest or, at least, that the interests of the predominant state taking on the burden of system management coincide with those of a broad number of states.

These are at best questionable assumptions. First, they are based on sparse and selective evidence that skews the historical record. European predominance and British hegemony in the modern period were both a cause and consequence of the unequal division of the world between dominant centres and dependent peripheries. While it is true that the *pax Britannica* in the nineteenth century was characterized by a long period of interstate peace and economic expansion in Europe, at the global level it was characterized by constant war-making in the colonial periphery and the construction of an unequal hierarchical division of labour. The post-1945 *pax Americana* was co-operative exclusively among the developed capitalist countries. Outside of the triad of USA, Western Europe and Japan, it was generally coercive.

Second, at the epistemological level, the theory naturalizes the *status quo*. All transformation of the international order, such as diffusion or redistribution of power at the economic and political levels, is seen as being risk-laden. Hence, a polycentric or plural world system is considered *a priori* more unstable and dangerous than a hierarchical one. This system-maintenance bias has been convincingly shown to reflect the particular concerns of American theorists (such as Susan Strange and Robert Cox) regarding the perpetuation of US hegemony from 1945. Moreover, by assuming that the state is a unitary rational actor behaving in accordance with unchanging interests, it also naturalizes domination by selective domestic social groups.

Hence Richard Ashley's critique: neorealism 'creates a theoretical perspective that parades the possibility of a rational power that need never acknowledge power's limits. What emerges is a positivist structuralism that treats the given order as the natural order.'

Liberal theorizing with regard to complex interdependence or international regimes (Hedley Bull, Robert Keohane, Joseph Nye and Stephen Krasner) does a better job of explaining the role of institutions, norms and principles in producing convergence in various issue areas. Yet it does not supply tools to challenge the existing order of things or to bring about democratic global governance.

Imagining new architectures

Today, new sources of democratic authority need to be imagined and established to secure the production of global public goods. Despite a significant body of political theory on the question (Walzer, Rawls etc.), such sources do not exist at present. The normative aim should be a non-hegemonic system transcending the logic of rivalry of the modern interstate system.

As Richard Falk points out, however, some 'post-Westphalian scenarios' have to be rejected as being either undesirable or unattainable, among them the notion of a self-regulating global market system, the limits of which are now plainly apparent, and the idea of a world government. Yet we can move forward by going back to and renewing the basic principles enunciated in the United Nations charter, in particular those on universal social, economic and human rights (see *International Organizations*).

Indispensable measures include the democratization of decision-making and reshaping the normative orientation of the multilateral institutions responsible for the governance of globalization (IMF, World Bank and WTO). Increasing the voting rights of emerging as well as poor countries would enhance democratic fairness among nations. At the same time, the composition of the UN Security Council must be made to reflect world diversity and plural interests. At the very least this implies ending the monopoly of the five permanent members by giving decision-making positions to countries such as Brazil, India, Japan, Germany and South Africa. Going a bit further one could imagine a system of representation at the regional or sub-regional level (the European Union, Africa, Latin America etc.).

More fairness among nations would have to be accompanied by

more social fairness worldwide to secure the basic economic and social rights of individuals. The renovated institutional system would thus have as its mission to act at the global level to reduce poverty, secure food supply and define common humane norms for dealing with migration and other pressing issues of human survival. As Pierre Bauchet has suggested, these aims could be given constitutional form through greater definition of the tasks of the international public institutions, their relations and the principles of their interventions. These include: the principles of 'subsidiarity' (devolution to the lowest capable level), global regulation (harmonization of fiscal regimes, employment conditions etc.), and consensual management practices.

A great deal of trans-disciplinary theoretical work is required to advance towards humane global governance, which is in turn a *sine qua non* for the production of global public goods. Even more difficult will be translation of this work to the political level. Overcoming rivalry is unlikely to occur spontaneously. As the experience of European unification shows, advances towards transnational integration and co-operation require the emergence of new 'shared meanings' that eventually become embedded in society. In the European case, these came out of a historic experience of tragedy.

Further reading

Ashley, R. (1986) The poverty of neorealism. In Keohane, R. (ed.) *Neorealism and its Critics*. Columbia University Press, New York.

Bauchet, P. (2003) *Concentration des multinationales et mutation des pouvoirs de l'État*. CNRS Éditions, Paris.

Falk, R. (2004) *The Declining World Order: America's Imperial Geopolitics*. Routledge, London.

Gilpin, R. (1981) *War and Change in World Politic*. Cambridge University Press, Cambridge.

Hugon, P. (2003) L'économie éthique publique: biens publics mondiaux et patrimoines communs. In *Publication du programme interdisciplinaire: Éthique de l'économie*. UNESCO, Paris.

Keohane, R. (1984) *After Hegemony, Cooperation and Discord in the World Political Economy*. Princeton University Pres, Princeton NJ.

Kindleberger, C. (1986) International Public Goods without International Government. *American Economic Review* 76 (1).

Kindleberger, C. (1996) *World Economic Primacy: 1500–1990*. Oxford University Press, New York.

Samuelson, P. (1966) The pure theory of public expenditure. In Stiglitz, J. (ed.) *The Collected Scientific Papers of Paul A. Samuelson* vol. 2. MIT Press, Cambridge, MA, pp. 1223–5.

Samuelson, P., Nordhaus, W. and William, D. (1985) *Economics*. McGraw Hill, New York.

Smith, A. (2009 [1776]) *An Inquiry into the Nature and Causes of the Wealth of Nations*. Classic House, New York.

Stiglitz, J. (1999) Knowledge as a global public good. In Kaul, I., Grunberg, I. and Stern, M. (eds) *Global Public Goods: International Cooperation in the 21st Century*. Oxford University Press, New York.

Stiglitz, J. (2002) *Globalization and its Discontents*. Norton, London and New York.

4

International Organizations

François-Xavier Merrien and Angèle Flora Mendy

What are IOs?

International organizations (IOs) are associations of states established by treaties that share the same mandate, constitution and structure, but have legal personalities distinct from that of their constituent members (member states). In the domain that concerns us here, a distinction should be made between Bretton Woods organizations (International Financial Institutions or IFIs) and those within the United Nations system.

The International Monetary Fund (IMF) and the World Bank are IFIs that were founded in 1944 in the wake of the Bretton Woods talks. The World Trade Organization (WTO) was established in 1994. The United Nations system includes both those bodies that were established to promote economic and social development (UN Economic and Social Council or ECOSOC) and the UN's special agencies, the most important being the United Nations Development Program (UNDP), the International Labour Organization (ILO), the United Nations Conference of Trade and Development (UNCTAD) and the United Nations Children Fund (UNICEF). All these organizations were set up to prevent a recurrence of the economic and social crises that led to the Second World War.

IOs have long been neglected as an object of study. Political science and development studies did not take them into consideration until the late 1980s and they were seen mainly as state agencies acting in the international arena or as instruments of capitalist hegemony. The international relations tradition regards them as tools of the ruling powers, while post-structuralist analyses of development (see *Development*) and the critical school of International Political Economy see them as agents and representatives of a hegemonic order. Although their points of view differ, these two currents have something in common. For the former, the international order reflects state interests and the balance of power between states, with international organizations helping to extend the neoliberal order on the international stage. For the latter, international organizations are agents for the construction of a hegemonic order dominated by the United States. They help to reinforce military, diplomatic and economic domination by disseminating ideas and cultural systems, but also by making concessions to those they dominate. IOs therefore have only a limited autonomy.

In recent years, this assumption has been challenged or qualified by analyses that see IOs as actors with a degree of autonomy on the international stage. The influence of the dominant powers varies over time and depending on the institutions concerned. They always have a degree of relative autonomy because of the nature of their power and the way they are financed, because their officials have some latitude or because of the missions entrusted to them. IOs have often defended goals to which even their most powerful sponsors objected. And they are not monolithic organizations. Even within the most highly structured organizations, there are minority schools of opinion which, in specific contexts, can make their voices heard or introduce alternative points of view.

IOs do a lot to shape international norms with regard to economic, social or environmental issues and human rights. It would be reductive, however, to see them as autonomous norm-generating agencies. IOs are always influenced by the ideas of outside organizations, social networks and groups. The paradigm shifts and changes of policy that punctuate the actions of international organizations do not result solely from internal paradigm shifts, but from interaction between the organization concerned and outsiders, especially Transnational Advocacy Networks (TAN). These networks include representatives of both civil society and the political world and have many supporters in governments and international organizations. Their voices are more likely to be heard when they can develop policy frames that offer a solution to the contradictions, impasses or new issues confronting IOs. The strength of such influences also depends on their own ability to develop networks and to communicate effectively.

A striking example of this process is how the gender paradigm was introduced into the discourse and programmes of International Organizations from the 1970s onwards. The Women in Development movement popularized the idea that a focus on women was essential if development programmes were to be effective. This movement, which was supported in the 1970s by liberal feminists in the US, Canada and Scandinavia, backed the declaration of a UN Decade for Women (1975–85) and organization of a series of international conferences on women in Mexico City, Copenhagen, Nairobi, Beijing and New York. Its influence was apparent in the adoption of the Convention on the Elimination of all Forms of Discrimination against Women, the establishment of specialist UN agencies such as UNIFEM and UNDAW (UN Division for the Advancement of Women) and the implementation of a large number of development programmes emphasizing women's productive roles (rather than just their reproductive role). Ten years later and against a groundswell of criticisms of WID, especially of its failure to take account of the dialectic of productive and non-productive gender roles, the Gender and Development movement came to the fore. GAD took the view that gender is a social construct. Gender analysis needed to be more aware of unequal access to resources in both domestic and productive spheres. The GAD movement has had a major influence on IOs and on programmes implemented in developing countries. It was behind the adoption of Gender Mainstreaming as a general policy principle by all the main international and bilateral organizations at the Beijing International Conference on Women (including the European Union, World Bank, UNDP, ILO, USAID and many others). As a result of Gender Mainstreaming, gender equality has been incorporated into policies, programmes and projects at every level.

One of the main obstacles to analysing IOs is that they are so diverse. They differ in terms of their mandates, their internal power structures (the way power is divided between stakeholders), their institutional structure, their history and their organizational culture. An organization's mandate defines its goals and objectives; the more specific the mandate, the more decisive its role. In that sense, a distinction can be made between organizations with strictly defined mandates (the IMF and the WTO) and those with broader mandates, such as the World Bank (the 'development' mentioned in its statutes has been interpreted as meaning many different things) or, even more, UNDP, UNCTAD and the ILO.

The Bretton Woods organizations either lay down strict rules (WTO) or grant loans (World Bank, IMF) – which most debt-stricken countries cannot do without – and work in ways that have more in common with companies than with UN organizations. Their staff have larger budgets and greater freedom to act than UN pro-grammes. They, and the networks they surround themselves with, come from similar, elevated backgrounds (neoclassical economics and usually a PhD from a British or American university) and tend to share the same analysis. This tendency has become more pro-nounced over the last thirty years.

The staff of UN organizations and programmes, although not immune to this tendency, come from a wider range of backgrounds and hold more varied worldviews. The UN is not very homogene-ous, except in terms of the universal goals it sets itself and defends. According to its charter, ECOSOC is a co-ordinator, but it has never been in a position to act as such. It is not unusual for competing programmes to be developed without reference to one another. Thus issues relating to education, health, food and trade are handled by different agencies, such as UNESCO, UNICEF, UNDP, UNCTAD or the FAO. On paper, the remits of ECOSOC and UNCTAD are practically the same. Moreover, the budgets available to UN pro-grammes are pathetic when compared with the Bank's.

From development to neoliberalism

While their goals have changed little over sixty years, the geopo-litical context and their intellectual and ideological inspiration have changed. In the twenty years that followed the establishment of the UN and the international financial institutions (IFIs), the emphasis was mainly on growth (meaning capital accumulation), increased investment and productivity and the balance of international pay-ments. The primary objectives of development policies then were industrialization and economic modernization. The big projects financed and recommended by UN programmes and the World Bank prioritized major infrastructural investment in roads and dams that were assumed to be the main vectors for economic modernization.

Social questions were not overlooked, but in general it was assumed that social well-being would come from development and that the countries concerned had an almost exclusive responsibility for social policy. During this period, the WHO devoted all its effort to programmes aiming to eradicate disease. The ILO tirelessly devoted itself to the task of improving workers' living conditions. It supplied technical support to governments, published recommendations and designed social and labour conventions that could be adopted by states. These were based on tripartite agreements between unions, employers and the state with the goal of improving the fate of the workforce. It was only in the 1970s that the issue of workers in the informal sector became part of its agenda (see *Informal Economy*).

The big organizations operate within a geopolitical context that was defined at first by the East–West conflict of the Cold War and then by a North–South divide; and this has greatly limited their scope for action, even ruling out certain policies. IOs refused to intervene in internal affairs of state and have backed the sometimes pharaonic and meaningless projects of dictators. Nevertheless, they did open up a space for discussions of development. They facilitated the emergence of new approaches, such as dependency and the new international economic order.

In the 1960s, the emergence of the countries of the South and especially the non-aligned movement led the UN to launch its 'Decade of Development' campaign. The United Nations Conference on Trade and Development played an innovative role in this. UNCTAD was, from its beginnings, part of a project to create a new economic order under the charismatic leadership of Secretary General Raül Prebish, the Argentinian development economist. During the 1970s, UNCTAD played a vital role in North–South discussions by defending the right of the countries of the South to demand a fairer international order. At the same time, some – the developed countries – saw UNCTAD, at best, as a talking shop that had no formal implications, while others –the southern countries in the Group of 77 (G77) wanted its decisions to be binding.

The United Research Institute for Social Development (UNRISD) was established in 1963. Ever since, this small Geneva-based organization, whose role often goes unnoticed, has carried out its own research and developed its own critique of social development. Thanks to the freedom of action given it by its charter – and the financial backing it receives from the Scandinavian countries and

Switzerland – UNRISD has pursued a critical analysis revealing, among other things, the inadequacies of 'mainstream' studies, the limitations of economic indicators, the negative effects of globalization, as well as the importance of the issues of gender, civil society and social welfare.

During this same period the World Bank's priorities changed. The emphasis shifted from infrastructures to the fight against poverty and to basic needs. The strategic emphasis was now on policies affecting education, health, nutrition, rural development and support for local projects and communities. The developing countries were now the main beneficiaries of loans from the Bank, which were facilitated by the creation of the International Development Association (IDA) in 1960. The WHO reorientated its actions and prioritized basic health care and the universal objective of health for all (the Alma–Ata Declaration of 1978), while UNESCO adopted similar decisions in the field of education. This period of optimism came to an end in the 1980s.

The financial crisis in Latin America, the collapse of the socialist bloc, the break-up of consensus among the developing countries, the growing influence of neoliberal ideas on political elites everywhere and the rapid acceleration of financial flows sounded the death knell for a whole period. The new context saw the rapid emergence of a dominant neoliberal ideology: government, industrial and social policies were criticized on the grounds that their guaranteed revenue streams resulted in economic inefficiency. Priority had to be given to cleaning up public finances, liberalizing economies and privatizing business and social services. The 'Washington Consensus' symbolized this policy reversal.

The IFIs criticized UN organizations and exercised hegemonic influence over conservative governments. They expanded their field of action considerably. The countries of the South were forced to accept harsh structural adjustment programmes (SAPs). The collapse of the socialist bloc accelerated this process. The developing countries and then the former communist countries became laboratories for experiments in reforming economic and social policy. The World Bank and the IMF each defended their 'shock therapy' strategy of reducing the role of the state and privatizing state-owned companies.

The ILO, which had a certain coherence during *les trente glorieuses* and the Cold War, was faced with a difficult challenge as the role of the state diminished and wage-earning, which had until then appeared to be the indisputable future of labour, became rarer in a world where the informal economy employs three out of four of all workers.

The World Bank championed the Chilean model of private pension funds financed through individual capitalization as a model for social policy. Privatization was justified on the grounds that health services were expensive and their main beneficiaries were in any case the middle classes. Governments should concentrate their efforts on providing public health resources for the poor. Health services were to be placed on a contractual basis (in accordance with the principles of New Public Management), thereby giving a major role to the private sector and non-governmental organizations (see *Third Sector*). The Bamako Initiative (1987) broke with the earlier tradition of public service by introducing the principle of user-fees.

The effects of these measures on growth and development have yet to be seen. Their immediate consequence was to destroy jobs, increase unemployment, reduce standards of living, increase inequality and encourage social exclusion and widespread poverty. The World Bank has had to implement social funds and policies to soften the effects of a crisis it made.

Along with the World Bank, the WTO has played an active role in liberalizing international trade. In this respect it looks like an agency that services the needs of economic globalization at the expense of the weakest states. The countries of the South have not received what they expected in turn: a reduction in the protection and subsidies enjoyed by farmers in the richer North. The implementation of the TRIPS agreement (Trade-Related Aspects of Intellectual Property Rights) appears, for example, to have had disastrous effects on health by reducing the South's ability to implement their own policies on drugs. The pressure brought to bear by NGOs on states and the WHO eventually forced them to retreat in this sector, but only partly. For a decade now, negotiating cycles have been blocked more often than they have made progress.

During this period, UN organizations have adopted a more critical stance. UNICEF has emphasized the negative effects of SAPs on children and women. The UNDP, an organization with offices in over 130 countries, has often adopted positions critical of the IFIs' orthodoxy. It supported early on concerns for human capital (health and education), international public goods and gender. It has defended a multidimensional analysis of development and poverty by calling on the economist Amartya Sen to draw up the human development index. The UNDP undeniably generates ideas and norms at the international level, especially with its *Report on Human Development*, which includes an appendix ranking countries according to that index.

UNCTAD, on the other hand, is a mouthpiece for the peripheral countries and has been confined to playing a secondary role. Its annual reports on 'Trade and Development', 'the Less Advanced Countries', World Investment' and 'the Less Developed Countries' are often critical of orthodoxy, but have not received the coverage they deserve. Its very existence has come under threat more than once, notably when the World Trade Organization was established.

After the Washington Consensus

As a result of structural adjustment's social costs, of the policies forced on Asian and Latin American countries in the 1997–8 financial crisis and of the social movements that have arisen in recent years (see *Alter-Globalization*), the Washington Consensus has unravelled. The big IOs have been forced to admit that their economic diagnosis was wrong and that institutional frameworks and social development are important because there can be no market without them. Social development is once more a priority. The World Social Summit (in Copenhagen, 1995) marked a major shift in priorities and has resulted in what some call a 'post-Washington consensus'.

After two decades of giving absolute priority to policies designed to stabilize and liberalize economies, a new concern for human development (the war on poverty, health, education, decent jobs, access to water . . .) and institutional reforms (the fight against corruption, democracy, good governance) are gradually becoming the top priorities, even though the earlier goals linger on in the international agenda.

The period around the millennium saw a new consensus on the need to reduce poverty. Reducing poverty is now being promoted as the basic objective of so-called 'development' policies. With the agreement of the international community, the IMF and World Bank now advocate Strategic Poverty Reduction Solutions, which must be drawn up by the poor countries themselves. The Millennium Goals approved by the UN General Assembly include the goal of reducing poverty by half by 2015. But while the Millennium Goals set medium-terms universal goals (2015), SPRS set short-term (three years) national goals and include a macroeconomic matrix, institutional reforms, action priorities and operating budgets.

The new approach marks a break with the period of structural adjustment in terms of both method and principle. Unlike the policies dictated by Structural Adjustment Programmes (SAP), the SPRS prioritize 'development' goals and basic social services at the national level. Whereas SAPs took no notice of the political regimes, there is a new concern for human rights and the rule of law. Unlike the top-down approach dictated by SAPs, the SPRS are based on a bottom-up approach and upon the idea of 'empowerment' of the people. The requirement to meet multiple *a priori* conditions gave way to mutual performance assessments and support was given to budgets rather than projects. Donor countries have adopted the Declarations of Rome (2003) and Paris (2005) to improve the co-ordination of aid and to make progress towards these international goals.

The World Bank, IMF, UNDP, the Organization for Economic Co-operation and Development (OECD) and bilateral organizations play the leading role in promoting these new international priorities and development approaches. In this they have often done little more than respond to the normative pressures brought to bear by other actors. The origins of the change in development policies can obviously be traced back to mass protests and the analyses of large NGOs, to criticisms emanating from UN agencies and departments – especially ECOSOC, UNICEF, ILO and UNDP – and to the big UN Conferences. No one can be unaware, for example, of such events as the 1987 publication of UNICEF's report on 'Adjustment with a Human Face' or the World Social Summit in Copenhagen, not to mention the Jubilee 2000 international coalition movement and the 'Make Poverty History' movement. This shift of emphasis in development policies reflects an overall change of attitude at the international level, a massive loss of trust in policies dominated by orthodox economic imperatives and the need to prioritize social objectives.

Opinions on SPRS and the Millennium Development Goals vary, with many experts taking the view that the former are nothing more than a continuation of structural adjustment programmes under another name, or a reframing of the neoliberal approach. For instance, the macro-economic frame of reference remains unchanged and the focus on good governance has had the effect of imposing political as well as economic conditions. The definition of poverty is often absolute rather than multidimensional. Civil society's involvement in drawing up the programmes is often more formal than real. And the decision to adopt a Strategic Poverty Reduction Document is conditional on its acceptance by the World Bank and the IMF. However, it cannot be denied that a SPRS does open up a political space and that many neoliberal development dogmas are no longer so imperative.

The Millennium Development Goals may not live up to the expectations of the third or voluntary sector (they do not, for example, include the aim of reducing inequality) and the financial resources available may be inadequate; but they do represent a major step at the international level towards recognizing human rights and the need for greater efforts to redistribute wealth. It is also true, however, that how the IOs define the means required to achieve these goals reveals continuing tensions between Bretton Woods and UN organizations. While both emphasize the need to increase the level of aid considerably, to make it more predictable and to harmonize and co-ordinate international aid, they take different views on what measures need to be taken at the national level. The former continue to prioritize trade liberalization, improving the economic environment for investment purposes, good governance and support for grassroots social initiatives. While they do not ignore these aspects, the latter tend to see human development as a greater priority.

Around 2005–7, the World Bank and IMF lost much of their influence and resources and they were on the verge of crisis. Developing countries' refusal to accept more stringent checks from the IFIs, uninterrupted global economic growth and China's emergence as an international financial power encouraged a growing number of countries to repay their debts ahead of schedule and not to borrow from either the IMF or the Bank. The 2008 crisis did allow both organizations, especially the IMF, to recover their influence. But both are now having to fight for funding as the world economic crisis deepens.

The governance of the IMF and the World Bank is still an issue. Europe and the United States still appoint the head of each respectively; and, despite recent reforms, power still lies with the West. The United States have 17 per cent of voting rights in the IMF and high-income countries 52 per cent, while the BRIC countries (Brazil, Russia, India and China) have only 11 per cent between them and the rest of the world (163 out of 185 countries) 37 per cent. Reform of the World Bank is also on the agenda. Topics for discussion include choosing a President irrespective of nationality, greater representation on the Executive Board for poor countries and an improved division of labour between the IMF and the Bank in order to allow the Bank to focus on the poorer countries and to emphasize grants rather than loans.

At the United Nations, the Security Council is being reorganized and reforms of governance and improved inter-agency co-ordination are also on the agenda. But, despite the urgent need for reform, the search for better ways to finance the organization has barely begun.

The difficulties encountered at Copenhagen in 2009 over reaching agreement on climate change are symbolic of the uncertainties facing the international order today.

Further reading

Barnett, M. and Finnemore, M. (2004) *Rules for the World: International Organizations in Global Politics*. Cornell University Press, Ithaca, NY, and London.

Cooper, F. and Packard, R. (eds) (1997) *International Development and the Social Sciences: Essays in the History and Politics of Knowledge*. University of California Press, Berkeley.

Cornwall, A., Harrison, E. and Whitehead, A. (2007) *Feminisms in Development: Contradictions, Contestations and Challenges*. Zed Books, London and New York.

Cox, R. W. (1987) *Production, Power and World Order: Social Forces in the Making of History*. Columbia University Press, New York.

Deacon, B. et al. (1997) *Global Social Policy*. Sage, London.

Dezalay, Y. and Garth, B. (2002) *The Internationalization of Palace Wars*. University of Chicago Press, Chicago.

Kelley, L. (ed.) (2002) *Health Impacts of Globalization: Towards Global Governance*. Palgrave Macmillan, London.

Keohane, R.O. (ed.) (1986) *Neorealism and its Critics*. Columbia University Press, New York.

Mkandawire, T. (ed.) (2001) *Social Policy in a Development Context*. UNRISD/ Macmillan, Geneva.

Risse, T., Ropp, S. C. and Sikkink, K. (1999) *The Power of Human Rights: International Norms and Domestic Change*. Cambridge University Press, Cambridge.

Stone, D. and Maxwell, S. (eds) (2004) *Global Knowledge Networks and International Development: Bridges Across Boundaries*. Routledge, London.

Toye, R. (2004) *The UN and Global Political Economy: Trade, Finance and Development*. Indiana University Press, Bloomington.

Wade, R. (2002) US hegemony and the World Bank: the fight over people and ideas. *Review of International Political Economy* 9 (2), 215–43.

Woods, N. (2006) *The Globalizers: The IMF, the World Bank and their Borrowers.* Cornell University Press, Ithaca, NY.

5

Development

Keith Hart and Vishnu Padayachee

What is 'development'?

In 1800 the world's population was around one billion. At that time only one in forty people lived in towns and cities. The rest lived by extracting a livelihood from the land. Animals and plants were responsible for almost all the energy produced and consumed by human beings. Two centuries later, world population had reached six billions. The proportion living in cities was close to a half. Inanimate energy sources converted by machines now accounted for the bulk of production and consumption. For most of this period, the human population has been growing at an average annual rate of 1.5 per cent; cities at two per cent a year; and energy production at around three per cent a year. This last figure is double the rate of population increase, a powerful index of the economic expansion of the last two hundred years. Many people live longer, work less and spend more than they did before. But the distribution of all this extra energy has been grossly unequal. A third of humanity still works in the fields with their hands and a similar number have never made a telephone call. Americans each consume four hundred times more energy than the average Ugandan, for example.

Development thus refers in the first instance to this hectic dash of humanity from the village to the city. It is widely assumed that the engine driving this economic growth and the inequality it entails is 'capitalism'. *Development* then comes to mean trying to understand both how capitalist growth is generated and how to make good the damage capitalism causes in repeated cycles of creation and destruction ('creative destruction', as Joseph Schumpeter put it). A third meaning refers to the *developmental state* of the mid twentieth century, the idea that governments are best placed to engineer sustained economic growth with redistribution. Pioneered by fascist and communist states, this model took root in the late colonial empires around the Second World War and became the norm for developed and newly independent countries afterwards, at least until the1970s.

The most common usage of *development* over the last half century, however, refers to the commitment of rich countries to help poor countries become richer. In the wake of the anti-colonial revolution, such a commitment was real enough, even if the recipes chosen were often flawed. But after the watershed of the 1970s, this commitment has faded. If, in the 1950s and 1960s, the rapid growth of the world economy encouraged a belief that poor countries too could embark on their own enrichment, from the 1980s onwards 'development' has more often meant freeing up global markets and applying sticking plaster to the wounds inflicted by exploitation and neglect. *Development* has thus been a label for political relations between rich and poor countries after colonial empire.

This has meant that *development* has been closely tied to the question of aid. The volume of aid from rich to poor countries or through the multilateral institutions such as the World Bank was never great and has declined relatively over the decades. It was always problematic in that the forms of aid were often more attuned to the interests of the donors than the recipients (see Judith Tendler's devastating critique, *Inside Foreign Aid*). Moreover, the gift relationship intrinsic to aid, a sort of latter-day alms (see *Gift*), reproduced an unequal world order with rich whites at the top and poor people of colour at the bottom. Finally, it was not obvious whether aid was intended to enrich the poor countries or merely to offer a palliative for their distress. In 2009 Dambisa Moyo, a Zambian economist who worked for Goldman Sachs, made an international impact with her book, *Dead Aid: Why Aid is not Working and How There is Another Way for Africa*, where she suggested that aid was an obstacle to development, not a solution. Needless to say, there are strong social forces in the rich countries opposed to this view and aid is still seen by many there as a moral commitment to make good the legacy of imperialism.

There are massive regional discrepancies in experiences of development since the collapse of European empire. After the anti-colonial revolution unleashed by the Second World War, many Asian countries did install successful capitalist economies, with and without Western help, eventually bringing about the eastward shift in the balance of global economic power that has accelerated in recent years. But other regions, especially Africa, the Middle East and much of Latin America, have stagnated or declined since the 1970s. These divergent paths have led to the circulation of a variety of development models, with an Asian emphasis on authoritarian states (notably China's) being opposed to Western liberalism and radical political alternatives coming out of Latin America in particular.

After the Second World War, there were two decades of general economic growth and relatively strong states (the 1950s and 1960s), followed later by two decades of economic stagnation and weakened states (the 1980s and 1990s) with the 1970s as the hinge between them. It soon became apparent that development in the sense of poor countries becoming richer was failing. By the 1980s, in the aftermath of the oil shocks and 'stagflation' of the1970s and with neoliberal conservatives in power, development was no longer seriously on the agenda. Instead the drive was to open up the world's economies to capital flows ('structural adjustment'), if necessary at the expense of states' ability to govern; and debt interest payments became a huge income drain from the poor countries. Under these circumstances, a 'post-development' critique arose suggesting that *development* was a sham discourse with no real achievements to its credit.

An unequal world

Since the formation of the United Nations in 1945, it has become normal to collect statistics on the world population; but thinking about humanity as a single entity has not yet taken hold. It is about time that it did. World society today is like the advanced centres of agrarian civilization before the modern revolutions swept them away. More than two centuries of political struggle and economic development have left the world in a condition similar to France's Old Regime when Jean-Jacques Rousseau wrote his discourse on inequality in the mid eighteenth century. How else can one describe a situation where a socially exclusive minority controls an impoverished mass whose powerlessness is now measured by how little money they have to spend? The latest wave of the machine revolution has granted one man a net worth of $40 billion and dominance of the global information industry, while billions of people lack material essentials, not to mention access to the internet.

There are two pressing features of our world: the unprecedented integration of markets since the Second World War and massive economic inequality between rich and poor nations. Becoming closer and more unequal at the same time is an explosive combination. *Forbes* magazine reported in March 2009 that the top ten richest individuals had a net worth between them of $250 billion, roughly the annual income of Finland (population five million) or of middle-ranking regional powers such as Venezuela (28 million), South Africa (49 million) and Iran (72 million). The same sum of a quarter trillion dollars equals the annual income of twenty-six sub-Saharan African countries with a combined population of almost half a billion or a twelfth of all those alive today.

Providing adequate food, clean water and basic education for the world's poorest people could all be achieved for less than the West spends annually on makeup, ice cream and pet food. The rate of car ownership in developed countries is 400 per thousand, under twenty in all developing countries. The rich pollute the world fifty times more than the poor; but the latter are more likely to die from the pollution. The UNDP *Human Development Report* for 1998 claimed that world consumption had increased six times in the previous two decades; but the richest 20 per cent accounted for 86 per cent of private expenditure, the poorest 20 per cent for only 1.3 per cent. Africa, with a seventh of the world's population (and rising), has two per cent of global purchasing power.

The world's poor are concentrated in what came to be called the Third World and latterly the Global South as a result of Western expansion over five centuries and particularly of colonial empires established in the nineteenth century. The world's young people are to be found predominantly in the South owing to a lag in the fall of birth rates there. The age distributions of rich and poor countries are skewed heavily towards the old and young respectively. There are tremendous inequalities within countries and regions; but a two-class model fits the above description quite closely. A rich, mainly white, ageing minority (about a sixth of the total, if we take North America, the European Union and Japan together) is surrounded by a majority that is a lot poorer, darker in colour and much younger. From the perspective of human reproduction as a whole, a dwindling Western elite will soon be replaced by non-Westerners from whom they are separated by a tradition of cultural arrogance and ingrained practices of social exclusion.

The *apartheid* principle of separating rich and poor spatially is to be found everywhere in local systems of discrimination, more or less blatant. But the Caribbean Nobel Prize-winning economist Sir Arthur Lewis makes a plausible case that twentieth-century world society was constructed along racial lines at a particular historical conjuncture. In three decades leading up to the First World War, fifty million Europeans left home for temperate lands of new settlement (three-quarters of them for the United States); the same number of Indians and Chinese ('coolies') were shipped to the colonies as indentured labourers. These two streams of migrants had to be kept apart since, although their work and skill-level were often similar, whites were paid on average nine shillings a day, while Asians received one shilling a day. In those areas where Asian workers were allowed to settle, the price of local wage-labour was driven down to their level. Western imperialism's division of the world at this time into countries of dear and cheap labour had profound consequences for their subsequent economic development. Demand in high-wage economies is stronger than in their low-wage counterparts. World trade has been organized ever since in the interests of the better-paid, with tax-rich states subsidizing their farmers to dump cheap food overseas at the expense of local agricultural development, while preventing poorer countries' manufactures from undermining the wages of industrial workers at home. South Africa and the United States each encouraged heavy immigration of working-class Europeans while seeking to retain a reserve of poorly paid black and Asian labour. The resulting dualism is inscribed on their shared history of racist urbanization.

The politics of African development

The project of developing Africa took hold in the late colonial period, around the Second World War and immediately after (see Fred Cooper's *Decolonization and African Society*). But independence from colonial rule, beginning in the late 1950s and culminating in the 1970s war against Portugal and the Southern white settler states, brought a new dimension to the search for economic development there. In 1960 Ghana, then the world's leading exporter of cocoa, had a bigger economy than Indonesia's and *per capita* income on a par with South Korea. But the economic failures of subsequent decades led to the situation today where Africa is the prime symbol of poverty in our world.

It is a curious fact that China occupied a similar slot in Western consciousness not long ago. In the 1920s and 1930s, Americans and Europeans often spoke of the Chinese the way they do of Africa today. China was then crippled by the violence of warlords, its peasants mired in the worst poverty imaginable. Today the country is spoken of as the likely global superpower, while its manufactures make inroads into Western dominance on a scale far greater than Japan's ever did. This profound shift in economic power from West to East does not guarantee Africa's escape from the shackles of inequality, but it does mean that structures of Atlantic dominance that once seemed inevitable are perceptibly on the move. We are entering a new phase of economic possibility worldwide, as well as of different constraints on development.

There has for a few decades now been a tendency to cleanse development bureaucracy of considerations of power, class and politics. By overlooking the violent social upheavals and struggles that characterize capitalist development, this makes it harder to understand the savage inequality typical of the South, not least in Africa. James Ferguson coined the apt phrase 'anti-politics machine' to describe this tendency. Based on anthropological research in the landlocked enclave of Lesotho, Ferguson argued that the World Bank's profile of that small country represented it as remote and isolated, a hopeless place cut off from the rest of the world by mountains and cultural tradition. In contrast, he demonstrated Lesotho's strong links to South Africa, especially as a migrant labour reserve for the mines. In the Bank's sanitized version of 'development' the same policies devised for Sri Lanka or Peru should apply in Lesotho. It is politics that makes these countries different and that dimension is normatively excluded by a narrow focus on poverty alleviation.

It would be no exaggeration to say that African development has been a site of class struggle between the bureaucracy, both national and international, and the people however they are classified (see *Informal Economy*). Human lives were overridden by bureaucratic planning recipes that could not accommodate people's real interests and practices. In a neoliberal climate this observation could be assimilated to a critique of the state, the core of bureaucratic order.

Consequently states were by-passed as corrupt and ineffective, their place taken by NGOs. But NGOs are not just Not Governments, they *are* Organizations, that is, bureaucracies (see *NGOs*). In many ways NGOs are driven by even stronger bureaucratic imperatives, more alien to the people concerned than many government agencies, because they depend on the image they can project to Western donors; and they are even less accountable to local people. The multilateral agencies too, who took it on themselves to co-ordinate development, have constantly struggled with the contradiction between their bureaucratic nature and the desire to stimulate self-organized human initiatives on the ground that are inevitably stifled by rational controls.

Africa appears in the Western media as little more than a playground for the four horsemen of the apocalypse: conquest, war, famine and death. Yet the continent's population is growing at 2.5 per cent a year and is projected to reach 1.8bn by 2050, near a quarter of humanity. Starting the twentieth century as the least densely populated and urbanized major region in the world, Africa is now close to the global average on both counts, having experienced a population explosion and urban revolution of unprecedented speed and size. The Asian manufacturing exporters have been quicker than the West to grasp the significance of Africa's potential share of the world market. The continent's development prospects could improve considerably in the coming half century, with the region's sole capitalist power, South Africa, playing a major role.

To speak of a possible economic upturn begs the question of what Africa's new urban populations could produce as a means of bringing about their own economic development. So far, African countries have relied on exporting raw materials, when they could. Minerals clearly have a promising future owing to scarce supplies and escalating demand; but the world market for food and other agricultural products is skewed by Western farm subsidies and prices are further depressed by the large number of poor farmers seeking entry. Conventionally, African governments have aspired to manufacturing exports as an alternative, but here they face intense competition from Asia. It would be more fruitful for African countries to argue collectively in the councils of world trade for some protection from international dumping, so that their farmers and infant industries might at least get a chance to supply their own populations first. But the world market for services is booming and perhaps greater opportunities for supplying national, regional and global markets exist there.

There was a time when most services were performed personally on the spot; but today, as a result of the digital revolution in communications (see *Digital Commons*), they increasingly link producers and consumers at distance. The fastest-growing sector of world trade is the production of culture: entertainment, education, media, software and a wide range of information services. The future of the human economy, once certain material requirements are satisfied, lies in the infinite scope for us to do things for each other – like singing songs or telling stories – that need not take a tangible form. The largest global television audiences are for sporting events like the World Cup or the Olympic Games. The United States' three leading exports are now movies, music and software; and this is why they have sponsored an intellectual property treaty (TRIPs) that seeks to shore up the profits of corporations whose products can be reproduced digitally at almost no cost. The central conflict in contemporary capitalism is between this attempt to privatize the cultural commons and widespread popular resistance to it.

There is a lot more to play for here and the terrain is not as rigidly mapped out as in agriculture and manufactures. It is also one where Africans are well placed to compete because of the proven preference of global audiences for their music and plastic arts. The world's second largest producer of movies after Hollywood is now Lagos in Nigeria ('Nollywood'), having recently overtaken Bollywood. Most of these movies cost no more than $5,000, a pattern reminiscent of Hollywood a century ago. American popular culture is still that country's most successful export. There is no reason why it couldn't be Africa's too.

Africa must escape soon from varieties of Old Regime that owe a lot to the historical legacy of slavery, colonialism and apartheid; but conditions there can no longer be attributed solely to these ancient causes. Developments in economy, technology, religion and the arts could offer fresh solutions for African underdevelopment. These would have to build on the conditions and energies generated by the twentieth century's urban revolution. Above all, new political forms must be found adequate to the task of bringing long-delayed emancipation to African peoples. These will include new models of economic integration across national boundaries.

The study of development

For a half century now, development studies has offered an interdisciplinary space within an increasingly formalized academic division of labour. It has thus performed a creative and innovative function comparable to area studies, Marxism, feminism and more recently cultural studies. The theories animating this field have shifted along with world history. In the 1960s, the dominant approach was *modernization*, the idea that poor people should become more like the rich. This meant replacing 'traditional' institutions with 'modern' ones, adopting a 'bourgeois package' that consisted of cities, capital, science and technology, democracy, the rule of law and education for all. Around 1970, it became clear that this wasn't working (see *Informal Economy*) and Marxist theories emanating from the other side in the Cold War, especially from Latin America and the Middle East, but also from France, became more generally accepted. These took the view that *underdevelopment* and *dependency* were caused by poor countries participating in a *world system* controlled by and for the rich capitalist countries. Development under these circumstances required them to withdraw from what was essentially a zero sum game, redistributing the wealth of the periphery to the core.

From the 1980s, when neoliberal policies became dominant, the focus of development theory moved away from the state's role in engineering 'national capitalism', the attempt to control markets, money and accumulation through central bureaucracy for the benefit of all citizens. Now it was on making markets work and getting prices right. This emphasis signalled the growing power of economics in contrast to an earlier inter- and multi-disciplinary approach to development thinking and practice. The development industry was controlled in the 1950s by engineering firms, since it was assumed that development meant blowing a hole in the rock and filling it with water. Around the 1960s economists, largely in an accountancy role, pointed out that development cost money and was supposed to yield economic returns, so cost-benefit analysis was introduced. Then it was discovered that the supposed beneficiaries of development – and the likely cause of planning failures – were people; so from the 1970s, sociologists, anthropologists and political scientists were recruited to monitor 'the human factor'. The neoliberal revolution of the 1980s installed the economists in full command and development studies' interdisciplinary ethos was effectively sidelined. The rationale for a separate area of academic study labelled 'development', as well as the need to think about development strategy beyond macro- and micro-economic policy, was called into question.

As Henry Bernstein points out, this was not just the triumph of economics, but of neoclassical economics (see *Building the human economy together*), one moreover that insisted on the totalizing primacy of mathematical modelling and econometrics, as well as on a highly technical concern with measurement, often directed to quantifying 'poverty'. Ever since the industrial revolution, elites were concerned to measure the material progress and deterioration of the poor urban masses. This concern now took a specific technical form. While mathematics, modelling and measurement all have their uses, we should also recognize their limitations. Another Nobel Prize-winning economist, Wassily Leontief, complained in 1970 that 'uncritical enthusiasm for mathematical formulation tends often to conceal the ephemeral content of the argument'.

We endorse a renewed drive to make development studies more open and inter- or multi-disciplinary. But this strategy too carries risks. Ravi Kanbur has pointed out:

> The social sciences need to come together to address specific and general problems in development studies and development policy. [But] there is the ever-present danger of the lowest common denominator. Instead of the strengths of each discipline, we may pick up the weaknesses of each. In the end, disciplinary narrowness may simply be replaced by lack of clarity.

So is 'Development Studies' a distinct academic field offering us a real degree of freedom from the disciplinary guilds or has it become an ossified irrelevance? Specifically, can the field now make a comeback from three decades of fighting the dominant trend of global politics?

Beyond development?

The premise of rich countries helping the poor to 'develop', first in their capacity as colonial masters and then within a framework of national independence, did have some force in the immediate post-war decades. But three decades of neoliberal globalization (see *Globalization* and *Alter-Globalization*) have undermined all that. When debt repayments have drained income from the poor countries, governments' ability to protect their citizens have been undermined by structural adjustment and aid levels have shrunk to the point of being merely symbolic, it is not surprising that many now see 'development' as a hypocritical claim to moral superiority on the part of the rich that obscures the economic realities of our world.

So advocates of a 'post-development' approach have suggested that 'development' is now over. To this has been added a growing insistence on ecological or environmental imperatives, usually referred to as 'sustainable development' (the French *développement durable*, development that lasts, is better). Here the premise is that the poor cannot become like the rich since there is not enough of everything to go around. Making a virtue of their own economic and demographic decline, Western and some Asian countries have revived a 'limits to growth' argument that was first aired in the 1970s. Elites have always been concerned that unchecked population expansion by the poor was a threat to their own security and this has now reached global proportions.

The 2009 Copenhagen summit on climate change that failed so signally to make any substantive progress offered clear evidence of this attitude. The rich countries proposed to cap the greenhouse gas emissions of developing countries at a lower level than those of the United States and the European Union. Brazil, India, China, South Africa and the other major players in the global restructuring of capitalism today not unreasonably objected, especially since the West is responsible for the great bulk of the carbon dioxide already in the atmosphere. Both the Brazilian and Chinese leaders made the same pointed joke – likening the US to a rich man who, after gorging himself at a banquet, then invites the neighbours in for coffee and asks them to split the bill. Imagine how Germany and the United States would have reacted if Britain, on losing its commanding position in the world economy, had suggested that they curb their development in the name of 'sustainability'.

The old premise of development still holds true for the vast majority of people alive. They want to be full citizens of a world whose privileges they can see on television. They want more than they have already, not to be told that it is time to tighten their belts. Africans still have lots of children because they lose them more easily. If their population doubles every three decades, this reflects limited improvements made in protecting them from war, disease and famine. But they know they have a long way to go before they enjoy the modern economic benefits that are taken for granted in the West (and may not last forever). Until then, the drive for development will drown voices urging limitation for the environment's sake.

Further reading

Bernstein, H. (2005) Development studies and the Marxists. In Kothari, U. (ed.) *A Radical History of Development Studies*. David Philip and Zed Books, Cape Town and London.

Cooper, F. (1996) *Decolonization and African Society: The Labour Question in French and British Africa*. Cambridge University Press, Cambridge.

Cowen, M. and Shenton, R. (1996) *Doctrines of Development*. Routledge, London.

Escobar, A. (1995) *Encountering Development: The Making and Unmaking of the Third World*. Princeton University Press, New York.

Ferguson, J. (1990) *The Anti-Politics Machine: 'Development', Depoliticization and Bureaucratic Power in Lesotho*. Cambridge University Press, New York. [Summary by Lohmann, L. (1994) The anti-politics machine: 'development' and bureaucratic power in Lesotho. *Ecologist* 24 (5), 176–81.]

Hart, K. (1982) *The Political Economy of West African Agriculture*. Cambridge University Press, Cambridge.

Kanbur, R. (2002) Economics, social science and development. *World Development* 30 (3), 477–86.

Lewis, W. A. (1978) *The Evolution of the International Economic Order*. Princeton University Press, Princeton, NJ.

Moyo, D. (2009) *Dead Aid: Why Aid is not Working and How There is Another Way for Africa*. Allen Lane, London.

Padayachee, V. (ed.) (2010) *The Political Economy of Africa*. Routledge: London.

Tendler, J. (1975) *Inside Foreign Aid*. Johns Hopkins Press, Baltimore, MD.

World Bank (2009) *World Development Report*. World Bank, Washington, DC.

6

Alter-Globalization

Geoffrey Pleyers

A global movement against the Washington Consensus

Since the mid 1990s, resistance to neoliberal policies in dozens of countries around the world progressively formed a global movement against the Washington Consensus that underpinned these policies. This movement gathered together a wide range of actors: indigenous peoples, Indian and Brazilian small farmers, Korean trade-unionists, South African movements against privatization, progressive intellectuals, green activists, the World March of Women, anarchists and anti-capitalist activists, fair trade networks and hundreds of NGOs. More than a strategic alliance, what unites these people in a global movement is a central claim: their refusal of neoliberal policies and their will to face up to globalization and to take part in the decisions that concern their common future.

The movement was first called *anti-globalization*. But after this movement brought together activists from over one hundred countries in the first World Social Forum, it soon appeared that it was not *against* globalization but for *another* globalization, where the economy could be regulated and where 'human beings are more important than transnational profits'. It thus came to be known as the 'Global Social Justice Movement', 'Alter-Globalization' or the 'Alter-Global Movement'.

This movement reflects the main challenges of our time: to build new institutions, mechanisms and solidarity adequate to the problems of increasing interdependency at the global level. Global warming, the 2008–9 world economic crisis, migration flows and new communications technologies all illustrate the need for a deep change in global standards, governance and solidarities. Pursuing social justice, wealth redistribution and risk protection within a national framework is no longer sufficient.

Neoliberal policies and international financial institutions (IFIs) have been the main target of these activists. Hegemonic throughout the 1990s, neoliberal ideology managed to control the direction and the meaning of globalization, limiting a progressive transition to world society to the image of a self-regulating global economy, beyond the reach of intervention by policy-makers. Driving these policies is the aim of promoting a purely economic rationality, liberated from obstructions imposed by regulations designed to moderate the economic system. After the fall of the Berlin Wall, neoliberal ideology and free trade were presented as the sole and inevitable path of modernization and of the transition to a global society: *There is no alternative,* as Mrs Thatcher stated.

Against this concept of globalization as domination by an economic system without actors, alter-globalization activists have insisted on the importance of social agency at the local, national, regional and global levels. Alter-globalization activists consider the major challenge to be the limitation of an economy that operates at a global level according to social, cultural, environmental and political standards that still largely rely on nation-state policies. Therefore, activists underline the urgent necessity of stronger and more democratic international institutions and of efficient rules for the world economy with the aim of establishing redistribution and participation at a global level. In the last decade, they have taken an active role in undermining the legitimacy of the Washington Consensus, notably by opening debates on trade, finance and economic policies that were hitherto restricted to international experts, and by demanding clear examination of Washington Consensus policies which have had questionable outcomes in terms of poverty reduction and have proven counterproductive when it comes to economic stability.

A brief history of alter-globalization

Three major periods can be distinguished in the short history of the alter-globalization movement. The first was marked by its formation out of diverse mobilizations against neoliberal policies in all regions of the world, from the Indian farmers' marches against the WTO and the Zapatista rebellion in Mexico to committed intellectuals' networks and civil society counter-summits. The globalism of the movement was readily apparent, particularly during mobilizations organized around global events, the most publicized of which was the Seattle mobilization against the third ministerial of the WTO in 1999. The alter-globalization movement was thus based on international campaigns (such as for the abolition of Third World Debt) and on international networks and meetings of committed intellectuals, but also on local and national mobilizations against neoliberal policies, such as 'water and gas wars' in Bolivia and South Korean workers' movements. During this first phase, intellectuals played an important role in attracting public attention to the issue of globalization and challenging the hegemonic Washington Consensus. They set up numerous international networks which became a feature of the alter-globalization movement, such as ATTAC, Global Trade Watch, the Transnational Institute and Focus on the Global South. Other global coalitions created during this period include the World March of Women, Jubilee South and Via Campesina, which claims to bring together over one hundred million small farmers.

All these actors gathered at the first World Social Forum (WSF), held in Porto Alegre in January 2001. This marked the beginning of the second phase, as the movement became organized around many Social Forums held at the local, national, continental and global level. These meetings were oriented less towards resistance than to bringing together alter-globalization activists from different parts of the world, in some cases with the aim of developing alternative programmes. The 2002 European Social Forum in Florence, the 2004 WSF in Mumbai and the 2005 WSF in Porto Alegre marked three high points of this period of alter-globalization; remarkable for their size (50,000, 120,000 and 170,000 participants respectively), for their openness to a wide range of civil society sectors and political cultures and for the active participation of grassroots activists in their organization and in the discussions that took place in the different thematic spaces they created. Although many columnists proclaimed the movement dead in the aftermath of September 11th 2001, maintaining that the 'war against terror' had replaced economic globalization as the central issue, this period may be considered in many ways to have been a golden age for the alter-globalization movement.

From 2000 to 2005, it grew rapidly on every continent. While alter-globalization activists mobilized massively against war between 2002 and 2004, the struggle against neoliberal ideology remained at the heart of the movement. The alter-globalization movement managed to win over a large part of public opinion in several countries and some right-wing politicians and representatives of the World Bank even wanted to take part in the WSF in Porto Alegre.

After an impressive ascendant phase from 1995 to 2005 – though not without its setbacks and retreats – the global movement experienced several less than successful events and entered a hesitant phase. Although they strengthened its geographical expansion, the 2006 'Polycentric' WSF held in Bamako, Caracas and Karachi and the 2007 WSF in Nairobi were in many respects less successful than previous events. With a reduced audience (15,000 to 50,000 fewer), these forums were also less horizontal and less able to integrate grassroots activists, giving stronger weight to NGOs and to those activists who were more oriented towards support for formal political actors and regimes. Major alter-globalization organizations had disappeared by now (e.g. the 'Movimiento de Resistencia Global' in Barcelona) or had considerably decreased (e.g. ATTAC, many social centres in Italy and the Wombles in the UK). Paradoxically, the alter-globalization movement appeared to have a difficult time adapting to the new ideological context it had helped to bring about. However, these difficulties do not diminish the fundamental success achieved by the movement at two levels: its geographic expansion and ability to undermine the legitimacy of the Washington Consensus.

The geography of the movement has indeed evolved considerably. New dynamic poles have emerged, while some of the former Western European strongholds were declining. The social forum dynamic has been reinforced in regions that are symbolically or strategically important (North America, the Maghreb, sub-Saharan Africa, South Korea) and infatuation with alter-globalization's ideas and forums has not diminished in Latin America, as is attested by the adoption of anti-neoliberal policies by several heads of state in the region and the participation of 130,000 activists in the WSF held at Bélem, Brazil in January 2009. This forum, held in the Amazon region, also provided an illustration of the growing importance of environmental concerns in the global movement, which became even stronger before and during the World Summit on Climate Change in Copenhagen. Moreover, the ever-increasing use of the internet led to a decline in the importance of civil society organizations for a movement that mostly relies on loose-knit networks of groups, small organizations, media sources and individual activists.

Beyond any doubt, the alter-globalization movement has enjoyed a certain success in delegitimizing the system. Many of the international institutions that supervised trade liberalization and encouraged Southern countries to adopt neoliberal policies are now discredited. The WTO has experienced a series of setbacks in Seattle (1999), Cancun (2003), Hong Kong (2005) and Geneva (2008). South American governments even buried the Free Trade Area of the Americas project at their 2005 continental summit. The 2008–2009 global financial and economic crisis provided a vivid illustration of the end of 30 years dominated by the Washington Consensus. The crisis vindicated much alter-globalization analysis, proving it to have been correct on many points. All over the world, political leaders have recognized the importance of state intervention in the economy, acknowledging the defects of the self-regulating market and of neoliberal policies. With the coming of the global crisis, some alter-globalization ideas and proposals have gradually been adopted, beyond their traditional constituencies. The right-wing French President Nicolas Sarkozy didn't hesitate to appropriate alter-globalization slogans: 'the ideology of the dictatorship of the market and public powerlessness has died with the financial crisis'. State intervention in the economy, the need to regulate speculation and global capital flows and the problem of tax havens have all become consensual elements in the discourse of G20 leaders. The plans adopted by developed and emergent states to face the crisis, however, were largely restricted to ensuring the perpetuation of the economic and financial system. Major changes have not been made nor have not stricter global regulations been set up. In the meanwhile, global warming, the food crisis and increasing poverty as a result of market failure have underlined the importance of global challenges and the need for more effective global governance.

A call for another economics

Alter-globalization intellectuals often share with their neoliberal adversaries and experts in the international institutions a tendency to reduce complex reality to a few calculable parameters, essentially drawn from economic analysis. From terrorism to cultural homogenization, they tend to perceive a common source for all evil: growing inequalities created by neoliberal globalization. Hence, attacks on the legitimacy of the neoliberal economic model and calls for another economics represent a major thrust of their struggle. Alter-globalization experts seek to demonstrate that the Washington Consensus policies are not only socially unfair but also economically irrational and invalid according to scientific criteria. Their major criticisms hence rest on two central values: *rationality* and *democracy*.

1. *From poverty to inequality*

The foundation of alter-globalization economic arguments is a move from a discursive emphasis on poverty and suffering to one on economic inequality, with its focus on the logic of social conflict and social agency. Poverty is thus not fatal, but a consequence of the dominant economic model and its highly unequal wealth distribution that 'impoverishes' a part of the population. Alter-globalization intellectuals argue that, contrary to neoliberal postulates, economic growth does not necessarily lead to the satisfaction of the needs of the greatest number. Thus the *United Nations Development Report* for 2006 showed that, outside China, poverty has increased in the world, in spite of the economic growth of the 1990s. They attribute this evolution to rising inequality during three decades of neoliberal policies.

The possibility of doing something is also underlined by alter-globalization activists who insist on the relatively limited amounts needed to implement alternative policies. They assert for example that poverty reduction and the implementation of the Millennium Development Goals only depend on political will: 'With less than the US budget for the Iraq war, the world could eliminate extreme poverty (cost $135 billion in the first year, rising to $195 billion by 2015); achieve universal literacy (cost $5 billion a year); immunize every child in the world against deadly diseases (cost $1.3 billion a year); and ensure developing countries have enough money to fight the AIDS epidemic (cost $15 billion per year).'

Rather than the pursuit of maximal profit or GDP growth, alter-globalization economists define economy as an 'instrument' to reduce poverty and satisfy human needs. Thus the International ATTAC network says: 'Humanity is the final end and there is no other measure of economic progress than the degree to which this end is achieved.' This central idea is expressed in slogans to be found worldwide, like 'People, not profits'. Activists thus assert 'Economists are very far off in their calculations when they do not take into account that their adjustment variables are human beings!' From this perspective, they consider it irrational to evaluate the economy solely on the basis of its own instrumental rationality. Since the 1990s, they have questioned GDP as a pertinent indicator of a population's wealth and well-being, developing positions echoed by Stiglitz, Sen and Fitoussi's 2009 report of the 'Commission on the Measurement of Economic Performance and Social Progress'.

2. Rationality: a factual evaluation of neoliberal policies

Deconstruction of 'neoliberal rationality' and of the scientific basis for the Washington Consensus became essential to any challenge posed to its hegemony. Alter-globalization activists attempt to demonstrate the irrationality of organizing globalization according to the domination of markets and finance by pointing out how dysfunctional and aberrant contemporary capitalism is.

Alter-globalization activists insist on evaluating neoliberal policies according to the objective test of facts. Thus Susan George once claimed that 'we can't find a single case where structural adjustment plans [imposed by the IMF and World Bank] have succeeded'. Activist experts argue that neoliberal formulas have failed to ensure growth, reduce poverty, decrease inequality or stabilize the economy. They emphasize how successive economic and financial crises afflicted countries that adopted neoliberal policies, such as Mexico, Turkey, Argentina, as well as the Asian crisis of 1997 and the US subprime crisis that eventually became a global financial, economic and social disaster. Activists consider that a model of market-oriented individuals seeking to maximize their own utility can never support long-term thinking, take the common good into account or effectively integrate economic, social and ecological constraints. The inevitable consequence therefore is systemic market instability.

Alter-globalization activists consider as false or obsolete some major axioms of neoclassical economics. They challenge Ricardo's theory of comparative advantage, Say's notion of nature as a 'free good' (that is, available in unlimited quantities and without cost), and more generally the economic 'externalities' that are falsely removed from the realm of economic calculations (e.g. the cost of environmental damages caused by a factory; the cost of thousands of years of radio-active waste treatment by the nuclear industry) (see *Ecological Economics.*) By demonstrating the irrationality of neoliberal theories, alter-globalization intellectuals seek to deconstruct its scientific claims and the idea that a free-market economy is inherently rational.

3. Democracy

Alter-globalization activists attempt to re-insert social and political questions into issues and decisions that are usually presented as the domain of experts and limited to the single question of maximizing efficiency. They seek to *create spaces of debate* in areas from economics to new technologies (GMOs, intellectual property, trade etc.) and encourage citizen participation in public discussions and political decisions. Seen from this perspective, more active participation and building a fairer world require citizens to become familiarized with scientific knowledge and debates, especially in public economics (see *Community Participation*).

As an anti-technocratic movement, alter-globalists oppose trusting unelected experts blindly in many international economic and trade matters. Elected officials have handed over a multitude of negotiations and decisions to independent administrative bodies of experts. These in turn were supposed to be able to act from a longer-term perspective than political actors, as F. Kydland, E. Prescott and R. Barro, winners of the Nobel Prize in economics, claimed to have demonstrated. Alter-globalization activists emphasize on the contrary the highly undemocratic character of the dominant influence of unelected and unaccountable experts in international decisions: 'It is a matter of re-conquering the spaces lost by democracy to the financial sector' (ATTAC). They have thus developed alternatives based on stronger regulation of the international economy under the control of citizens through civil society organizations such as Global Trade Watch, the Transnational Institute and ATTAC.

As the major bodies managing the transition to a more global society, the G8, G20, World Bank, IMF and WTO are the core targets of alter-globalization debates on global governance. Activists want structural reform or the replacement of these international financial institutions (IFI), for which they have formed images that are often simplified and homogeneous (see *International Organizations*). To their mind, these institutions have come to embody both *neoliberal ideology* and the *technocratic aspect* of the new governance. The most telling criticisms relate to the technocratic, opaque and anti-democratic way these bodies function: voting is rare, countries are unequal, and delegates are unaccountable to their populations. Alter-globalization activists support the creation of new institutions and the reinforcement of others that already exist in order to set up global regulations and deal with global concerns, notably social and environmental standards, while making international treaties, such as the Human Right Declaration or ILO conventions, more enforceable.

Three major tendencies

After their successful struggle to delegitimate the Washington Consensus, alter-globalization activists now believe that the time has come to focus on implementing concrete alternatives. But, although the massive demonstrations and social forums provided both media coverage and a united image of the movement, alter-globalization activists are far more varied in how they believe their alternative policies might be implemented. Three major tendencies may be distinguished in this respect.

1. Citizens' and experts' advocacy networks

One tendency believes that concrete outcomes may be achieved through efficient single-issue networks able to direct coherent arguments and advocacy towards citizens, policymakers and international institutions. Issues like food sovereignty, Third World debt and financial transactions are considered to be ways of introducing the imposition of limits on the financial sector and broader questions concerning a new world order. Through the issue of water protection, for instance, activists raise the question of global public goods (see *Global Public Goods*), oppose some activities of global corporations and promote the idea of the long-term efficiency of the public sector. After several years of intense exchanges between citizens and experts focusing on the same issue, the quality of arguments within these thematic networks has increased considerably. In recent years, they have become the dynamic core of discussions at the social forums. Although they receive little media attention, these networks have often proved to be effective. During the autumn of 2008, the European Water Network contributed to the decision by the City of Paris to re-municipalize its water distribution, which had been managed previously by private corporations. Debt cancellation arguments have been adopted by political commissions in Ecuador and some of the movement's experts have joined national delegations to major international meetings, including the Geneva WTO negotiations in 2008.

2. A focus on the local level

(See *Local Development*). A broad cultural trend within the alter-globalization movement considers that social change will occur only by implementing horizontal, participatory, convivial and sustainable values in daily practices, personal life and local spaces. The Zapatistas and other Latin American indigenous movements focus on developing communities' local autonomy by implementing participatory self-government, alternative education systems and improving the quality of life. This aspiration to a world based on local communities that are much more self-reliant also became central for many movements in Western countries. 'Relocalization' movements develop a wide range of local experiments aiming to reduce consumption and increase local production, while building community resilience in response to climate change and seeking to preserve and promote local knowledge and culture. Urban activists appreciate also the convivial aspect of local initiatives and the fact that they allow the implementation of small but concrete alternatives to corporate globalization and mass consumption. Local 'collective purchase groups' and community-supported agriculture networks organize collective purchases from local producers, often of organic food, in Japan, Western Europe and North America. Their goal is to make quality food affordable, to bring an alternative to anonymous supermarkets and to promote local social relations. The movement for convivial *décroissance* (de-growth) reflects this tendency and aims for a lifestyle that reduces waste and imposes less strain on natural resources. Other 'convivial' urban movements include associations promoting the use of bicycles and local initiatives to strengthen social relations within neighbourhoods.

3. Supporting progressive regimes

A third component of the movement believes that broad social change will occur mainly through progressive policies implemented by national policy-makers, governments and institutions as key actors. Alter-globalization activists have struggled to strengthen state agency in social, environmental and economic matters. Now that state intervention has regained legitimacy, this more 'political' component of the movement believes that the time has come to support progressive political leaders' efforts. These have notably included President Hugo Chavez of Venezuela and President Evo Morales in Bolivia. Alternative programmes and projects are implemented both through national social and economic policies and through international alliances between progressive regimes. New regional projects and institutions have been launched on this basis, like the Bank of the South, which has assumed the main tasks of the IMF in the region. For reasons of history and political culture, Latin American and Indian activists are used to working closely with political parties and leaders. Similar developments have also occurred recently in Western countries. For example, in the United States the impetus produced by the first national social forum in 2007 was largely redirected towards the presidential campaign of Senator Obama.

These three tendencies within the alter-globalization movement are based on distinct conceptions of social change. The different political options they propose have animated countless debates among activists in the last few years. But they may be seen as complementary strategies in many respects. Taken together, they offer concrete guidelines for a global and multi-dimensional approach to social change and poverty reduction that acknowledges simultaneously the key roles to be played by local communities and grassroots social actors, global citizens' activism, international institutions and national political leaders.

By debating rarely discussed issues, in particular in the economic field, promoting citizens' discussion of global issues and policies, working for new global regulations and co-ordinating activists from all over the world, the alter-globalization movement has undoubtedly contributed to defining a global public space, stronger global consciousness, multiplication of activities on a world scale and more active citizenship at local, national, continental and global levels.

Further reading

Bello, W. (2007) *World Social Forum at a Crossroad*. Focus on the Global South, Bangkok.

Cardoso, F. E. (2008) A surprising world. *Idées pour le débat* 10, 32–7.

Held, D. and McGrew, A. (2007) *Globalization/Antiglobalization*, 2nd edn. Polity, Cambridge.

Kalinowski, W. (ed.) (2009) *Looking for Solutions to the Crisis*. International Initiative for Rethinking the Economy, Paris.

Passet, R. (2003) Rationalité et cohérence d'une mondialisation à finalité humaine. *Grain de Sable* no. 415 7 April.

Pleyers, G. (2010) *Alter-Globalization. Becoming an Actor in the Global Age*. Polity, Cambridge.

Sen, A. (1999) *Development as Freedom*. Oxford University Press, Oxford.

Stiglitz, J., Sen, A. and Fitoussi, J. P. (2009) *Report of the Commission on the Measurement of Economic Performance and Social Progress*. OFCE, Paris.

Teivainen, T. (2002) *Enter Economism, Exit Politics: Experts, Economic Policy and Damage to Democracy*. Z Books, London.

Whitaker, F., de Sousa Santos, B. and Cassen, B. (2006) The world social forum: where do we stand and where are we going? In Glasius, M., Kaldor, M. and Anheier, H. (eds) *Global Civil Society 2005/6*. Sage, London.

Part II

Economics with a Human Face

7

Plural Economy

Jean-Louis Laville

Two characteristics of economics

Karl Polanyi stresses the heuristic value of taking a new reflexive look at definitions of the economy. The term 'economic', which is commonly used to describe a certain kind of human activity, shifts between two poles of meaning. Its first, or formal, meaning derives from the logical nature of the relationship between end and means: when we define the economic with reference to scarcity, we use the term in that formal sense. The second, or substantive, sense places the emphasis on relations between human beings and the natural environments from which they derive their means of sustenance. The substantive definition sees this interdependence as a constituent element of the economy.

These definitions of the possible meanings of the human economy derive from 'essentially different sources' and both are 'primary and elementary', according to the Austrian economist Carl Menger. This discussion is not taken into account (since it has been forgotten) by neoclassical economics, which typically understands the term 'economic' only in its formal sense. Polanyi suggests that this reduction of the field of economic thinking has resulted in a complete break between economics and biology, and his argument has been developed by a number of economists who take a reflexive interest in their science.

If we take this distinction as a starting point, we can underline two characteristics of modern economics: *1. The economic sphere is regarded as autonomous and is equated with the market*. Relegation of the substantive meaning of the economy to obscurity leads to a confusion between economics and market economics that persists throughout the long 'retreat' signalled by the adoption of the formal definition of the economic. Passet traces its history from the physiocrats to the neoclassical economists. *2. The market is self-regulating*. Rationalist and atomistic hypotheses about human behaviour underpin the claim that the economy can be studied by using a deductive method: individual behaviour is aggregated by the market and no consideration is given to the institutional framework that shapes it. If we see the market as a self-regulating mechanism, or one that uses prices to match supply to demand, we overlook the institutional changes that were required to bring it into being and the institutional structures that make it possible.

In addition to these two points made by Polanyi, we can add another that is made by many authors, including Marx as well as Weber and Mauss: *3. The firm is identified with capitalist enterprise*. In a capitalist economy based on private ownership of the means of production, the creation of goods presupposes that the owner of capital can make a profit. The enterprise is a profit-making unit and capital-accounting is therefore basic to the rational form of a profit-making economy because it makes it possible to calculate whether there will be a surplus, given the monetary value of the resources invested in the enterprise. When joint-stock companies were made legal, capital could be concentrated in unprecedented ways, since property rights could be traded without their owners having any personal acquaintance with each other. At the same time, the stock exchange guaranteed their assets a measure of liquidity.

This definition of the economy as a combination of the self-regulating market and joint-stock companies has one further implication: the vision of society comes to be synonymous with its own market mechanism. When it knows no limits, the market economy tends to incorporate and organize society: the pursuit of private self-interest is thought to promote the common good and there is therefore no need for political deliberation. The irruption of this utopian idea of a self-regulating market marks the difference between democratic modernity and other human societies where there were market elements but never any intention of organizing them as an autonomous system.

The reaction of society

Given that it has always proved impossible to realize the utopia of a market society, society's reaction is to fall back on the notion of solidarity, which is a point of reference for all attempts to regulate the economy in a democratic way. Regulation can take many different institutional forms. Marcel Mauss asks us to consider this possibility in the conclusion to his essay on the gift, where he underlines the relationship between reciprocity and redistribution.

The principle of redistribution may be invoked to prevent the economy from being reduced to the market. The non-market economy, in which the allocation of goods and services is organized through redistribution, is just as much a constituent element of democratic modernity as the market economy. The growing importance of social questions posed by capitalism revealed the need to promote institutions that could counter its politically undesirable effects. While the idea of an economy based on reciprocity has gradually faded, the non-market principle of redistribution was mobilized in response to popular pressure. The welfare state granted citizens individual rights insuring them against social risks or benefits that provided a safety net for the most disadvantaged (see *Citizenship and Welfare*). Public services were thus defined as the supply of goods and services with a redistributive dimension (from rich to poor and from the active to the inactive), with rules laid down by public authorities that were subject to democratic controls.

In order to prevent the market becoming a self-regulating market, it has been limited by being embedded in institutions. While modernity does have an inherent tendency to disembed the market, this has been counterbalanced by recurrent reactions on the part of society. The goal is to socialize the market, in other words to inscribe it with a set of rules drawn up through a process of political deliberation. The tension between embedding and disembedding may be regarded as a constituent element of the modern market economy. In history, the attempt to establish a self-regulating economy has led to the establishment of regulatory institutions. Most of the markets that exist today consist primarily of rules, institutions and networks that frame and control them, shaping the way supply matches demand. These frameworks are in turn challenged by enthusiastic calls for deregulation and for markets to be brought into line with the ideal and impersonal norms of competition, that is, for the desocialization of markets.

Attempts have also been made to found and secure legitimacy for non-capitalist companies. The goal of companies where property rights are held by investors is to maximize profits and labour is subordinated to that logic of accumulation. Although this is the dominant model, it has been shown that *ownership can take different forms* and that various types of owners can have property rights. Unlike capitalist firms, some companies are not owned by investors, but by other parties whose goal is not to accumulate capital. The stimulus to economic action then has more to do with a reciprocity in which *'le lien prime sur le bien'* [bonds matter more than goods] than with the maximization of individual self-interest.

The social market is a utopia in its own right and reactions to it vary. Other economic principles may be invoked; institutions may be created to limit and lay down rules for the market sphere; and non-capitalist forms of ownership may be adopted. In democratic modernity, the economy is thus affected by two tendencies: on the one hand, there is a tendency to disembed the market and on the other hand a tendency to re-embed it in democratic ways. When the latter prevails, the political principle of solidarity is likely to come to the fore (see *Solidarity Economy*).

The expansion of the market comes up against what Polanyi called a 'counter-movement' checking its expansion in specific ways. Thus the 'great transformation' brought about by self-regulating markets generates the political impulse to free society from the threats posed by (neo)liberalism.

What social transformation?

As Dumont reminds us, this upheaval gave birth to both fascist and communist regimes, the destruction of freedom and a reign of oppression. According to him, the transformation totalitarian regimes sought to bring about could never reconcile freedom with equality. The two may, on the other hand, be reconciled by the 'ill-defined alloy' typical of social democracy. Because he defines the compromise between the market and the state typical of the post-war period of expansion in these terms, Dumont underestimates the cohesion of the Fordist and welfare industrial societies in which social rules were imposed upon the market economy through legislation and collective bargaining. They also organized a vast redistributive and non-market economy whose rules were established by the welfare state. He is right, though, to point out that these compromises can be reversed and that the neoliberal offensive has undermined their foundations by freeing the market from certain social rules on the grounds that they were too rigid, and by denying the legitimacy of a non-market economy whose weakness was that it was too bureaucratic or subject to the whims of its users. That reversibility is now obvious.

Given that neoliberalism has revived the utopia of a market society, the nature of the democratic response will be crucial. If there is no such response, there is a danger that the desire for liberation will be turned into its opposite and that the globalization of the market and its expansion into areas that were hitherto untouched will have as their corollary the rise of fundamentalism and a defensive identity politics. While recent events have confirmed that this is a real threat, the spectre of a market society has so far proved to be incompatible with democracy throughout the twentieth century. When the economic worldview becomes an end in itself, it denies democratic processes the right to define a human project with a human meaning and this has always been the case. Any attempt to reinstate earlier compromises is doomed to failure. Social progress, for example, can no longer be guaranteed by taxing the market economy because this now faces new difficulties. On the one hand, it would be preferable to restrict the market in order to prevent it from expanding to include all spheres of human life and to preserve relationships based on solidarity; on the other hand, it might also be wise to allow the market to expand as much as possible in order to maximize the availability of resources to finance the redistributive systems that bear witness to the ongoing solidarity that exists between social groups.

If we want to get out of this seeming impasse, we have to take into account every concrete attempt that is made to resist the growing commodification of social life. That is why experiments in 'social economy' are so important. Because they take so many different forms, they are a challenge to the monochrome version of economy that neoliberal ideology describes as inevitable. If these initiatives are able to transcend the limits of their sectoral origins, to provide a clear definition of their aims and of what they imply in terms of public regulations, and to ally themselves with social movements that share the same goals of social economy, they may have a contribution to make to the democratization of both economy and society.

Economic pluralism and the aspiration to democracy

We may ask which institutions might guarantee that the plural character of the economy could be legitimated and inscribed within a democratic framework, given that the pursuit of material profit compromises that project whenever it becomes the only permissible logic and knows no limits. The answer to that question must lie in institutional innovations grounded in social practice. Only such practical experiments will show how the economy may be shaped by democratic norms. How to reconcile equality and freedom is still the principal issue of democracy in a complex society and discussions of future policy directions will lead nowhere unless society's reactions are taken into account. This is a further point on which Mauss and Polyani agreed: we must begin by recognizing and analysing existing practices. We must, in other words, take as our starting point actual economic trends and not a project for social reform that is wrapped up in a veneer of realism. As Mauss argues, such an idea of social change does not force us to choose between radical alternatives or between contradictory forms of society. Social change occurs as new groups and institutions are built on top of the old.

Mauss and Polanyi have laid the theoretical foundations for a plural approach to the economy. They outlined a way of thinking about social change that is not content with making ritual obeisance to overthrowing the system. If we accept that concept of change, we have to work within a democratic framework to develop a balance of power that recognizes that the economy may, quite legitimately, be institutionalized and socialized in more ways than one. A plural approach to the economy will allow us to renew the terms of the debate between reformism and radicalism.

Further reading

Callon, M. (1999) La Sociologie peut-elle enrichir l'analyse économique des externalités? Essai sur la notion de débordement. In Foray, D. and Mairesse, D. J. (eds) *Innovations et performances: Approches interdisciplinaires.* Editions de l'École des Hautes Études en Science Sociales, Paris, pp. 399–431.

Dumont, L. (1983) Préface. In Polanyi, K. *La Grande Transformation: Aux Origines politique et économique de notre temps.* Gallimard, Paris.

Laville, J.-L. (2000 [1994]) *L'Économie solidaire: Une perspective internationale.* Desclée de Brouwer, Paris.

Maréchal, J-P. (2001) *Humaniser l'économie.* Desclée de Brouwer, Paris.

Mauss, M. (1990 [1925]) *The Gift: The Form and Reason for Exchange in Archaic Communities.* Routledge, London.

Menger C. (1923) *Grundsätze der Volkswirtschaftslehre.* Edition Carl Menger, Vienna.

Passet, R. (1996) *L'Économique et le vivant.* Economica, Paris.

Polanyi, K. (1977) *The Livelihood of Man.* Academic Press, New York.

Polanyi, K. (2001 [1944]) *The Great Transformation: The Political and Economic Origins of our Times.* Beacon Press, Boston.

Roustang, G. (2002) *Démocratie: Le Risque du marché.* Desclée de Brouwer, Paris.

Weber, M. (1981 [1922]) *General Economic History.* Transaction Books, New Brunswick, NJ.

8

Ecological Economics

Sabine U. O'Hara

The term 'ecological economics' seems to be a contradiction, even though ecology and economy share a root in the Greek word for household (*oikos*). Yet *oikonomia,* the management of the household, has had little in common with ecology, the science of relations between organisms and their environment (a term coined by Haeckel in the late nineteenth century). It was not until Kenneth Boulding's *Spaceship Earth* that the concept of an economy embedded in the larger physical, biological and ecological context of planet earth gained attention.

For much of its history, economic theory drew tight boundaries around its key concerns. It focused almost exclusively on the management of the *human* household and on the systems, institutions and policy measures that 'optimize' human household management or at least meet household management goals. Impacts outside these boundaries were termed 'externalities' and deemed outside the purview of economists. The 'optimal' allocation of resources to address the key questions of economics consequently was also limited by these boundaries: what to produce (production), how to produce it (resource allocation) and for whom to produce it (distribution) were based on economic value (generally expressed in monetary terms), economic indicators and economic timeframes (generally short term compared to geological, physical, ecological, or biological timeframes).

At the microeconomic level, the main players in the allocation project of economics are firms and households. Firms make resource allocation and production decisions based on 'what' and 'how' to produce and households make consumption decisions, thereby addressing the question 'for whom' to produce. And while the picture at the macroeconomic level is more complex, with banks and government sectors adding topics like money supply, interest rates, savings, investments and government spending, here too, larger social and environmental context systems are generally absent.

The sources and sinks that support much of the productive capacity of the economy and supply the resourcing and absorptive capacity of environmental and human systems are missing at virtually every level of aggregation. The result of this neglect is not surprising: natural resources, absorptive sink capacities of the environment, restorative and recreative contributions of human communities and households and contributions outside the valuation mechanism of the market economy are generally overused and undervalued. As Herman Daly and others have argued, the critical question that has been absent from economic theory is 'how much to produce'.

Economics in context

The question of refocusing economics to take neglected contexts and functions into account has principally two answers: (1) one approach is to internalize social and environmental contexts into the valuation and allocation framework of economics; (2) the second is to internalize economic activity into social and environmental contexts. Since economic, social and environmental systems have different measures and timescales, the two approaches will yield different answers to the economic questions concerning what, how, and for whom to produce.

Much work during the past three decades has focused on the first approach and on defining and refining valuation methods to internalize externalities. Typically these valuation methods are based on recognizing that ecological and biological systems and non-human made resources contribute significant value to the human economy. Human economic activity would be significantly limited without a steady supply of water, clean air, protective ozone, flora and fauna. In addition to these resourcing (source) and absorptive (sink) functions, the aesthetic and recreational benefits of the natural environment sustain and restore physical, emotional and spiritual dimensions of human life.

Assigning economic value to these contributions is not easy. The very reason they are termed 'externalities' is that there are no markets where their prices can be established (see *Global Public Goods*). Valuation techniques therefore seek to assess the monetary value of environmental contributions measured in terms of their exchange value, use value, options value, and intrinsic (existence) value. The primary tools for solving the internalization problem and for assigning value to unaccounted – for environmental services have been valuation techniques like hedonic pricing, travel cost assessment, techniques that calculate the replacement value of natural resources and amenities and various types of survey-based contingent valuation approaches.

One of the most debated studies by Robert Costanza and his associates calculated the monetary value of global ecosystem services using a modelling approach. The study gave a replacement value to ecosystem services based on the premise that essential services would need to be offered through various technical means should the services provided by nature become overused, exhausted and thus unavailable. The estimated value of the global ecosystems services was $16 to 54 billion per year.

Yet assigning monetary value does not necessarily solve the underlying measurement problems associated with assessing the value and impact of environmental services. Such techniques remain firmly embedded in the very conceptual framework that causes the inadequate representation of environmental and social context systems in the first place. The very systems and institutions that are central to managing the human household seem inadequate when it comes to capturing the value of ecosystem functions. Some ecological economists point out that much of what is termed 'economic development' has been shaped by the biases of monetization; that is, creating markets for cutting down, digging up, or selling the natural and human capital that was once outside of the market. Development thus implies a preference for moving restorative, recreative, reproductive and resourcing services from the informal sphere of communities, households and underground economies to the formal sphere of the market. The result may be the creation of monetary value (for example increased GDP), but often the depletion of non-market or non-measured value captured in the ecological and social support systems that make the creation of economic value possible. For example, defensive expenditures like the restoration of an old cathedral suffering from pollution damage or the attempt to increase the pH of a lake suffering from the effects of acid rain are GDP positive, but they at best re-establish the status quo rather than adding positive value.

Ecological economics, also referred to as the science of sustainability, is therefore generally closer to the second approach – internalizing economic activity rather than internalizing externalities. Ecological economics emerged as a field in the 1980s and the journal *Ecological Economics* began publication in 1989; the International Society for Ecological Economics (ISEE), founded in 1986, now has chapters around the world. There is a substantial literature, as well as newsletters, listservs and electronic discussion groups.

Yet the roots of ecological economics predate this. One of the early ecological economists was Nicolai Georgescu-Roegen who distinguished between *stocks* and *funds*. A stock is capable of producing a physical flow at any desired rate, but a fund is capable of producing a service only at a given rate since it is limited by biophysical reality and context. For example, we can burn a ton of coal a day for thirty days, or we may burn the entire thirty tons in one day; yet one worker can only dig one ditch a day for a month, he cannot dig thirty ditches in one day. Funds include the sustaining functions which support the economic inputs of labour power, all capital and land in Ricardo's sense. Funds are the 'agents of production' that make the generation of economic flows possible. Without the sustaining functions of funds the availability of flows will be impaired. Flows include inflows from nature, inflows from manufacturing processes and outflows of useful products and waste. Flows thus represent physical quantities while funds represent an amount of services contributed. Every economic process requires both flows from nature as inputs and sink services for the disposal of waste generated. The relationship of source flows and sinks to production may be used to describe a *feasible* technology, that is, technology that is capable of producing a specific economic product. Not all feasible technology is also *viable*, however. A technology is viable only if it can maintain the corresponding material structure that supports its resource and sink functions, and consequently the human species. A technology that substitutes irreplaceable stocks or generates irreducible pollution or violates the ability of funds to provide assimilative and restorative services is not viable. This understanding places economic processes squarely within the context of physical, biological and ecological systems. Water filtration capacities of the soil, absorptive capacities, biological diversity that enhances resilience to droughts and other extreme climate conditions – all these sustain economic activity. Their loss is costly and often irreversible.

Herman Daly, Georgescu-Roegen's student, published his seminal work, *Toward a Steady State Economy*, in 1974. Drawing on the principles of thermodynamics, Daly argued for an economy that seeks to minimize energy throughput and thus entropy generation. Other ecological economists sought to take their cue from ecologists like Howard Odum. This line of enquiry focuses on ecosystem functions and services and on managing the tasks of production, resource allocation and distribution in ways that are more aligned with ecological systems and principles, and are therefore less destructive of them. Ecological economics thus points beyond conventional economic valuation and systems approaches to the natural context of the economic household. When the economy as an open sub-system is placed within a wider environmental context system that is materially limited and thermodynamically constrained, management rules change dramatically.

At the same time, ecosystems evolve, change and adjust to new humanly created conditions and challenges, unless of course, they reach the limits of their adaptability and simply collapse. Viewing the economy as an embedded dynamic sub-system thus brings deeper philosophical dimension of ecological economics to the fore. One fundamental question focuses on the overall 'scale' of the economy and its ethical implications. Questions like 'how much is enough?' and 'what satisfies our needs and makes for the good life?' are central to ecological economics.

Some ecological economists have addressed the non-commensurability question that results from abandoning money as common denominator and sole measure of value. The resulting methodologies include multi-indicator and discourse-based approaches to valuation. Multi-indicator approaches identify various measures that capture the social, economic, and environmental impact of economic activity in their respective units of measure – number of jobs created, tons of emissions or the proportion of pollutants in the waste water stream etc. The result is typically a mix of growing, diminishing or neutral impacts that defy easy conclusions regarding the overall effects of economic activity or of changes in its intensity and are generally more difficult to interpret. Moreover, the selection of indicator categories and the evaluation of trade-offs between them cannot be easily generalized, but must be flexible in order to allow for context-specific conditions and variations. This task is not only unfamiliar but uncomfortable for many economists. The challenge of evaluating trade-offs is generally left to other experts such as development planners and these are often hidden by value assumptions wrapped in elaborate terminology. Rarely are people with context-specific, local knowledge or whose knowledge systems have been marginalized consulted by professionals when it comes to making valuations. Yet it is the knowledge of context held by these unofficial experts that is best suited to identify the specific social and ecological characteristics of a community or region.

No matter how carefully one selects generalized 'objective' measures of economic, environmental and social activity or well-being, these measures can easily ignore the specific needs, options and perceptions of individuals or social groups, especially of those whose opinions have been made marginal. As Amartya Sen has pointed out, objective measures may in fact reinforce existing cultural, class and gender biases.

One way of broadening the valuation process is a discourse-based approach that relies on the contributions of stakeholders to bring their respective life-worlds to bear on it. While these may differ in their assessment of the trade-offs associated with different levels and types of economic activity, a discourse process that lays bare operative assumptions and valuation biases of stakeholders, who are in turn informed and impacted by the discourse process itself, can often yield assessment outcomes at least as valid as those generated by official experts. This also points to an added dimension of ecological economics, namely the social context of economic activity. The sustaining, restorative and recreative services offered in households, communities and other spheres of social interaction can be similarly undermined when their support is neglected. Feminist ecological economists have made this dimension particularly explicit in their work (see *Feminist Economics*).

Some work in ecological economics not only takes environmental and social impacts into account, but also lays bare the valuation biases of the dominant economic model whereby market activities (the public sphere) are deemed more valuable than the household's

(the private sphere); universalized concepts and measures are preferred to local context-specific ones; and single-stranded theories
are preferred to variable experience. The bias here lies not simply in
the choice of indicators, however multiple, to capture complexity. It
is also a matter of power and of who selects the indicators and who
evaluates the trade-offs between different scenarios of economic
activity. If such underlying biases are not made explicit, they simply
perpetuate those implicit in the short-hand assumptions of economic
theory itself. The result is invariably destruction of the long-term sustainability of the economic process, as the social and environmental
inputs and the context conditions that underpin the economy are
neglected and undermined.

To account for complexity, ecological economics must have
norms that go much further than those of the Pareto Optimality
notions of mainstream economics. The world of ecological economics deals explicitly with the constraints of nature, acknowledging that
in reality there are limits to growth in real income and to the substi-
tutability of capital. Hence, the question of just income distribution
can neither be dispensed with by aspiring to boundless affluence
nor can it be diffused by unlimited economic growth as mainstream
economics implies. Rather, the question of quality and of what makes
for the good life comes to the fore. Malte Faber identifies three
principal characteristics of ecological economics that differ from the
mainstream discipline:

1. Nature is taken seriously (intrinsic value)
2. Justice and human dignity are taken seriously (normative
   perspective)
3. Time is taken seriously (irreversibility and uncertainty)

Seeking solutions

So how does ecological economics alter the management of the
household in light of the laws of habitat that form its context? One
approach is to measure value generation differently, as in the Indicator
of Sustainable Economic Welfare (ISEW) offered by Herman Daly
and John Cobb which seeks to correct the misrepresentation of value
contained in the most common existing measure, Gross Domestic
Product (GDP). A similar approach, put forward by Clifford Cobb,
Ted Halstead and Jonathan Rowe, is the General Progress Indicator

(GPI). Both ISEW and GPI take personal consumption as a starting point and adjust for (1) defensive expenditures necessary to repair social and environmental destruction, (2) non-renewable energy resources borrowed from future generations and (3) shifts in the functions provided in households and civil society. These aggregate measures of welfare thus start with basic economic needs and adjust for changes in social and environmental quality or non-economic and non-material needs. As with GDP, they also create a single numerical indicator that can be easily tracked by policy-makers and analysts. The downside of this aggregation is a significant loss of information. Multi-criteria measures like the United Nations' Sustainable Development Indicators disaggregate social, economic and environmental dimensions and provide more transparent information about the social and environmental dimensions of welfare.

Much of the work of ecological economists is policy-oriented and relies on a variety of approaches employing models, indicators and stakeholder surveys to inform policy objectives and strategies for their implementation. Simulation models, for example, may provide information about the anticipated impact of various pollution levels or the seasonal fluctuations in water levels resulting from dams, or the impact of irrigation on groundwater levels. Ecological economists favour fairly sophisticated models that are inclusive, based on transparent assumptions, flexible and allow for cross-influences and context changes. Such models can complement discourse-based approaches that introduce the messy interaction of real people and communities, located in the spatial, ecological, social and cultural contexts of life. Assessment of these impacts can be the result of a stakeholder process that balances competing interests and ideally arrives at a viable policy option.

Much of the work of ecological economists therefore takes place in the concrete context of local communities and regions, in a context of social relationships involving local government, neighbourhood associations, private sector businesses, non-profit organizations and advocacy groups. The approach is often intentionally participatory since, when professionals rely on expert judgements alone without examining their epistemological assumptions and valuation biases, they usually miss a great deal. For example, should economists listen to the needs of those who are unaware of, yet materially dependent on invisible ecosystem services? Should they listen to people for whom an ecosystem is merely an abstract concept, or perhaps, a recreational opportunity? Both expert and popular perspectives must be taken into account, yet they may not have equal weight. Making explicit and prioritizing the judgement of people who perceive their well-being as inseparably linked to the health and functioning of non-human ecological and human social support systems is needed to point the way toward viable policy solutions. If existing power relations are not transparent, then economic constructs will simply perpetuate the influence of those whose priorities have always been heard, as well as the passivity of those who have been excluded from the valuation process. Most commonly it is the latter who bear the burden of providing socially sustaining functions and who suffer most from the negative economic impacts.

If we wish to take the complexities of real-life-contexts into account, we must respect people's subjective perceptions about their own life-worlds; and economists, including some ecological economists, have long been sceptical of the value of human actors' actual perceptions and opinions. An individual's stated preferences and revealed preferences are, in this view, two different things. And it is no small task to admit diverse and often unfamiliar perspectives and measures into the valuation and decision process. It requires new approaches and sensibilities, detailed empirical observation, historical awareness and guidelines concerning functions and services deemed to be indispensable. This implies collaboration and communication between experts and their local counterparts who may challenge standard methods and models. Without the effective representation of situated agents, economic measures and models will continue to ignore the social and environmental dimensions of long-term sustainability in favour of short-term unsustainable 'quick fixes'.

Scholars from the global South have been particularly prominent in articulating multi-dimensional perspectives and in calling attention to the inadequacies of standard economic valuation methods. They include Bina Agarwal, Asoka Bandarage, Manfred Max-Neef, Vandana Shiva and Clement Tisdell, to name just a few. By assessing the effects of economic development, industrialization, structural adjustment, population policies and imported agricultural methods, these scholars have not only articulated the specific social and ecological dimensions of economic development strategies, but they have also pointed to underlying systemic problems (see *Development*). Recurring themes in this body of work are global-local connections (see *Globalization* and *Alter-Globalization*), power structures and the relationship between gender and the environment. They explain the systemic effects of development policies biased toward the monetary economy and its particular definitions of efficiency, growth and wealth creation. When economists work face-to-face with stakeholders in communities and regions, they invariably gain insights about environmental, ecological and social processes that go beyond standard perspectives on knowledge and valuation. As Richard Norgaard has argued, the field must necessarily be characterized by methodological pluralism. This pluralism makes room for diverse context-specific conditions and perspectives; and it unpacks the 'black box' of cost-benefit analysis, giving voice to multiple knowledge systems and context-based expertise.

In order to meet the demands of such complex, non-hierarchical, and nuanced models, ecological economists often have to start from scratch collecting their own data, building their own models and designing their own policies. They often take on community-based 'volunteer' work as a way of advancing their chosen field of scholarship while remaining connected to people and places in their own life-worlds. The result is participatory research and assessment that may capture more complexity and information about context. Case-study approaches and others that seek to capture economic, environmental and social impacts through direct observation, social accounting matrices and surveys are also prominent in this regard. In committing to methodological pluralism, ecological economists also commit to being open to learning *with* those who have grassroots expertise rather than learning *about* them.

The ongoing dialogue about methodological pluralism will result in more than just a refinement of methods that aim to capture environmental and social impacts and values. In advancing the theory and practice of ecological economics, it should influence mainstream economics as well.

Conclusion

Management of the human household – the economy – has often ignored the *logos* of the natural home we all inhabit. The consequence of this neglect has been the destruction of valuable context systems that provide essential ecological and social services sustaining the economy itself. Ecological economists seek to change this by focusing attention on what traditional economic constructs have deemed 'externalities' and by seeking to integrate them back into the environmental and social context of households, communities and ecosystems.

This radical shift in perspective has been accompanied by theoretical and methodological innovations, such as methods that rely on data collection rather than existing statistics; research design that is participatory rather than distanced; an interest in stakeholder discourse rather than individual preferences; transparency and collaboration between stakeholder groups and experts; and new theoretical models that redefine the core economic activities of production, consumption and welfare creation.

In bringing such innovations to the field of economics, ecological economists also highlight the biases that stand behind the neglect of ecological and social-cultural context systems. This work of 'uncovering' and 'reconnecting' has implications for theory and practice, for policy measures and for real-life solutions to the unsustainable character of current economic practice. Advancing this important work requires new dialogues and practices. Ecological economics thus does more than define a new sub-field of economics; it has the potential to change economics itself by placing it within a context of social and environmental systems and constraints.

Further reading

Bandarage, A. (1997) *Women, Population and Global Crisis: A Political-Economic Analysis*. St Martins, New York.

Common, M. and Stagl, S. (2005) *Ecological Economics: An Introduction*. Cambridge University Press, New York.

Costanza, R. (ed.) (1991) *Ecological Economics: The Science and Management of Sustainability*. Columbia University Press.

Costanza, R., Cumberland, J., Daly, H., Goodland, R. and Norgaard, R. (1997) *An Introduction to Ecological Economics*. St Lucie Press, Boca Raton, FL.

Costanza, R., Segura, O. and Martinez-Alier, J. (1996) *Getting Down to Earth: Practical Applications of Ecological Economics*. Island Press, Washington, DC.

Daly, H. (1999) *Ecological Economics and the Ecology of Economics*. Elgar, Cheltenham.

Daly, H. and Cobb, J. (1989) *For the Common Good*. Beacon, Boston, MA.

Georgescu-Roegen, N. (1975) Energy and economic myths. *Southern Economic Journal* 41, 347–81.

Gowdy, J. and O'Hara, S. (1996) *Economic Theory for Environmentalists*. St Lucie Press.

Krishnan, R., Harris, J. and Goodwin, N. (eds) (1995) *A Survey of Ecological Economics*. Island Press, Washington, DC.

Martinez-Alier, J. and Ropke, I. (eds). (2008). *Recent Developments in Ecological Economics*, 2 vols., Edward Elgar, Cheltenham.

O'Hara, S. (1998) Sustaining Production: Material and Institutional Considerations. *International Journal of Environment and Pollution* 9 (2/3), 287–304.

O'Hara, S. (1999) Economics, ecology and quality of life: who evaluates? *Feminist Economics* 5 (2), 83–9.

Silliman, J. and King, Y. (1999) *Dangerous Intersections: Perspectives on Population, Environment and Development*. South End, Boston, MA.

Victor, P. (2008) *Managing Without Growth: Slower by Design, not Disaster*. Edward Elgar, Cheltenham.

9

Feminist Economics

Julie A. Nelson

Feminist economics examines gender and the economy from a liberatory perspective. It challenges economic policies that treat women as invisible. It challenges practices that reinforce situations and stereotypes that are oppressive to women. At a more academic level, feminist economists also point out that the sort of economic analysis that currently dominates academic and policy circles is masculine-biased in its definitions and methods; and they explore more adequate alternatives.

Because of its liberatory and critical perspective, feminist economics is different from 'women-and-the-economy' or 'feminine' approaches to economics. The 'women-and-the-economy' approach, for example, simply uses data on women, makes gender a variable within existing models or looks at how women fit into economic practices shaped around a typical male model of market participation. While such studies may serve to advance awareness of women's issues, they can also be shallow or even attempt to make situations of oppression or exclusion appear just or rational. 'Feminine' economics, on the other hand, gives a one-sided priority to women or to aspects of the economy, such as gift-giving and co-operation, that have been stereotypically associated with women. In contrast, feminist economists generally take a critical view of stereotyping and (though anti-feminists often portray feminists as hostile towards men) the vast majority consider the goal to be liberation for women, men and children.

While these boundaries shape feminist economics, however, they do not define a single perspective. Within the field, a wide diversity of projects and viewpoints has flourished.

The origins of feminist economics

While feminist thought on economic topics has appeared at various times in history, feminist economics in its contemporary form originated with the equal rights movements that took place in many industrialized countries during the 1960s and 1970s. During that period, political movements for equal employment rights for minorities and women brought new attention to the economic status of marginalized groups. These movements challenged the explanations for sex and race differences in work and pay that had been promulgated by mainstream academic economics.

In many countries, the mainstream of economic research and policy-making has been dominated by a single approach, neoclassical economics. The neoclassical approach takes markets and exchange as the definitive economic phenomena, and assumes that behaviour in markets reflects self-interest, rationality, and competition. Rather than seeing the economy as human-created, social, organic, and complex, it assumes that the economy is an a-social, mechanical, law-driven phenomenon. In order to study this imagined mechanical economy, it adopted mathematical modelling techniques that mimic physics. Well-being is often more or less equated with growth in Gross Domestic Product. While not all neoclassical economists hold conservative political views, this type of economics has often been used to defend neoliberal (free-market) policies, on the grounds that government 'interference' with the smoothly running 'gears' of unrestrained markets puts harmful grit into the economic 'engine of growth'. Within this approach, observed patterns of work, income and wealth are generally considered to be the result of individuals acting freely and rationally, in their own interests.

Up until the 1960s, neoclassical economics subsumed women and women's traditional activities into the 'black box' of the household. A household was generally understood to be represented by its male head, whose preferences, it was assumed, determined household decisions. Studies of paid labour generally focused on men only, and everyone in a household was assumed to enjoy the same level of well-being. All time not spent at paid market labour – including time

spent on household work – was called 'leisure', and as a result household production was not (and still is not) included in national GDP
accounts. Women's lesser participation in paid labour and segregation into certain sectors of the labour market, when it was noticed,
was explained as being the result of free choice. It was presumed
that innate differences between men and women in tastes and abilities explained their different 'choices' of education and subsequent
'choices' of time allocation at home and in the paid labour market.
Women, women's traditional activities, the well-being of women and
children, and the roles of differential power and discrimination were
invisible.

Starting in the 1970s, however, women in many countries increasingly moved into the labour market and into formerly all-male
occupations. Neoclassical economists sometimes tried to explain
this shift without leaving the rational choice paradigm by attributing
it to changes in technology or underlying relative prices. Feminist
economists, however, recognized these shifts as the result of the
breaking down of legal restrictions and social norms that had previously limited women's educational and job opportunities. A key
distinction feminists often make is between *sex*, understood as
the biological difference between the sexes, and *gender*, the social
beliefs that society constructs on the basis of sex. While traditional
economists saw household and labour market outcomes as reflecting only innate sex differences, feminists investigated the impacts of
misleading stereotypes and rigid social and legal constraints. During
the 1970s, feminist academic economists called into question, for
example, the ideas that specialization in household work would be an
optimizing choice for a woman, and that labour markets were free of
discrimination.

During the 1980s, feminist economics continued to develop.
Myriad studies of women's economic history, economic status, and
progress towards gaining economic equality were accomplished,
covering many countries and regions. Surveys of policies related to
gender equity were begun. An early landmark in the popular movement for feminist economics was the publication in 1988 of Marilyn
Waring's book, *If Women Counted*. Waring, a former member of
the New Zealand Parliament, argued that the absence of women's
unpaid labour in the national production accounts severely biased
the design of national policies. Within academic circles, some
feminist economists incorporated the insights of unconventional (or

heterodox) schools of economic thought, such as radical economics or institutional economics, to explain societal shifts. Recognition of the importance of social beliefs and structures of power in creating gendered economic outcomes has remained a hallmark of feminist economics.

By the end of the 1980s, a cogent critique of neoclassical economics was developing among academic economists, while at the same time the idea of taking a feminist approach to economics was also influencing a number of neighbouring academic disciplines, policy debates and grassroots movements.

The development of a critical movement

While feminists' dissatisfaction with mainstream economic scholarship was originally rooted in its neglect and distortion of women's experiences, by the late 1980s feminists were also raising a more thoroughgoing critique. Many feminist economists were finding that traditional neoclassical rational-choice models and a narrow focus on mathematical and statistical methods were a Procrustean bed. When it came to analysing phenomena fraught with real human issues including connection to others, tradition and relations of domination, such disciplinary strictures cut off the most interesting and salient parts. Feminists began to raise questions about the mainstream definition of economics, its central image of 'economic man' and its exclusive use of a particular set of methodological tools.

Essays on this theme were brought together in a 1993 volume published in the United States, *Beyond Economic Man: Feminist Theory and Economics*. One essay suggested that economics be defined by a concern with the provisioning of life in all spheres where this occurs, rather than only being concerned with choices and markets. Several essays explained how a particular set of professional values, emphasizing culturally masculine-associated factors such as autonomy, separation and abstraction had come to take precedence over culturally feminine-associated factors such as interdependence, connection and concreteness. The contributors argued that rather than taking masculinist tendencies as a sign of 'rigour' in the discipline, the truncation of methods created by this bias has weakened the discipline's ability to explain real-world phenomena. While many mainstream economists have feared that feminist economics would introduce a political agenda and subjective biases into otherwise pure and objective research, this volume turned the tables, pointing out that the neoclassical agenda is itself permeated by biases and that its status-quo-preserving theories are themselves a political stance. Questions were raised about mainstream economics not because it is too objective, but because it is not objective enough.

A conference, *Out of the Margin* held in The Netherlands in 1993, further developed these themes, and contributed innovative discussions on economic methodology. While many feminist economists continue to make use of traditional mainstream tools, on the whole the field has come to be characterized by inclusion of a broader range of concepts and methods. Theories of human behaviour that include a balance between individuality and relationship, autonomy and dependence, reason and emotion, and competition and co-operation have been developed. The use of historical studies, case studies, interviews and other qualitative data, as well as greater attention to issues such as data quality and replication in quantitative work, have been explored. Feminist economists tend to find that such serious efforts to create and promote more adequate forms of economic practice lead to new insights across the board, whether or not the topic being studied is explicitly gender-related.

With the publication of a number of books and articles, and meetings at early conferences, feminist economics coalesced into an organized field in the early 1990s. The International Association for Feminist Economics (IAFFE) was formed in 1992 and its journal, *Feminist Economics*, commenced publication a few years later. A review by Ferber and Nelson of developments during the first ten years of feminist economics was published in 2003. Reference works containing selected important historical and critical writings have been recently compiled. IAFFE continues to sponsor conferences which bring together people from many continents, disciplines, and backgrounds at different international locations each year. International and wide-ranging in scope, feminist economics now includes work on a number of subjects, some of which can be mentioned here.

Labour markets and entrepreneurship

True to its roots, feminist economics continues to develop analyses of gender issues in labour markets. Studies of women's paid labour supply, labour market discrimination and the origins of occupational segregation have been numerous. Feminist economists have also investigated topics related to labour unions; employment in global corporations; job-tied retirement policies; migration for work; formal versus informal labour markets; the effects of equal wage, fair employment, and affirmative action (or employment equity) laws; the availability and consequences of part-time work and family-friendly employer policies; sex work and trafficking; and many other topics. Often these studies are directly tied to legal issues or are intended to inform policy or public opinion.

Some feminists make use of conventional methods including mainstream theories, large-scale surveys, and/or econometric models to examine these topics. Other feminist economists raise questions about the ability of such tools, used alone, to shed light on the underlying causes of inequality and encourage increased investigation into the social, political and institutional structures of gender and labour markets, including using methods such as historical investigation and case studies.

Many women, however, do not participate in labour markets as employees, but instead are self-employed. In industrialized countries, it has been suggested that this is sometimes a reaction against workplace policies that fail to take into account the needs of employees' families. In countries of the global South, many women work in subsistence or small-scale agriculture, or microenterprises in sectors such as handicraft manufacture, food processing and retail trade. Feminist economists have analysed how marginalization into such areas of work can trap women in poverty, compared to more formal sorts of employment. But research and innovation by academics working with local groups and non-governmental organizations have also investigated how, with interventions, such work may help strengthen women's economic positions. The significance of microloans as a means to alleviate women's poverty remains a topic of controversy (see *Microcredit*).

Households and care

While family life was long considered 'non-economic' by mainstream economists, it has often been adult women's sole means of accessing economic resources for themselves and their children. Issues of intra-household distribution and decision-making have been investigated by many feminist economists. Pro-male gender biases in the distribution of food, medical care and education within families has been shown to have had dramatic effects on economic outcomes, and even survival, particularly in some countries of South and East Asia. Questions of marriage, divorce, fertility, property rights, domestic violence and the well-being of children have been investigated from feminist perspectives. A number of feminist economists go beyond neoclassical bargaining models to examine legal, social and psychological issues related to intra-household decision-making and well-being.

Much of women's traditional work in sex-segregated occupations (such as nursing and childcare) and within households can be described as 'caring labour'. Care-work presents a challenge to neoclassical economics since the traditional image of 'economic man' is of an autonomous, self-interested individual who neither requires care nor has any inclination to provide it. The conceptual and empirical study of work with dependency, emotional and/or other-regarding components has become a focus of much work by feminist economists. They have developed critiques of theories and policies that assume that economic agents are unencumbered prime-age workers, delving into the economic problems of elderly women, parents of young children and lone mothers who are faced with simultaneous responsibilities for income generation and family care.

The issue of valuing unpaid work within households remains controversial among feminists. Some feminists argue that is important for public policy that this work be measured, preferably in monetary terms. Time-use surveys have been used to obtain estimates of the number of hours devoted to such work by various family members, and a monetary value is often assigned by multiplying these hours by the going wages for jobs in house-cleaning or childcare. Others point out, however, that these monetary valuations tend to be understated, since the wages used in valuation are themselves depressed by sexist societal biases. Still others object to this whole field of research, arguing that to focus on the issue of unpaid work and care reinforces stereotypes about women and draws energy away from efforts to advance women into positions of greater economic and political power.

Macroeconomics, trade and development

Feminist economists have also made innovations in the analysis of economies at the national and global levels. Some have studied how including unpaid production in GDP changes macroeconomic patterns of economic growth. A number have studied the changes in women's status that have come about during transitions from socialism and during other forms of macroeconomic restructuring. Others have made detailed analyses of government budgets or tax systems according to their consequences for gender equity.

The effects of liberalization of global trade and finance – and in particular the macroeconomic policies imposed on debtor countries by the World Bank and International Monetary Fund – have been examined from a feminist point of view. It has been pointed out, for example, that programmes which prescribe macroeconomic belt-tightening through cutbacks in health care often have their most immediate impact on women, as women are expected to take on, unpaid, the work of providing services no longer provided by governments. Men and women may also be affected differently, depending on the degree to which they work in subsistence or trade sectors. At the theoretical level, feminist work challenges the models that justify neoliberal policy. The neoclassical image of perfectly functioning 'free' markets or trade is challenged by recognition of the real world complexity of human motivations and interrelationships, and concentrations of political and economic power.

As many theories of economic development have come to emphasize 'human capital' – that is, labour skills and capacities embodied in human beings – increased attention has been paid to women's and girls' access to health care and education in countries of the global South. Feminist economists have also challenged the definition of economic development in terms of industrialization and GDP growth, turning attention more directly to issues of growth in human well-being and capabilities. Investigations into topics such as gender differences in access to education; the effect of female education on fertility, occupational outcomes, and national productivity; and the effect of HIV-AIDS on women and national economies are now numerous.

Historical topics and the discipline

Feminist economists and historians have investigated the history of women's economic activities, from early times to the present, and in the context of many nations and cultures. In a more inward turn, a substantial literature has developed describing the history of economic thought in regards to women. They have also looked at the history of women and feminists within the economics discipline itself. Recent studies in major countries indicate that women are still underrepresented in the top ranks of academic economics, receiving tenure less frequently than men even when controlling for factors such as publications and family. Sexual harassment, sex discrimination and inhospitable environments are among the barriers yet to be overcome in some departments and universities. The academic teaching of economics has also been examined. Feminist economists have investigated how the content of economics courses can be made less biased concerning women, how courses can be enriched by feminist revaluation of theories and methods, and how pedagogy can be adapted to better reach students with diverse backgrounds and learning styles.

Overlaps with other initiatives

Academic feminist economists have also been involved in a wide variety of initiatives that intersect with the field on various grounds, and/or which can be subjected to feminist critique. Studies on the interplay of gender with race, caste, class and sexual preference have proliferated. On a philosophical front, feminist economists have pursued discussion concerning the epistemological and methodological foundations of economics in dialogue with thinkers from post-modernist, post-colonial, critical realist, pragmatist and other perspectives. Academic feminists have also investigated possible mutuality of aspects of aims and methods with various heterodox schools of economics including institutionalist economics, social economics, radical economics, post-Keynesian economics, 'post-autistic' (now 'real-world') economics and ecological economics. Both the activities of the International Association for Feminist Economics and the initiatives of various individuals have developed closer ties and cross-critiques among academics in fields including economics, women's studies, sociology, economic sociology, philosophy, finance, management, economic geography and political science.

The academy, however, has not been the only base for the growth of feminist economics. Many people 'on the ground', working in governmental policy offices, businesses, or non-profit and community groups, have challenged sexist economic practices in myriad and important ways. Increased interaction between feminists in these locations and those in the 'ivory tower' would be to the benefit of both.

An evaluation

Feminist economics has become a large and quite diverse initiative, with a number of different growth areas. While the field is still fairly young, some successes, failures and problematic developments may be noted. Perhaps one of the more successful aspects of feminist economics has been the increased acceptance by many in the development community of the idea that a country cannot truly improve its economic situation while leaving the female half of its population behind. Although many feminists in the development field undoubtedly would like even more feminist engagement, some perceptible progress has been made.

A notable failure, so far, has been of feminist economists' attempts to affect the assumptions and methods used by the mainstream academic discipline of economics. While economics departments have become somewhat more tolerant, over time, of studies of women's market behaviour using relatively conventional assumptions and methods, feminist critiques of neoclassical models and methodologies have been not so much disputed by mainstream economists as simply ignored. Whether the pressure from feminist and other critical and human-centred groups, and the patent inadequacy of mainstream theories demonstrated by the recent financial collapse, will change the discipline itself – or will allow alternative sources of economic knowledge outside the discipline to gain increased recognition and influence – remains to be seen.

The diversity of the field has its benefits, limits and problems. The variety of theoretical, national, historical and personal perspectives brought to the field so far has been stimulating for all involved. However, while very many different voices have joined in this project, not all have had equal hearing: Matters of power differences by race, class, and nation are still very much present. And differences in disciplinary background, political ideology and imagination about what liberation is and how it may be achieved can make it difficult for participants to understand each other and work together. Some feminist economists, for example, seek primarily to improve conditions within market-oriented economies; others equate 'capitalism' with 'patriarchy' and see hope only in alternatives such as socialism or localism. It can be difficult to communicate across these gaps.

Overall, feminist economists have made significant strides in increasing recognition of the female half of the human economy; have made significant contributions to critical thought about human economic organization; and have helped to influence policy in many places around the world. It is this writer's hope that feminist economics will continue to develop a critical and constructive voice, bringing the concerns of women and girls to attention when they are (again and again) neglected, and contributing to visions of how economies could be organized to serve human and ecological well-being. In the view of this author, market commerce is neither the wonderful machine that physics-mimicking neoclassical economists imagine, nor the evil machine that some fear, but rather a human-created institution that contains opportunity for ethical deliberation and creative design. Recognition of this may help us move towards a better world.

Further reading

Agarwal, B., Humphries, J. and Robeyns, I. (eds) (2005) *Amartya Sen's Work and Ideas*. Routledge, New York.

Barker, D. and Kuiper, E. (eds) (2009) *Feminist Economics: Critical Concepts*. Routledge.

Benería, L., May, A. M. and Strassmann, D. (eds) (2010) *Feminist Economics*. Edward Elgar, Cheltenham.

Ferber, M. A. and Nelson, J. A. (eds) (1993) *Beyond Economic Man: Feminist Theory and Economics*. University of Chicago Press, Chicago.

Ferber, M. A. and Nelson, J. A. (eds) (2003) *Feminist Economics Today: Beyond Economic Man*. University of Chicago Press, Chicago.

Folbre, N. (1995) 'Holding hands at midnight': the paradox of caring labor. *Feminist Economic* 1 (1), 73–92.

Grown, C., Cagatay, N. and Elson, D. (eds) (2000) Special issue on growth, trade, finance and gender inequality. *World Development* 28 (7).

Kuiper, E. and Sap, J. (eds) (1995) *Out of the Margin: Feminist Perspectives on Economics*. Routledge, London.

Nelson, J. A. (2006) *Economics for Humans*. University of Chicago Press, Chicago.

Waring, M. (1988) *If Women Counted*. Harper and Row, San Francisco.

10

Fair Trade

Alfonso Cotera Fretel and Humberto Ortiz Roca

What is fair trade?

Fair trade is a process of exchange linking production, distribution and consumption with the aim of promoting solidarity and sustainable development. It seeks above all to benefit excluded or impoverished producers, by improving economic, social, political, cultural, environmental and ethical conditions at all levels of the process. These improvements include fair prices for producers, education for consumers and human development for one and all, with full respect for human rights and the environment. Fair trade can be understood as the fundamental meeting point between responsible producers and ethical consumers.

Fairer conditions are sought for producers, especially the more disadvantaged, through the development of international trade practices and rules based on the criteria of justice and equity, with consumer support for these ends. The impact of fair trade lies not in figures showing who were made rich and became even richer through this trade, but in the number of those it has helped to lift out of poverty, exclusion and disadvantage.

Fair trade is not simply a commercial relationship. It seeks to establish co-operation and partnership between the producers of the South and the consumers of the North based on equality and mutual respect. Through fair trade the conscientious consumer does not just acquire products but also makes committed relationships with producers, learning in the process about the origins of products (in ethical and environmental terms). It is underpinned by all the work for a fair and solidarity economy at the level of world society. When seen from a truly global perspective, the concept is more far-reaching than versions created by European networks such as FLO (Fairtrade Labelling Organizations International), IFAT (International Federation for Alternative Trade), NEWS (Network of European World Shops) and EFTA (European Fair Trade Association).

International trade has developed traditionally through a model of exchange that generates injustice, inequality and marginality. To take just agriculture, the countries of the North import products for their populations' consumption that are not produced in their climates, such as bananas, coffee, cocoa, sugar etc. Similarly, these countries import products that would require high labour costs if produced locally, in comparison with the cheap prices paid in the countries of the South, where labour is less well paid. At the same time they subsidize their agriculture, and industry too, but do everything possible to prevent the countries of the South from doing the same.

International trade agreements, supervised by the World Trade Organization (WTO), have stipulated that industrial countries should reduce duties on agricultural imports by 36 per cent over six years, and that developing countries should reach a level of 24 per cent in ten years. In practice, the developed countries maintain their high agricultural subsidies, while developing countries cannot maintain theirs owing to an international financial system that facilitates dumping and keeps producers in the South less competitive.

The consequence of this situation is the continued export of agricultural products and raw materials by countries and regions whose populations are suffering from hunger to other countries which overproduce food. Products that had always been consumed locally by the peoples of the South have become the intellectual property of transnational companies who know nothing of these ancestral traditions, despite the provisions of International Labour Organization convention 169 concerning the rights of indigenous and tribal peoples in independent countries.

For almost fifty years, NGOs in the North, especially Europe, have been in dialogue with NGOs and producer groups in the South to develop an alternative to the traditional pattern of international trade. Using terms like *fair trade* or *commerce equitable*, they have sought to reverse the tendency for unequal exchange 'from the bottom up', promoting and recognizing the work of producers from the South through the payment of fair prices for their products and raising awareness of consumers in the North to the meaning of healthy consumption and purchasing power, substituting ethical for narrowly economic considerations.

The fair-trade movement has established alternative markets in the North, with specific standards being set for each product. The number of these products is increasing and their production is already much more diversified, being sold in solidarity shops and even some supermarkets. (Mexico has solidarity supermarkets, but in Europe and North America these are more likely to be organic.) These markets offer wealthy consumers a more direct relationship with producers from the South and generally provide better commercial conditions. This direct relationship is not so much due to reduced physical distance, but to ethical closeness which, for all the great geographical distances involved, can be termed an 'economy of proximity'.

North and South

The original concept of fair trade involved replacing North/South aid relations with exchange relations based on solidarity (the slogan being *Trade, Not Aid*). Then national certification of fair-trade, organic and quality labels was initiated in nearly all of Europe and North America. The agencies responsible for this certification also often imported and promoted products from co-operatives, associations and small producers from the South.

In 1997, all these initiatives were brought together under the FLO (Fair-trade Labelling Organizations International) to provide them with an internationally valid fair-trade label. Since then, these agencies have begun to work together to facilitate exports and promotion of products from organizations of small producers, with the aim of reducing North–South inequality. In Mexico, domestic fair trade is being developed with the aim of promoting small producers, with a brand label that certifies fair marketing as well as production. A solidarity production and marketing network has also been formed between producers in Mexico and the United States, called the *Coalición Rural*.

The Ecuadorian 'Fraternal marketing' initiative (*Comercializando como Hermanos*) has been the driving force behind a community movement based on popular organizations from both rural and urban components of the home market. This 'Latin American Community Marketing Network' (RELACC) has bases in eighteen Latin America countries. The Rural Coalition was formed with the objective of becoming an alternative to free trade (NAFTA), in an alliance of more than ninety small producers' and agricultural workers' organizations in Mexico and the United States. In Peru, the Peruvian Fair Trade and Ethical Consumption Network includes networks of domestic producers connected to international fair-trade networks, such as in the coffee sector, under the National Coffee Council (JNC), and of craft workers in the Peru Inter-Regional Centre for Craftspeople (CIAP). This last covers nineteen associations of craftsmen and women from both rural and urban areas forming a whole movement, with solidarity fair-trade shops in several Peruvian cities and networks for solidarity tourism, organic producers and ecological consumer organizations, prison producers (supported by the Episcopal Social Action Commission), the child and teenage worker movement (MANTHOC) and solidarity economy initiative groups.

Various fair-trade marketing experiments have emerged in other Latin American countries. Women's organizations in Chile ('buying together') have sought to link producers directly to consumers. Along the same lines, there are consumer markets in Venezuela (the CECOSESOLA experiment), Solidarity Farmers' Markets in Colombia and community currency schemes in Argentina, Mexico, Ecuador, Brazil and other countries. Within this same perspective, the Santa Maria Co-operative Market in Brazil does not just exchange products, but also involves a rich process of *knowledge exchange*. The Latin American Co-ordination Table for Fair Trade was established in 2004, formed of various national and regional networks and organizations aimed at South–South fair trade.

Fair trade therefore involves developing strategies for dialogue between states, multilateral organizations and social networks in pursuit of legal standing for fair trade at the national and international levels. In the case of the European Union, for example, the European Parliament unanimously approved a resolution for the promotion of 'ecological and solidarity trade' in July 1998.

At the start of the twenty-first century, the programme of solidarity certification in the countries of the South themselves has advanced substantially. In 2006, the Latin American fair-trade network proposed the creation of a continental label which also involves 'cross certification', through which a body in one country, complying with the standards and legal requirements laid down, would be able to certify products from another country and so on. The network has been carrying out studies preparatory to launching this 'label of the South' which will increase access for a much larger number of small producers.

The concept of fair trade has expanded, with the definition being extended to trade within countries, enhancing the local market and not just exports, trade between the countries of the South as well as with the North and the East. The accords proposed during the first Latin American Meeting for Free Trade, Ethical Consumption, Social Money and Exchange, organized in Lima, Peru, in March 2001 had this project very much in mind.

The wider social agenda of fair trade

Fair trade is also related to ethical consumption, as two sides of the same concept; one cannot exist without the other. Barter (direct exchange) and community currencies are therefore preferred as the means of exchange in local and regional economies, especially for more disadvantaged groups and the poor, while demonstrating their viability across the social spectrum. The multiple functions of fair trade are increasingly being recognized: it is not just a marketing strategy, but also a way of promoting permanent and sustainable local production, job creation, the establishment of gender and generation equality and the mobilization of ethnic-cultural values and all the other aspects of local development.

The transformative power of fair trade allows other kinds of relationships to be established between producers and consumers, based on equity, co-operation, trust and shared interest. The principles of this form of marketing are:

(a) creation of new forms of exchange, founded on solidarity, in pursuit of a sustainable and equitable future for regions and their inhabitants;

(b) co-operation as the basis and condition for exchange, implying trust, transparency of information and fair and lasting relationships;

(c) incorporation of social and environmental costs to ensure the sustainability of exchange relations adopted consciously by producers and consumers;

(d) formulation of criteria and standards conducive to greater fairness in commercial transactions between North and South, modifying the established international division of labour;

(e) establishment of a more direct relationship of solidarity between producers and consumers, not just as a mechanism for cheaper product prices, but also as a process of socialization, with a view towards constructing a responsible and sustainable world; and

(f) humanization of markets by integrating fair trade into a vision of the economy centred on the person, not confined to commercial and monetary exchange.

Fair trade has several objectives. The first of these is the evolution of trading practices with a view to sustainable development and the incorporation of social and environmental costs into prices, thereby raising public awareness in support of national and international legislation. This consumer awareness favours fairer exchange. Another objective is to develop a strategic balance between local and international markets. The promotion of gender and generation equality aims to stimulate full human participation, through more equitable relations between men and women and people of different ages, thereby allowing women to play a more active role in the development process, in decision-making and in administration of organizations. This is linked to a broader political process of female emancipation (see *Feminist Economics*). By supporting the expression of local cultures and values through intercultural dialogue, the fair trade movement argues that products do not just have exchange and use value, but also express the characteristic realities and experiences of the culture that produces them. They are vehicles of communication and exchange that enable an intercultural dialogue between consumers, whose tastes and desires are partly shaped by respect for identities. Finally, fair trade aims to promote rounded development in economic, organizational, social and political terms. In the economic arena the focus is on improvements in production techniques and diversification so that people do not depend on just one product for income.

In organizational terms, fair trade aims at improving the management and administrative abilities of present and future directors of organizations, while encouraging the full participation of members in formulating strategies and distributing any additional income from achieved sales. At the level of society, fair trade focuses on improving the living conditions of members of the participating organizations and those of their families and communities, through health and education policies and programmes, such as improvements to housing and drinking-water systems and a host of similar projects.

The development of fair trade is based on some fundamental principles. The most direct possible relationship needs to be established between producers and consumers, reducing the intervention of conventional intermediaries and speculators. Exchange should be carried out at a fair price that allows all producers and their families to live decently from the fruits of their labour. The conditions of paid labour need at least to meet the standards of the International Labour Organization (ILO) or those of the relevant country, if they are better than the ILO's. Workers' rights of association must be respected and forced labour outlawed. In the case of self-employed producers, partial advances of funds should be authorized prior to harvest or manufacturing, if required. Contractual relationships should be established on a long-term basis of mutual respect and ethical values. The aim of such relationships is not just to establish a fair price for products, but to create conditions for the sustainable development of all workers. These minimal criteria can be summed up as solidarity, justice, responsibility and rights. Some fair-trade organizations establish criteria for measuring 'progress' towards these ends.

The participants in fair trade

The fair-trade movement is based on a constant process of creation and development in different forms, evolving according to the socio-economic, political, cultural and environmental contexts of each region. Various types of actors participate in this process by directly intervening in economic activity to implement, promote and develop fairer exchange.

The *producers* are all those who make products sold in the fair-trade market, according to given requirements, technical standards and conditions. The vast majority of these producers are found on the margins of traditional trade and come from countries in the South and the East. The *consumers* are all those people buy products in the fair-trade market, often reflecting their awareness of the unfair international system of commerce and/or solidarity with those on the margins who are excluded by the dominant system. These consumers are largely found in the countries of the North. The *companies* involved in the fair-trade system are private-sector bodies with a sense of social responsibility who are willing to work within this trading perspective. This category should not be extended to those for whom social responsibility is just a marketing mechanism for infiltrating the fair-trade movement (see *Corporate Social Responsibility*). Unlike these companies, *co-operative organizations* offer economic, technical or promotional contributions to the development of fair trade. Finally, *governments* are those local, regional or national administrations which assist the market, minimally through its regulation according to environmental and social criteria or by establishing a legal framework for fair trade.

Another group of actors consists of *institutions*, bodies and organizations created specifically to advance fair trade. *Producers' organizations* are co-operatives, producer associations, workers' unions or other bodies representing the interests of their members in negotiations within the fair-trade movement and in institutional relationships with other bodies. *Consumer organizations* are associations and co-operatives of consumers working for the promotion of fair trade and raising citizens' awareness concerning the challenges of ethical and responsible consumption. Some of these have established their own systems for fair distribution of regional products or imported goods. In the late 1980s certain criteria were formed and developed for each product. The *certification agencies* are dedicated to certifying whether products fulfil the conditions for qualifying as fair-trade items, with a view in particular to their distribution through supermarkets. Other agents, *the importers or buying centres*, are responsible for acquiring and placing products on the market (distributors, whole world shops, retail sales points). Direct sales to consumers are handled by *fair-trade shops*, which are often supplied by fair-trade buying centres, although these shops may also have direct commercial relationships with producers. Finally, *distributors* and *points of sale* are commercial members of fair-trade organizations (producers, labelling and buying centres) responsible for the distribution of products, particularly food, on the open market.

Twelve proposals for developing fair trade

1. Expand the range of the concept

The concept of fair trade needs to take into account the diversity of practices, models and scales of trade that seek to incorporate the criteria of fairness into market transactions and to foster relevant values in these transactions. This presupposes more effective links between fair-trade players and political leaders as a way of renewing agreed criteria of fairness in the light of common experience and raising public awareness at all levels, including South/South and North/North trade. Above all, the restrictive view taken by the European Union and the United States/Canada, which only recognize the North/South dimension, needs to be replaced.

2. Recognize producers and employees as parties with full rights

This involves the incorporation of producers and employees into discussions concerning criteria for fair certification as well as evaluation and compliance with these criteria. This should also cover the definition of new strategies for the extension of fair trade to new products and markets, especially for locally transformed products. There should thus be a focus on strengthening the production, organization and management capacities of disadvantaged producers.

3. Develop communications between all fair-trade parties

In order for the practice and knowledge of fair trade to make progress, the circulation of information between groups of producers, consumers, importers, certifiers, shops, employees and politicians must be enhanced. Backward regions and disadvantaged producers should be compensated by infrastructure facilitating access to information that would allow them to use the media currently available as well as new information and communication technologies.

4. Strategies for local development (see Local Development)

The best way for such producers to be exposed to globalization is by affirming the central role to be played by local regions, for which new local strategies of development should be explored. These strategies should be based on the following principal objectives: food security, employment, health, diversified production, local economic integration, expansion of regional markets and equitable development.

5. Build platforms articulating fair-trade parties at all levels

The work of the fair-trade movement must be guided by common platforms. Shared objectives should be agreed between all the institutions taking part in the fair-trade movement from the local to the global level. These would then become lines of action for the development and promotion of society and would inform concrete demands put to states and supranational organizations.

6. Collaboration between the fair-trade and organic movements

Duplication of the work of the organic movement and that of the fair-trade movement should be avoided, where possible. Environmental criteria should therefore be incorporated into fair-trade labels and social solidarity criteria into organic labels, with the aim of making a broader unified movement of producers, consumers, institutions and organizations.

7. Incorporate environmental criteria into the assessment of fair trade

Environmental protection criteria need to be integrated into the processes of international production and exchange, within the framework of the goal of sustainable trade. All organizations should participate in efforts to implement a Multilateral Agreement on the Environment that would combine the environmental and social costs of production, distribution and consumption.

8. Fair standards for new products and sectors

Fair trade should foster the transformation of primary products by their own producers as near as possible to the places of origin of such products. Fair trade should develop standards for products which play an important part in food security.

9. Encourage the holistic approach of solidarity economy (see Solidarity Economy)

The fair-trade movement forms part of the holistic approach to solidarity economy and therefore needs to connect with other efforts to promote social solidarity in economic activities (solidarity finance, local development, responsible tourism, ethical consumption, community currencies, knowledge exchange, proximity services etc.). These might generate economic and social synergies and in the process become more prominent in the public arena.

10. Mass distribution of fair-trade products

Fair trade products must find channels of mass distribution at home and abroad which means being integrated into traditional channels of distribution. Oligopolistic practices must be avoided of course and pressure put on the major distributors to conform with ethical trade practices and norms of social responsibility.

11. Fight for an improved international and national legal status for fair-trade products

Fair trade is part of the search for equitable markets and the war against disadvantage and poverty. A sustainable and responsible world should accord to fair trade a legal status consistent with promoting and facilitating its development.

12. Reform markets and trade integration at the international level

Dialogue should be promoted between civil society organizations and nation-states concerning the implications of multilateral agreements on investment, international financial institutions, free-trade negotiations, agreements and all the other accords reached at world summits. Agreements for fair economic integration at the level of the South's regions and local areas should be promoted, with the aim of developing a critical and purposeful stance towards multilateral treaty proposals on investment and free trade.

Further reading

ALOE (2008) *Intercambiando visiones sobre una economía: Responsable, Plural y Solidaria*. FPH, Paris.

Cooper, A. (2007) *Fair Trade (Issues in Our World)*. Franklin Watts, London.

Cotera Fretel, A. and Simoncelli-Bourque, E. (2002) *Manual sobre Comercio Justo*. GRESP, Oxfam GB, SUCO, Lima.

Fassa, R. (1998) *Rapport sur le commerce équitable*. Commission du Développement et de la Coopération, Paris.

Fundación Consumidor Consciente (2001) *El planeta necesita un consumidor consciente*, http://www.fairtrade.net.

Grodnick, A. and Conroy, M. (2007). *Fair Trade: The Challenges of Transforming Globalization*. Routledge, London.

Hayes, M. G. (2006) On the efficiency of fair trade, *Review of Social Economy*, 64 (4), 447–68.

Johnson, P. (2001) Alianza para un mundo responsable, plural y solidario. In Mayer, C. L. (ed.) *Cuaderno de propuestas para el siglo XXI: Comercio Justo.*

Murray, D., Raynolds, L. T. and Taylor, P. L. (2003) *One Cup at a Time: Poverty Alleviation and Fair Trade in Latin America*, http://www.colostate.edu/ Depts/Sociology/FairTradeResearchGroup.

Nicholls, A. and Opal, C. (2004). *Fair Trade: Market-Driven Ethical Consumption.* Sage, London.

Simoncelli-Bourque, E. and Cotera Fretel, A. (eds) (2002) *Directorio de Comercio Justo.* GRESP.

Soares, F. and Diehl, N. (2001) Alianza para un mundo responsable, plural y solidario. In Mayer, C. L. (ed.) *Cuaderno de propuestas para el siglo XXI: Consumo Ético.*

Stiglitz, J. and Charlton, A. (2007) *Fair Trade for All: How Trade Can Promote Development.* Oxford University Press, Oxford.

11

Labour Economy

José Luis Coraggio

Labour economy vs. capital economy

The *Capital Economy*, organized into enterprises, aims constantly to increase and reproduce capital (accumulation) following the strict logic of instrumental rationality. The *Labour Economy* aims to reproduce and develop human life and its ways of organizing work, so that social and natural processes are governed by reproductive rationality. In the first type of economy, workers merely own a resource, their labour, that can only be engaged and organized by capitalist owners of the means of production and consumption; whereas in the second type of economy they are the autonomous agents of production, fighting for autonomy within the capitalist system. In the first, the force of labour has been transformed into the power of an automaton, capital; while in the second, labour is at the centre of the economic process in harmony with nature.

In a mixed economy, the organizational forms through which labour power is reproduced and realized are part of the 'popular economy', whether they are based on solidarity or not, and include production for the market managed by workers themselves: individual or family firms, co-operatives providing goods or services, and all those communal, mutual, and non-commercial entities that contribute directly to the conditions of life, such as the 'domestic' work of reproduction which is currently ignored in official accounts of the economy. It also includes various associated kinds of work that aim to improve the terms of trade for workers and their organizations (systems providing the means of consumption or supplies, systems of marketing or co-operative financing). To this should be added the reproduction and sale of salaried labour, the main social (heteronymous) form of work organization, imposed from above by capitalist or state agencies. This form of work is structured by tensions between employers and workers, in disputes over rights of access to and conditions of work, when the latter seek increased autonomy and emancipation from exploitative systems of production, whether 'Taylorist' or 'Toyota-ist'. Meanwhile the social struggle calls for the solidarity of (unionized) workers in their confrontation with the capitalist organization of work.

The *Labour Economy* may thus be counterposed to the *Capital Economy* which has produced, among other things, a particular way of organizing and understanding work that is specific to what we term capitalism. One of its features is the commoditization of labour, through the separation of individuals and their labour power, as Marx put it, and the buying and selling of this labour power on the market as a fictitious commodity, in Polanyi's terms. The idea of a 'labour market' implies a self-regulating market where the price (wage) and the conditions of the work contract are fixed by supply and demand, without reference to the needs of the workers. Actual markets, however, are not merely self-regulating mechanisms that aggregate quantities and balance supply and demand, but are instead real multidimensional force fields in which culture, values and the structure of different 'capitals' contribute to the differentiation, segmentation and regulation of techno-economic practices. These in turn reproduce or introduce variation into the structure, such as the recent appearance of a differentiated category of 'knowledge workers'.

From the first 'great transformation', organized capitalism has regulated the labour market, through heavy state intervention and with the help of powerful union organizations. This meant that workers and society in general acquired a culture of rights for workers and their families which limited the free play of the labour market and prevented wage levels from sinking to 'free-market' levels. This gave rise to what Robert Castel calls the 'salaried society' in which work for others, through the regulation and institutionalization of the labour market, becomes the universal basis of social integration. As Polanyi anticipated, the labour market, together with markets for the fictitious goods of land and money (to which we could now add the knowledge market), came to operate under heavy restrictions placed on it by the state and civil society organizations.

The capitalist organization of work also includes the actual management of the labour process and direct manipulation of the subjectivity, desires and daily lives of the workers. The control of science and technology by capital, which turns knowledge into an instrument for the pursuit of monetary gain, contributes to the formation of the proletariat as a mass of worker-consumers subordinated to systems of production, whose labour power becomes one more resource to be economized and substituted by other resources if profitability so requires. Capital's inherent tendency to replace 'live' labour power with the force of a productive apparatus ('machine power') has become obvious following the break in recent decades with the model of organized capital and the conservative attack on the state, whether in its socialist or social-democratic forms. Actual work is increasingly being carried out by machines, robots or automatic production systems mediated by markets which, in the case of many highly fungible goods, also operate automatically.

Thus work-for-capital has become of late the integrative and orientating institution that forms the life choices and strategies of the majority of society's members. This is despite the fact that it is alien in the double sense of every productive process being directed by the dictates of capitalism, its representatives and its productive systems and by being imposed through a system of needs and scarcity generated as a function of the accumulation of private capital, something that the inventors of Toyota-ism have been unable to overcome. This is all currently undergoing dizzying transformations as a result of neoliberalism, with the weakening of trade unions and work becoming precarious, while losing its central place within the capitalist system, but without being replaced by any equivalent processes of integration. Thus, for enormous numbers of workers, deregulated work is no longer sufficient to provide those necessities of life historically defined as essential to the labour force; and there has arisen a need to find other ways of organizing work itself. Capital produces whatever is most profitable and not whatever satisfies wider and more pressing needs. Work-for-capital has proved to destabilize people's perspectives on life, because it now includes only a reduced proportion of the population and even those included experience a 'precarious security'; so that society is split apart and lacks social protection. This development is designed to force those who own nothing but their labour power to take whatever work is available, for fear of hunger or destitution. At the same time it fuels their search for other ways of fulfilling their own capacities and needs.

Because the vision of a waged society is so ingrained, however, and obvious alternatives are so few, traditional wage work is still missed and desired even more than the things it produces. So we are once again learning to seek it out, keep it and defend it from competition with other workers. This much-desired work is still salaried work, work for a boss, whether private or public, and although it cannot be the basis for autonomy, it can still be valued as 'worthy', because it is obtained through the market, the place where 'you know who's who' and you know how much things and people are worth. Whether we consider the level of particular production processes or the more general social level, such work does not produce any solidarity nor shared understanding nor any meaning that transcends its instrumental function as a means of earning the money that buys what we need or desire.

From the point of view of capital, a desirable economy – with capital automatically conceived as the central subject – is one operating solely through market principles defined by the logic of accumulation and based on the utilitarian calculations of individuals whose ability to compete and earn provides them with access to wealth and to the possibility of human development. From the point of view of *Labour,* a desirable economy is one with self-recreating labour at its heart, a system combining five principles of integration that I have identified, following Polanyi, as social processes that ensure the sustenance of all:

(a) self-sufficiency of domestic units (households);
(b) reciprocity within and between communities;
(c) redistribution at different levels of society;
(d) exchange in regulated or free markets;
(e) planning of complexity (especially the unintended consequences of individual actions).

For the *Capital Economy,* quantitative increase in the amount of goods through the higher productivity of labour is the defining criterion of the economy's efficiency; whereas for the *Labour Economy,* it is the quality of life, well-being, the fulfilment of individuals linked together by relations of solidarity, with justice and in peace. While the goal of the *Capital Economy* is the maximization of capital itself, the *Labour Economy* is a means to a transcendent end, that of a full life for all in society. Although goods may have meanings attributed to them by society, they are not an end in themselves and strategic manipulation of interpersonal relations should diminish, to be replaced by mutual recognition, negotiation and agreements between equals.

For the *Labour Economy*, the social question is not, how do we return to full employment (overseen by capital) so that everyone can have an income and consume what is most profitable for capital? but rather, how do we recognize, reclaim, foster, invent and develop other forms of active life, other ways of motivating and co-ordinating human actions, so that we can create other products, seek more desirable outcomes and make human life fulfilling, a life that includes work for sure, but work performed willingly and in fraternity?

Popular, public and mixed economies

Within existing capitalist societies, just as the *enterprise* is the basic microeconomic form of organization for capital accumulation, the *household* is the basic microeconomic form of organization for reproducing not only labour power for capital, which workers depend on to exist and develop, but also their lives and capabilities through the generations. Households may be extended, drawing on the same logic of reproduction of life, to take the form of associations, organized communities and various kinds of formal and informal networks that consolidate relations with their members' well-being and reproduction in mind. Taken as a whole, they comprise what I call the *Popular Economy* which, as part of a mixed economy under capitalist hegemony, enters into relations with the capitalist enterprises and state agencies. The main content of these exchanges is labour power itself.

Solidary relations within the *Popular Economy* can provide certain aspects of reproduction: these include trade unions fighting for fair contracts and value for wage labour, associations of independent producers sharing the means of production or marketing channels, self-run service co-operatives, supply networks, movements demanding resources and assets – housing, health services, education etc. In a kind of reverse primitive accumulation, all of these may obtain resources from the capitalist economy not through economic exchange but through pressure, force and assertion of rights. The same is true for local neighbourhood associations which manage their own area and also create spaces for primary social interaction. Such networks may also have a more inclusive focus on society as a whole: ecological or human rights movements, struggles over land, water or territory, movements of gender, cultural or ethnic affirmation, demands for popular education or influence over specific state policies and many others. They may have transnational strategies, such as migration and income transfers to maintain families; remittances are the first or second item in the balance of payments of many Latin American countries.

Both forms of economic organization – popular and capitalist – are capable of developing intermediate systems for self-government, for strategic planning and for representing their own interests. Both forms have links – not without contradiction – with the *Public Economy*, its policies, its arenas for discussion and politico-administrative organizations. Between them these three sub-systems form an open *Mixed Economy*. This is the basis for a predominantly capitalist system which generates multiple spaces of resistance under the contradictory hegemony of a culture of capitalism.

With their zeal for accumulation and totalizing instrumental rationality, capitalist enterprises view all aspects of the social, political, ecological and symbolic context as either resources or obstacles and strive to co-opt or eliminate them, as far as their enrichment project requires and their power allows. At the middle level of economy, however, competition sets limits to this power while, at the most inclusive level, limits are set by so-called 'extra-economic' forces, whether social or ecological.

In general, a capitalist enterprise will not spontaneously limit its exploitation of the environment or human labour power nor put an end to unequal exchange or the degradation of the quality of life, if these enable it to maximize profits. Capital, particularly footloose global capital, being captive to market fluctuations, is by nature not concerned with any social, political, psychological or ecological dis-equilibrium produced by its own actions or by other enterprises in the territories where it finds a temporary home. The owners of capital may, of course, personally place moral restrictions on the unintended consequences of their strategies for society and the environment, but this is not intrinsic to the dynamics of capital. Workers, however, may in their own interest strive to win a measure of democracy from the state or federation of states, thereby opening up a political space for debate about the common good and making a critique of the capitalist system's overtly irrational tendencies. Forms of popular collective power (trade unions, ecological, feminist and ethnic movements, consumer associations etc.) may act as representatives of the common good, putting forward more *socially* efficient forms of the enterprise system based on an ethics that is not in thrall to the logic of accumulation and capable of limiting its destructive tendencies.

Polanyi, here agreeing with Marx, has demonstrated the perversity of reducing social integration to a free-market mechanism that sets prices through supply and demand, leading to a self-destructive form of society that degrades both human and natural life. In Marx's terms, an abstract system is set up which is perceived as natural but in fact has been and continues to be constructed and institutionalized through particular projects of domination. In such a vision of the economy, workers are not subjects but objects; they are 'human resources', a term now joined by 'human capital', 'social capital', 'the capital of the poor' and the whole terminology of stock markets applied to people.

The transition to a labour economy

Practices found within the *Social Economy* may be seen as being transitional between the *Mixed Capital Economy* and the *Mixed Labour Economy*. They open up the possibility of moving from mere political limitation of tendencies within capitalism towards the development of a *Labour Economy* that would satisfy the legitimate needs of all, through being organized and co-ordinated with a high degree of critical reflexivity and mediated not just by a regulated market but by structures of solidarity. In such an economy, the predominant forms of work would no longer resemble alienated, fragmented wage labour, organized by capital in sufficient quantity for everybody to become, in Arendt's term, *homo laborans*, mere adjuncts of the machinery of production.

Achievement of the social conditions for another kind of work, for the material and subjective achievement of self-governing and autonomous workers, involves a cultural struggle, not just to change the social evaluation of self-managed work, but to change the market behaviour of citizens in the daily reproduction of their immediate lives. In fact, in their capacity as consumers, workers may make the many forms of disequilibrium produced by capital even worse and thereby contribute to capital's growth, before other forms of work based on solidarity can develop. Even when profit is not their primary objective, the proponents of the *Social Economy* (defined as alternative and socially aware economic practices) may end up internalizing forms of work organization with the same values and criteria of efficiency as those of private enterprise. This trend may be reinforced by the common sense idea that sees 'the market is never wrong', when economic organization is defined in terms of a narrowly financial notion of sustainability and respect for negative freedom.

In the *Labour Economy* the meaning of economy is the fulfilment of the legitimate needs and desires of everyone through a rational organization of the division of labour. Its strategic horizon is not one where attainment of 'the kingdom of liberty' depends on over-coming 'necessity'. Nor does its realization hinge on some utopian outcome where no economy is needed at all. Nevertheless, it does develop a practical critique of the structure of desires and demand for goods and services generated by the idea of the good life in a capitalist economy, as well as of the utilitarian tendencies of the mass of middle-level, poor and destitute consumers. This is a question of finding a democratic means of formulating a range of practical defini-tions of what is necessary, sufficient, useful and legitimately desirable, as well as agreeing on more rational forms of production and con-sumption. It also involves recognizing the unity of the work involved in both production and consumption at the local level and the need to increase local self-sufficiency while maintaining an ecological bal-ance, while reining in market speculation in foodstuffs.

All this implies recognizing the importance and potential of the existing *Popular Economy* while generating a critique that goes beyond it, since this reactive and adaptive popular economy is unable to guarantee the survival *of all* in the context of transformations in global capitalism. It will require a systemic approach to transform this chaotic whole into an organically connected unity of production and consumption that is able to link work (of a different kind) with the satisfaction of needs defined historically by democratic societies.

In addition to whatever is necessary for domestic consumption and production, households also need access to other shared and collective resources for housework and the immediate reproduction of life (and hence of the capacity for labour) and this will involve some material accumulation, but as a means rather than an end in itself. From the point of view of the *Labour Economy*, control of general conditions – infrastructure, collective consumption – needs to be placed in the hands of workers' organizations or in those of decentralized and truly democratic structures of authority and management.

Although the *Capital Economy* has had a homogenizing effect, there are very wide socio-economic and cultural differences between households. A range of exchange relations between communities and individuals can already be found, based on utilitarian co-operation, centralized reciprocity, generalized reciprocity or community feeling, as well as on strong competition, depending on the values and institutions involved in such relations. The idea of a (different kind of) *Labour Economy* implies starting from this rich plurality of forms, counteracting capital's tendency to impose a model of abstract labour and unending consumption as a social leveller. It should be possible for multiple definitions of the good life to co-exist, although all definitions should guarantee people's ability to choose a new way of life or to remain attached to their original culture. From the micro point of view, two hypotheses emerge from this idea: (a) wage labour has never been, is not and even less will be the only way a household's labour can be put to work so as to obtain the conditions and means of life; and (b) it is possible for relations of production, work and distribution *not* to be objectivized and *not* to be experienced as unconscious abstractions, but to be structured by more transparent interpersonal relationships ranging from kinship to citizenship in a participatory democracy.

Such a prospect is difficult to imagine if our starting point remains the omnipresent market model. How can workers desire, initiate, sustain and develop forms of production capable of competing with capitalist forms? How can we change modern capitalist culture? How can we alter a balance of forces in which the means of production, communications and the army are concentrated in the hands of elites? Writers are optimistic or pessimistic on this question depending on whether they imagine capitalism has made a theoretical success of integrating society or assume its inevitable failure. In any case, we may rely on capitalism's contradictions at least to facilitate experiments in this direction, even if they will not generate a non-capitalist economy by themselves.

Confrontation between the *Capital Economy* and the *Labour Economy* is expressed in the political sphere. Here lies the possibility for organizing linked systems of production or territorial groupings through convergence between the many forms of workers' organizations and those of small or medium capital (for whose owners economic success is seen as being indispensable to the possibility of a good life). Integrated local development can make particular interests more visible and thus encourage possible alliances that conform to the principle of reproduction in its wider sense. Within the current technological paradigm a conflict with big capital in the struggle for the reproduction of life is inevitable. The alienation of workers' knowledge, the super-exploitation of labour and the despoliation of nature make this so. The common good will never be realized until the hurricane of capitalist centralization and globalization abates.

While the benefits and relative efficiency of productive processes commanded by capital can be quantified – or at least reduced to quantifiable form – the quality of life is of course inherently qualitative, although some aspects may be quantified. Capital can economize on labour costs, although in doing so it degrades social life, and on those incurred in extracting material resources, although in doing so it destroys nature. When labour is organized to reproduce life in general, it is sparing of nature and careful not to upset its balance, recognizing that we are ourselves part of the natural cycle rather than assuming that *homo sapiens* dominates nature as if he were somehow 'outside' it. Hard and soft technologies are selected on the basis of the social relationships they foster as much as for their material results. While for the *Capital Economy* productive labour is whatever generates value and surplus value, the *Labour Economy* considers labour useful to the extent that it produces use value and satisfies social needs that are in themselves sources of satisfaction. Prices are not left to market mechanisms but are regulated by strategic social and political interventions. Certain spheres will develop in which – given the type of goods and subjects of exchange – 'fair' prices will operate, while the price system as a whole should bear a relation to reproductive reason (another aspect of 'fairness').

The *Popular Economy* that exists already, along with a *Public Economy* responsive to a democratic project fuelled by solidarity, could together form the basis of a *Labour Economy* capable of representing and putting into effect life projects in a more egalitarian, solidary, just and self-governed society. This presupposes a strategic vision that seeks to go beyond the micro-social level of enterprise or micro

networks based on solidarity for survival, but will rather democrati-
cally develop new definitions of wealth, of nature and of productive
work, new ways of organizing the social division of labour, in short,
a *Different Economy*.

Further reading

Arendt, H. (1999) *The Human Condition*. University of Chicago Press,
Chicago.

Castel, R. (2003) *From Manual Workers to Wage Labourers: Transformation of the
Social Question*. Transaction Publishers, New Brunswick, NJ.

Coraggio, J. L. (1999) *Política social y economía del trabajo: Alternativas a la política
neoliberal para la ciudad*. Miño y Dávila Editores, Madrid.

Coraggio, J. L. (2007) *Economía social, acción pública y política*. Editorial
CICCUS, Buenos Aires.

Gorz, A. (1999) *Reclaiming Work: Beyond the Wage-Based Society*. Polity,
Cambridge.

Marx, K. (1973) *Grundrisse: Foundations of the Critique of Political Economy*
(rough draft). Pelican Books, Harmondsworth.

Max-Neef, M. A. (1989) *Human-Scale Development: Conception, Application and
Further Reflection*. Apex Press/CITA, New York.

Polanyi, K. (1957) The economy as instituted process. In Polanyi, K. et al.
(eds) *Trade and Market in the Early Empires: Economies in History and Theory*.
The Free Press, Glencoe, IL.

Postone, M. (1996) *Time, Labor, and Social Domination: A Reinterpretation of
Marx's Critical Theory*. Cambridge University Press, Cambridge.

Salmon, A. (2002) *Éthique et ordre économique: Une entreprise de séduction*. CNRS
Éditions, Paris.

12

Microcredit

Jean-Michel Servet

Overview

The term 'microcredit' refers to small loans made either to groups of borrowers or individuals. Such loans are advanced by a variety of institutions ranging from non-governmental organizations to banks and public programmes. Their stated targets are low-income groups and individuals, or groups and individuals subject to social, ethnic, religious, sexual or other forms of discrimination. Their goal is to allow them to develop income-generating activities. It is assumed that their increased wealth will allow them to meet other needs in the areas of health and education, and to develop other capacities, including equality between men and women and the rights of minorities.

In the so-called developing countries, microcredit is targeted mainly at broad sectors of the population that find themselves in a situation of financial exclusion without necessarily being poor. In Argentina and Central/Eastern Europe, for example, which have experienced the sudden impoverishment of large fractions of the population, microcredit is targeted mainly at the 'new poor', who come from the educated strata. In the so-called developed countries, where the wage-system is dominant, microcredit is targeted at a limited proportion of workers: self-employment may be only one solution to the question of unemployment and poverty among workers. These countries have recently seen the emergence of forms of social microcredit designed not to stimulate activity, but to allow deprived fractions of the population to cope with their financial exclusion by allowing them to meet their basic needs: furnishing a house, having a vehicle repaired or buying a pair of glasses, and so on.

In the early 1990s, microcredit was almost unknown outside a narrow circle of specialists, but it now attracts growing media attention. It is often described as one of the most effective ways of eradicating poverty or guaranteeing local development. In many countries, it is used by the authorities as part of a strategy to achieve the Millennium Goals of eradicating poverty by 2015 (the goals themselves were defined mainly by UN institutions). In the strategic plans that have been adopted to implement this strategy, microcredit is seen primarily as an effective way of raising incomes. Financial inclusion is not an end in itself and the fight against insecurity and vulnerability takes priority.

Bangladesh's Grameen Bank is often described as the first modern organization to have adopted a microcredit policy. It was not active in fact until 1976. Opportunity International, a Christian-based non-profit-making organization began to advance small loans in Colombia in 1971 and the non-governmental organization Accion International advanced its first credits in Brazil in 1973. Grameen Bank has 7.4 million borrowers, but other microfinance organizations have many more active borrowers: India's Nabard (National Bank for Agriculture and Rural Development) has almost thirty-nine million members in mutual aid groups. If the description of the activities of microcredit organizations is extended to include savings, Grameen looks like an organization operating on a modest scale compared with Indonesia's 'people's bank' BRI, with its twenty-eight million savers.

The notion that the main actors involved in microcredit are small-scale organizations also requires qualification. The sector is in fact highly concentrated and is becoming more so as a result of the pressure brought to bear by backers who are encouraging the normalization of microcredit. According to a 2009 Report from the Microcredit Summit Campaign, 88 per cent of 106 million of the 'poorest' out of 154 million people who borrow from microfinance organizations were financed by only seventy-six institutions and six networks (data for 2007). Those networks have 45 per cent of the 'poorest' clients, and the ten biggest institutions (which each have at least one million clients) represent 26 per cent of all clients. The thousands of institutions that have fewer than 10,000 clients each account for no more than four per cent of all clients.

The term 'microcredit' is in fact now used to describe a great variety of models. It should be noted in passing that many organizations that began by lending to groups, which is still often seen as symbolic of microcredit, now make loans to individuals. In 2002, Grameen Bank was forced to abandon what appeared to be one of its basic policies. The methods favoured by microfinance institutions (social microcredit, individual loans, bank affiliates) are largely determined by stimuli from public bodies, including financial support for 'commercial' microfinance from public co-operative agencies. Which method is used in any given country usually also depends on regulatory norms. Some organizations that began life as non-governmental organizations become banks when inflows of savings are deposited with them. They then become profit-making organizations and many abandon their stated goals of human development in the process. Organizations also tend to begin to offer services other than credit, such as insurance and the transfer of funds. There is also a tendency for venture capital to acquire greater holdings in them. That is why the term microfinance is used more often than 'microcredit'. The recent adoption of the term financial inclusion marks a further retreat from the original goal of fighting poverty.

The threat of neoliberalism and speculative investment

Neoliberals view microcredit as a means of encouraging job-creation through self-employment. When defined in those terms, it is a particularly insidious way of dismantling welfare policies aimed at the unemployed and the destitute in the weakest and most marginalized zones. The provision of welfare is supposedly a passive form of social spending, whereas support for microloans is considered an active form of social spending and a more effective way of stimulating economic development at the local level. There is also a danger that the growth of micro-enterprises whose activities might begin to compete with wage labour will further undermine traditional welfare and solidarity systems, that competition will reduce wages, take little heed of environmental norms and encourage child labour. Hence the need to evaluate microloans in terms of their social and environmental impact and not just in financial terms.

Neoliberal discourse has been accompanied by an extraordinary media campaign designed to attract multilateral and bilateral co-operation funds. At a time when the volume of public development aid is supposedly being increased, there is now a danger that money will be diverted away from what might be more effective ways of fighting poverty, since the odds are that microcredit will not fulfil its promise and will not reduce poverty. Only a small proportion of public development aid is, however, taken up by microfinance: the World Bank and the UNDP devote only one per cent and three per cent of their respective resources to microfinance.

The World Bank has played a major role in using advertising to promote microcredit as a development tool, mainly through the CGAP (Consultative Group to Assist the Poor). Media interest in microcredit has been strongly backed by the Microcredit Summits, which were organized by the RESULTS Educational Fund (a US-based grassroots advocacy organization) and their equivalents at national and continental levels (such as the Asian-Pacific Regional Microcredit Summit held in Bali, Indonesia in 2008 and the Latin American/Caribbean Regional Microcredit summit held in Cartagena, Columbia in November 2009). As in other domains, there is a striking contrast between the stated goal of reducing poverty and the display of wealth that accompanies such meetings.

The first Summit (Washington, February 1997) brought together over 2,900 people from 137 countries. The last Global Microcredit Summit brought 2,000 delegates from 110 countries together in Halifax (Nova Scotia, Canada) in November 2006. It marked the success of campaigns targeted at 100 million poor clients and defined the new goals of campaigns to promote microcredit: making micro-credit available for '175 million of the world's poorest families' by the end of 2015 and allowing '100 million families [to] rise above the US $1 a day threshold (adjusted for purchasing power parity) between 1990 and 2015'.

A series of lectures given in 2005, which was declared the World Year of Microcredit by the UN, marked the apogee of public demon-strations of support for microcredit. The award of the Nobel Prize for Peace to Grameen Bank and its founder Muhammed Yunus in 2002 sparked ever greater media interest. This fostered a largely illu-sory belief in microcredit's ability to reduce poverty.

The belief that profitable microcredit institutions could be quickly established proved very seductive. Norms were therefore defined for the good management of microfinance institutions, which were encouraged to place the emphasis on financial criteria. Campaigns, some of them successful, were launched to lower penal rates of interest for the benefit of microcredit organizations. It was recognized that such credit was expensive, but it was also argued that this was the price that had to be paid for the services rendered. It was claimed that their ability to finance a project mattered more to borrowers than the rate of interest, but no one raised the question of whether all categories of borrowers could support that rate. There was no discussion of the danger of indebtedness, of the possible impoverishment of borrowers . . . or of the enrichment of certain lenders.

Microcredit institutions receive support from private donors, private non-profit-making investors and ethical or joint investors, but their objective is also competition, and this may transform them into vehicles for investment that may, it is promised, bring an annual return of up to 15 per cent. While some of these investments (which can take the form of either share-holdings or loans) are primarily designed to make a profit, many also have social or ethical goals. Symbiotics SA, for example, supplies its customers with indicators that allow them to invest in full knowledge of the facts.

International investment in microfinance institutions by investment funds tripled between 2004 and 2006 and rose by an annual 25 per cent until 2008, by which time they reached the equivalent of $7 billion divided between some one hundred funds; this figure does not take into account the big international banks and institutional investors. One quarter of the funds (which are actually a combination of public and private funds) are of German origin; 24 per cent are from the US, 19 per cent from the Netherlands, 14 per cent from Luxembourg and nine per cent from Switzerland. Public and private actors are reported to have invested $15 billion (figures for late 2008) in microcredit, mainly in Eastern Europe, Latin America, and Central and South Asia. Rating institutions for microfinance also profit from this ideology, which allows some of the aid destined for microfinance projects to be siphoned off because financial exclusion is confused with poverty.

Can microcredit have a positive effect on the incomes of 'poor' populations?

Neoliberalism's supporters are by no means the only ones to have been seduced by microcredit. The belief that microcredit has been a success is based on the publicity given to stories about borrowers (most of whom are women) whose lives have been transformed by small loans. Not only have they increased their income considerably and made other small but productive investments, they have improved their environment habitat, find it easier to send their children to school and to obtain health care, have successfully challenged the alcoholism and violence of their menfolk and have won some autonomy of action for themselves. The financial success of some organizations, which often reflects the fact that women are better than men at repaying their debts, is seen as proof that such credit has positive benefits for borrowers. The image of microcredit that is publicized by the media and some academic studies, as well as the hopes placed in it by the authorities, is based on economistic dogma when it comes to analysing the causes of poverty and a biased understanding of the borrowers' circumstances, of the services that are supplied to these populations and of the real effects of microcredit. Let us look at some of these beliefs. The essential need for the most deprived communities is supposedly the need for credit and the poor are assumed to have a well-known preference for self-employment rather than wage-earning. Financial institutions do not have the resources to meet the almost unlimited demands of their potential customers. It should, therefore, be possible to create microcredit institutions that can quickly make a profit even though their customers are poor or even very poor.

The clients of the institutions offering microcredit must belong to the 'poor' category of the population. There are, however, growing doubts: the poor and especially the poorest may not be the best targets for such loans. This is because financial inclusion is very limited in most developing countries and large fractions of the population living above the poverty threshold find themselves in a situation of financial exclusion. Populations that experience financial exclusion but are not poor offer better guarantees of repayment. Because lenders want to balance their finances, they often lend to fewer of the poor in order to achieve their financial goals, and the definition of the poverty they are targeting remains vague. The widespread need for financial services therefore allows microfinance institutions to expand their activities with a view to reducing their costs. It appears that nine preconditions have to be met if microcredit is to have a positive and rapid effect on the income of the poorest.

1. When microcredit targets customers who are living above the poverty threshold, it helps not to reduce, but to increase the income inequalities between them and the most deprived strata of the population. If the extension of microcredit to strata that are not poor is to have a positive effect on the poorest, it has to be demonstrated that there is a 'trickle down effect', or that making the rich richer has a positive effect on the incomes of the most impoverished strata. The experience of the last sixty years does not prove that it has any such effect. The extension of microcredit to populations that are not poor but are financially excluded has a positive effect in terms of financial inclusion, but that is not the same as increasing the income of poor populations or as providing them with subsidies.

2. If microcredit is to be an effective way of promoting development – in the minimalist sense of raising incomes – the loans granted must actually be used by the borrowers to increase their productive capacities. Microfinance is often seen as an economic initiative because it is reduced to meaning advancing credit to create self-employment or micro-enterprises. It main goal is supposedly to increase incomes by developing such enterprises. Microloans that are intended to encourage economic activity on the part of the poorest in fact seem to have only a limited effect, mainly because the credit is short-term and because the profitability of these units of production's capital is limited. But in many cases there are few checks, and the financial resources of a household are liable to be used for other purposes. Small credits do help them to time-manage their resources and expenditure more efficiently. But that does not mean that more of those resources are devoted to additional investment in productive activities. Families can manage their budgets better, but that does not necessarily have the positive effect of allowing them to expand their income-generating activities. If the loans are used to buy medication or to cover the costs of sending children to school, they do have an indirect positive effect, but they rarely have any immediate effect in terms of increasing the family's income.

3. If microcredit is to have a positive effect on incomes, any investment must be made in an activity for which there is a market. We often find that the men and women who benefit from these loans imitate one another. This considerably reduces their effect in terms of generating new resources. They accumulate debts and the loans

are either re-scheduled or decapitalized to mask the fact. If these practices are taken into account, the advertised repayment rates are often lower than in reality.

4. If microcredit is to be successful, the man or woman concerned must have the appropriate managerial and technological abilities. Credit is not itself enough to encourage micro-entrepreneurship. A lot of resources must be devoted to providing professional, technical and commercial support for the creators of economic activity. But this broader interpretation of microfinance, which includes finance for training and information policies, is very often rejected in favour of a minimalist and purely financial vision of microcredit. That vision tends to ignore non-financial (but expensive) institutional activities on the grounds that specialist financial skills are being provided. And it is indeed difficult to pressurize borrowers into repaying their loans by managing the non-financial side of the relationship.

5. There must be some willingness to accept a higher level of risk. Studies of poverty show that the most deprived fractions of the population are handicapped not so much by their low incomes as by their precarious position and by the fact that they do not have the means to deal with a crisis such as illness. Populations that are exposed to risk therefore avoid further risks and tend to turn to less risky activities, but those are the activities that generate the lowest incomes. From that point of view, such populations need service transfers from migrants (savings and insurance) rather than loans that are advanced for productive purposes. The development of institutionalized welfare is essential if the social pressure brought to bear on the resources of micro-enterprises is to be reduced.

6. If microcredit is to be a success, the profitability of micro-activities must be higher than that of more capital-intensive activities. The case for small loans is based on the illusion that the marginal profitability of capital falls at all times and in all places. It is assumed, in other words, that falling marginal profitability and productivity are directly proportional, in the mathematical sense, to increases in the scale of units producing goods and services. While that may be true of individual units of production (with the exception of productive activities involving a high degree of skill; in such cases, production costs are now falling), the same is not true in overall terms. It can

just as easily be argued that certain types of companies have an average level of productivity (which rises as they expand) and that the productivity of large or medium-sized units will be higher than that of small units. Once units expand beyond a certain size, productivity falls in all these categories. In Africa, entrepreneurship among the poor has been promoted at the expense of other productive models. Yet if we look at the policies adopted by the two locomotives of contemporary world growth, China and India, it is obvious that economic development in those countries is based on the promotion of companies of a certain size and of wage-earning. And while microfinance services are available there, they are a way of allowing certain strata of the population to survive rather than being an instrument of policies designed to increase incomes.

7. The cost of loans, as expressed by the rate of interest that is paid, must be lower than the profitability of the activity they are invested in. This explains why microcredit tends to be used to finance commercial activities rather than craft industries, and craft industries rather than agriculture. When interest rates rise above 60 per cent, as in Latin America, while agricultural activities rarely have a return of more than 15 per cent or even eight per cent, loans are requested to finance part of those activities (such as buying fertilizer or seed). Both labour and property are under-rewarded and resources are diverted from agriculture to the financial sector and from the rural world to the urban world.

8. Investments made thanks to microloans must result in endogenous spending that generates a demand for locally produced goods and services and not for the import of goods. When, for instance, loans are actually used to buy medicines, the state of the population's health does improve. That is a positive outcome, but financial resources are exported and have no internal multiplier-effect on incomes. Microcredit thus acts as a growth factor in countries that use the loans to finance exports and that enjoy the financial flows generated by interest on the loans, but not in the so-called developing countries. This reveals the macro-economic limitations of microcredit.

9. If the overall effect of microcredit on incomes is to be positive because of the interest paid by borrowers, it must not allow resources

to be siphoned off for the benefit of outside lenders. If financial resources for investments are inadequate at the local level, capital has to be imported, but funding from outside is often a substitute for the mobilization of local resources. In many countries where per capita incomes are among the lowest in the world, banking institutions are experiencing excess liquidity. This is the case in forty of the forty-four countries in Africa south of the Sahara, as well as in Egypt, Algeria and Morocco, and in other parts of the world, such as Guyana in the Caribbean. International guarantee funds may make it possible to create an endogenous financial dynamic.

It is highly unusual for all nine preconditions to be met at the same time. As recent studies have demonstrated, the overall performance of microcredit institutions is poor in terms of the fight against poverty, especially in the growing number of countries where borrowers' levels of indebtedness are rising. Microcredit therefore is unlikely to be an efficient way of reducing poverty significantly in the developing countries.

When it comes to fighting unemployment in the developed countries, one has only to compare the number of companies that could be created by microcredit with the number of unemployed and poor workers to see the limitations, and especially the dangers, of this type of policy. While it is described as the main, or only, alternative to the loss of wage employment, support for microfinance can undermine the right to work even further. That those who wish to create jobs should be given all possible support goes without saying. That is a question of rights. Positive discrimination in favour of those who are economically excluded and who want to create economic activity is an innovative policy. But presenting this as almost the only solution – and one that can be applied everywhere– is a covert way of dismantling wage-earner's self-defence systems and prohibitions on usury. It took two hundred years for those systems to gain acceptance and now this is being lost.

Microcredit and the fight against social exclusion

The economic limitations of microcredit explain why it would be dangerous to see these small short-term loans as the main weapon in the fight against poverty at the global level. Direct action in the fields of health, education, training and the defence of rights is still the priority, and we should have no illusions about the immediate effect of increased purchasing power in these areas.

It would, however, be a mistake to ignore some of microcredit's potential. While it is not an instrument that will increase productive resources to any great extent, microfinance (including microcredit) does enhance the ability of the most deprived to improve the time-management of their resources, and that is vital if their vulnerability is to be reduced.

Microcredit can act as a stimulus to local development if it creates a synergy between public and private actors. It has, for instance, proved to be a very effective way of using financial bonds to strengthen social ties and of providing essential resources in post-conflict or post-crisis situations in Uganda, Cambodia, Bosnia and Kosovo.

In terms of North–South relations, microcredit may also create and strengthen new forms of solidarity, especially when the loans do not come in the form of outside investment in strong currencies that are expected to produce a high return and when they are supported by guarantee funds that make accountable use of local resources.

If microcredit is to reinforce a local logic of solidarity, it must be part of the fight against financial exclusion; but it has to be understood that the need for loans is only one aspect of financial exclusion. In that respect, savings, transfers from migrants and guarantees are much more effective, especially for populations that have almost no access to formal financial services. These are the needs that the populations concerned emphasize. Financial services other than microcredit appear to be indispensable if micro-entrepreneurship is to develop. It has also to be noted that, in many countries, postal services, international co-operatives and mutual aid savings and credit services provide many more financial services than the microcredit institutions that have received so much attention from the media. The emphasis should be placed on training, but also on micro-insurance and protection for both property and individuals.

Microcredit may be an effective weapon in the fight against various forms of exclusion in a wide variety of situations, provided that both its real potential and its limitations are properly understood.

Further reading

Armendariz de Aghion, B. and Murdich, J. (2005) *The Economics of Microfinance.* MIT Press, Cambridge, MA, and London.

Armandariz, B. and Leabie, M. (eds) (2010) *The Handbook of Microfinance*. World Scientific Publishing, Singapore.

Balkenhol, B. (ed.) *Microfinance and Public Policy: Outreach, Performance and Efficiency*. Palgrave-Macmillan and ILO, London.

Daley-Harris, S. (2009). *State of the Microcredit Summit Campaign: Report 2005*. Washington, DC.

Demirgüç-Kunt, A., Beck, T. and Honohan, P. (eds) (2007) *Finance for All? Policies and Pitfalls in Expanding Access*. BIRD, Washington, DC.

Fernando, J. L. (ed.) (2006) *Microfinance: Perils and Prospects*. Routledge, London.

Kholiquzzaman, A. Q. (ed.) (2007) *Socio-Economic and Indebtedness-Related Impact of Micro-Credit in Bangladesh*. The University Press Limited, Dhaka.

Guerin, I. and Palier, J. (eds) (2005) *Microfinance Challenges: Empowerment or Disempowerment of the Poor*. FIP, Pondicherry.

Muhammad, A. (2009) Grameen and Microcredit: A Tale of Corporate Success. *Economic and Political Weekly* 44 (35) August, 35–42.

Roodman, D. and Murdoch, J. (2009) The impact of microcredit on the poor in Bangladesh: revisiting the evidence. *Working Papers 174*. Center for Global Development.

Servet, J-M. (2006) *Banquiers aux pieds nus: La microfinance*. Odile Jacob, Paris.

UNCDF (2005) Microfinance and the Millennium Development Goals. International Year of Microcredit.

Van Oosterhout, H. (2005) *Where does the Money Go? From Policy Assumptions to Financial Behaviour at the Grassroots*. Dutch University Press, Utrecht.

Wampfler, B., Guerin, I. and Servet, J-M. (2006) The role of research in microfinance. *European Dialogue* 36, September, 7–21.

13

Informal Economy

Keith Hart

Antecedents

The informal economy (or informal sector) became current in the early 1970s as a label for economic activities that escape state regulation. It arose in response to the proliferation of self-employment and casual labour in Third World cities; but later the expression came to be used with reference to industrial societies, where it competed with similar epithets – the 'hidden', 'underground', 'black' economy and so on. The social phenomenon is real enough and of some antiquity, but its definition remains elusive.

Most readers of this book live substantially inside the formal economy. This is a world of salaries, monthly mortgage payments, clean credit ratings, fear of the tax authorities, regular meals, good health cover, pension contributions, school fees and summer holidays. What makes this lifestyle 'formal' is the regularity of its order, a predictable rhythm that we often take for granted. For the world to become calculable in this way it must be made amenable to reason, 'rationalized'; and this means that many elements of uncertainty – other people, machines, the material environment – have to be brought under a measure of formal control.

'Form' is *the rule*, an idea of what ought to be universal in social life; and for most of the twentieth century the dominant forms were those of bureaucracy, particularly national bureaucracy, since society was identified to a large extent with nation-states. The formal and informal aspects of society were always linked; so the idea of an 'informal economy' is entailed in the institutional effort to organize society along formal lines. The term 'informal sector' (later 'informal economy' and now often just 'informality') arose almost four decades ago to describe the unregulated activities of the Third World urban poor. But the problem of proliferating urban masses, supporting themselves in invisible ways and at some perceived risk to public safety, is an older one.

In the eighteenth century, Scottish economists wrote about the 'urban riffraff' of Glasgow and Edinburgh. Later, the inhabitants of English city slums were called 'the dangerous classes'. London's East End in the mid nineteenth century, as captured by Charles Dickens in *Oliver Twist*, is a stark example of informal economic organization which rivals in scale any of today's tropical slum areas. More recently, Martin Scorsese's film *Gangs of New York* shows how criminal gangs and political corruption were rampant there at the same time. Some notable attempts have been made to document the economy of the streets. Henry Mayhew's investigations of *London Labour and the London Poor*, published in the 1860s are a classic source, as are Oscar Lewis's several accounts of the 'culture of poverty' (for example, in his ethnographic novel of Puerto Rico and New York, *La Vida*).

The anthropologist Clifford Geertz identified two economic ideal types in a Javanese town. The majority were occupied in a street economy that he labelled 'bazaar-type'. Opposed to this was the 'firm-type' economy consisting largely of Western corporations that benefited from the protection of state law. These had *form* in Max Weber's sense of 'rational enterprise' based on calculation and the avoidance of risk. National bureaucracy lent these firms a measure of protection from competition, thereby allowing the systematic accumulation of capital. The 'bazaar', on the other hand, was individualistic and competitive, so that accumulation was well-nigh impossible. Geertz considered what it would take for a group of reform Muslim entrepreneurs to join the modern 'firm' economy. They were rational and calculating enough; but they were denied the institutional protection of state bureaucracy, which was the preserve of the existing corporations.

History of the concept

Very little of this impinged on the thinking of development economists for whom the dominant influence in the 1960s was W. Arthur

Lewis's dualistic model of a transfer of underemployed labour from traditional agriculture to cities, where they could find more productive employment working for capitalist firms and the government. In the twentieth century, capitalism was organized through the nation-state. 'National capitalism' was thus the attempt to manage markets and money through central bureaucracy and 'development' consisted in its displacement of more backward economic forms (see *Development*). The antithesis of national capitalism could be said to be the informal economy. It soon became recognized as a universal feature of the modern economy. Independence from the state's rules unites practices as diverse as home improvement, street trade, squatter settlements, open source software, the illegal drugs traffic, political corruption and offshore banking.

Welfare-state democracy was sustained by 'macroeconomics', a term associated with Maynard Keynes. In this view only the state could regenerate a damaged market economy, mainly by spending money it did not have to boost the purchasing power of the masses ('consumer demand'). The economic boom of the 1950s and 1960s depended on the co-ordinated efforts of the leading industrial states to expand their public sectors. It all began to unravel in the 'stagflation' of the 1970s. The neoliberal conservatives who have dominated politics of late sought to counter inflation with 'sound money' and to release the potential of the market by getting the state off its back. Their policies often combined 'privatization' with a strengthening of state power. In the process they dismantled twentieth-century social democracy.

The idea of an 'informal economy' has run as a submerged commentary on these developments. It came out of the lives of Third World city-dwellers, whose lack of money makes them about as conventionally poor as it is possible to be. By the 1970s it was becoming clear that development was a pipe-dream for Third World countries. Populations had exploded; cities were growing rapidly; mechanization was weak; productivity in predominantly agricultural economies remained low; and the gap between rich and poor was widening. The malaise was conceived of as 'urban unemployment'. The spectre of the 1930s dominated development discourse. Anyone who visited, not to mention lived in, these sprawling cities would get a rather different picture. Their streets were teeming with life, a constantly shifting crowd of hawkers, porters, taxi-drivers, beggars, pimps, pickpockets, hustlers – all of them getting by without the benefit of a 'real job'. But the antithesis of the state-made modern economy had not yet found its academic name.

In a paper presented to a 1971 conference on 'Urban unemployment in Africa', based on fieldwork in the slums of Ghana's capital city, Accra, I argued that the urban poor were not 'unemployed'. They were working, although often for low and erratic returns. 'Informal' incomes, unregulated by law and invisible to bureaucracy, were a significant part of urban economies that had grown up largely without official knowledge or control. What distinguished these self-employed earnings from wage employment was the degree of *rationalization* of working conditions. Following Weber, I argued that the ability to stabilize economic activity within a bureaucratic form made returns more calculable and regular for the workers as well as their bosses. That stability was in turn guaranteed by the state's laws, which only extended so far into the depths of Ghana's economy. 'Formal' incomes came from regulated economic activities and 'informal' incomes, both legal and illegal, lay beyond the scope of regulation.

I did not identify the informal economy with a place or a class or even whole persons. Everyone in Accra, but especially in the slum where I lived, tried to combine the two sources of income. Informal opportunities ranged from market gardening and brewing through every kind of trade to gambling, theft and political corruption. My analysis had its roots in what people generate out of the circumstances of their everyday lives. The laws and offices of state bureaucracy only made their search for self-preservation and improvement more difficult. Moreover, I suggested that the relationship between formal and informal sources of employment might be of some significance for models of economic development in the long run. In particular, the informal economy might be just a way of recycling income generated from elsewhere or it could be a source of enterprise and capital formation leading to economic growth in its own right.

The dualism (formal–informal) and some of the thinking behind it received immediate publicity through its adoption in an influential International Labour Office report on incomes and employment in Kenya, which elevated the 'informal sector' to the status of a major source for national development by the bootstraps. This report suggested that self-employed or 'informal' incomes might reduce the gap between those with and without jobs and so could contribute to a more equitable income distribution. Following the 'growth or bust' policies of the 1960s, they advocated 'growth with redistribution', that is, helping the poor out of the proceeds of economic expansion. This reflected a shift in World Bank policy announced by its president, Robert McNamara, in Nairobi a year later. By now the multilateral institutions were worried about potential social explosions; and they felt that more attention should be paid to peasants and the urban poor. A vogue for promoting the 'informal sector' as a device for employment creation fitted in with this shift, since the dominant development paradigm was still Keynesian.

This was enough to encourage legions of researchers to adopt the term. Before long a substantial critique of the 'informal sector' concept had emerged. Marxists claimed that its proponents mystified the essentially regressive and exploitative nature of this economic zone, which they preferred to call 'petty commodity production'. The study of Third World urban poverty rapidly became a new segment of the academic division of labour; as a key term in its discourse, the informal economy attracted an unusual volume of debate. In writing my paper, I had no ambition to coin a concept, just to insert a particular vision of irregular economic activity into the ongoing debates of professionals in the development industry. The ILO Kenya report, on the other hand, did want to coin a concept and that is what it has subsequently become, a keyword helping to organize a segment of the academic and policy-making bureaucracy. So the idea of an 'informal economy' could be said to have a double provenance reflecting its two sides, bureaucracy (development administration) and the people (ethnography).

Most economists saw the idea in quantitative terms as a sector of small-scale, low-productivity, low-income activities without benefit of advanced machines; whereas I stressed the reliability of income streams, the presence or absence of bureaucratic *form*. When the bureaucracy tried to promote the informal sector – by providing credit, government buildings or new technologies, for example – it killed off the informality of the enterprises concerned and exposed participants to taxation. The association of the idea with the sprawling slums of Third World cities was strong; but the 'commanding heights' of the informal economy lay at the centres of political power, in the corrupt fortunes of public office-holders who often owned the taxis or the rented accommodation operated by the small fry.

The 1980s saw another major shift in world economy following the lead of Reagan and Thatcher. Now the state was no longer seen as the great provider. Rather 'the market', freed of as many encumbrances as possible, was the only engine of growth. The informal economy took on a new lease of life as a zone of free commerce, competitive because unregulated. This coincided with the imposition of 'structural adjustment' policies that reduced public expenditures and threw responsibility onto the invisible self-help schemes of the people themselves. By now, the rhetoric and reality of development had been effectively abandoned as the Third World suffered the largest income drain in its history, in the form of repayment of debts incurred during the wild banking boom of the 1970s.

After the millennium, the attitude of the international agencies changed again. By now there had been substantial inward investment in some poor countries and foreign businesses were feeling the lack of an effective regulatory environment. To some extent this meant boosting national bureaucracy, which was hard, given that states were deliberately undermined by structural adjustment in order to secure the free movement of capital. Now the call was for regulation and standardization. 'Informality' has come to be perceived by the World Bank as a threat to 'private sector development'. Business corporations are undercut by informal operators who pay no taxes, evade costly regulations and take advantage of numerous devices, legal and illegal, to reduce their prices. Accordingly, whereas the informal economy was once seen as a positive factor in development, it is now, in an update of its nineteenth-century designation as 'the dangerous classes', more likely to be represented as an obstacle to development. Today the model of success is the highly bureaucratic type of economy achieved by Western countries only in the second half of the twentieth century.

Hernando de Soto, a Peruvian economist, has drawn attention to this issue in two books, *The Other Path* and *The Mystery of Capital*. Bureaucratic red tape in countries like Peru makes it very difficult for migrants to the cities to set up new businesses, get loans or establish formal property rights in their possessions. Although this was at first an effect of local elites jealously holding onto inherited privileges, it is now reinforced by the international system of bureaucracy controlled by the USA and Europe. The irony is that these regions took full advantage of the flexibility afforded by informal arrangements in their own drive for development a century or two ago, but deny it to those who would develop from behind today.

Links between the formal and informal economy

It would not be hard, in post-colonial Africa for example, to conceive of the relationship between formal and informal 'sectors' as a war waged by the bureaucracy on the people, allowing informal economic practices to be portrayed as a kind of democratic resistance. Yet, however much we might endorse the political value of self-organized economic activities, there are tasks of large-scale co-ordination for which bureaucracy is well suited; and its origins were closely linked to aspirations for political equality, even if historical reality has often been different. So the task is not only to find practical ways of harnessing the complementary potential of bureaucracy and informality, but also to advance thinking about their dialectical movement.

Forms are necessarily abstract and a lot of social life is left out as a result. This can lead to an attempt to reduce the gap by creating new abstractions that incorporate the informal practices of people into the formal model. Naming these practices as an 'informal sector' is one such device. They appear to be informal because their forms are largely invisible to the bureaucratic gaze. Mobilizing the informal economy will require a pluralistic approach based on at least acknowledgement of those forms. Equally, the formal sphere of society is not just abstract, but consists also of the people who staff bureaucracies and their informal practices. Somehow the human potential of both has to be unlocked together.

For any rule to be translated into human action, something else must be brought into play, such as personal judgement. So informality is built into bureaucratic forms as unspecified *content*. This is no trivial matter. Viable solutions to problems of administration invariably contain processes that are invisible to the formal order. Thus workers sometimes 'work-to-rule': they follow their job descriptions to the letter without any of the informal practices that allow these abstractions to function. Everything grinds to a halt as a result. Or take a chain of commodities from their production by a transnational corporation to their final consumption in an African city. At several points, invisible actors fill the gaps that the bureaucracy cannot handle directly, from the factories to the docks to the supermarkets and street traders who supply the cigarettes to smokers. Informal processes are indispensable to the trade, as variable content to the general form. It has never been resolved whether the informal economy refers to casual labour in formal enterprises or not. This has become more pressing in the context of widespread privatization of public services, leading to low pay and precarious rights, and of outsourcing by businesses, often to unregulated workers on the other side of the world.

Of course, some of these activities may break the law, through a breach of health and safety regulations, tax evasion, smuggling, the use of child labour, selling without a licence etc. Another way that informal activities relate to formal organization is thus as its *negation*. Rule-breaking takes place both within bureaucracy and outside it; and so the informal is often illegal. This compromises attempts to promote the informal sector as a legitimate sphere of the economy, since it is hard to draw a line between colourful women selling oranges on the street and the gangsters who exact tribute from them. When the rule of law is weak, the forms that emerge in its place are often criminal in character. A good part of modern society consists in protecting the public image of bureaucratic processes from a reality that mixes formal order with corruption and criminality.

Some 'informal' activities exist in parallel, as *residue*: they are just separate from the bureaucracy. It would be stretching the logic of the formal/informal pair to include peasant economy, domestic life and much else within the rubric of the 'informal'. Yet the social forms endemic to these often shape informal economic practices and *vice versa*. What is at stake here is whether society is just one thing – one state with its rule of law – or can tolerate a measure of legal pluralism, leaving some institutions to their own devices. Communities use implicit rules (customs) rather than state-made laws and usually regulate their members informally, relying on the sanction of exclusion rather than punishment. European empires, faced with a shortage of administrative resources, turned to 'indirect rule' as a way of incorporating subject peoples into their systems of government on a semi-autonomous basis. This legal pluralism delegated supervision of indigenous customary forms to appointed chiefs and headmen, reserving the key levers of power to the colonial regime. Any serious attempt to link the formal and the informal economy today requires a similar openness to plurality of form.

There is a gender component to the informal economy in that men have a disproportionate share of formal positions and women's work is predominantly informal (see *Feminist Economics*). This has led activist groups, such as 'Women in Informal Employment: Globalizing and Organizing' (WIEGO) and the Self-Employed

Women's Association (SEWA), to use the concept as an umbrella
term drawing attention to discrimination worldwide. Here then is
one example of how the idea of an informal economy can be put to
positive political ends in negotiations between international bureaucracies and NGOs representing a substantial segment of the excluded
poor (see *NGOs*).

Informality reconsidered

It is inconsistent to claim that the urban poor have an informal economy but their rich masters do not; or that the developing countries
have an informal sector but not the developed. As long as there is
formal economic analysis and the *partial* institutionalization of economies around the globe along capitalist lines (see *Communism*), there
will be a need for some such remedial concept as the informal economy. Its application to concrete conditions is stimulated by palpable
discrepancies between prevalent models and observed realities. Such
a discrepancy provoked the emergence of the concept in the 1970s,
when developing economies bore the brunt of the depression that
marked the end of the West's post-war miracle. Later the accelerat-
ing decline of the same industrial economies encouraged some social
scientists to adopt the term there. The common strand is the growing
inability of modern states to control the wider economic environment that sustains them. Hence the need for a dualistic model, such
as that offered by the 'informal economy' concept.

The formal/informal pair, representing bureaucracy and popular
self-organization as they do, mirrored to some extent the poles of the
Cold War, 'state socialism' vs. 'the free market'. After three decades
of welfare-state democracy, the profound shift in economic policy
to what we now call neoliberalism was well under way in the 1970s;
and we are now witnessing the start of another long swing back from
over-reliance on the market to increased state intervention in some
form or another. So the state/market pair has not faded away. The
formal/informal dualism first saw light in a development context
during the world crisis of the early1970s – a sequence of events that
took in America's losing war in Vietnam, the dollar's detachment
from gold in 1971 and the subsequent dismantling of the Bretton
Woods regime of fixed parity exchange rates. Then the energy crisis
of 1973 plunged the world economy into a depression from which
has not yet recovered.

No-one could have anticipated what happened next. Under a neoliberal imperative to reduce the state's grip on 'the free market', manifested in developing countries as 'structural adjustment', national economies and the world economy itself were radically informalized. Not only did the management of money go offshore, but corporations outsourced, downsized and casualized their labour forces, public functions were privatized often corruptly, the drugs and illicit arms trades took off, the global war over 'intellectual property' assumed central place in capitalism's contradictions, and whole countries, such as Mobutu's Zaire, abandoned any pretence of formality in their economic affairs. Here was no 'hole-in-the-wall' operation living in the cracks of the law. The market frenzy led to the 'commanding heights' of the informal economy taking over the state-made bureaucracy. The formal/informal pair, now more clearly reflecting the opposition between state and market, leaked into each other to the point of being often indistinguishable. What is the difference between a Wall Street bank laundering gangsters' money through the Cayman Islands and the mafias running opium out of Afghanistan with the support of several national governments?

The idea of an informal economy has drawn attention to activities that were previously invisible to the bureaucratic gaze, but it was founded on a fundamentally *static* analysis. I wanted to establish that no single idea ('the state') can ever capture the complexity of real life, leaving the residue to leak out as potential material for another idea, its negation (in Hegelian terms). But I conceived of informal income opportunities as at best a minor appendage of the state-made economy, perhaps a bit more than the economists' dismissive 'taking in each other's washing', but essentially going nowhere. I did not join the rush to announce a new means of development by the bootstraps. My first criticism of the concept now is that it was insufficiently dynamic. Perhaps we didn't want the two sides to move dialectically, since the result could be the annihilation of all life on the planet. In that sense, the informal economy could be said to be a Cold War concept.

The label 'informal' may be popular because it is both positive and negative. To act informally is to be free and flexible; but it also refers to what people are not doing – not wearing conventional dress, not being regulated by the state. The 'informal economy' allows academics and bureaucrats to incorporate the teeming street life of exotic cities into their abstract models without having to know what people are really up to. A second criticism would thus be that 'informality' tells us too little about what is actually going on. Is the informal economy in fact a term for the unregulated markets that spring up under conditions of rapid urbanization? If so, we need to understand better what are the positive principles organizing these markets. To the extent that neoliberalism has succeeded in reducing state controls, the world economy itself has become largely an informal zone. This extension of the scope of the concept – to embrace rich and poor countries, government and business, casual labour and the self-employed, corruption and crime – when taken with the wholesale devolution of central bureaucracies compared with four decades ago, leaves a question-mark over its continuing usefulness today.

We are living through the period of humanity's rapid disengagement from the soil as the chief object of labour and matrix of social life. The hectic growth of cities over the last two centuries could not be organized immediately as ruling elites would like. The informal economy is one way of pointing to how people devised their own means of survival and sometimes of prosperity in the urban markets that spring up spontaneously to meet their needs.

Further reading

Davis, M. (2006) *Planet of Slums*. Verso, New York.

De Soto, H. (2000) *The Mystery of Capital: Why Capitalism Triumphs in the West and Fails Everywhere Else*. Bantam, London.

Geertz, C. (1963) *Peddlers and Princes*. University of Chicago Press, Chicago.

Hart, K. (1973). Informal income opportunities and urban employment in Ghana. *Journal of Modern African Studies* 11, 61–89.

Hart, K. (2005). *The Hit Man's Dilemma: Or Business, Personal and Impersonal*. Prickly Paradigm, Chicago.

Guha-Khasnobis, B., Kanbur, R. and Ostrom, E. (eds) 2005 *Linking the Formal and Informal Economy: Concepts and Policies*. Oxford University Press, Oxford.

International Labour Organization (1972) *Incomes, Employment and Equality in Kenya*. ILO, Geneva.

Lewis, O. (1964). *La Vida: A Puerto Rican Family in the Culture of Poverty: San Juan and New York*. Random House, New York.

Mayhew, H. (1861–2). *London Labour and the London Poor*, 4 vols. London.

Portes, A., Castells, M. and Benton, L. (eds) (1989) *The Informal Economy: Studies in Advanced and Less Developed Countries*. Johns Hopkins University Press, Baltimore, MD.

Weber, M. (1981[1922]) *General Economic History*. Transaction Books, New Brunswick, NJ.

Women in Informal Employment: Globalizing and Organizing (WIEGO) (2009) About the informal economy, http://www.wiego.org/about_ie.

Part III
Moral Politics

14

Citizenship

Paulo Henrique Martins

Citizenship is an ambivalent legal, political and moral construct. It appears historically in complex and open societies where the problem of the relationship between the individual and society is resolved through the emergence of a public sphere constituted as the 'common world'. With the advent of modernity, this sphere reduced the influence of the private realm and emphasized the importance of equality as a political and legal achievement. This meant that individual property was combined with communal or social property. In moral terms, the basic value underlying citizenship is that of equality, which, in the case of societies attempting to be democratic, co-exists with the new value of liberty, meaning no longer freedom of the oppressor but that of the ordinary individual. Promoting equality means privileging society as a whole, the collective will, a moral obligation reaching beyond the sphere of the individual who must accept that social property implies a transfer to the public sphere of what was previously private property.

Taken together, the basic moral values of equality and freedom find historical expression through the political activities that emerge from the tensions between the maintenance of collective beliefs and values on the one hand and increasing stress on the liberation of desires and individual uniqueness found in contemporary individualism on the other. In practice, this ambivalence, which lies at the heart of citizenship, is resolved by the co-existence of movements towards increasing differentiation (of gender, ethnicity, nationality, culture and so on) and those that aim to preserve the established social order.

In addition to its moral and political aspects, citizenship must be embodied in a juridical process. Seen in this perspective, citizenship acquires legal force and sanction only through written language, in the form of legal codes and republican constitutions which, by positing the public interest as central to collective life, enable the idea to acquire judicial, legal and even constitutional standing. We should note here the influence of Greek and Roman traditions. For the Greeks the idea of the citizen was not to be confused with that of the concrete individual. Respect for the laws of the *polis* was the only way of preventing the community from being dominated by a single master or oppressor, as among the supposedly barbarian peoples of those times. Roman tradition later emphasized the legal and representative aspects of citizenship. For Cicero, citizenship was related to the existence of a community of rights. This Roman definition of the citizen in legal terms also enabled the introduction of a further set of values, including the notion of universal rights which was taken up over the following centuries by Christianity and spread by European colonial expansion.

The State of Right

Citizenship appears in history only with the transition from the Right of the State to the State of Right, where the interests of the ruler are replaced by those of the ordinary individual, lacking a noble title but possessing constitutional guarantees embodied in universal legislation. The construction of this State of Right and the corresponding destruction of aristocratic privilege were not simple historical processes, however. The emergence of modern citizenship from the early eighteenth century came about only though bloody uprisings like the French and American revolutions. While Renaissance thought had paved the way for the return of the republican ideal of citizenship, it was systematized by those thinkers who came to be seen as founders of the modern idea of the individual.

Thomas Hobbes put forward the idea of a vertical contract, imposed from the top down by a sovereign legislator. He believed that, since human beings were by nature hostile to each other, they were incapable of any spontaneous deliberation on matters of collective interest. In contrast, John Locke maintained that society was the result of a contract between free individuals who formed an organized plurality. Jean-Jacques Rousseau believed that all individuals had an interest in seeking the shelter of the collective good. For him, a social contract deriving from a pact on this scale and built on consensus was the precondition for all citizens to adopt freedom and obligation as common virtues. Basically, Rousseau connected the idea of citizenship with that of community. The tendencies of political thought associated with these three authors underlie different modes of organizing citizenship: a limited, top-down model, as found in various authoritarian regimes, is inspired by Hobbes; liberal conceptions derive from Locke; and the community or associative model comes from Rousseau. These conceptions still predominate today, as manifested in the debate between defenders of a liberal understanding of citizenship, such as Norberto Bobbio and Richard Rorty, and those who promote a communitarian and multicultural notion of citizenship, like Charles Taylor and Will Kymlicka.

Recently there has been a pronounced tendency – particularly among authors influenced by contemporary political philosophy – to define citizenship in terms of rights. T. H. Marshall considered the development of citizenship rights to have gone through three distinct phases: civil and political rights, which he saw as first-generation rights; social and economic rights, being the second-generation; and a more recent bundle of third-generation rights. First- and second-generation rights were acquired in the eighteenth and nineteenth centuries. Thus civil rights, conceived of as individual rights of freedom, equality, property, mobility, security and so on, were won in the eighteenth century; political rights were attained during the nineteenth century in the form of electoral participation, freedom of association and assembly and the right to form political organizations and labour unions. Social and economic rights were institutionalized in the twentieth century, following working-class struggles and were expressed in labour, health care, education and pension rights, in other words, guaranteed access to welfare and social benefits. Finally, Marshall believed that in the second half of the twentieth century we could begin to talk of third-generation rights, possessed not by the individual but by collectives like the nation, ethnic groups or humanity itself. Examples of these rights would be the rights of self-determination of peoples, environmental rights, consumer rights and the rights of women, children and the elderly. Some authors are now talking of fourth-generation rights, such as those relating to bio-ethics and focused on preventing the destruction of life or the unrestrained creation of life in laboratories.

Some authors have reservations about Marshall's work, considering that rights of citizenship were not established in the sequence that he suggests. They note that, when we examine the mosaic of citizenship at a global level, its manifestations vary enormously between societies and cultures. So they suggest that it would be more relevant to examine rights of citizenship within a framework of cultural diversity. Writers like Kymlicka have proposed a notion of *differentiated citizenship*, resulting from the superseding of old nationalisms and the adoption of a multicultural perspective. This thesis draws support from ongoing conflicts over linguistic rights, regional autonomy, immigration and naturalization, territorial disputes and religious differences, among others. Similarly, Taylor argues that new struggles for citizenship can no longer be controlled by classical forms of social administration and that a politics of recognition and dignity is needed in order to respond effectively to new demands. Jürgen Habermas is also concerned with the issue of new forms of citizenship and with re-opening discussion on the relationship between the nation and rights, but his emphasis is on the idea of *post-national citizenship*. When considering the challenges of European integration, he stresses the importance of discussing alternative modes of integration and social inclusion based on a new relationship between the State of Right and democracy.

Citizenship and democracy

It would be a mistake to identify citizenship with democracy and summarily reduce one to the other. Although the latter could not exist without the former, citizenship can exist without democracy. The Greeks were aware of this difference. While defining citizens as those who exercised judicial or deliberative power within the collective group of individuals termed the *polis*, Aristotle recognized that citizenship could exist in non-democratic, despotic or tyrannical regimes. The legal, political and moral equality that is standard today has been no easy achievement and those who consider social property more important than the individual and those who hold the opposite view have held sway in different contexts.

In the bureaucratic-socialist regimes of the twentieth century, duties were more valued than freedoms, whereas in bourgeois democratic regimes, particularly those influenced by neoliberal ideology, the opposite can be seen: individual freedom is prized more than collective obligations. In both cases the relationship between citizenship and democracy is problematic. While the overwhelming weight of collective equality suffocates citizens' liberties, excessive individual liberty threatens the survival of the 'common world'. Somewhere between these poles lie attempts to reconcile citizenship and democracy through experiments in participation which seek to harmonize the gains of representation (indirect and individual choice) with the system of assembly (direct and collective choice).

While morality, politics and rights are considered to be the unquestionable foundations of citizenship, its stability and even permanence depend on other historical factors. We may recall here the principle of universal rights, which seeks to make the primary values of equality and freedom compatible in a more institutionally complex way that unites national differences within a common globalized sphere. Irrespective of this principle, citizenship is not, despite what common sense may suggest, a kind of universal human or 'natural' right. Evidence shows that it is a local phenomenon and that societies organized on the basis of a citizen ideal have been a minority throughout human history. The feeling that citizenship is something natural is only the result of a long process whereby a particular moral order has been internalized. This order is modern and it mistakenly claims to be an *a priori* universal truth, while neglecting, as Taylor suggests, a view of the public sphere as a historically emergent space for discussion and organization of common ends that are as yet unclear. The value of universality is at base a kind of transnational symbolic political operator, drawing its legitimacy from the possibility of successfully mediating between and adapting national, religious, historical and cultural meanings, in all their differentiation and particularity. Such a synthesis is far from being guaranteed in historical reality.

Citizenship as a universal right has been reinforced by another principle, the idea of human rights. The belief is common in the West that citizenship is a universal value of democracy, necessarily founded on human rights. As an intangible asset of the human being, modern democratic citizenship should consequently be taken as a reference for political organization as a whole, irrespective of particular cultural contexts. Attempts to put these humanistic ideals into practice have experienced significant difficulties, however, such as those arising out of the problematic attempts over the past two hundred years of European colonizers to impose on other peoples the democratic republican ideal from the top. Construction of citizenship requires a series of inter-subjective agreements that are not confined to the simple redistribution of material wealth and the trappings of power. In many societies such agreements have to include recognition of difference in culture, religion and politics. These pressures, manifested in struggles for material and symbolic assets, influence social institutions in general and have to be regularly renewed, necessitating the creation of fresh mechanisms of participation, regulation and negotiation of citizenship rights at various levels of social organization, from the central authority to regional and local bodies.

Finally, we should emphasize how neoliberal thinking applies strong pressure towards confining discussion of citizenship to economic and commercial issues, with its exclusive stress on market autonomy and reducing the regulatory power of the state, so that citizens' rights amount to little more than productive consumption and flexible labour. This reductionist view needs to be contrasted with older traditions and more modern thinking which, as shown above, were open to a more complex conception of the foundations of citizenship and repositioned economic issues within social frameworks. Anti-utilitarian critical theory is indispensible to such a process (see *Gift*), so that the moral, political and legal aspects of citizenship might be brought back to prominence rather than being impoverished by what is little more than a mercantilist ideology. In this respect it is useful to recall B. S. Santos, for whom the creation of a complex understanding of citizenship, responsive to demands for the abolition of current forms of oppression and exclusion, cannot be accomplished by the mere concession of rights, as is usually supposed. Such a renewal requires a global reconstruction of public education and of development models. This observation is particularly relevant for peripheral societies where the construction of citizenship is constantly hindered by structural problems entailed in dominant traditional values as well as in modernization processes.

Some new approaches to global citizens' rights

The systematic development of subaltern studies and post-colonial studies by authors with knowledge or personal experience of the problem of citizenship in societies subject to colonial domination has recently made it possible to bypass the dilemma of choosing between national and global citizenship, which some European theoreticians consider to be insoluble. When national citizenship is examined from the perspective of former colonial societies of the South, the formation of the nation-state in a process of modernization can only superficially be represented as being based on an original community, whether religious, ethnic or cultural. In general, the nation was directly linked to the colonizers' techniques of domination when they sought to classify human and non-human resources.

As Partha Chaterjee explains, in societies subject to colonization such as India, the idea of a unified national society was linked to the adoption of technologies of government used by the British to organize the populations and natural resources required for the success of the colonial enterprise. For example, censuses were useful in building up colonial armies and bureaucracies and electoral registration helped to legitimize the presence of the colonizer as a political mentor. This means that in these societies, the idea of rights arising from citizenship cannot be understood simply on the basis of an abstract thing called a nation; rather, concrete political and cultural questions must be asked about the techniques employed by colonial bureaucracies to organize national states as homogeneous cultural entitites. There are significant differences also in the impact of such mechanisms in Asia, Africa and the Americas.

A critical approach to the idea of a nation and therefore of citizenship in relation to the colonial process forces us to recognize both cultural pluralism and the moral damage generated by colonial violence. In 'Can the subaltern speak?', Gayatri Spivak calls attention to how symbolic colonial violence led to the humiliation of being subaltern. Since the end of the 1970s, an increasing number of authors such as Said, Bhabha, Hall, Gilroy and Quijano among others, have sought to draw attention to the importance of critiquing the violence of the colonial process in order to recuperate the value of citizenship in its various historical, cultural, ethnic and religious representations. As a result of this effort, epistemological questions have been brought sharply to the fore.

The force employed generated a symbolism of inferiority deeply rooted in the populations subjected to colonial domination and this continues to affect the moral, affective and reflective capacities of these peoples. Global social injustice is directly related to the epistemic violence inflicted on non-European cultures by the colonizing process, thus making it impossible to conceive of citizenship as an *a priori* universal moral category. The only way to begin to overcome this invisible symbolic domination is through a systematic critique of the unequal hierarchy of colonialism. In the view of some authors, the European model is not the only form in which modernity may be expressed; it is just one way that modernity is revealed. There are good grounds for accepting the possibility of multiple modernities and various forms of citizenship. Overcoming the symbolism of inferiority calls for a new emancipatory paradigm to help deconstruct the cognitive violence exercized against the colonized by the colonizers, so making possible a sociology of absence, as well as a sociology of emergence capable of expanding the range of possible social experience in future, and thus opening the door to plural, differentiated citizenship at various levels of organization, including the local, national and global.

The experience of moral and cognitive devaluation suffered by colonized individuals has thus produced a significant intellectual reaction in the last decades of the twentieth century, leading some authors to seek to link capitalist exploitation to the question of colonialism. In their view, this is indispensible if the relationship between citizenship rights and globalization is to be understood in a new way. These critiques from subaltern and post-colonial studies propose to relocate the theme of citizenship and human rights beyond the dichotomy between national and global citizenship, by insisting on the importance of alterity and cultural difference. This is not just an academic issue, since the epistemic and physical violence of colonialism are involved. Any discussion of human rights and emancipation associated with alternative forms of collective and community life depends on being clear about this.

Conclusion

A contemporary understanding of citizenship requires us to acknowledge that law is only one of its constitutive dimensions and that moral and political aspects should also be taken into account. Each of these considered by itself is an inadequate explanation for the emergence of citizenship. For citizenship to succeed as a historical project, it must benefit from a confluence of struggles for recognition and dignity, free and equal representation and participation and enjoyment of civic, political, social, economic, cultural and environmental rights in common. In this debate, it is equally important to bear in mind the importance of the struggles against the hierarchies of social and cultural inequalities produced by the project of colonialism, contributing to different values being placed on those born in the colonizing countries and those born in the colonized countries, as extensively demonstrated by subaltern studies and post-colonial studies. Such a confluence has to be built on our shared experience of a common world that cannot be privatized by individuals or corporations. This is particularly important if the construction of democratic citizenship is at stake, for it constantly fluctuates between the polarities of social life – individual and collective interests, established and developing orders, and global and local spaces, as well as the colonial and post-colonial worlds.

Further reading

Ashcroft, B., Griffiths, G. and Tiffin, H. (eds) (1995) *The Post-Colonial Studies Reader*. Routledge, New York.

Bobbio, N. (2005) *Liberalism and Democracy*. Verso, New York.

Bulmer, M. and Rees, A. (eds) (1996) *Citizenship Today: Contemporary Relevance of T. H. Marshall*. Routledge, London.

Chaterjee, P. (1994) *The Nation and its Fragments: Colonial and Postcolonial Histories*. Princeton University Press, Princeton, NJ.

Gilroy, P. (1993) *The Black Atlantic: Modernity and Double-Consciousness*. Verso, London and New York.

Habermas, J. (2002) *The Inclusion of the Other: Studies in Political Theory*. Polity, Cambridge.

Kymlicka, W. (2002) *Contemporary Political Philosophy: An Introduction*. Oxford University Press, Oxford.

Memmi, A. (1973) *Portrait du colonisé, précédé du portrait du colonisateur* (preface Jean-Paul Sartre). Payot, Paris.

Santos, B. S. (2005) Law and globalization from below: toward a cosmopolitan legality. *Cambridge Studies in Law and Society*.

Santos, B. S. (2008) *A gramática do tempo: para uma nova cultura política*, 2nd edn. Cortez, São Paulo.

Taylor, C. (1995) *Philosophical Arguments*. Harvard University Press, Cambridge, MA.

Wallerstein, I. (2006) *European Universalism: The Rhetoric of Power*. New Press, New York.

15

Corporate Social Responsibility

Anne Salmon

Introducing CSR

The terms 'ethics' and 'corporate social responsibility' (CSR) are now commonplace and have become an integral part of managerial discourse. These notions are used by the management of international firms to improve their image and to counter that of the predatory company whose interests are purely financial; they are a way of legitimating capitalism by making it look ethical. They are an attempt on the part of big companies to represent themselves as economic agents who promote the common good. The evidence of their direct, voluntary contributions to health and development aid programmes – and they are far from negligible in financial terms – is certainly a rising index of acknowledgement of their social responsibilities. Although these philanthropic acts are often seen as an expression of CSR, the two should not be confused. Corporate Social Responsibility, as defined by various international organizations (such as the International Labour Office, Organization for Economic Co-operation and Development, European Consumer Centres Network), has much wider social and environmental implications. Agreements with trade unions may, for example, commit companies to respect union rights or to refuse to employ child labour, even when they operate in countries where the law permits it. As both these organizations and the companies involved emphasize, such undertakings sometimes go beyond their legal obligations in a context where multinationals can still take advantage of the relaxed legal frameworks recommended by neoliberal governments.

From the 1990s onwards, governments were beginning to take more interest in these issues: could a trend that was initiated by the multinationals offer a new model for the private regulation of a globalized economy? As they began to operate at an international level, companies certainly claimed, in the name of promoting greater social harmony, to be able to establish normative systems that would be respected by their employees, their subsidiaries and, increasingly, their sub-contractors. While some complacently dismiss CSR as a passing fad, it is becoming so entrenched that it lends itself to other interpretations. This suggests that it should be analysed as a socio-logical object in its own right. The multinationals are using these notions to enhance their own legitimacy as actors who can establish normative systems inside the economic perimeters they control. They are also using them to initiate and structure public debates about regulation and they can therefore be analysed as a contem-porary reformulation of some long-standing questions about the relationship between ethics and economics, indeed between capital-ism and democracy.

Ethics and economics

Although their approaches differ in many respects, neither Émile Durkheim nor Max Weber took at face value the argument that eco-nomics should be independent of ethics, as neoliberals working in what they consider to be the tradition of Adam Smith would have us believe. Both articulated a vision through a study of the division of labour in society in the case of Durkheim and of the spirit of capital-ism in that of Weber. In Durkheim's view, the division of labour is so closely bound up with a moral perspective that one begins to wonder if he is arguing that the division of labour is not so much an economi-cally determined phenomenon, but a purely social fact to be analysed in its own right. For Weber, it is pointless to look for purely eco-nomic explanations for the emergence of modern capitalism in the West. If we wish to understand its rationality, we also have to look at cultural phenomena whose origins lie in the Protestant Reformation, and especially at the ethics it shaped.

By distancing themselves from economists' attempts to reduce actors' motives to pure self-interest and to adapt regulations to the strict laws of the market, both Durkheim and Weber theorized relationships that economics has long tried to exclude from its field of interest. For his part, Durkheim sees an intrinsic relationship between economics and ethics. The division of labour in society is an ethical phenomenon in its own right and it leads to a specific form of solidarity, namely organic solidarity. Weber analyses the links between the Protestant ethic and capitalism in terms of 'elective affinities'. He stresses that the ascetic morality of Puritanism originally had nothing to do with capitalism and sees their coming together as fortuitous. Ultimately, it was 'despite itself' that the Protestant ethic provided an 'intellectual backdrop' that helped to justify a devotion to the 'calling to make money' and to 'work', and helped to establish both as regular, rational activities involving calculation and forecasts.

Yet both authors found the 'demoralization' of economic life problematic. Durkheim's analysis concentrates on the dangers of anomie, while Weber feared that the growing rationalization of an economy that no longer had any ethical basis would lead to a loss of meaning. These theses are very familiar, but even a brief examination of them can teach us some lessons and it is worth outlining them here. By emphasizing that there are links between social structures and moral orientations, Durkheim challenged the notion that an ethics based upon an *a priori* idea can have any practical effects. Studying a moral phenomenon therefore means examining a set of correspondences. Quite apart from the fact that moral principles can survive structural modifications and can therefore fill the void they leave by supplying sets of rules, an ethics that is decreed from on high is inconceivable. From that point of view, the reestablishment of an ethical economics implies structural reforms. The revival of 'corporations' is therefore one of the major elements in the programme of reforms advocated by Durkheim. Moral principles simply cannot take root if the structure itself implies a different form of ethics.

Weber also raises the question of the practical effects of ethics, but he takes a very different approach. Two points must be stressed. The first relates to Weber's insistence that an ethical system cannot be reduced to a set of dogmas or a list of values and precepts. An ethical system is a form of psychic mobilization that gives rise to specific forms of belief. The Protestant ethic has practical effects because it is based not only on a religious ideal, but also on the doctrine of predestination and on the fears it aroused in the believer in the absence of any certain guarantee of salvation. It thus influences the very structure of the believer's personality and therefore promotes a worldly asceticism. Weber also warns us against using ethics to justify or legitimize the system. The Protestant ethic was not, he asserts, designed to prop up capitalism or, for that matter, to socialize it in one way or another. The ethical goals and practical implications the doctrines of the reformers were in fact purely religious. And the ideal motifs supplied by the Protestant ethic have practical effects precisely because they do not belong within the economic sphere and are designed for very different purposes, namely the salvation of souls. Habermas reminds us of this when he warns against treating the symbolic production of meaning as being purely instrumental.

When contemporary management theory talks about ethics, the results look to the observer like the product of a colourful assemblage of religious, cultural or philosophical references intended as a source of self-justification or legitimation. They are often mannered but they are rarely rigorous. Enshrined in what are sometimes sumptuous publications, these are norms that are defined by economic actors and for economic purposes. The top-down and instrumental nature of these ethical charters give a new relevance to the sociologists' warnings about the dangers of ethical systems that are dictated from on high and of the utilitarian production of ideas that are expected to have a real historical impact.

Capitalism and Democracy

Business ethics certainly looks like a system of norms and values, but it is also a representation of social groups that can be reshaped and described in new ways. There are norms involved, but the issue of identity is determinant: it is the key to a company's institutionalization. If they are to look to the public like socially responsible actors, multinationals must get away from the traditional image of the company as a theatre of class conflict. Putting it into historical perspective is a good way of analysing how managerial ethics has found a new way to construct company identity

There is nothing new about employers' attempts to lay down norms for labour. From the late eighteenth century onwards and throughout the nineteenth, workshop regulations were posted everywhere in the factories; and this practice continued into the first half of the twentieth century. With the tacit approval of the authorities, factory owners, acting in their capacity as private individuals, were able to lay down sets of obligations and punishable offences. These texts adopted a quasi-legal style to make it appear that they had the force of law.

> *Art. 4. Any worker who shouts or sings in the workshop will pay a fine of 0.25 centimes. If the worker who shouted cannot be identified even though it is clear that the shouts came from certain looms, all workers operating those looms will be fined, unless the worker responsible makes himself known. (Textile mill in Roubaix, France 1863)*

Such rules, which were unilaterally laid down by employers, are a reminder that we are always talking about two watertight worlds and that they are in conflict. There is an 'us' (the employers and their 'allies') and there is a 'them'. The very nature of these rules implies that it is the employers who construct the identity of their workers. Trying to control singing, playing or shouting on the shop floor is an admission that such behaviour is probable or at least likely. These documents typically infantilize the world of work. They help to legitimize the authority of employers, who are implicitly identified with rationality, while the labouring masses are equated with irrationality and impulsiveness and are therefore denied the ability to organize their own labour.

Business ethics redefines these identities. Unlike the rules of old, charters do not establish a hierarchy of moral capacities by assuming that the employers, defined as a class, possess qualities that wage-earners do not. They address all the staff, with no distinctions and they define directors as staff members. Shopfloor regulations implied explicit power relations and, in symbolic terms, were an expression of contempt for the workforce, but all that is now concealed: 'one big family with the same values' is a point of anchorage for PR operations that promote a consensual vision of social relations on the one hand and, on the other, the idea that the firm is a collective whose members all share a common moral purpose.

The so-called ethical mobilization of employees is in that sense a way of legitimizing the actions of a socially responsible firm. It is part of a new ideological construct and many observers have already noted where this can lead: now that they have become the moral equivalent of citizens, companies can play down their new duties while at the same time claiming citizens' rights that have the effect of marginalizing natural persons when it comes to the exercise of democratic power. Ethics and CSR therefore provide us with a tool for analysing the conflicted relationship between capitalism and democracy.

Companies now claim that their economic might allows them to play a new role when it comes to world governance. This role is problematic. The European Parliament and Commission have emphasized its problematic nature by trying to restrict the exercise of this claim while encouraging enterprises to adopt the CSR approach. The notion of CSR actually calls into question the division of labour between business and the state, as well as the boundaries between economics and politics and between private and public. 'The good of society' and 'the general interest' are regarded as legitimate goals for productive activity. CSR is an expression of multinational enterprises' desire to extend their prerogatives. As the petroleum company TOTAL puts it, the group is not only a 'social actor', but also a legitimate actor involved in a public debate.

> *Because we are a responsible company, we believe that it is our duty to become involved in public debates relating to our activities. We try to*
> *— provide the competent authorities with the technical information they need to take decisions;*
> *— take part in national and international debates about key issues such as the protection of human rights and climate change.*

In a context where political spaces based upon nation-states are beginning to look fragile and it is increasingly difficult to construct an international political framework, firms operating on a world scale regard the spaces they define and control as an arena in which they have the authority to establish new social ways of organizing the globalized economy. At the same time, they are attempting to structure debates about social and environmental issues, mainly through their lobbying activities.

Paternalism saw authority still bound up with the personal figure of the employer/factory owner. CSR is changing that. It is now the *company* that has the power to act, which implies that is in an institutional and moral position to justify its actions and the stances it takes and it is increasingly implied that the company acts as a citizen. Companies are arrogating the citizen's right to freedom of expression. They are also arrogating the rights of political institutions, as well as certain prerogatives. Managerial discourse commonly uses politically connoted terms like 'company governance', though frequent reference to ethics makes it unclear just what this means. Companies switch between the political and ethical registers, but they always place the emphasis on the latter because they cannot justify the former in democratic terms.

Conclusion

The notions of ethics and social responsibility promote the image of a company or institution whose members share the same values. Those values supply the social basis for a solidarity that extends beyond the company itself and that in itself justifies new prerogatives. This image has a real ideological coherence. Given that one of its goals is to promote a model for a 'welfare company' that can co-exist alongside nation-states, one can understand why the company identity enshrined in ethical charters promotes the idea that social relations inside the company are consensual and that this proves it is a socially responsible enterprise. The private solidarity promoted by enterprises cannot in fact demonstrate its legitimacy by proving that it has any real effects or by showing that it has democratic roots.

Growing job insecurity, especially in the countries of the North, is one of the effects of the out-sourcing of jobs on a large scale. Out-sourcing means that large numbers of workers are excluded from the most advantageous collective agreements and labour regulations. Forms of social welfare that were once associated with big companies within the context of a Fordist compromise backed by the welfare state are now enjoyed by only small numbers of employees. Companies' willingness to extent their commitment beyond their legal obligations has to be seen in a context where the labour force is becoming increasingly fragmented. Company statements about solidarity do nothing to prevent the naturalization of economic constraints that justifies the undermining of social welfare provision on the grounds that the right to work must become more 'flexible'. It is rather on the contrary. In that sense, statements about CSR actually sanction the removal of legal safeguards by encouraging governments to introduce further deregulation.

In the countries of the South, the situation is different but it is still problematic. Democratic states and labour legislation are weaker there. In some cases, initiatives taken by 'welfare firms' can therefore represent a form of social progress. But it is not clear what effect they will have on the coherence of social policies at the national level and especially on the growth of democracy.

Be that as it may, a critical examination of CSR must go beyond the issue of the authenticity of commitments made by the management of multinationals and an evaluation of company performance in terms of CSR. The evaluations of company decision-making structures on which the rating agencies base their reports conceal the need for an analysis of the political significance of multinationals' CSR practices. While they claim that the demand for efficiency is in response to a social demand, CSR practices are being used to justify the calculated or self-regulating responses of 'welfare companies' whose activities are not subject to democratic debate or controls.

It seems likely that some mix of the welfare-state and the welfare-company (which has always been the case in the United States more than Europe) will be advocated. Their respective roles are yet to be determined. This will depend no doubt to a large extent on the future balance of power and on debates about the tensions between capitalism and democracy. The recent rise of an emphasis on business ethics and corporate social responsibility means that those debates are more important than they have ever been.

Further reading

Capron, M. and Quiarel-Lanoizelée, F. (2004) *Mythes et réalités de l'entreprise responsible: Acteurs, enjeux, stratégies*. La Découverte, Paris.

Cattani, A. D. and Salmon, A. (2006) Responsabilidade social das empresas. In Cattani, A. D. and Holzmann, L. (eds) *Dicionário de trabalho e tecnologia*. Editora da UFRGS, Porto Alegre, pp. 244–8.

Durkheim, E. (1997 [1893]) *The Division of Labour in Society* (trans. Halls, W. D.). Free Press, New York.

Habermas, J. (1976) *Legitimation Crisis* (trans. McCarthy, T.). Heinemann, London.

Hart, K. (2005) *The Hit Man's Dilemma, or Business, Personal and Impersonal*. Prickly Paradigm Press, Chicago.

International Labour Office (2006) Tripartite Declaration of Principles Concerning Multinational Enterprises and Social Policy [online]. Available at: http://www.ilo.org/public/english/employment/multi/download/english.pdf.

Logsdon, J. M. and Wood, D. J. (2002) Business citizenship: from domestic to global level of analysis. *Business Ethics Quarterly* 12 (2), 155–87.

Preston, L. E. and Post, J. E. (1975) *Private Management and Public Policy: The Principles of Public Responsibility*. Prentice-Hall, Englewood Cliffs, NJ.

Reich, R. (2007) *Supercapitalism: The Transformation of Business, Democracy and Everyday Life*. Knopf, New York.

Salmon, A. (2007) *La tentation éthique du capitalisme*. La Découverte, Paris.

Salmon, A. (2009) *Moraliser le capitalisme?* CNRS Éditions, Paris.

Weber, M. (1994 [1905]) *The Protestant Ethic and the Spirit of Capitalism* (trans. Parsons, T.). Routledge, London.

16

Welfare

Adalbert Evers

Studies have been made of how the development of the market complemented that of the state during the formation of modern industrial societies. It is also possible to make similar studies of the interactions between public policies and regulations on the one hand and the development of the third sector and charities on the other. The hypothesis that increased welfare provision from the third or voluntary sector will reduce the role of the state, as in a zero-sum game, may in that respect prove to be deceptive (see *Third Sector*).

If, on the other hand, contemporary democracies and welfare states have only one thing in common, it may well be the growing interpenetration of different spheres and sectors and the irrelevance of the boundaries between political, economic and private space, and between the monetary and non-monetary economies. It is mainly for this reason that welfare-provision has always been financed from a variety of different sources, even though it has been described only recently as a product of a plural economy and welfare pluralism (see *Plural Economy*). If we are to find theoretical underpinnings for the political debate about welfare, we need sociological concepts that can explain the relationship between different sectors of society.

Concepts: civil society and public space

Notions such as those of 'civil society' and 'public space' assume that modern democracies have developed a social field structured mainly by voluntary associations as an arena for the representation of social and political interests, solidarity and mutual aid. The general metaphor of 'public space' thus refers to the space that opens up between the state, the market and families, which are seen as the cornerstones of a triangular space of tensions. Developments, orientations and strategies deployed within this public space do have an influence, but at the same time they are exposed to that environment, as defined by these three major poles. It has to be emphasized that the very existence of a public space and of associations with a minimal degree of autonomy does represent a real democratic conquest based upon the liberal reforms that stem from what Walzer calls 'the art of separation'. The expression refers to the separation of public and private spheres, of economic and political power, and of state and society, thereby guaranteeing the independence of citizens and their freedom of association. It is society's capacity for self-organization within this public space – in part through voluntary associations – that helps to define it as 'civil'. Authoritarian and totalitarian regimes do not permit such self-organization. Under communist and fascist regimes, even the least political expressions of social solidarity – such as the Red Cross or religious charities – are either banned or incorporated into the state and lose their voluntary status.

At the structural level, it may be argued that the spaces of state, market and community all prioritize specific rationalities. In an economic world where social relations are mediated through money, instrumentalist thinking, individual choice and anonymity are the predominant forms and are constantly encouraged. At the level of the central government, strongly universalist orientations requiring general rules and standardized procedures are dominant; at the community level, in contrast, norms and traditions that encourage interpersonal bonds and duties prevail. At the infra-political and decision-making level, these spheres overlap. Constant processes of commodification and market penetration may, for instance, reduce the space needed for the provision of public goods and services by the state or the voluntary sector. They may also undermine the desire for self-regulation, solidarity and public commitment, and this historical dynamic has been well described by Wuthnow. Relations that are mediated by money open up new prospects in terms of individual choice and anonymity, but they can also undermine social relations based on solidarity. Unlike the other spheres, which are characterized by the clear predominance of one form of rationality, the specific characteristic of the voluntary sector is that it encourages the co-existence and combination of different rationalities.

History

The same structural pluralism and diversity is apparent if we adopt a historical perspective. On the one hand, confessional associations (one has only to think of the revival of voluntary church-based associations in Eastern Europe) or organizations associated with the labour movement (such as the old co-operatives) are testimony to the continued presence of traditional rationalities that encourage self-organization, even though they have lost much of their significance. The same variety can be seen in the increasingly different ways that 'the art of family life' can be defined.

Associations and their modes of regulation need to be analysed as a component part of different welfare regimes. We therefore have to expand the existing typology, which does not take them into account. In some countries, such as the USA, these organizations play a vital role; in others, such as the Nordic states, there are impressive numbers of social and solidarity organizations, but their activities are restricted to the defence of private interests and lobbying.

Although they enjoy legal guarantees in all democracies, the form taken by associations is simultaneously influenced by public institutions, the market economy and an 'informal sector' organized around the family and local solidarity networks. Such organizations then generate ideas and conflicts within a space that transcends the usual barriers between the worlds of the market, states and local communities because of the innovations and disagreements they articulate and organize. This analysis, which reveals the many inter-relations possible between a public space, composed of the state, the market and the third sector, and informal groups, can be analysed in both structural and historical terms.

The future

In a context where the welfare state is being deregulated and destabilized, the neoliberal approach that combines consumerist ethics with a managerial orientation can still be opposed by invoking a contrasting approach based on two key ideas:

Re-evaluation and strengthening of the role of community bonds, and especially the family, insofar as they are the (co)-producers of many aspects of welfare and social well-being. As Titmuss has demonstrated, the state is not the sole provider of social services. The family has a major role to play in this domain, and it is still usually women who care for children, the elderly and dependent adults. The community concept of the family requires changes in gender relations, at work and at home. This will make the concept of a 'multi-dimensional life' accessible to men and women alike. The way roles are divided between the genders is also broadly determined by conditions of access to the labour market and by the structure of public safeguards.

Re-evaluation of the role of civil associations, not only as service-providers but also as agencies for social integration. This role has to be reconsidered both internally (by their membership) and externally (by the groups targeted by these associations). Such considerations must also be taken seriously to the extent that they promote the values of co-operation and solidarity. Civil associations are in effect 'schools of democracy' that are trying to establish interrelations between the universal rights of the citizen and the right to different and particular life styles and conceptions of welfare in a plural society.

This perspective is sometimes described as the 'well-being society' or *Wohlergesellschaft*. The emphasis falls on strengthening the role of individuals as members, co-producers and citizens, as opposed to their status as taxpayers or voters. The role of the state is not restricted to the regulation of markets and the supervision of specific services; it also extends to the implementation of policies that foster the infrastructures required for the development of this associative and civil life. The main difficulty lies in defining the investment required to finance a domain that has long been under-financed and under great pressure from its users, but which is of great importance in that it constitutes a society's 'social capital' (see *Social Capital*).

Further reading

Cohen, J. and Rogers, J. (1994) Solidarity, democracy, association. *Politische Vierteljaheresschrift, Sonderheft 25: Staat und Verbände.*

Edwards, M. (2004) *Civil Society.* Polity, Cambridge.

Esping-Anderson, G. (1990) *The Three Worlds of Welfare Capitalism.* Polity, Cambridge.

Evers, A. (1983) The welfare mix approach: understanding the pluralism of welfare systems. In Evers, A. and Svetlik (eds) *Balancing Pluralism: New Welfare Mixes in Care for the Elderly.* Avebury, Aldershot, pp. 3–32.

Evers, A. and Olk, T. (1996) Consumers, citizens and co-producers: a pluralistic perspective on democracy in social services. In Flösser, G. and Otto, H. U. *Towards More Democracy in Social Services.* De Gruyter, New York and Berlin.

Gilbert, N. (2009) Welfare Pluralism and Social Policy. In Midgely, J. (ed.) *The Handbook of Social Policy.* Sage, Los Angeles, pp. 236–46.

Lewis, J. (1995) *The Voluntary Sector, the State and Social Work in Britain.* Edward Elgar, Aldershot.

Mayo, M. (2008) Understanding the mixed economy of welfare. *International Journal of Social Welfare* 17 (1).

Mertens, S. (1999) Nonprofit organizations and social economy: two ways of understanding the third sector. *Annals of Public and Cooperative Economics* 70 (3), 501–20.

Powell, M. and Barrientos, A. (2004) Welfare regimes and the welfare mix. *Journal of Political Research* 43 (1), 83–106.

Titmuss, R. M. (1963) *Essays on the Welfare State.* Allen and Unwin, London.

Walzer, M. (1988) Socializing the welfare state. In Gutman, A. (ed.) *Democracy and the Welfare State.* Princeton University Press, Princeton, NJ.

Walzer, M. (1992) The civil society argument. In Mouffe C. (ed.) *Dimensions of Radical Democracy. Pluralism, Citizenship, Community.* Verso, London and New York.

Wuthnow, R. (1991) The voluntary sector: legacy for the past, hope for the future? In Wuthnow, E. (ed.) *Between States and Markets: The Voluntary Sector in Contemporary Perspective.* Princeton University Press, Princeton, NJ.

17

Gift

Alain Caillé

The spirit of the gift

For anyone who wishes to break free from the constraints of economics, either by attempting to build a completely different economy or by looking for something other than the economy – something that lies outside or beyond economics – the notion of the gift is an obvious, even inevitable, point of reference. If goods and services are not to be produced on the basis of individual self-interest or for profit, and if they are not intended to be sold, then they must obviously be given or shared. There must, at the very least, be an element of disinterestedness. Indeed, how could an economy be based on 'solidarity' if those who invoke it were not, in one way or another, inspired by the spirit of giving? This raises the question of what we are to understand by the spirit of giving.

There are two main and contrasting positions on this point, and they can be described, respectively, as non-utilitarian and anti-utilitarian. The former has all the attractions of what appears to be a radical argument. Because it refers to an uncompromising conception of the gift, it encourages us to reject completely any idea of individual self-interest, contract, return or reciprocity and to leave the economic domain for good. In their day, Stalin and Mao Tse Tung, for example, called on workers to reject 'material incentives' and to produce only in order to build a communist society. On a very different register, a whole theological and then philosophical tradition argues that there can be no gift unless it is absolutely pure, or in other words devoid of all intentionality or any expectation of getting something in return. When I give, explains Derrida, for example, I am not giving because, acting in the knowledge that I am giving, I watch myself giving and at least enjoy the pleasure afforded me by my position as donor. And, as Marion once argued, if there is to be a gift (a true or pure gift), there must be no subject who gives, no object that is given, and no one who receives the gift! As we can see, these conceptions reduce the 'gift' to a 'donation' that has no subject.

The anti-utilitarian concept, in contrast, is certainly less grandiose, but it is more adaptable to reality. It does not call for the elimination or sacrifice of utility, self-interest, intentionality or subjectivity. Nor does it call for any sacrifice. It regards the gift as a sociological operator that creates alliances, friendship and solidarity. It is thanks to the gift that we have social relations and co-operation rather than nothing or war. In order to establish alliances and create trust, we must display or bring into being those elements of disinterestedness and unconditionality on which social relations are based. But it is clear that this unconditionality works to the advantage of all. To sum up: the non-utilitarian gift is purely free and absolutely unconditional. Although it does not demand its abolition, the anti-utilitarian gift simply subordinates the moment of utility, calculation and self-interest to the imperatives of a primal disinterestedness and unconditionality. It obeys a logic of conditional unconditionality.

An anthropological perspective

It may be argued that the anti-utilitarian conception of the gift derives from an anthropological perspective that is supported by many studies. Ever since the publication of Mauss's famous *The Gift* in 1924–5 – Mauss was the nephew and sole theoretical legatee of Durkheim, the founder of the French school of sociology – investigating practices associated with ceremonial gifts has been central to the work of ethnologists. Mauss discovered that the obligation to give – or, rather, the threefold obligation to 'give, receive and return' – is the basic social rule of at least a certain number of savage or archaic societies and is nothing more than a concrete translation of the principle of reciprocity that supplies the basis for Claude Lévi-Strauss's structural anthropology and which Karl Polanyi contrasts with exchange and redistribution.

And economic sociology (or in other words, a way of theorizing economics in non-economic ways) must by definition ask itself about the role played in every kind of modern economic activity by the respective logics of the market, the redistributive hierarchy and reciprocal giving. But, to extend the argument beyond economic sociology, we may conclude that the theory of the gift is something that general sociological theory and political philosophy cannot do without.

Mauss's essential discovery has, therefore, more general implications: the earliest societies or social bonds were not constructed on the basis of a contract or the exchange of commodities, but in obedience to the obligation to compete by being conspicuously generous. Rivalry? Ostentatious giving? The savage gift in fact has nothing to do with Christian charity. Full of aggression and ambivalence, it is an agonistic gift. We do not enhance the standing of our names or acquire prestige by economizing, but through expenditure that takes the extreme form of waste and the acceptance of loss. This discovery obviously throws down a fantastic challenge to the assumptions of economic theory and especially to the theory of rational choice because it demonstrates that, as Mauss puts it, *homo economicus* is not behind us but ahead of us. *Homo eonomicus* is not as natural or universal as the economists claim. In most cases, the goods that are given, accepted and returned within the framework of the obligation to be mutually generous do not in fact have any utilitarian value. They are valuable only because they symbolize the social relationship they create by causing a debt to circulate endlessly between the partners. The debt may – and must be – inverted, but it can never be redeemed. The gifts are symbols and the symbols are gifts. They are not returned immediately and it is not an equivalent that is returned; they are returned much later, and much more is returned than was given. It is not just positive goods or acts of kindness that circulate; so too do insults, acts of vengeance, curses and wrongdoing, and they circulate in precisely the same way. If we cannot give evil, how can we give good? The most famous examples of the practice of agonistic giving are the *potlatch* of the Kwakiutl Indians of British Columbia in Western Canada and the *kula* of the Trobriand Islands to the northeast of New Guinea.

And now?

What remains of the primitive world of the gift, apart from the practice of giving Christmas and birthday presents? Not a lot, it would seem, especially as our conception of the gift has been modified and modelled by two thousand years of Christianity. All the great religions must in fact be interpreted as transformations of the archaic gift system. They have tried to universalize it (give to those who are not relatives), radicalize it (really *give* the desirable object and not just its sign) and to internalize it (no ostentatious giving). And yet if we look more closely, a whole host of goods do still circulate in the way that the gift once circulated and it would therefore be a serious mistake to think that gift practices only concern savage societies and have more or less disappeared in contemporary societies. The most famous example given by Titmuss is that of blood donation, while Godbout has shown that the characteristic feature of the modern gift is that it is also a gift to strangers. In more general terms, however, we may put forward the hypothesis that the obligation to give is still the basic rule of *primal sociability* of one-to-one relations – and in this sphere the personality of those involved is more important than their function. Even in the supposedly impersonal sphere of *secondary sociability* – the sphere of the market, the state and science in which the requirement for individuals to be efficient in functional terms counts for more than their personality – the obligation to give, receive and return gifts plays a subordinate but still decisive role to the extent that functional actions are always performed by persons. So much so that no company, administration or research laboratory would be efficient if it did not, in one way or another, succeed in mobilizing on its own behalf the creative energy (the impulse to give), loyalty and fidelity of its members. It is at this point that the link between Mauss's discovery and the new economic sociology appears most clearly. As Granovetter explains, the explanation for social actions does not lie in individual rationality or in over-arching holistic rules, but in networks, and in the trust that unites and binds together members of networks. The same theme can be seen in the work of Callon and in Actor Network Theory. All that is perfectly true, provided that we add that it is the gift that creates networks and that it is the reproduction of those networks that inspires trust. Network relationships are gift relationships (and the first great network to be studied was the *kula* circle observed by Malinowski).

Some theoretical implications

It is, however, possible to go beyond these notes. Indeed, it is both possible and necessary, if we are to believe the *Revue du MAUSS* group, which thinks that the specificity of sociology, as opposed to economic science, lies in anti-utilitarianism – a strand that can be found in Durkheim, Weber, Marx and even Pareto – and that anti-utilitarianism can become a reality only if it is organized around Mauss's discovery and if it takes the 'gift paradigm' seriously. What Mauss actually demonstrates in his study of the archaic gift is that social action does not simply obey the logic of rational self-interest, but also a primal logic of sympathy and that the tension between self-interest and disinterestedness overlaps with that between obligation and freedom. The social bond is therefore based on neither rational self-interest, as methodological individualists believe, nor, as those who believe in methodological holism would have it, on an always already present or over-arching law. These theoretical and methodological positions, and most schools in the social sciences that oscillate between the two, in fact have one thing in common and it transcends the differences between them. They both attempt to explain action and history by reducing them to choices and decisions that are made by an always-already substantial subject: the individual and society are assumed to be entities. They therefore fail to see the emergent dimension of the social bond or of the individual psyche. If we explain them in terms of the gift, we do not, as is all too often believed, explain them in terms of charity or altruism, but in terms of their emergence. Viewed in this light, the gift represents the privileged modality of what might be called constitutive action. It has something in common with action, in Arendt's sense of the term, or with the concept of *the* political.

Let us look, to end, at two of the gift paradigm's implications for the critique of economism. If, on the one hand, we assert that there are, and must be, actions that do not stem simply from calculated material self-interest (as in the case of the market) or obligation (as is the case with the state and redistribution), but also and primarily from a logic of alliance and a certain disinterestedness, then the anti-utilitarian paradigm is obviously close to the arguments of the supporters of the economics of solidarity and a valorization of all that is done in the name of the principle of association. The fact remains that while, in theory, the spirit of the gift takes hierarchical precedence over the logics of individual self-interest and obligation within the voluntary or non-profit making [*associatif*] sector, that is not necessarily – or completely – the case in reality. By the same criterion and, as we have seen, a certain element of disinterestedness must, of necessity, be present within the firm or the state apparatus.

Because it undermines clear-cut oppositions between the pure gift and self-interest, or between the market, the state and associations, the gift paradigm implies that we have to understand not only the difference between their logics, but also the dialectical continuities that exist between them and the ways they may be inverted. On the other hand, and this is where the gift paradigm may be identified with a truly political conception of the social bond, it clearly implies that the first and necessary precondition for the effectiveness of any human community is to be found in the modalities of its constitution as a subject. A country cannot be prosperous unless it is first and foremost a country or fatherland. No association can be based upon solidarity unless the principle of association takes priority over functional imperatives. No laboratory can do anything and no sports team can be successful unless it is first and foremost a community.

It follows that the alternatives to contemporary mega-capitalism – and the need to find alternatives is imperative – are not in fact truly economic alternatives. In one sense, there is not – or is no longer – any plausible economic alternative to the market economy. The fact remains that the role of economics can be restricted. It must, in other words, be constituted on a different basis and subordinated to, among other things, the demand for disinterestedness, the gift, and democratization.

Further reading

Caillé, A. (2000) *Anthropologie du don. Le tiers paradigme*. Desclée de Brouwer, Paris.

Caillé, A. (2004 [1994]) *Don, intérêt et désintéressement: Bourdieu, Mauss, Platon, et quelques autres*. La Découverte/MAUSS, Paris.

Callon, M. (ed.) (1998) *The Laws of the Markets*. Blackwell, Oxford.

Derrida, J. (1994) *Giving Time*. University of Chicago Press, Chicago.

Godbout, J. (2001) *Le don, la dette, l'identité*. La Découverte/MAUSS, Paris.

Godbout, J. and Caillé, A. (2000) *The World of the Gift*. McGill-Queen's, Montreal.

Gregory, C. (1982) *Gifts and Commodities*. Academic Press, New York.

Hart, K. (2007) Marcel Mauss: in pursuit of the whole. *Comparative Studies in Society and History* 49 (2), 473–85.

Hyde, L. (1979) *The Gift: Imagination and the Erotic Life of Property*. Vintage Books, New York.

Malinowski, B. (1961[1922]) *Argonauts of the Western Pacific: An Account of*

Native Enterprise and Adventure in the Archipelago of Melanesian New Guinea. Dutton, New York.

Mauss, M. (1990 [1925]) *The Gift: The Form and Reason for Exchange in Archaic Societies.* Routledge, London.

Perret, B. (2004) *La société comme monde commun.* Desclee de Brouwer, Paris.

Strathern, M. (1988) *The Gender of the Gift.* University of California Press, Berkeley.

Titmuss, R.M. (1972) *The Gift Relationship: From Human Blood to Social Policy.* Vintage Books, New York.

18

Moral Economy

Chris Hann

The modern social sciences compartmentalize. My university education began with courses in politics, philosophy and economics, before I switched to social anthropology. The concept of moral economy straddles all four of these disciplines. Its popularity in the last half century is largely due to the work of the Marxist historian E. P. Thompson, so history must certainly be added to this list. Sociology can hardly be excluded. In short, the idea of moral economy exemplifies the need to think beyond the familiar academic boundaries and return to more holistic approaches in the human sciences. Even then, moral economy should not be treated as a separate topic of investigation, but considered alongside solidarity economy, plural economy and the other categories of this guide. In the first part of this contribution I argue that its congruence with cognate terms addressed here is overwhelming. In the second part I outline the concept's trajectory in recent decades, focusing on the pioneering contributions of Thompson and James Scott. I then draw on my own field research in China and Hungary to illustrate the complexities we encounter when applying this idea to socialist rural transformation and its aftermath. I conclude by generalizing the key points which emerge from this empirical discussion. Moral economy has been a helpful term in critiquing crude economism and exploring the roots of social protest, but it cannot remain immune to critique itself.

Preliminary remarks: wholes, parts and individuals

The demarcation lines of my undergraduate courses were quite clear. We explored morality in particular branches of philosophy and political theory. As for economics, its essence was revealed in the title of our first textbook, *Positive Economics*. True, this implied that there might be another, normative dimension to that discipline. We were introduced to sub-fields such as 'welfare economics'. But even in these fields the dominant paradigm was the 'neoclassical synthesis', deriving primarily from English utilitarian philosophy. It was epitomized in the notion of Pareto optimality, which described a position where no further market transactions can increase the utility of one economic agent without reducing the utility of others. In my classes and tutorials, we spent a lot of time struggling with the mathematics of these solutions and almost none in questioning how Pareto optimality was related to distribution. Vilfredo Pareto, a political economist and sociologist, has in recent decades been partly superseded in these economics classes by the mathematician John Nash. Students now learn how to specify the Nash equilibrium in a discipline that has detached itself ever more completely from questions of politics and society – and morality.

But neoclassical economists are not the only ones to blame. Other social scientists have been complicit in modern divisions of academic labour which assign economy and morality to separate domains or oppose them to each other simplistically, rather than explore their links holistically. For example, social anthropology has recently seen a revival of interest in morality, but much of this work has stressed the reflexive moral decisions of 'free' individuals and hardly engaged significantly with the economy. This recent anthropology tends to be dismissive of Émile Durkheim, Pareto's contemporary, who approached *society* as a moral system.

A similar emphasis on society as a whole is found in the work of Karl Polanyi, whose *The Great Transformation* shares much with Thompson's analysis of the moral economy. For both, the spread of the market principle from the late eighteenth century threatened the foundations of society. Whereas in all previous human communities the economy had been shaped by a variety of 'forms of integration', such as reciprocity, redistribution and householding, Polanyi argued that in nineteenth-century England market exchange achieved an unprecedented dominance. According to Polanyi's moral critique, humanity needed to rediscover the deeper meaning of economy, its ability to satisfy substantive human needs and not merely to maximize short-term individual greed. He used the metaphor of 'embeddedness' to indicate that pre-modern economies could not be analysed apart from their social and political contexts. He later suggested that the modern economy could be 'disembedded', thereby excluding it from the purview of his 'substantivist' school of economic anthropology. In spite of this concession to the economists, Polanyi's approach has been a continuous source of inspiration for unorthodox economists. He did not actually use the term moral economy, but many people think he did.

Louis Dumont drew on the holistic traditions of both Durkheim and Polanyi for his study of the Indian caste system. The models of Pareto and Nash were irrelevant in a society where the merchants were clearly subordinated to kings and warriors and a complex division of labour was ultimately regulated not by the market principle, and still less by the principle of individual utility maximization, but by notions of hierarchy and ritual purity upheld by ascetic religious specialists. Although the term was not yet available to him in the 1960s, Dumont's account of India exemplifies a holistic approach to the economy. The core activities of production, consumption and trade are governed by an encompassing moral code, sanctioned ultimately by religious beliefs assumed to be thoroughly internalized throughout the society (including by 'untouchables' and tribal communities outside the formal hierarchy of caste).

This is of course an ideal-type. Durkheim found it easier to exemplify his notion of the *conscience collective* in the totemic beliefs of Australian aborigines than in contemporary France, where the moral convictions of the Dreyfusards clearly differed from those of their opponents. Later historical scholarship on South Asia has revealed that the pre-modern agrarian economy was in fact strongly influenced by 'market forces' arising from the impersonal calculation of economic agents. The ideology of caste might continue to exercise a certain hegemony in India even today, e.g. in shaping marriage patterns; but there are many other social boundaries and we cannot assume that the moral economies of castes and sub-castes with very different endowments and interests will be the same. Whether we privilege the whole or the part will depend on how we define moral economy. The concept turns out to be elusive. Let us now turn to the term's deployment in the works of its most influential theoreticians.

Thompson, Scott and their followers

The English historian Edward Palmer Thompson was almost single-handedly responsible for the great popularity of the term moral economy in Anglophone history and social science over the last half century. He used the term in opposition to 'the new political economy of the free market' as it began to develop in England in the eighteenth century. The ground for the bifurcation of economy and morality in modern neoclassical economics was prepared by Adam Smith, who followed up his study of *Moral Sentiments* (1767) with an analysis of the *Wealth of Nations* (1776). Even in the latter (despite subsequent simplification of his ideas by free-market ideologists), Smith did not advocate a political economy that was disembedded from society and morality. Nor was it Thompson's intention to oppose the moral to the political. Until the marginalist revolution of the 1870s displaced political economy from the core of mainstream economics, it was taken for granted that economy dealt with the welfare of the people, which was inherently a matter of both politics and morality.

Thompson was no Durkheimian either. As a Marxist, he applied the concept of moral economy to the popular culture of the plebs. The causes of the bread riots that he studied in eighteenth century England were more complex than price increases and 'actual deprivation'. Thompson drew attention to a popular consensus about right and wrong in a subordinated part of society. This consensus was:

> grounded upon a consistent traditional view of social norms and obligations, of the proper economic functions of several parties within the community, which, taken together, can be said to constitute the moral economy of the poor.

Thompson mocked those social and economic historians who portrayed the English crowd in the reductionist terms of *homo economicus*. He showed that, just like the Trobriand Islanders studied by anthropologist Bronislaw Malinowski, the behaviour of English workers was comprehensible only when you had understood their values, which were rooted in their agrarian traditions, in 'the old moral economy of provision'. At the core of this economy were notions of need and 'reasonable price', which Thompson acknowledged were by no means peculiarly English.

The genealogy of the term moral economy is not unlike that of 'civil society'. In both cases, a term current in intellectual discourse in the early industrial era disappeared for more than a century, only to be revived by Western Marxists (or at any rate scholars leaning to the left) in the late twentieth century. This resemblance is superficial, however, since moral economy was never as prominent in the older literature as civil society. Thompson later confessed that he was unable to trace exactly when the term was first used in England. It was certainly current in Chartist polemics of the 1830s. Thompson revived it briefly in *The Making of the English Working Class* (1963), but he did not consider it important enough to warrant inclusion in the Index of this work. It was fully elaborated in his article 'The moral economy of the English crowd in the eighteenth century' (1971). Thompson developed his argument in *Customs in Common* (1991), where he dealt with numerous criticisms and reviewed some of the wider literature he had generated.

Scholars immediately began to apply Thompson's concept in very different contexts from the 1970s. In *The Moral Economy of the Peasant*, American political scientist and anthropologist James Scott argued that peasants in Southeast Asia adhered to a strong conservative ethic which prioritized the subsistence of all members of the local community. Whenever this was threatened, political rebellion was likely to ensue. In later work Scott showed how, in practice, informal methods of resistance were far more widespread than open rebellion. His first book drew a sharp critique from Samuel Popkin, who accused Scott of romanticizing the unity of the rural community and insisted that peasants in Southeast Asia, like economic actors everywhere, were rational utility maximizers. These exchanges repeated the long-running debate in economic anthropology between 'substantivists' and their 'formalist' opponents who represented the neoclassical position inside anthropology. These debates were themselves a re-run of the celebrated 'Battle over methods' (*Methodenstreit*) in late nineteenth-century German historiography.

Thompson approved of Scott's adaptation of his concept, though he was less enthusiastic about other adaptations. He concluded his 1991 review optimistically: further enquiry into 'the moral' was recommended as a promising research agenda. Thompson added:

> . . . if I did father the term 'moral economy' upon current academic discourse, the term has long forgotten its paternity. I will not disown it,

but it has come of age and I am no longer answerable for its actions. It will be interesting to see how it goes on.

Two decades on, Thompson's paternal rights have not been forgotten, but even he might be surprised by the sheer variety of contexts in which scholars from many disciplines continue to identify moral economies – from corruption and AIDS in Africa to the history of science in the West, from localized case studies to world religions and transnational movements of protest or 'humanitarianism'. Didier Fassin has recently provided a creative survey of this literature; in spite of proliferating diffuse and 'anodyne' usages, he remains convinced of its heuristic value as well as its potential for emancipatory politics.

Extension of the concept's use was perhaps predictable. So long as mainstream economics defines itself as the science of economizing behaviour, in the sense of maximizing utility under conditions of scarce resources, there is a need for a concept that embraces all those factors shaping human action that cannot be reduced to a calculus of rational individual choice. On this broad understanding, moral economy may cover everything from consumer tastes and desires to the work ethic and values derived from religious convictions. A distinct moral economy might then be attributed to every social group or 'subculture'. Since there is individual variation within every such group, it is then a short step to recognize individual moral economies. This is arguably to trivialize the concept and it would clearly contradict Thompson's definition, which derived the moral economy from a social consensus. But Thompson's original formulation is itself open to critical scrutiny, as I argue in the next section with reference to my own research.

The moral economy of decollectivization

I first used the concept of moral economy in research on the break-up of collective farms in the former Soviet bloc after 1990. The main interest of these case materials is that they engage with socialism, whereas the dominant thrust of the moral economy literature has been a critique of new forms of capitalist market economy. The introduction of the market and privatization of land owned previously by the village collective farm or by the state did not lead to improved economic performance but rather, in almost every

case throughout the former 'second world', to severe social dislo-
cation and diminished economic efficiency. Various explanations
were put forward. So-called 'new institutionalists' drew attention to
shortcomings in the implementation of the changes, e.g. in issuing
land titles, providing credit, and in general, creating 'effective' markets. My research group sought to probe deeper into how villagers
reacted to the introduction of the new rules. In the case of Russia,
for example, where private property in land was not widespread
before collectivization, we found strong notions of 'limited good',
which led villagers to criticize and resist reforms that were bound to
accentuate social differentiation by favoring the emergence of a new
class of commercial farmers . From the point of view of the authorities and their neoliberal international advisers, such sentiments were
either the regrettable consequence of socialist rule or evidence of
backwardness in the *longue durée*, or some combination of the two. As
in earlier formulations of modernization theory, the advocates of the
market were adamant that such vestiges of an older, egalitarian moral
economy should not be allowed to obstruct progress.

   But the moral context of decollectivization across Eurasia turns
out to be immensely complex, as further examples from China and
Hungary reveal. The former claims still to be a socialist state, but it
too implemented a variety of decollectivization thirty years ago. The
replacement of brigades and communes by households as the key unit
of rural production was a crucial step in China's more general opening up to the market. The 'responsibility system' devolved land to
household management on an egalitarian basis. Although there have
been problems, caused by demographic variation within communities, for example, or by the predatory appropriations of state officials
in peri-urban zones, this reform process has been overwhelmingly
popular with villagers and it has been an economic success. Unlike
privatization in Russia and Eastern Europe, land has not become a
commodity. In Marxist terms, we can conclude that the country's
most numerous social class has not been dispossessed of the means
of production and that the commercialization that has transformed
the economy in recent decades is not yet definitively a capitalist
transformation. In Polanyian terms we might call this 'embedded
socialism'. In the ethnically Uyghur villages I studied in Xinjiang, I
found that households did their best to avoid co-operation outside
the immediate family and attributed this strategy to the excesses of
the Maoist period. There was nonetheless strong solidarity at the

level of the community, expressed through the revival of Islam and in ritual events generally. The moral community destroyed under Chairman Mao has been effectively reconstituted in the framework of the household responsibility system.

These examples from Russia and China seem to speak of a singular 'traditional view of norms and obligations', in line with Thompson's definition of the moral economy, even if certain individuals in both cases might well be interested in acquiring more land and becoming entrepreneurial. By contrast, the case of socialist and postsocialist Hungary, a much smaller country, illustrates the difficulty of generalization and the dangers in one-sided applications of the concept of moral economy. As elsewhere across the landmass, collectivization was experienced by the great majority of villagers as a violent intervention and an affront to the evolved norms of private property. The largest political party emerging from the last relatively free election of 1948 was the Independent Smallholders' Party (ISP), strongly committed to private ownership and the market. This party was eliminated soon afterwards and mass collectivization was completed at the end of the 1950s. However, before the end of the 1960s Hungary had embarked upon decentralizing reforms which encouraged private initiatives, in agriculture as in other sectors. The socialist property ideology was never formally abandoned, but in practice market incentives allowed for massive embourgeoisement, based on an efficient symbiosis of large-scale socialist institutions and the labour resources of the household. Like China's responsibility system, these reforms were welcomed by villagers; but this welcome was economistic, based solely on the material accumulation which the reforms enabled; market socialism never received a deeper moral legitimation.

This moral deficit became crucial when the rural symbiosis disintegrated following the collapse of socialist power. Pressure came not only from external agents but also from within the countryside, notably the revived ISP, to restore full private ownership by dismantling collective farms according to the pre-collectivization plot boundaries. This demand was justified in moral terms. Opponents pointed to the obvious economic irrationality of such a scheme, and there were some who attempted to defend socialist ideals in moral terms. After all, Hungarian collective farms had allowed the industrious to prosper as a reward for their hard work, while continuing to provide a safety net for their weaker members, and why should the children and grandchildren of appropriated landowners now benefit from restitution? There was no moral consensus. The solution of the first post-socialist government was a compromise which did not give full satisfaction to anyone: the principle of 'compensation' allowed for thorough-going privatization, but did not guarantee that one would be able to regain control of the patrimony to which one felt emotionally and morally attached. Many of those allocated land were too old to be able to farm it independently. The entire sector plunged into a deep depression, from which even new subsidies following Hungary's entry into the European Union have failed to bring a full recovery.

Meanwhile the moral landscape continues to evolve. As in Russia, one comes across resentment towards those who, by one means or another, have emerged as capitalist farmers. There is now widespread nostalgia for the last decades of socialism, however crude their economism, and regret that the ISP was able to destroy the entire system of collective farming by manipulating emotions. Yet some villagers continue to insist that this decollectivization and commoditization of land was the *right* path to follow, even if they concede that it was both economically irrational (in terms of production and productivity) and socially unfair (because it gave windfall endowments to persons who had not worked to deserve them). The ISP eventually split into squabbling factions and many of its former members nowadays vote for extreme right-wing, nationalist parties. Such trends are common in the region, and indeed in much of rural Europe. This is the other end of the spectrum from the revolutionary, subaltern groups which figure most prominently in the moral economy literature. Yet it needs to be recognized that the institutions of the market and private property may also command moral support. Sometimes, as in post-socialist Hungary, the support may be strong enough to result in behaviour which contradicts the economist's model of *homo economicus*. Of course, that is exactly what Thompson wanted to get at with his concept of the moral economy. The problem is that the villagers' behaviour may equally contradict the diagnosis of the Marxist analyst, who must regretfully conclude that the exploited have once again been deluded by a dominant ideology. But if moral economy is primarily a nexus of beliefs, practices and emotions among the folk, rather than an analytical concept designed to register only those beliefs, practices and emotions which conduce to action which the observer considers to be progressive, then we must conclude that even the reactionary right is entitled to its moral economy.

Conclusion and critique

The concept of moral economy has been brilliantly applied by E. P. Thompson and James Scott to critique economism and high-light the values that have provoked sections of society (urban and rural respectively) to resort to political action and, more generally, behaviour which puts the long-term values of community before the short-term maximization of individual utility. The concept was useful in directing the attention of a generation of historians and social scientists to local norms underpinning the economic and political behaviour of 'underdog' sections of society. But there are dangers inherent in a term which, compared to other terms used to counter economism (such as *social* or *community*), so explicitly privileges the normative. Among the major difficulties are that elites have moral norms too, that the distribution of norms and values in any particular social context is complex, and that the norms of subaltern groups may often be invoked to legitimate actions far removed from the moral preferences of the analyst. E. P. Thompson could never really deal with the fact that the English working class was also strongly imbued with nationalist sentiments.

I have suggested that, even if he never used the term, Polanyi deserves to be viewed as the most sophisticated theoretician of the moral economy *writ large*. It is no accident that the current global crisis of capitalism has led many to rediscover his oeuvre (Dale 2010). However, when Polanyi wrote about the self-defence of 'society' in response to market disembedding, he too was referring to dominated groups rather than to a Durkheimian col-lectivity. Like Thompson, Polanyi had trouble recognizing that society's defences against the incursions of the market were not limited to the foundation of trade unions and friendly societies but included nationalist protectionism and an accompanying jingoism. An adequate updating of his theory of the 'double movement' in the context of global interconnectedness will have to address this issue.

As the Hungarian example showed, it is difficult to defend a pure Durkheimian position. Moral economy has proven useful in mounting critiques of the market and its lack of morality, but some citizens may sincerely believe that the market and private property offer the best moral guarantees available. Strongly held conventions of justice in small-scale rural communities, in which the greater part of the world's population still lives, may not only stifle and repress entrepreneurial energies; they may in some circumstances subvert due legal process and promote a punitive vigilantism. In urban contexts, too, for example when linking the concept of moral economy to the 'informal sector' (see *Informal Economy*), it is important not to idealize the concept; we need to be continuously alert to the fact that the very same norms which underpin resistance to the market and to rapacious power holders may also have repressive, destructive potential.

As a result of the dominance of the English language, the term moral economy has spread in recent decades into other languages (*économie morale*, *Moralökonomie* etc.). If it has not yet been widely taken up by French scholars, the reasons are not hard to perceive. Given the strength of the tradition of Durkheim and Mauss, which never ceased to define sociology as a moral discipline, not to mention the greater diversity of the economics community, France did not need the concept of moral economy to counter hegemonic utilitarian legacies. The works of Thompson, Scott and others who have followed them have a lot to offer non-Anglophone readers. But these authors would be the first to approve if such readers prefer to translate their central concept into local terms such as *économie solidaire*, and to deplore the proliferation of redundant Anglicisms. Moral economy deserves the space it has been allocated in this guide, but let us save it from academic reification.

Further reading

Abrahams, R. (1998) *Vigilant Citizens; Vigilantism and the State*. Polity, Cambridge.

Dale, G. (2010) *Karl Polanyi*. Polity, Cambridge.

Fassin, D. (2009) Les Économies morales revisitées. *Annales, Histoire, Sciences Sociales* 64 (6).

Hann, C. (2003) (With the 'Property Relations' Group) *The Postsocialist Agrarian Question: Property Relations and the Rural Condition*. LIT, Münster.

(2006) *Not the Horse We Wanted! Postsocialism, Neoliberalism and Eurasia*. LIT, Münster.

(2009) Embedded socialism? Land, labour, and money in eastern Xinjiang. In Hann, C. and Hart, K. (eds) *Market and Society: The Great Transformation Today*. Cambridge University Press, Cambridge, pp. 256–71.

Hann, C. and Hart, K. (2010) *Economic Anthropology: History, Ethnography, Critique*. Polity, Cambridge.

Polanyi, K. (1944) *The Great Transformation: The Political and Economic Origins of our Times.* Beacon, Boston.

Scott, J. (1976) *The Moral Economy of the Peasant: Rebellion and Subsistence in Southeast Asia.* Yale University Press, New Haven.

Thompson, E. P. (1991) *Customs in Common.* New Press, New York.

19

Communism

David Graeber

Communism may be divided into two chief varieties, which I will call 'mythic' and 'everyday' communism. They might as easily be referred to as 'ideal' and 'empirical' or even 'transcendent' and 'immanent' versions of communism.

Mythic Communism (with a capital C) is a theory of history, of a classless society that once existed and will, it is hoped, someday return again. It is notoriously messianic in its form. It also relies on a certain notion of totality: once upon a time there were tribes, some day there will be nations, organized entirely on communistic principles: that is, where 'society' – the totality itself – regulates social production and therefore inequalities of property will not exist.

Everyday communism (with a small c) can only be understood in contrast by rejecting such totalizing frameworks and examining everyday practice at every level of human life to see where the classic communistic principle of 'from each according to their abilities, to each according to their needs' is actually applied. As an expectation of mutual aid, communism in this sense can be seen as the foundation of all human sociality anywhere; as a principle of co-operation, it emerges spontaneously in times of crisis; as solidarity, it underlies almost all relations of social trust. Everyday communism then is not a larger regulatory body that co-ordinates all economic activity within a single 'society', but a principle that exists in and to some extent forms the necessary foundation of any society or human relations of any

kind. Even capitalism can be seen as a system for managing communism (although it is evidently in many ways a profoundly flawed one).
Let me take each of these in turn.

Mythic Communism

This is an idea of a society that either once existed or might exist at
some time in the future, which is free of all property divisions and
where all things are shared in common. Secondarily, it refers to social
experiments, often religious in inspiration, which try to recreate
such arrangements on a smaller scale in the present day. Finally, the
term has been applied more loosely to mass political movements or
regimes that aim to bring such a society about in the future.

Social movements that aimed to abolish all property divisions are
occasionally attested for the ancient world, from the Chinese 'School
of the Tillers' (c. 500 BCE) to Persian Mazdakites (c. 500 CE), as are
smaller sectarian groups (such as certain groups of Essenes) who
formed utopian communities based on communistic principles.
Owing to the very limited nature of our sources, it's extremely difficult to establish how common such movements really were, let
alone to get an accurate picture of their aims and ideologies. Most
of human history – especially the history of Africa, the Pacific and
the Americas – is simply lost to us. Yet these are precisely the parts
of the world where such movements are likely to have been most
widespread and successful. Many of the notoriously egalitarian societies of Amazonia and North America, for example, lived on lands
that, centuries earlier, had seen complex urban civilizations. Are they
better seen as refugees from the collapse of those civilizations or as
descendants of the rebels who overthrew them? If the latter, might
this suggest that their ideas and practices with regard to land, nature,
and property (which inspired many early European conceptions of
'primitive communism' in the first place) are themselves successful
revolutionary ideologies of generations past? It seems likely, but we
simply do not know. Even African hunter-gatherers like the !Kung,
Hadza or Pygmies, so often treated as living fossils of the Paleolithic,
or egalitarian pastoralists like the Nuer or Maasai, live in areas where
there have been farmers, states and kingdoms for thousands of
years. It is not at all clear how much their rejection of individualist
property regimes or, for that matter, anything else about their social
organization really resembles what was common in the Paleolithic or

how much they represent a self-conscious rejection of the values of surrounding populations.

To return to what we still like to call, for no particularly good reason, the 'Western tradition', the idea that property divisions have not always existed recurs often in ancient authors and seems to have been commonly held. It came to be enshrined in Roman Law through certain passages of Justinian's *Digest* which hold that property divisions are not based on the laws of nature but, like war, government, slavery and all forms of social inequality, arose only later through the *ius gentium* (law of nations) – essentially, the usages of war. These passages were widely discussed when Roman law was revived in twelfth-century Western Europe, where attempts were made to square them with biblical accounts of Eden and with the teachings of Jesus, the practices of the Apostles and the writings of some of the early Church Fathers (such as Saint Basil) who opposed the private ownership of wealth. The debate over 'apostolic poverty' that raged throughout the thirteenth century, most famously between the Franciscans and Dominicans, was above all about the legitimacy of private property itself and the feasibility of creating a society without it. Such arguments within the Church echoed those of popular religious movements – now remembered as 'heresies' – that became quite common during the later Middle Ages in Europe, many of which, like the Taborites, whose armies came to dominate much of Central Europe in the fifteenth century, were explicitly communist. Similar movements of religious communism emerged in early modern times, from the Diggers in England to the Anabaptists in Germany, almost always to be harshly suppressed by the authorities. One can find similar Christian communism reflected in movements such as the Taiping rebels who at certain times controlled substantial portions of nineteenth-century China.

It is a notorious feature of popular insurrections in traditional societies that they tend to appeal either to a utopian view of a past social order or to a messianic view of a future society shown by divine revelation or sometimes both. The idea that there was once a time when social divisions did not exist ('when Adam delved and Eva span, who then was the gentleman?') and that such a time will come again follows naturally from this messianic vision.

It is not surprising then that a similar historical vision often came to be invoked within the workers' movements of the nineteenth century. It was in this context that the word 'Communism' first came to be employed in its present sense, somewhere between 1835 and 1845. For Marx, Communism was the final end of revolutionary struggle, to be fully achieved only after an indeterminate political conflict, and while he argued that in one sense communism was already immanent in workers' present-day self-organization against capitalism, he saw that struggle as an ongoing process whose end simply could not be imagined using the bourgeois categories that existed in his day. Hence his notorious refusal to describe what communism might be like. In the one, famous instance where he even came close to such a description, in *The German Ideology*, he did not even attempt a science fiction vision but preferred to fall back on images clearly inspired by 'primitive communism' once more:

> As soon as the division of labour begins, each man has a particular, exclusive sphere of activity which is forced upon him and from which he cannot escape. He is a hunter, fisherman, shepherd or a critic and he must remain so if he does not want to lose his means of livelihood; whereas in communist society, where nobody has one exclusive sphere of activity but each can become accomplished in any branch he wishes, society regulates the general production and thus makes it possible for me to do one thing today and another tomorrow, to hunt in the morning, fish in the afternoon, rear cattle in the evening, criticize after dinner, just as I have a mind, without ever becoming a hunter, fisherman, shepherd, or critic.

Obviously all this is in a manner of speaking; Marx was not suggesting that after the revolution most people would actually spend their time occupied mainly in hunting and fishing – although he might have used those examples in order to suggest that, under communism, the artificial division we make between (painful) work and (pleasurable) leisure would no longer make much sense. His real point here is that what we call 'private property', 'the division of labour' and 'social inequality' are all ultimately the same thing; and a free society, therefore, could only be one that abolishes all three of them. This is why he insisted that under Communism we would become, as he put it, a Species Being, defined only by our common humanity, rather than being split into different sorts of person who do different things. A practical manifestation of this would have to be one where we are all free to move back and forth between roles – even, apparently, gender roles, since Marx begins his discussion of the division of labour with the division between men and women – but, by appealing to an obviously fanciful primitive vision, Marx intentionally avoids even speculating about how this might actually work out.

Above all, for Marx, Communism meant overcoming the alienation produced by property regimes, whereby our own deeds return to us in strange unrecognizable forms, making it impossible for human beings to create together a world that we might actually wish to live in:

> *Communism* as the *positive* transcendence of *private property* as *human self-estrangement*, and therefore as the real *appropriation* of the *human* essence by and for man; communism therefore as the complete return of man to himself as a *social* (i.e. human) being – a return accomplished consciously and embracing the entire wealth of previous development. This communism, as fully developed naturalism, equals humanism, and as fully developed humanism equals naturalism; it is the *genuine* resolution of the conflict between man and nature and between man and man – the true resolution of the strife between existence and essence, between objectification and self-confirmation, between freedom and necessity, between the individual and the species. Communism is the riddle of history solved, and it knows itself to be this solution.

After the release of Marx and Engels' *Manifesto of the Communist Party* in 1848, the word came to be almost indelibly identified with their specific political project, and the equally specific theoretical analysis of class, capitalism, labour and exploitation on which it was built. Nonetheless, it took some time before 'communist' simply became a word for a kind of Marxist. For instance, the term 'libertarian communist' was often used as a synonym for 'anarchist.' During much of the nineteenth century, references to 'communists' in mainstream literature most probably referred neither to Marxists nor to anarchists but simply to proponents and creators of communes or similar utopian experiments – 'intentional communities' as they would be called today – a form of political action almost uniformly disdained by Marxists. A good example of this usage is Charles Nordhoff's famous study, *The Communistic Societies of the United States*, published in 1875. This usage of 'communism' never completely went away, and has returned in essays like *Call* and *The Coming Insurrection* by the 'Invisible Committee' today, where 'communism' is used to refer simply to the internal organization of communes.

With the success of the Russian revolution this emphasis did largely change, and over the course of the twentieth century 'Communism' has been used more and more to refer to the ideology of Communist

Parties and then, by extension, to what came to be known by their opponents in the Cold War as 'Communist regimes'. As a result, for many, if not most of the world's population, 'Communism' has come to mean 'that economic system that prevailed under the command economies of the former Soviet Union and its allies, Maoist China, and other Marxist regimes.' There is a profound historical irony here, since none of those regimes ever claimed to have actually achieved Communism as they themselves defined it. They referred to their own systems rather as 'socialist' – embodying a transitional period of the dictatorship of proletariat that would only be transformed into actual Communism at some unspecified point in the future, when technological advance, greater education and prosperity would eventually lead to the withering away of the state.

Everyday communism

The phrase 'actually existing socialism' was coined as a term of critique: socialist revolutionaries talked incessantly about regimes they wished to create, but in almost no case wished their visions to be judged by the actual achievements of regimes that referred to themselves as 'socialist'. This raises the question: is it possible to speak of 'actually existing' communism? If we view things within a statist framework and look for some unit which can be designated a 'society' organized on communistic principles, then clearly the answer would have to be no. However this is not the only possible approach. I prefer to identify a principle that, in combination with others, can be found in all human societies to a variable degree. Because of its mundane character, making it almost invisible to the normal gaze, I call it 'everyday communism'.

In order to do so, it seems best to start from the classical definition of communism – 'from each according to their abilities, to each according to their needs' – and then examine those forms of organization or human relationships that are organized according to that principle, wherever one happens to find them. The origin of this phrase, incidentally, is interesting. It is widely, but incorrectly attributed to Karl Marx. It appears to have been a slogan current in the French workers' movement in the first decades of the nineteenth century; and it first appears in print in a book called *L'Organisation du travail* by the socialist agitator Louis Blanc in 1839. Blanc used it to describe the organizational principles of the 'social workshops' he wished the government to set up as a new basis for industry.

like asking for a light or even a cigarette. In such cases the costs of providing are clearly considered to be so minimal that we comply without even thinking about it. The same is true if another person's need – even a stranger's – is spectacular and extreme: if they are drowning, for example. If a child has fallen into the subway tracks, we assume anyone who is capable of helping them up will do so.

I call this 'baseline communism', the understanding that, unless people consider themselves so completely inimical to one another and if the need is considered great enough or the cost reasonable enough, the principle of 'from each according to their abilities, to each according to their needs' will apply. Of course, different communities apply very different standards to the question of what is a reasonable need: in an impersonal urban environment it might be limited to lights and directions; in many human societies, a direct request for food or some other item of common consumption may be impossible to refuse. This is especially true of the most ordinary, everyday sorts of food, which in many societies, for this very reason, become ways of maintaining social boundaries: as for instance in many European and Middle Eastern societies where blood-feuds prevailed, men would hesitate to eat bread and salt with a potential rivals because, if they did, it would no longer be permissible to harm such a person.

Sharing food is indeed still considered to be the foundation of morality, but of course it's also one of the chief forms of pleasure (who would really want to eat a delicious meal by themselves?). Feasts are in most places seen as the apex of sociability. The elaborate games, contests, pageants and performances that mark a popular festival, are, like the structures of exchange that characterize society itself, built on top of a kind of communistic base. In this case the experience of shared conviviality is not only the moral basis of society but also its most fundamental source of pleasure. Solitary pleasures will always exist no doubt, but for most human beings, even now, the most pleasurable activities almost usually involve sharing something: music, food, liquor, drugs, gossip, drama, bed. There is thus a certain communism of the senses at the root of most things we consider fun.

Conclusions

The sociology of everyday communism is a potentially enormous field, but one which, owing to our peculiar ideological blinkers, we have been unable to write because we have been largely unable to see the object. Marcel Mauss for instance spoke of 'individualistic communism', such as exists between close kin such as mothers and their children, usually siblings, but also between close friends or blood brothers. In this sense any 'society' might be imagined as threaded by endless communistic networks. In such relationships, everything might be shared if the need arises. In other relations between individuals, each is limited to only a certain kind of claim on the other: to help them repair their fishnets, aid them in war, or provide cattle for a wedding feast. Still these can be considered communistic if the claim can be exercised whenever there is a need. Similarly, there are groups within which all members can make certain unlimited claims of this sort when in need: mutual aid societies, mutual insurance associations, and the like. Modern insurance firms are, ironically, commercial transformations of an essentially communist principle. Finally any self-organized social group, from a corporation to a football club to a religious confraternity, will have particular rules about which sorts of things must be shared, and about collective access to their common resources. This of course shades into the literature on the collective management of the commons, but it's important to note that often, social groups (starting with clans, villages, or the like) will make entirely artificial rules to create mutual communistic dependence. Anthropologists for example are familiar with the existence of moiety structures, where a community divides itself into two arbitrary divisions, each of which must rely on the other to build their houses, provide ritual services, or bury each other's dead, purely whenever the other has a need.

Communistic relations exist in endless variety, but two common characteristics always leap to the fore. The first is that they are not based on calculation. It would never occur to one side of an Iroquois village, for example, to complain that they had buried six of the other side's dead this year and the other side had only buried two of theirs. This would be insane. When keeping accounts seems insane in this way, we are in the presence of communism. The reason it seems so is because everyone must die and the two sides of the village will always presumably be there to bury one another's dead, so keeping accounts is obviously pointless. This brings out the second point: unlike exchange, where debts can be cancelled out immediately, or in the relatively short term, communism is based on the presumption of eternity. One can act communistically with those one treats *as if* they will always exist, just as society will always exist, even if (as with, say, our mothers) we know at a more cerebral level that this is not really true.

We might thus analyse human relations as tending to take one of three forms: communistic relations, hierarchical relations, or relations of exchange. Exchange is based on principles of reciprocity, but this means that either relations are cancelled out immediately (as in the market, when there is immediate payment), or eventually, when a gift is returned or a debt repaid. Human relations based on exchange are inherently temporary, but egalitarian at least in the sense that when the payment is made, the two parties return to equal status. Hierarchy is not based on a principle of reciprocal exchange but rather of precedent: if one gives a gift to a superior or inferior, one is likely to be expected to do it again under similar circumstances. Hierarchy resembles communism in that it is assumed to be permanent, and therefore tends not to involve the calculation of accounts; except that communism, of course, tends to be resolutely egalitarian in its basis.

Several radical implications follow. I will end with one. If we accept this definition, it gives us a new perspective on capitalism. It is one way of organizing communism. Any widely distributed economic principle must be a way of organizing communism, since co-operation and the trust intrinsic to baseline sociality will always be the foundations of human economy and society. The question for those of us who feel capitalism is a bad way of organizing communism or even an ultimately unsustainable one is what would a more just way of organizing communism look like? One specifically that would discourage the tendency of communistic relations to slide into forms of hierarchy. There are grounds for believing that the more creative the form of labour, the more egalitarian the forms of co-operation will tend to be. So perhaps the key question is: how might we contrive more egalitarian and creative forms of human co-operation that are less hierarchical and stultifying than those we currently know?

Further reading

Blanc, L. (1839) *L'Organisation du travail*. Au Bureau de Nouveau Monde, Paris. [First to say 'from each according to their abilities, to each according to their needs']

Cohn, N. (1972) *The Pursuit of the Millennium: Revolutionary Millenarians and Mystical Anarchists of the Middle Ages.* Oxford University Press, New York. [A classic, but critical approach to medieval communistic movements]

Dawson, D. (1992) *Cities of the Gods: Communist Utopias in Greek Thought.* Oxford University Press, Oxford. [Good summary for the ancient world]

Graeber, D. (2010) *Debt: The First Five Thousand Years.* Melville House, New York. [Contains chapter on everyday communism in its various manifestations]

Invisible Committee, The (2004) *Call.* US Committee to Support the Tarnac 9, New York. [Contemporary reassertion of 'communism' as communalism]

Kropotkin, P. (1902) *Mutual Aid: A Factor of Evolution.* William Heinemann, London. [Classic anarcho- communism, Kropotkin's 'mutual aid' is close to 'everyday communism']

Marx, K. and Engels, F. (1846 [1970]) *The German Ideology.* International Publishers, New York.

Marx, K. and Engels, F. (1848 [1998]) *Manifesto of the Communist Party.* Penguin, New York.

Mauss, M. (1990 [1925]) *The Gift: Form and Reason of Exchange in Archaic Societies.* Routledge, London. [Mauss's classic essay introduces the idea of 'total reciprocity', which is small-c communism]

Morgan, L. H. (1965 [1881]) *Houses and House-Life of the American Aborigines.* University of Chicago Press, Chicago. [Influential ethnography of communal living, especially for Engels]

Nordhoff, C. (1875) *The Communistic Societies of the United States.* Harper and Brothers, New York. [Especially good on religious societies]

Priestland, D. (2006) *The Red Flag: Communism and the Making of the Modern World.* Allen Lane, London. [The standard recent scholarly history]

Testart, A. (1985) *Le Communisme primitif.* Maison des Sciences de l'Homme, Paris. [The best recent version of old-fashioned 'primitive communism']

Part IV

Beyond Market and State

20

The Third Sector

Catherine Alexander

Definition

The simplest and most common definition of the third sector is that it is not part of the government, any profits are usually reinvested for social, environmental or cultural aims, and participation is largely voluntary. The term indicates a space for social, economic and political activities that offer an alternative to both state command and free-market economies. Although the term has only been in vogue since the late 1980s, it has enjoyed popularity on the right and left wings of politics alike. What marks the third sector out from other alternative economies is that it includes organizations with links to government, the market and communities, whether these relationships are conceived of as intermediary or oppositional. But even this minimal definition is up for debate. There are two broad schools of thought and policy, based on different understandings of the third sector. In part, these differences can be explained by examining the specific legal frameworks and histories of third-sector activities by country and region.

The North American approach, typified by Salomon and Anheier, takes the third sector to be synonymous with non-profit organizations, focuses solely on economic activities and assumes the third sector 'exists with some meaningful degree of independence from the state and the corporate sector'. Based on these assumptions, the

Johns Hopkins Civil Society research project has been scoping the economic activities of non-profit groups worldwide. In 2007, *The New York Times* suggested that a fourth sector was on the rise, marked by integrating business, or profit-orientated methods, with social purposes. The unique selling point of this latest sector is apparently the combination of financial and social capital with philanthropic or re-investment aims. This hybrid form, however, only appears completely new if the American designation of the third sector is used.

European scholars have vigorously criticized this definition. At the core of the disagreement is an insistence that history should be taken into account. This changes the landscape dramatically; and three key differences from the North American classification immediately become apparent. First, in defining third-sector organizations, European legislatures have long been more concerned with the legal status of beneficiaries than with the generation of profit *per se*. Thus, legally, the European third sector also covers organizations that aim to meet the social and financial needs of their members. The distinction here therefore is not between profit and non-profit making groups, but between maximizing returns for individual investors and collective or mutual benefit. In Europe, co-operatives, mutuals, associations, foundations and charities are all part of the third sector; in America they are not. This is why, in Europe, the term 'third sector' often appears to be the same as the 'social economy' or 'sustainable economy' and is sometimes theorized as being in opposition to capitalist economies.

A second feature of European research is that, far from characterizing the third sector as distinct from state and market, it is taken to be integrated with politics, the market, local communities and households, to different degrees. Evers and Laville suggest that this allows third-sector economic activity to be seen as a pluralist hybrid of market, non-market (e.g. redistribution by the welfare state) and non-monetary (based on reciprocity) forms of economy. Moreover, this awareness that the third sector overlaps with other domains means that, in addition to its economic significance, it can be seen as an important site for political resistance, social research and campaigning. This holds true beyond the European region.

A third feature is that traditions of third-sector organizations are markedly different from one country to another as a result of specific socio-economic and political histories, public policies and legal frameworks. One theoretical response has been to generate nuanced taxonomies of such organizations and to stress how they change over time. What this kind of history gives us is a sense of long European traditions combining collective action, mutual aid and welfare economies provided by a mixture of churches, local and central government and private philanthropy.

Different traditions within Europe show varying attitudes towards the state and relations between the state and popular organizations. Thus the French *économie solidaire* stresses mutualism and the communal economy (see *Solidarity Economy*); Italian *associationismo* acts as a local counterweight to the power of state and church; in Germany, the tradition of *subsidiarity* provides a framework for the relationship between the state and third sector in the provision of social services; in Sweden social movements tend to make demands on the social democratic state and legislature rather than providing social services themselves; and the British welfare system is a mixed economy of nationalized health care, with both local government and charities providing social services. The 'pragmatic patchwork' of British welfare has its roots in the medieval period. A 'private third sector' has emerged in Latin America where public universities are increasingly being displaced by privately funded social science research and policy units.

Just as each country's third sector has its unique traits, so too do national politics and law pose particular challenges to the operation of these groups. The extent of the German Catholic charity Caritas' operations, for example, appears to contravene anti-monopoly legislation. In one view, the European Union offers a supranational space that allows organizations to side-step such national restrictions. Such a shift of direction could support the creation of a genuinely European civil society. Some organizations answering to the broad definition of the third sector given above, such as Greenpeace or the Red Cross, already operate on an international scale. The main difference is that these promote universal versions of the public good and make no claim for legitimacy from being embedded in and responsive to local society, as many third-sector groups do.

The third sector therefore acts as an umbrella term for a range of enterprises that differ according to local contexts and histories. It draws on ideas of social capital and community action emphasizing the common good (see *Social Capital* and *Community Participation*). It is commonly confused with the voluntary or community sector, social economy and social enterprise (see *Social Enterprise* and *Solidarity*

Economy). Nevertheless, the term has real force in that government and supra-state institutions, such as the European Union, promote, fund and engage with the idea of the third sector, thereby endowing it with considerable instrumental potency.

The micro-politics of interactions between the third sector, public institutions and private firms are, however, still under-researched. This is of relevance both where the third sector is established, and in areas, such as the former Soviet Union, where it is being promoted, alongside a market economy, as an essential plank in building democratic societies. Frequently, generic ideal models of both the third sector and a free market have been exported, irrespective of local conditions and histories, often with poor or disastrous results. The third sector does, however, play a notable role in assisting and advising migrants across the former Soviet space. Attention to the past thus needs to be complemented by awareness of current transformations to the roles and functions of states and markets. As these change, often becoming more closely linked in the provision of public services, so too the third sector changes its forms and operations.

History

The history of the third sector may be considered in two parts: the emergence of the term; and the development of activities and organizations that came to be subsumed under it.

The idea of a third sector originated in the United States during the 1970s, where it was used by Amitai Etzioni and others in public policy and management studies to think about emerging economic and organizational forms in a post-industrial context. The term then lapsed until it was rediscovered and championed in Europe during the late 1980s. This renaissance mirrored a shift in emphasis within the development industry from top-down projects towards grass-roots initiatives conceived of in terms of a more distributed model of governance (see *Development* and *NGOs*). It also coincided with the rise of New Public Management (NPM), which endorsed market principles for running state assets and services, outsourcing many such services to private firms or the third sector.

The initial interest in voluntary work was twofold. Etzioni drew up a taxonomy of why individuals engage with different kinds of organization, suggesting that, whereas the state has coercive power and the market negotiates agreements, voluntary groups function through shared values and consensual decisionmaking. At a more inclusive level, the third sector was thought to be the most effective way of providing services that contribute to the public good (education, health and welfare), when these were not profitable enough to attract businesses and might be entangled in bureaucracy if left to government. Etzioni also mentioned pollution in this context, even though environmental issues only became a common third-sector concern in the late 1990s. From the beginning, broad-brush characterizations of the state, market and third sector were employed that are still commonplace. The state's role, in this view, is to ensure the public good, but it is burdened by red tape; the market is efficient, but seeks only to maximize shareholder value; the third sector unites the best of both worlds: efficiency and public interest. Of course, these pure types leave out a lot of social complexity. Although Etzioni stressed that the third sector could deliver public services effectively, others pointed out that it also provided an arena for social activism.

The context for a revival of the concept from the late 1980s was a wider move away from state provision of services. The 'Washington Consensus', which was taken at the time, and since, to be a blueprint for neoliberal globalization (see *Alter-Globalization*), formalized the shift from excessive reliance on government to reliance on the market and individual responsibility. Typically associated with conditions attached to IMF loans to poor countries ('structural adjustment'), this shopping list of privatization and deregulation was also applied within the global North, most enthusiastically by the United States and Britain. The end of the Cold War appeared to sanction such a move away from state control.

Understanding the context of the 1990s and after is essential for grasping the nature of the third sector today. Change was not only quantitative but qualitative. With the retraction of the state in many regions of the world, together with the displacement of much industry to the global South, unemployment for manual labour rose. The growth of service and cultural sectors in place of smoke-stack industries went hand-in-hand with a modification of the voluntary sector's gender and class composition. More men began to enter what had been traditionally a sector dominated by middle-class women. At the same time, the ageing populations of the global North generated growing demand for support services.

The European Union's enthusiasm for the third sector took off

with the 1989 Delors Commission which established the Social
Economy Unit, followed by the 2001 White Paper on European
Governance, where civil society was identified as the key mechanism
for bringing together the EU and its citizens. But particular national
instances have been shoe-horned into a one-size model for the purpose of policy and endorsement. Thus, even within the EU, various
terminologies proliferate. 'Private non-profit institutions serving
households', 'NGOs', 'non-profit sector', 'non-profit associations'
and 'voluntary organizations' and 'voluntary organizations and foundations for the third sector' are all used in European discourse for the
third sector; while 'third system', 'social economy', *économie solidaire*
and most recently CMAFs (co-operatives, mutuals, associations and
foundations) also refer to it, often without qualification. One result
is that it can be hard for third-sector organizations to know how to
steer their way through Brussels funding agencies without resorting
to intermediary bodies, which then become an additional bureaucratic layer.

A historical perspective further gives a sense of how certain
activities have moved from one area to another. In Europe, many
schools and hospitals were originally set up by the third sector. In
the mid-twentieth century most education and health functions
were managed by the state. In the last twenty years, many services (e.g. education, health, waste management and prisons) have
changed hands again to be managed by third-sector or private firms.
Withdrawal of state-provided services has been undertaken at various speeds, with correspondingly different levels of involvement of
the third sector. While debate continues in Europe over how far the
third sector should complement or replace state services, it should be
noted that in Zimbabwe, church missions provide two-thirds of all
hospital beds in rural areas, while in Zambia the third sector – which
is mostly church-based – provides almost half the health services in
rural areas.

Two theories seek to account for the emergence of the third
sector. The first, echoing the North American approach, casts the
third sector as a distinct area of activity that arose in response to the
failure of both state and market to provide for welfare needs. The
second, European version frames the development of a third way or
sector as part of the expansion of modern democratic states, where
a range of public spheres, or civil society, plays an active role. From
the start, the relationship with public institutions was vital, whether

third-sector organizations sought co-operation with the state or an alternative base for political action. Power and the history of local political configurations are therefore central to this version of the European third sector.

This is well illustrated by the distinction between what would now be called third-sector activities in nineteenth-century England and France. In the former, philanthropy and charity were morally endorsed objectives, the wealthier members of society contributing in a private capacity to help the poor. The legislative framework supported the autonomous creation of such organizations to assist a distinct class of beneficiaries. In France, an emphasis on communal solidarity after the Revolution led rather to the establishment of mutual aid associations and workers' co-operatives. The French model has dominated the EU's categorization of the third sector as co-operatives, mutuals, associations and foundations. In the twentieth century many mutual organizations, such as trade unions, became enervated or were increasingly integrated into the market economy.

Evers and Laville suggest a further typology of amalgamations involving state, market and third-sector enterprises. Scandinavian universalism gives primacy to the state's redistributive function with the third sector mainly lobbying for social demands, such as childcare. In liberal systems, such as Britain, state assistance is provided for the most socially deprived section of the population, supplemented by third-sector services. Italy, Spain and Portugal focus on state monetary transfers rather than services, but access may be hindered by clientelist bureaucracies. In the corporatist regimes of Germany, Austria, France and Belgium many public welfare and infrastructural services are provided by associations, closely regulated and largely funded by the state. Even so, any emphasis on the historical emergence of the third sector still needs to be complemented by detailed empirical accounts of how this hybrid sector operates.

Activities

The traditional focus of third-sector activity has been on social welfare, encompassing education, housing, health and social justice. In the Anglo-Saxon context, this has been extended in the last two decades to cover infrastructural services such as community waste management. Support for the unemployed now ranges from provision of basic necessities to giving work experience or re-skilling people for a changed work environment. This accords with the Anglophone political mantra in the last decade that welfare should not be an end in itself but should channel people back to work.

This is not as straightforward as it might appear. In the first place, voluntary labour can be classed both as a gift of time and effort and as a rehabilitative process producing the active, responsible citizen demanded by neoliberal ideology. Second, some who participate in voluntary work for the latter purpose are either unable or unwilling to rejoin the mainstream labour market. Third, the classification of activities by surveys and funding bodies often artificially separates fields that are merged in practice. Thus a faith-based organization that collects and passes on second-hand clothes and furniture to those in need may be staffed by a mixture of paid workers and volunteers. The latter group may comprise workers from religious institutions, people who prefer community to mainstream work, mandatory placements of unemployed people, young people on work training schemes and prisoners assigned to learn new skills. The combination of all these kinds of workers affects the delivery of social services, health and education, as well as having consequences for employment and the environment.

The diffuse nature and effects of third-sector activities can make government funding problematic; in the context of NPM ideology, devolved government budgets demand value for money in the supply of narrowly defined services. The broader and longer-term benefits of activities often go unmarked, while services appear to be more expensive than those offered by a commercial firm supplying a single product. Such difficulties in accounting for services provided can result in third-sector organizations subsidizing state institutions. Again, where government contracts are informed by the principles of NPM, third-sector organizations must present themselves and perform as firms with a robust financial turnover in order to be competitive and allow governments to demonstrate transparency and public accountability. It is only through detailed examination of the interactions between third-sector organizations, state institutions and corporate bodies that these kinds of micro-politics begin to emerge.

Scope

Despite its heterogeneity, attempts to aggregate the sector in terms of its economic value, employment or the range of activities undertaken are common. This has, however, been hampered by the lack of reliable statistics before the 1990s and by the ephemeral nature of many organizations. The justification for scoping the third sector is often because its vitality is seen as an indicator of the health of the economy, rather than society. The Johns Hopkins project aimed to analyse the extent, structure, financing and impact of non-profit activities in forty-six countries. Apart from quantitative assessments and comparisons, the project also has detailed country reports. In 2007, for example, the project reported that Canada's non-profit organizations accounted for nearly eight per cent of the country's GDP, exceeding each of agriculture, mining, oil and gas extraction, retail trade, accommodations and food services and motor vehicle manufacture. The project estimated that an average of ten per cent of the adult population in thirty-six developed and developing countries volunteer labour. For the thirty-six developed countries, the total value of this labour in 1995–2000 was estimated to be $3 billion. Christopher Gunn suggests that non-profit corporations, co-operatives and credit unions together make up ten per cent of economic activity in the United States. On average, the European third sector expanded by 20–30 per cent between 1990 and 1995.

Many third-sector schemes rely heavily on government funding. The Johns Hopkins project shows that government support for third-sector operations in developed countries provides over a third of their revenue, while for developing countries it is a sixth. One result of the NPM approach has been less public money available for the third sector in Europe, particularly in Germany and France where public funding has long been the main source of its revenue. This has led to increased competition with private sector companies. In Britain, by contrast, the amount directed towards third-sector organizations has risen along with more severe divestment of state services. The emphasis here, in line with NPM, is on start-up rather than continuation funding and the ability to demonstrate the financial value of contracted deliveries of services. Third-sector funding in Latin America is markedly different. Non-profit organizations in Argentina, Columbia, Peru, Brazil and Mexico all source over 60 per cent of their funds from selling services. The Catholic church is arguably the largest third-sector organization anywhere in terms of its social welfare activities. Caritas alone has 350,000 employees. Again, the legislative and tax systems of each country contribute to making the third sector's size and revenue highly variable. Tax breaks for charitable donations in the US, for example, are conducive to a higher figure than would be likely otherwise.

As has been observed for NGOs (see *NGOs*), normative accounts at a high level of abstraction predominate rather than studies of micro-politics and local contexts, so that it is hard to compare the value of each country's third sector without taking specific contexts into account. Nevertheless, it is still of interest to account for the growth of economic activity that does not fit neatly into either public or private sectors, especially when the prevailing neoliberal ideology applauds self-determination and an abridged state. Whatever the method of calculation, the third sector is clearly significant both economically and as an idea for organizing or mobilizing society.

Conclusion: critiques and possibilities

The current enthusiasm for the third sector on the part of the powers is remarkable. In common with NGOs, it has been imagined as an all-round 'magic bullet' for social and economic woes. The truth is, as always, more complicated. This last section discusses both common criticisms of the third sector and its positive features, showing that they are often two sides of the same coin.

A key strength of third-sector groups is that they are often rooted in locality and community and can act as intermediaries between households, state and market enterprises (see *Fair Trade* and *Local Development*). This emphasis on local economies and 'closing the loop' locally, may counteract the effects of flexible capitalism and post-industrial urban ghettos. Locally provided service provision is arguably more responsive to needs. Certainly, in forming alliances with the third-sector, governments emphasize its grassroots legitimacy, creativity and ability to kick-start local economic development drawing on social capital. Civic values are reinforced. Household economies are supported through sharing labour. Economic and social domains are reunited. Mutual trust and commitment to common endeavours are established.

Thus, what distinguishes the third sector from the polar extremes of state and market is considered to be its morality and effectiveness. The first draws on the long-term, reproductive moralities of kin, household and locality in contrast to the rapacity of market relations focused on short-term individual profit maximization. This stresses the recuperative capacity of the third sector both for individuals and as a social counterweight to the market; the virtues of care and mutuality can restore social equilibrium to a world out of joint. Further, local knowledge of communities means that the third sector is best placed to know how and where effort should be directed for the public good.

This is undoubtedly true, but needs qualification. The assumption that local communities are always homogeneous is dubious (see *Moral Economy*). This poses difficulties for organizations claiming to represent disparate groups that happen to be in the same place; neither the public good nor the local good are clear cut. Representation is less of a problem for mutual aid societies or associations whose members elect to join them. Nevertheless, there have been calls from within and outside the third sector for more attention to governance, accountability and transparency. The emergence of a third sector in the former Soviet Union has often been marked by an elite membership which is not in touch with its purported constituencies. The efficacy of local empowerment can turn out to be practically empty in the absence of capacity to provide basic needs. The complementary value of the third sector, in other words, should not be mistaken for fundamental infrastructural provision.

The very strength and unique position of the third sector, situated between community, market and state, can also generate delicate tensions. Reliance on government or supra-government funding may, in many cases, compromise the sector's independence. For example, when government bureaucracies, as the main source of funding in many cases, insist on competitive commercial criteria when assessing the capacity of third-sector organizations, they are often placed at a disadvantage. The result is that third-sector groups contractually yoked to the state must often learn to demonstrate long-term financial viability, value for money in narrow service areas and continuation strategies, all the while absorbing risks that contribute to the high turnover of establishments in this sector. Again, the potential advantage of occupying an intermediate space also makes the third sector vulnerable to economic downturns as government funding and private philanthropy are reduced. Championing the virtues of the third sector is all very well but, without understanding and acknowledging the complexity of their operations on the ground, their very viability can be threatened.

The range of third-sector forms and relations to state, market and community is such that generalizations concerning the value of the third sector are suspect. This is exacerbated if we take into account the convergence and interdependence of all three sectors in contemporary neoliberal societies. A moral middle ground between state and market, the impersonal twins that gave us the Cold War, has often proven to be easier to identify as an idea than as social practice; and this may account for the overlapping terminologies that seek to define it, of which the third sector is currently the leading candidate.

Further reading

Alexander, C. (2009) Illusions of freedom: Polanyi and the third sector. In Hann, C. and Hart, K. (eds) *Market and Society: The Great Transformation Today*. Cambridge University Press, pp. 221–39.

Anheier, H. (2002) The third sector in Europe: five theses. *Civil Society Working Paper* 12, Centre for Civil Society, London School of Economics.

Bridge, S., Murtagh, B. and O'Neill, K. (2008) *Understanding the Social Economy and the Third Sector*. Palgrave Macmillan.

Etzioni, A. (1973) The third sector and domestic missions. *Public Administration Review* 33 (3), 314–23.

Evers, A. and Laville, J.-L. (2004) *The Third Sector in Europe*. Edward Elgar, Cheltenham.

Gunn, C. (2004) *Third Sector Development: Making up for the Market?* Cornell University Press.

Hemment, J. (2004) The riddle of the third sector: civil society, international aid, and NGOs in Russia. *Anthropological Quarterly* 77 (2), 215–41.

Levy, D. (1996) *Building the Third Sector: Latin America's Private Research Centers and Nonprofit Development*. University of Pittsburgh Press.

Salomon, L. and Anheier, H. (1997) *Defining the Nonprofit Sector: A Cross-National Analysis*. Manchester University Press.

Salomon, L., Wojcieck, S. and List, R. (2003) *Global Civil Society: An Overview*. The Johns Hopkins Comparative Non-Profit Sector Project.

21

Solidarity Economy (*Économie solidaire*)

Jean-Louis Laville

Since the 1980s, there has been renewed interest in organizations that are neither public nor private for-profit initiatives. These organizations are most often referred to as the 'third sector'. The North-American approach – that adopted by the Johns Hopkins Project – which is dominant at the international level, defines this third sector as one grouping together all non-profit organizations. But European experience has given birth to another theoretical approach, defining the third sector as a social and solidarity economy. This contribution aims to present and explain the European conception and to confront the North American one with it in order to stimulate international debate.

Criticisms of the non-profit approach

This emphasis on non-profit organizations is based on the perspective of neoclassical economics which understands them in terms of market failure in the provision of individual services and state failure in the provision of collective services. In these approaches to the economy, often referred to as 'theories of institutional choice', the aim is to explain why the market, the state or the non-profit sector are resorted to. This approach supposes a separation between these three 'sectors' and a hierarchy among them, the non-profit sector being a second- or third-rank option when the solutions provided by the market and the state prove inadequate.

The first criticism concerns the status of the non-profit criterion. The theory of institutional choice makes the non-profit constraint autonomous and takes this constraint as a privileged channel of the trust provided by non-profit organizations to users of their services. But this is not the only way to generate trust; standards adopted by for-profit organizations can do so also. Other means are available to all types of organization (ethical codes, certifications, labels . . .), as various studies have confirmed. It is consequently difficult to perceive when and why the non-profit constraint proves decisive in the decisions made by the individuals concerned. Adverse selection and moral risk exist in many activities and may indicate market difficulties. These characteristics did not prevent the development of markets in many instances, such as consultancy services for firms or professional services; but the market, in such cases, is a network-market, typically for high-quality goods and services, and a market for organizations, where customers do not choose this or that product or service, but the organization (consultancy firm, hospital centre, . . .) that provides it because the latter is well known and well positioned. The limits of the orthodox market model may thus be overcome by markets based on rules of quality and institutional guarantees.

The second criticism relates to the weak explanation given for setting up non-profit organizations. What is detailed are the reasons why users or donors resort to non-profit organizations, but the implicit statement is that of their pre-existence, making it possible for non-profit organizations to be chosen. The disinterestedness of promoters of non-profit organizations, which clearly manifests itself in the non-distribution constraint, is supposed to generate trust and to explain the individual economic interest of consumers who then resort to these organizations to optimize their satisfaction. This theoretical dead-end is brought to its extreme by the economic theory of altruism, which shows how disinterestedness itself is economically rational and constitutes, in sum, a form of realization of the individual interest, the satisfaction resulting from the fact to help others being introduced in the utility function of the consumer.

The third criticism is the focus on a narrow range of interests with regard to service provision. They reduce all human decisions to rational choices framed by instrumental behaviour, i.e. behaviours oriented towards the result of action; this leads, as Etzioni (1988) put it, to denying the existence of society. Society, in this perspective, is only the result of individual choices oriented towards interests and individuals are considered only as consumers. Their decisions tend to maximize their advantages. The role of organizations is thus only perceived through their function of providing services; other dimensions are not taken into account. The issues of social integration and democratic participation are overlooked. Some of these utilitarian theories can even go so far as to interpret rich and complex cultural legacies as a hindrance to logical decisions or as data of less importance than efficiency in provision.

The fourth criticism relates to how the sectors are conceptualized which authorizes a functional and pacified version of the relations between the market, the state and non-profit organizations. An approach through market and state failures can obviously be used ideologically when the non-profit sector is summoned to justify the withdrawal of the state. The shift towards a valorization of civil society as an alternative to state intervention can thus follow on the heels of a theory of rational choice in which the agents choose among the market, the state and non-profit solutions.

The fifth criticism relates to the implicit hierarchy contained in the theory of institutional choice. The latter does not content itself with considering the market, the state and non-profit organizations as distinct entities and with placing them in separate compartments; it goes further by putting forward an analytical grid in which the market and the state are apprehended as the pillars of society and non-profit organizations as a complement. As underlined by Godbout, according to this approach, 'the market and the State represent the normal way to circulate goods and services' and if the state can be replaced by non-profit organizations, it is because the latter succeeds to the former, because the state has failed in its task of protection by falling into bureaucracy.

But such a conception is invalidated by history, associationism having pre-existed public intervention – hence the necessary shift towards conceptions based on other prerequisites, which do not overlook a history more than two centuries long. In this regard, a historical rather than hypothetico-deductive approach, based on the European reality, allows us to develop two complementary conceptions: the social economy and the solidarity economy.

A European approach: the social economy

The notion of social economy as it is understood in Europe defines a set of organizations that is broader than the non-profit sector in the North American approach. The latter excludes co-operatives and mutual societies on the grounds that they distribute part of their profits to their members; but such an exclusion cannot be justified in the European context. First, some co-operatives, such as building co-operatives in Sweden, have never distributed any profits. Secondly, the distribution of profits is in all cases limited, since co-operatives and mutual societies have their roots in the same ground as associations: they are not created with the goal of obtaining a return on capital invested, but with one of satisfying the general or mutual interest, to contribute to public welfare or to meet social demands made by some sections of the population.

A definition according to the limit placed on profit-making

In Europe, the struggles of the nineteenth century led to compromises legalizing the existence of organizations in which a class of agents other than investors had property rights. The legal forms so recognized (co-operatives, mutual societies, associations) define a set of social economy organizations in which a ban on the distribution on profits is not the decisive criterion, but rather the material interest of investors is subject to limits. Consequently, the boundary is not between for-profit and non-profit organizations, but between capitalist and social economy organizations, the latter giving priority to a shared patrimony over returns to individual investments. In other words, in Europe, what is stressed at the organizational level is legal limits on private appropriation of benefits.

Consequently, the definition adopted by the Johns Hopkins comparative Non-Profit Sector Project has an American bias because it is based on the non-distribution constraint, which structures the configuration of the sector in North America, with a correspondingly important role for foundations. This criterion does not allow for the legal specificities of European countries, where the decisive criterion is limitation of the distribution of profits. This is what gives social economy organizations their specificity compared to other productive organizations. Beyond their differences, European initiatives share a common tradition – different from North America's – which insists less on not distributing profits, philanthropy and voluntary

work than on collective actions based on mutual help and the participation of the citizens who are concerned with social problems.

A legal and normative definition

The idea of a social economy differs from the non-profit sector in
that it draws on the lessons of history, recognizing that experiences
of association in one period led to the creation of different legal
forms in another. The social economy approach has thus always been
principally legal; it can discriminate statistically between three types:
co-operatives, mutual societies and associations. But, as Defourny
and his colleagues acknowledge (see *Social Enterprise*), although the
adoption of one of these legal forms is 'a significant step towards
joining the social economy – this in itself does not guarantee that it
will become part of it. In certain countries, enterprises are frequently
co-operative in name only. Similarly, an associative or mutual status
sometimes provides a legal cover for para-public agencies and for-
profit economic activity.'

A normative approach has consequently been put forward in
combination with the legal one. The resulting definition states that
'the social economy includes all economic activities conducted by
enterprises, primarily co-operatives, associations and mutual benefit
societies, whose ethics express the following principles: placing service to its members or to the community ahead of profit; autonomous
management; a democratic decision-making process; the primacy
of people and work over capital in the distribution of revenues'.
This gives a more accurate description of how these organizations
function, but it poses a question-mark over the simple classification
offered by the legal approach. Hence there is an ambiguity in writing about the social economy which oscillates between including all
the organizations that meet the legal specification – when the aim
is to assess their importance in the economy – and excluding some
organizations because of the gap between their affirmed principles
and observable reality.

A definition by a system of rules

In order to avoid simply juxtaposing the legal forms and general ethical principles, an integrated approach to the social economy has been
proposed that focuses on its system of rules. It aims to go beyond

debates about the values considered to be specific to the social economy in order to carry out a more thorough analysis of the specific
characteristics of the organizations belonging to it. Social economy
organizations may be understood in terms of the voluntary contributions of an enterprise's members, their principles of combination and
activities. The body of rules expresses both sides of this association:
the members have equal rights in relation to the functioning of the
organization; operating surpluses, if any, are proportionate to their
level of activity.

The *co-operative model* becomes the *point of reference* for the whole of the
social economy, so that only entrepreneurial associations that have a
company form are included. The social economy is composed of non-
capitalist enterprises operating in the market and the main indicator of
their success is the volume of their market activities, thereby burying
from view any questions concerning their internal functioning and
non-market operations. Thus, associations whose resources largely
come from redistribution and volunteers are on the border of a social
economy whose charter in France states that its components 'live in
the market economy' and develop 'institutions that the traditional
market economy does not generate'. This definition evaluates co-
operatives, mutual societies and associations in terms of how members
achieve a measure of integration into the market economy.

A plural approach: the solidarity economy

The social economy, through defining itself as a set of organizations,
leaves open the broader question of its relationship to the contemporary economy and democracy. An emphasis on these two aspects
gave rise to the 'solidarity economy' (*économie solidaire*). This theoretical
perspective was elaborated to account for the emergence and existence of numerous initiatives in Europe over the last two decades.

The economic dimension

From an economic point of view, the solidarity economy approach
is based on recognition that economic principles are plural (see
Plural Economy), as attested by numerous authors such as Boulding,
Mauss, Perroux, Polanyi and Razeto Migliaro, all of whom advance
an extended definition of the economy in which three principles are
distinguished.

The market principle allows supply of and demand for goods and services to meet; exchange happens on the basis of price-setting. The relation between supply and demand is established through contracts informed by calculation of interest. The market principle does not presuppose immersion in social relations and it is not necessarily produced by the social system, unlike the other economic principles described below.

Redistribution is the principle according to which a central authority is responsible for allocating what is produced, which presupposes a procedure defining the rules of levy and their use. A relation establishes itself over time between the central authority which imposes an obligation and the agents who submit to it.

Reciprocity corresponds to relations established between groups or persons through actions that only make sense insofar as they express a will to demonstrate a social link among the stakeholders. The cycle of reciprocity contrasts with market exchange in that the former is inseparable from human relations involving the desire for recognition and power; reciprocity also differs from redistribution, insofar as it is not imposed by a central authority.

Today, as in the past, reflection on the possibility of economic democracy is enriched by using this more realistic perspective which is less ideological than reliance on the market economy: namely, a plural economy, in which the market is just one of the components alongside redistribution and reciprocity (see *Plural Economy*).

The way that the economy is divided between the three principles has varied greatly throughout history and each of them has been profoundly affected by the rise of modern democracy. There is, however, much more to this than diffusion of the market principle alone. Despite a drive to make the market largely autonomous and 'disembedded' from social relations, democratic solidarity also emerged in a distinctive form: public redistribution had its rules enacted through representative democracy; and reciprocity was able to unfold on the basis of the voluntary public commitments of free and equal citizens. Recognition of individual rights made possible the emergence of a solidarity that expressed social esteem as witnessed by acts of egalitarian reciprocity. This in turn fed a demand for a more abstract solidarity that contributed to widening of the scope of social rights to which public redistribution gave expression, allowing citizens to escape from dependency on traditional forms of philanthropy. In the context of a market economy, democratic solidarity thus defined itself through a combination of egalitarian reciprocity and public redistribution. The three economic principles thus endure, even though their forms and respective weight vary.

The solidarity economy approach stresses a mix of all three principles. According to this perspective, by combining the resources and opportunities contained in all three principles in their projects, social economy organizations can protect themselves against the perils of marginalization. But why would such hybridity be desirable? An answer depends on linking economic concerns to a political dimension.

The political dimension

In the nineteenth century, self-protection from the market led to associations being set up and a welfare state being built. Associations were society's 'first line of defence' before the state took a hand.

The European point of view seeks to integrate these civil society initiatives within a public sphere created by democratic modernity. Relations between these initiatives and the public authorities are then linked through politics, the relationship between the community's potential for action as a whole and the exercise of power. Associations combine both these dimensions of politics: on the one hand, non-institutional politics centred on citizens' potential for action if they make use of the positive freedom to which they are formally entitled and, on the other hand, institutional politics as defined by the exercise of power.

All interactions between public authorities and civil society translate into mutual effects whose intensity and modalities greatly vary over time. On the one hand, the initiatives of various social actors contribute to the evolution of forms of public regulation. On the other hand, rules enacted by public authorities influence the trajectories of these initiatives. We should never consider organizations in isolation from their relations with the public sphere. This is what constitutes their institutional dimension.

Theoretical approaches

The European approach replaces the idea of a sector with an emphasis on the structuring power of the principle of solidarity and with studying the close relations between associative action and the public authorities.

From the notion of sector to that of solidarity

In contrast to neoclassical economics' hypothetical-deductive approach, a significant number of works have adopted more comprehensive methodologies. This research relegates the notion of sector to a minor role and uses the concept of solidarity to explain various social practices grouped under the generic term, 'civic associationism'. Such an approach is not exclusively European, since quite similar orientations permeate the Latin American literature. It could be claimed that recognition of human and civil rights destabilized the old social order without eliminating conditions inherited from traditional society. When the social question arose, as early as the nineteenth century, the issue of the compatibility between citizenship and economic development generated heated debates, giving rise to the emergence of associations (see *Citizenship*).

From the notion of sector to one of public action

The European perspective links associationism to public action, since its roots lie in resistance to the market utopia and are deeply intertwined, whereas theories of institutional choice consider associations to be organizations that intervene in the case of market or state failure. A more historical analysis highlights the fact that associations 'are not only producers of goods and services, but important factors of political and social co-ordination'. This is what the Johns Hopkins research project recognized when they moved from the notion of a 'non-profit sector' to the idea of a 'civil society sector'. This rapprochement with the European view can account for how associations are embedded in society, but it assimilates the association sector too quickly to civil society as a whole and cannot adequately analyse its interactions with the state and the market.

A strictly sector-based vision fails to take into account the intermediate dimension of associations, which may be thought of as a space facilitating links between the private and public spheres. Associative action, born from encounters among persons, gives them the possibility of contributing to the construction of that common world which is essential for true democracy, through voluntary commitments that respect a plurality of opinions, conflicts of interest and different perspectives. This mediation between private and public spheres, which takes place in many different ways, and the mix of resources and logics of action on which it is founded, are poorly translated by representations that suppose well-separated sectors, with clear-cut boundaries. Study of the genesis and institutionalization of associations underlines the significance of the interdependence between associative and public action.

If, following Cohen and Arato, we define civil society as a sphere that is distinct from both the state and the market, associations belong to an organized civil society since they influence the configuration of public space through whatever innovations and dissent they manage to express there, including for their own production. But, as Barthélémy rightly says, 'the activities of civil society cannot be dissociated from political society' and associations are not only the expression of civil society, they are also implied in relations of power because they 'publicize the ideological conflicts of the wider society, contribute to the formation of elites and to the forms of local power and participate in the definition of public policies while legitimizing the political and administrative sphere'.

In sum, as Walzer notes, civil society, if it recognizes interpersonal ties, is marked by inequality. As far as the state is concerned, since it results from a universalist orientation, it guarantees social rights while establishing general rules and standardized procedures that correct inequalities, but also neglect the contribution of local relations. The real question thus does not concern the substitution of civil society for the state nor the dissolution of civil society in the market, but the way the democratic process in civil society and the democratization of public institutions reinforce each other.

Further reading

Barthélémy, M. (2000) *Associations: un nouvel âge de la participation?* Presses de Sciences Po, Paris.

Borzaga, C. (1998) *The Economics of the Third Sector in Europe: The Italian Experience*. Department of Economics, University of Trento.

Boulding, K. (1973) *The Economy of Love and Fear.* Wadsworth, Belmont, CA.

Chanial, P. (2001) *Justice, don et association: La Délicate essence de la démocratie.* La Découverte, Paris.

Cohen, J. and Arato, A. (1994) *Civil Society and Political Theory.* MIT Press, Cambridge, MA.

Defourny, J., Develtere, P. and Fonteneau, B. (eds) (2000) *Social Economy North and South*. HIVA and Centre d'Économie Sociale, Leuven and Liège.

Godbout, J. (2000) *Le don, la dette et l'identité: Homo donator vs homo economicus.* La Découverte, Paris.

Laville, J-L. and Sainsaulieu, R. (1997) *Sociologie de l'association.* Desclée de Brouwer, Paris.

Maucourant, J., Servet, J-M. and Tiran, A. (1998) *La Modernité de Karl Polanyi: Introduction générale.* L'Harmattan, Paris.

Perroux, F. (1960) *Économie et société: Contrainte-échange-don.* Presses Universitaires de France, Paris.

Salamon, L. M. and Anheier, H. (1995) *Defining the Nonprofit Sector.* Manchester University Press, Manchester.

Vienney, C. (1994) *L'Économie sociale, collection Repères.* La Découverte, Paris.

Walzer, M. (2000) Sauver la société civile? In *Mouvements* no. 8, La Découverte.

22

Community Participation

Marilyn Taylor

The turn to community

The award of the 2009 Nobel Prize in Economic Sciences to Elinor Ostrom, famous for her work on 'the commons', might be regarded as recognition at last that human behaviour is not always governed by self-interest. While 'community' has always been with us, it reached a fairly low point with the advance of individualism and consumer choice in the heyday of neoliberalism in the 1980s. Margaret Thatcher's much quoted assertion at the time – that there was no such thing as society, only individuals and their families – seemed to sound its death knell. But, to paraphrase Mark Twain, reports of its death were greatly exaggerated. The subsequent two decades have seen a revival of its fortunes. Along with associated concepts such as social capital, civic engagement and civil society, it is now a dominant theme in policy discourse. The concept of social capital, in particular, has been embraced by international institutions such as the World Bank and the International Monetary Fund, who have also, since the 1990s, required community involvement as a condition of investment and support (see *Social Capital*). But why is this? And what can this portfolio of ideas offer as a way through the complexities of a post-modern, post-welfare state society?

The history of 'community' in theory and policy is well rehearsed. Most contemporary accounts take the work of Ferdinand Toennies as their starting point. The distinction he made between *Gemeinschaft* and *Gesellschaft* contrasts traditional, holistic, organic communities (usually seen as rural and pre-industrial) with the newer fragmented relationships of (urban) industrialized society. Similar distinctions have been made by many writers since, usually lamenting the inevitable passing of the solidarities of traditional communities with the advance of capitalism. Indeed, since this time, Al Hunter argues, community has been 'variously lost, found, liberated, mislaid and limited': lost by the Chicago School, who saw social disorganization as the root of many of the social problems of the 1930s; found by the community studies tradition of the 1950s and 1960s; liberated by new ways of connecting between people through new technology; mislaid by the dominance of survey research in the social sciences which focused on interpersonal ties at the expense of a more holistic picture of the institutions which embed community; limited by the multiple ties and loyalties of contemporary life.

Before exploring these developments in more detail, we should ask what we mean by community. There are many ways of approaching this task. Communities may be defined in terms of the characteristics their members share, which could be personal (age, gender, ethnic origin, sexuality); beliefs and values (political, ideological, religious); activities (leisure, arts, music, sport); use of services or goods (commuters, patients); location (where members live, study and work). But characteristics held in common do not make a community. This requires common interests, which might include a cultural heritage, social relationships, economic interests and shared experience of power or oppression.

Hunter describes community as a variable rather than a given. He identifies three dimensions on which communities vary. These are: ecological, in terms of the space and time they occupy; social structural, in terms of the interpersonal networks and institutional density within them; and symbolic/cultural, in terms of the extent to which they confer a common identity and culture. When all three are combined, they characterize a strong community.

Community is often used normatively, as I have indicated above, signifying solidarity and cohesion. Then again it may be used instrumentally – identifying community as a target for particular services and policies or, more actively, as an agent that can maintain or change its own circumstances. It is in the last two senses that policy engages with community and it is to these that I now turn.

The community in policy

As capitalism advanced, the decline in solidarity that it brought was lamented by supporter and foe alike. In the eighteenth and nineteenth centuries, some leading industrialists sought to revive the notion of community with the building of model villages, while Adam Smith, the foremost advocate of the market, urged self-restraint, arguing that the state has an important role to play in promoting and supporting an overarching moral framework and societal values – an argument that has received scant attention in the work of many of his followers. In the mid-twentieth century, sociologists promoted community rather as a mediating agent between the state and the citizen, while the 1960s and early 1970s saw a flurry of state-sponsored community initiatives in the global North to tackle the poverty that persisted despite the welfare state. Community development was already established in the global South, emerging initially out of the colonial era and the journey towards independence, but subsequently, as already noted, it was promoted by major international economic institutions as a condition of aid.

As the 1990s progressed, community was emphasized in policy not only as a counterbalance to the state but also as a corrective to the excesses of the market and the individualism fostered by the neoliberal agenda. Indeed, by the end of the century, 'third-way politics' positioned community as a third force balancing both market and state (see *Third Sector*). This interest in community has since played out in policies to promote 'community capacity' and 'community empowerment', and to foster a social economy through encouraging community-based social enterprise (see *Solidarity Economy, Social Enterprise*).

Some have taken these ideas further, seeing community as an *alternative* to state and market, arguing, for example, for an associative democracy, based on small associations and enterprises. Others have celebrated community as a site of resistance to the power of capital and the rampant individualism that they associate with it, pursuing strategies of radical community organizing and community development, based on the ideas of Saul Alinsky and the liberation theology of Paolo Freire.

The theory

Much of the contemporary emphasis on community focuses on that enduring distinction between the ideal utopian *Gemeinschaft* based on close ties and common values and the more fragmented and instrumental relationships of the limited liability *Gesellschaft*, on the one hand, or the alienated, socially disorganized and dysfunctional 'defeated communities' of the Chicago School, on the other.

The most recent revival of community values has been strongly associated with the communitarian school, whose chief advocate has been Amitai Etzioni. Community, for him, is characterized by strong interlocking ties and shared values. He sees the family first and then the community as the site of moral norms and obligations, emphasizing the need to balance rights with responsibilities and seeking to revive the institutions that mediate between the individual and the state.

While influential, the communitarian school has attracted growing criticism – for its assumptions of homogeneity, for being rooted in the American way of life and for its conservatism. As the 1990s progressed, another potentially more flexible concept was to take centre stage. 'Social capital' was popularized through the work of Robert Putnam, who defined it as 'features of social life – networks, norms and trust' that enable participants to 'act together more effectively to pursue shared objectives'. He and others described it as a collective resource embedded in informal networks, and associated it with a range of positive outcomes, including good governance, health and economic prosperity. Participation in social and civic activities was, for Putnam, a strong indicator of social capital. He saw social capital as a moral resource, lamenting its decline in an increasingly individualistic society but, in a departure from the communitarian discourse, he emphasized that it was not simply the close bonding ties within communities that constituted social capital. He and subsequent writers have stressed also the importance of bridging ties across different communities.

The popularity of social capital was a welcome counterbalance to the individualism of the neoliberal agenda that had reigned supreme in the 1980s. It was also a concept that resonated with the predominantly economic discourse of these times. Thus, James Coleman described it as a fourth and previously neglected form of capital in the production process, alongside financial, physical and human capital. Like Putnam after him, he defined social capital as essentially a collective resource, although both scholars recognized that it could have benefits for individuals. However, others have conceptualized it as an individual good and in doing so have stressed that social capital, like any other form of capital, is unevenly distributed. Thus, Alejandro Portes defines it as 'the capacity of individuals to command scarce resources by virtue of their membership in networks or broader social structure'. As Pierre Bourdieu argued, it can operate in the same way as other forms of capital, often interacting with them to reproduce existing inequalities (see *Social Capital*).

Robert Sampson is another who sees social capital as a collective good. Drawing on the Chicago School tradition and particularly on their concern with dysfunctional communities, he has explored the concept of collective efficacy. Against the voices that claim that community has been lost, he argues instead that it has been transformed as the capacity for deep, long-lasting relationships is supplemented by one for more restricted, surface relationships, and by the bridging weaker ties of social capital. Alongside the need for social relations, he argues for the importance of structural connections and institutional strength in local communities, as well as vertical integration with the wider society. Unlike the communitarians, he champions the role of the state, arguing that it needs to mount aggressive strategies to address the social and ecological changes that have restricted the ability of inner cities in the US to realize their common values and maintain effective controls (see *Solidarity Economy*).

Community participation

Community participation can be seen as a response to five major policy concerns towards the end of the twentieth century. The first was the *crisis of development* across the globe. The perceived weakness of many states in the global South, then described as the 'developing world', combined with the economic shocks of the 1970s and 1980s, provoked global economic institutions to introduce structural adjustment policies as a basis for investment and support but also to look beyond the state to the population as the key to development success (see *Development*).

The second was the need for *radical service reform*. The perceived failure of both market and state in meeting welfare needs, coupled with rising demand, led governments to look to the community and the third sector for a role they could play in the 'welfare mix'. While the transfer of services from the state might have been inspired initially by privatization and neoliberal philosophy, developing the potential of the third sector and communities themselves to deliver mainstream services has become an increasingly central theme in public discourse, along with the promotion of social enterprise and the European concept of a social economy, which can combine economic with social (and environmental) value (see *Third Sector*).

Communities might be involved in service reform as both co-producers and consumers. The third policy concern – about the *democratic deficit* – involved them as citizens. The march of democracy across the globe in the twentieth century – with the fall of the Berlin Wall in Europe, and of apartheid in South Africa, towards its end – has paradoxically contrasted with increasing disenchantment in what we might call the more established democracies. Voting figures have fallen in many of these countries, while opinion polls show decreasing trust in politicians. Meanwhile, the democratic deficit in international institutions, such as the European Union, has led them to set up their own mechanisms for dialogue with civil society (see *Citizenship*).

A fourth incentive for promoting community participation relates to the *moral agenda*. A number of trends has increased concern globally about increasing fragmentation, the loss of a moral compass, and racial tension. One is the increasing displacement of populations across the globe, and the tensions raised (or provoked) in communities in relation to immigration. Another has been the geographical concentration of unemployment, low income, poor health and a range of associated social problems in isolated 'deprived' neighbourhoods, as a result of economic restructuring. A third has been the perceived loss of community already described, with the growth of the consumer society and individualization.

A final factor in the growth of the community participation agenda, paradoxically, has been *globalization*. Some argue that, as this has 'hollowed out' the nation-state, with supranational institutions sucking power upwards, people are seeking a renewed sense of identity and control at local rather than national level. In parallel, commentators observe a shift from 'government' to multi-level 'governance' in recognition of the fact that, in a globalized world, the state no longer has the resources, legitimacy or knowledge to govern on its own (see *Globalization*). The resulting focus on new forms of partnership working along with the devolution of power from the centre has the potential to give communities a much greater say in the decisions affecting their neighbourhood.

Can community participation deliver?

Many commentators have criticized the utopianism attached to the community discourse. For some, it is unrealistic to expect community participation to achieve all that is required of it; others argue that communities should resist being co-opted into this agenda.

In the first camp, critics remind us that 'community' has a darker side. Because community is defined as much by what it is not as by what it is, communities often become active in response to what they perceive as a threat from outside. The tight policing of community boundaries as a result can lead to oppression within and exclusion of those outside. As such, community is fraught with contradictions. The contradiction between the security that community provides and the freedom that is demanded in contemporary society is evidenced by Zygmunt Bauman's comparison between the gated communities of the rich and the ghettoes of the poor. The rich buy their way into status and security by living in enclaves; the poor are forced together in ghettoes that are not of their choosing and which are often unstable and unsafe. Indeed, Bauman argues that the new global elite increasingly live in a 'community-free zone', but that their choice to opt out of communal insurance against misfortune renders life more uncertain for the rest of society. This uncertainty easily translates into mutual mistrust, creating a vicious cycle whereby people retreat into their own circles.

In this camp, critics also question how representative those who engage actively in community participation or partnership exercises are. They cite examples of community leaders who act as 'gatekeepers', preventing rather than enabling access to the wider community. They suggest that new processes of governance are creating 'expert citizens', with community leaders or representatives becoming increasingly divorced from their constituencies as they learn the new rules and language of the game. There is an inevitable tension between leadership, expertise and widespread participation, however committed these 'expert citizens' may be to keeping a strong link with their community roots. This is a particular issue as participation scales up to national or even global levels. Jan Aart Scholte has commented, for example, that: 'At a global level, citizen involvement rests on an overly narrow cultural base.'

In the second camp, critics observe the continuing resistance of many state players to the concept of community participation. As a result, many community participants in partnerships still feel marginalized or ignored as partners and in consultation. But the exercise of power is more subtle than this. Building on the work of Michel Foucault, adherents of the 'governmentality' school acknowledge that, as power has become increasingly dispersed, governing is happening at a distance from the state. But, they argue, the assumptions behind these new forms of governing and the 'rules of engagement' remain those of the elite, so it is taken for granted that those who are governed are willingly compliant in the exercise of power. Thus, Foucault has argued that forms of power beyond the state can often sustain the state more effectively than its own institutions, enlarging and maximizing its effectiveness. This is not achieved through coercive control, but through a more complex and subtle diffusion of techniques and forms of knowledge through which, Nikolas Rose argues, communities 'can be mobilized, enrolled, deployed in novel programmes'. Indeed, Bill Cooke and Uma Kothari have described participation as 'the new tyranny', showing how it often falls short of its promise, being manipulated or misapplied by its practitioners.

Governmentality theorists also note how community is overwhelmingly prescribed for 'the poor', with the implication that the causes of disadvantage lie in these communities themselves. In this way, they argue, communities are also ironically made responsible for their own fate, but without the resources or control over external forces that would be needed to address the conditions that shape their destiny.

A third critique in this camp relates to the co-option of communities for external agendas. Community players are meant to bring distinctive qualities to the services they provide and the contributions they make to policy and decision-making. But, in the arena of service delivery, tightly defined and policed contracts, along with procurement policies that privilege economics of scale, render this increasingly unlikely. More widely, meanwhile, as community has become a site of governance, to quote Nikolas Rose again, the 'community discourse', has hi-jacked a 'language of resistance and transformed it into an expert discourse and professional vocation'. In partnerships, it is easy for community players to get sucked into existing cultures of decision-making and to collude with existing patterns of power. An overwhelmingly consensual culture, meanwhile, discourages dissent and leaves community representatives facing two ways, vulnerable to accusations of being unrepresentative from both partners around the decision-making table and their own constituency.

One particular question that the current policy drive for community participation raises is the extent to which, as community energies go into delivering on state agendas, partnership has become the 'only game in town'. John Gaventa and Andrea Cornwall have distinguished between 'invited' governance spaces, into which community participants are invited by government and 'created' or 'popular' spaces, created by communities themselves. As traditional mass organizations lose membership and trade unions, political parties, and adult education opportunities become increasingly centralized, those who find the official 'invited' spaces disempowering or who do not 'fit' find themselves with nowhere else to go. Experience in the UK suggests that there is a danger that extreme right-wing parties could fill this political vacuum.

For all these reasons, the potential of community participation is open to question. Devolving too much power to communities could give up the field to the 'Not in My Back Yard' activists; dealing with community leaders could lead to individuals within the community who don't fit being even further marginalized; communities could be held to blame for factors well outside their control; or they could get sucked into existing patterns of power and influence, losing their distinctive voice and ceasing to represent those who are most marginalized in society.

Moving forward

Such a focus on critique masks many positives. New, fluid forms of power create new opportunities. There are countless examples of effective community practice across the globe where devolving powers to and building on capacities within communities has achieved real gains for those who live there. For some authorities, international and national requirements and incentives may be treated either as a tick-box exercise or actively resisted, but elsewhere change agents within and beyond the state have seized on the opportunities offered to transform the way they operate and create new forms of dialogue. Both communities and those they engage with have learnt new skills. There are also powerful examples of effective community organizing 'from below' as people create their own spaces for change. Some of these are based on faith organizations – particularly in the Alinsky-inspired community organizing movement – some on rich local social movement traditions, as in Latin America.

A particularly interesting development in recent years has been the growing influence in the global North of initiatives in the South. The best-known example is the model of participatory budgeting developed in Porto Alegre, which spread in Brazil under the umbrella of a sympathetic state committed to change and has been adopted by governments across the globe. International NGOs, meanwhile, are applying models like Civic Driven Change, developed in the South, to communities in the North (see *NGOs*).

A further source of inspiration for the future has been described as globalization from below – the opportunities provided for organizing across localities and countries, as well as other traditional divides, by the internet (see *Globalization*). Like community participation itself, the internet is not a universal panacea: differential access to technology means there is still scope for marginalization and exclusion; like any other part of the media, the technology can be appropriated and controlled by the elite or by the state; the loudest voices may not speak for many people. But the scope for making connections, for spreading knowledge and for engaging different communities is enormous.

Nonetheless, research suggests that, rather than being a 'spray-on' solution, communities are complex and community participation is a site of tension in itself: between diversity and cohesion; between accountability and flexibility; between representative and participatory democracy; between the responsibilities of state and citizen; between expert leadership and widespread participation; between negotiating change from the inside and demanding it from the outside; between focusing energies at local level and scaling up to regional, national and supranational level. Effective community participation will require imaginative approaches to addressing these tensions.

Navigating the tensions

So what has been learnt from this wealth of experience? The challenges of community participation will vary from country to country according to the socio-political context and history at national and local level. But comparative research suggests that there are common issues too.

Experience across the globe suggests that a strong *drive from the top* – with incentives and sanctions – has been crucial in pushing community participation up the agenda at all levels. But too much central control will drive out the flexibility and innovation that community participation can bring to policy and practice.

Clarity about the different roles and legitimacy of the various players can help to address the tensions between representative and participatory democracy. State or professional resistance often comes from those who feel their own role threatened.

Social capital that bridges between communities and links across power differentials is the glue that can make participation effective. But it is not something that can easily be built in highly structured formal settings. Formal opportunities for engagement need to be embedded in *informal opportunities to build trust* and knowledge across sectors at all levels.

A lot has been said and written about capacity building in the community. But *partners too need capacity building* if they are to build the skills and knowledge that effective participation requires. Engaging with diverse communities, meanwhile, requires *new skills in all sectors of mediation, facilitation and conflict resolution* and a willingness to engage with difference and dissent. Research and experience have stressed also the importance of *boundary spanners*, who can command respect across sectoral and other boundaries, along with recognition of the growing importance of these roles and skills in a complex and fragmented society.

For communities themselves, maintaining independence and distinctiveness, as well as effective accountability, will depend on a strong and well-informed public that will hold community providers and representatives to account and provide a variety of ways into engagement. This needs an investment of time and resources in *community development*, that can build from the bottom up rather than being tied to targets and goals external to the community. It also needs community leaders and third-sector organizations themselves to recognize the importance of building a strong community base.

Finally, and related to this, social change will need communities who are *working for change on the inside and the outside* – 'in and against the state'. As Mitchell Dean – a prominent governmentality scholar puts it: 'You can simultaneously work together and be restive.' Boundary spanners can do this. Communities can also find an independent voice through alliances, while larger NGOs nationally and internationally provide resources and support for communities to find their voices, learn political skills as well as acting as a channel for voices who do not themselves have access to power holders (or may not want it). But alternative spaces and opportunities for political education, where communities can find their own independent voice, are essential for a thriving democracy, if decision-makers are to be held to account, and their erosion and colonization are a major source of concern.

Further reading

Barnes, M., Newman, J. and Sullivan, H. (2007) *Power, Participation and Political Renewal: Case Studies in Political Participation.* The Policy Press, Bristol.

Cnaan, R., Hunter, A. and Milofsky, C. (2005) *The Handbook of Community Movements and Local Organizations.* Springer, New York.

Cornwall, A. and Coelho, V. (2007) *Spaces for Change: The Politics of Citizen Participation in New Democratic Spaces.* Zed Books, London.

De Filippis, J. and Saegert, S. (2007) *The Community Development Reader.* Routledge, New York.

Gaventa, J. (2006) Triumph, deficit or contestation? Deepening the 'deepening democracy'. In debate. *IDS Working Paper* 264. Institute of Development Studies, Brighton.

Gilchrist, A. *The Well-Connected Community.* The Policy Press, Bristol.

Hickey, S. and Mohan, G. (2004) *Participation: from Tyranny to Transformation? Exploring New Approaches to Participation in Development.* Zed Books, London.

Scholte, J. (2002) *Civil Society and Democracy in Global Governance.* Global Governance 8, pp. 281–304.

Taylor, M. (2003) *Public Policy in the Community.* Palgrave Macmillan, London.

23

Local Development

John M. Bryden

Approaches to local development

The concept of local development emerged and evolved in two main ways. The first and earlier definition emerged in opposition to growing state power and, subsequently, to globalization and growing corporate power. The second and generally later definition related to public management, based on ideas about the need to improve the effectiveness and efficiency of public policies organized from centres of government. The first started as a project of anarchists and communitarians; the second as a project of the state. In both cases, 'local' was conceived of as a geographical community below the level of nations and federal states. In the first case, however, the emphasis was on community, identity and power and in the second on 'devolution' of responsibilities to the lower (usually lowest) level of government, notably the municipality, county or district within the authority of the state and its rules. More important, the first was also seen as a means of furthering democracy and dealing with growing economic inequality and hence with distorted economic (and hence political) power. I argue here that at least since the early 1980s the 'managerial' approach has come to dominate. In the post-crisis world, however, we need to return to the first approach and reconstruct an idea of local development based on human values, community and identity. Although local development in this sense is *necessary* for a more human development in future, it is not *sufficient*.

'Local development' is sometimes used interchangeably with 'community development', 'self-reliant development', 'bottom-up development', 'development from below', 'place-based development', territorial development' and indeed 'place development'. Although all of these have elements in common, they are not the same. What they have in common is a contrast with national planning, centralized decision-making, uniformity of action across national space, reliance on corporate power and disempowerment of citizens and lower levels of government. They equally share a focus on 'place', although they differ in how the notion of 'place' is constructed and by whom.

The urban geographer John Friedmann has argued that 'place refers to *patterns of affectively valued social relations embedded in a physical environment*'. Friedmann suggests that 'place-making is . . . a way of creating and/or strengthening place-bound relations'. He stresses, however, that if we accept his definition of place, then 'places can neither be planned for nor designed from the outside, for example by architects, but emerge spontaneously from within civil society itself: embedded in the physical world . . . *they are a purely social creation*'. Place is thus a geographical space, with real physical borders, but with significant place-based relations. As such it comes close to Ferdinand Toennies' concept of *Gemeinschaft* or place-based community, as well as to the idea of 'locality' and hence to the 'local' as a focus for 'development'.

'Self-reliant' development on the other hand represents a definite 'alternative' path sometimes termed 'radical practice' and grounded in different values. In other words, it has a clear ideological component. Thus John Friedmann argues that its historical roots lie in utopian, anarchist and Marxist thought of the nineteenth century. To him the set of alternative social values commonly associated with self-reliant development includes:

An orientation that assigns priority to the basic material and psychological needs of people;

An ethic that stresses harmonious and enduring relations between people and their physical environment;

Social recognition of the use value of voluntary work in households and community;

The democratization of capital involving both its internal accountability to workers and its external accountability to territorial
communities;

A strong preference for non-hierarchical forms of social organization, such as small group and network structures;

The practice of territorial self-governance inclusive of the
lowest levels of political organization in street, village and
neighbourhood;

Equality of access to the bases of social power, including surplus
time, knowledge and skills, organizations, the instruments of
production and good health, adequate space for life, work and
political assembly, strategic information, social networks, and
financial resources.

Thinking about self-reliance today contains a notion of a 'human
scale' – emphasizing local democratic, participatory and co-operative
structures as a means of 'getting control' of our lives, and escaping
domination, dependence and control by giant private corporations
and 'big government'.

This idea of the human scale, linked with self-reliant and 'bottom
up' development, is also reflected in E. F. Schumacher's *Small is
Beautiful* and Ivan Illich's *Tools of Conviviality*. To Schumacher, people
are alive when they are 'self-dependent'. Illich's idea is that 'A society
is . . . convivial when man controls the tool', where 'tool' is used in
its broadest sense. Schumacher argued that 'One does not make a
people viable by grouping them to form a large community', rather
'People can be themselves in small groups'. The human scale, then, is
likely to approach the 'local' scale, and 'local development', encompassing also 'self-dependence', may also be interpreted as a 'tool' for
a more convivial society.

The closely related concepts of 'bottom-up development' and
'development from below' are virtually the same as 'self-reliant'
development and need no separate discussion here, except to note
that many of the ideas associated with these labels came from scholars and practitioners working in the poorer and more peripheral parts
of the world, where the marginalization of rural regions and poor
people is extreme and the role of the state is commonly seen as being
perverse.

Local development and globalization

In parallel debates, 'localism' or localization was seen as the counterpart of globalism or globalization (see *Globalization* and *Alter-Globalization*). The relationship between global and local was also described as problematic in that locality is sometimes cast as a form of opposition or resistance to the hegemonic global sphere. If we consider the modern origins of 'self-reliant or autarkic development', the infant industry arguments of the nineteenth-century national economist Friedrich List were clearly hostile to the idea of 'global competition'. But just as local development is not only about autarky or indeed economics, so too globalization is not only about global competition. Even so, it was increasingly clear by the 1980s that global competition was at the core of the neoliberal agenda and that localities benefiting from some kind of 'protection' (for example through agricultural or industrial policies or government preference for local producers) would now lose it. The general response to this pressure was for local communities to exploit their less mobile and less tangible assets, often in the form of public goods that were particular to 'place'. This was because other assets, especially capital, were destined to become ever more mobile.

In the 1970s, the centralized development policies of national governments seemed incapable of responding to the challenges of structural change caused by resource scarcity, new technologies and globalization of capital. State-level financial crises also usually made it fiscally impossible for national governments to deal with the local-level impacts of restructuring. These factors, together with a spread of neoliberal policies of non-intervention in the economy and a lower commitment to full employment goals, directly and indirectly encouraged a new interest in sub-national or 'local' areas as arenas for development efforts.

A further factor was growing recognition that localities are not homogeneous. For example, rural areas differ markedly in their economic structure and activities, natural and human resources, location and demographic and social conditions. Rurality represents a very diverse set of characteristics, perceptions, problems, opportunities and constraints in all countries. Consequently, despite widespread crisis and the conventional wisdom regarding spatial development, some localities experienced a measure of success based on local organization of development initiatives. This was also reflected in emerging data on the economic performance of the smaller regions of the OECD countries as a result of territorial development initiatives taken after 1990. The spread of such 'success' stories was reinforced by the fiscal crisis of central governments and by an ideological shift towards an emphasis on the potential benefits of transferring responsibility and control of development to local areas and people themselves, towards an *endogenous* approach to development.

By the late 1980s, developments in policy and politics within Europe emphasized a more flexible, integrated and decentralized approach to rural policy on grounds of efficiency or effectiveness, or, more cynically, of saving money. In the context of rural development, a new approach emerged, with a local and territorial focus and an integrated, participatory approach. The European LEADER observatory from 1995 to 2000 provided the opportunity to observe the initiatives taken by local communities in rural regions across the European Union, when empowered to tackle their own development, at least initially with little central government control or interference.

From the 1980s then, at least three schools of thought could be identified. First, there were those who viewed state downloading of responsibilities to the local level as an abrogation of previous responsibilities and indeed an attack on the social contract itself – an attack on the idea and practice of citizen equivalence across national space and social groups, as well as on the political values underpinning those. Second, were those who welcomed such devolution and considered *subsidiarity* to be positive and necessary to improve the effectiveness of development and welfare policy in a complex modern world. Third were those who believed in a more radical agenda of self-reliance, with much greater local control over key assets like one's own labour, land and capital, usually in co-operative or other joint forms.

Critique

Several criticisms have been levelled at the related concepts of local, endogenous or bottom-up development and these are reflected in Fraser Taylor and Fiona MacKenzie's, *Development from Within*. They include critique of the theoretical underpinning of these notions; questions concerning the concepts of 'locality' and 'community'; the nature and effects of conflicts between 'locality' and the 'state'; and the state's motives for engaging in 'local development'.

Theories of 'development', especially when they take the form of bureaucratic projects, must be subjected to critique of course. Nevertheless, we should be clear about whether we are criticizing the gulf between rhetoric and practice, the results of practical application of the theory or the theory itself. It is relatively easy to criticize on *a priori* grounds the World Bank's adoption of the rhetoric of 'bottom-up development', 'local empowerment' and a 'participatory approach' (see *Social Capital*) or the EU's LEADER programme or the UN Capital Development Fund's adoption of the principle of local development. Yet the real consequences of these shifts, which are – or ought to be – long-term in nature, are not immediately apparent.

Equally, to criticize a project for its weak theoretical basis presumes that a strong theoretical base is a necessary or sufficient condition for good 'practice'! Indeed, Taylor and Mackenzie follow an 'inductive approach', starting not with theory, but by examining case studies of local and community development in Africa and then seeking to develop theory on the basis of practice. Such an inductive approach recognizes the complex diversity of the real world; whereas theory seeks to simplify it and thus builds the central power of the state, while weakening local power by claiming objectivity and universality. Yet we do need better theory about development from below or, for that matter, 'development from within' or 'development from above'. In their absence, other theories simply fill the gap, such as currently fashionable theories of 'city regions' which relegate local communities and rural regions to the role of being mere bystanders or 'green space'. On the other hand, local development should not necessarily be thought of as 'self-reliant', the question being rather what power localities have over their future, how this can be exercised and what difference it would make.

The assumption of undifferentiated community that is implied by proponents of 'local development' is clearly untenable. Power-holders at the community level may subvert local initiatives in their own interests, just as they do at the national level. On the other hand, there is a general issue of the gap between economic power and political democracy which applies at all levels of society and government, always made worse by inequality between citizens in income, wealth and education. With any given pattern of material inequality, the mechanisms of control at the local level are potentially more effective and less disastrous, since they are often more transparent and subject to scrutiny. Outcomes also depend on the nature and functioning of local democratic systems. So although it is fair to point out internal divisions within communities, this does not by itself invalidate the bottom-up approach. Power relations are also obscure at the national and supranational levels.

As I have said, two common rationales for the state becoming involved in the contradictory business of sponsoring 'bottom up' development are saving money (government expenditure) and improving the efficiency of public programmes. Others include the suppression of local revolt or unrest and, more altruistically, improving national democracy, fairness and cohesion. In the period during and after Thatcher, 'downsizing of the state' in Britain did involve passing down some responsibilities to local government and voluntary organizations (NGOs). Similar processes occurred in the US during and after Ronald Reagan. The profusion of 'local initiatives' in the richer countries involving everything from health, social welfare and education to development and the environment has put great pressure on local volunteer resources. Yet a good deal of voluntary effort goes into these and other local initiatives and is offered freely. One is moved to ask why? Is it indeed an expression of alternative values or 'radical practice'? Is it merely self-interest? Is it a willingness to offer this as a *quid pro quo* for a transfer of (some) power (or relief at getting rid of bureaucratic, codified schemes)? What are the limits to such voluntary offers? What are the conditions which encourage them, or inhibit them? As Friedmann argued, radical practice is about changing reality, not administering it!

Given that state engagement with 'local development' is inherently contradictory, one must ask what is 'going on' when the state sponsors local initiatives. The answers concern the changing function and role of the state and relate to both the 'demand side' (people insisting on more say, not trusting central power etc.) and the 'supply side' (the state is no longer able to 'deliver' through top-down, centralized schemes).

The late Charles Tilley reviewed an eclectic selection of literature on the top-down-bottom-up duality. He concluded that we should be

> looking for processes that undermine, counter or render pernicious the sorts of interactive mechanisms that usually mediate uniform schemes and local practice: polyvalent performance, accommodative bargaining,

category formation, intellectual brokerage, and improvisation. When they involve encounters between local and large scales, these mechanisms are most likely to fail or to generate destructive incompatibility where little previous communication between local and large scale has occurred, where local connections and resources have diminished, where time horizons have shortened, and where authorities are responding to serious struggles with their own peers or predators rather than to relations with their subordinates . . .

Neoliberalism and its local discontents

Modern governments have espoused 'local development' and decentralization as part of 'new public management', as developed in Britain by New Labour from Thatcher. Yet, as many have pointed out, this political project is contradictory in both ideology and practice. For some, decentralization has gone hand-in-hand with, and even acted as a cloak for, re-centralization. For others, it is a way of saving central budgets, by passing down responsibilities with rules but no money to 'lower' levels of government or to NGOs. For yet others it has been an attempt to 'capture' the radical agendas of self-reliance and local empowerment and head off threats to the status quo. The values underlying these different interpretations vary, but taken together they provide elements of an outline of what an agenda for 'alternative' local development might look like when state-sponsored neoliberalism or 'new public management' is replaced by a post-liberal agenda. One thing is sure: the new liberal approach to 'local development' is a far cry from the kind of 'self-reliant development' embodied in Gandhi's philosophy of *Sarvodaya* which underpinned his idea of the Panchayati Raj as the village-based republic and bedrock of a participatory democracy in India.

Research undertaken in the late 1990s reinforced the view that, although the development of rural regions required a locally specific approach, supported by relatively autonomous local government, strong civil institutions and good co-operation between various actors, appropriate action by central authorities was also required, for example to redress imbalances between rich and poor regions. Given a 'level playing field' in terms of reasonably equal access to public services, infrastructure and local government structures, the more successful localities retained significant ownership of land, houses and other assets, established effective use rights over local public goods and resisted large-scale dominant public- or private-sector initiatives such as megastores or nuclear power plants and disposal facilities. Conditions fostering these features included autonomous and effective local government, good co-operation between local institutions and actors, local ownership of key assets and a strong sense of community and identity. Under such conditions, localities even in marginal rural regions could become economically and socially successful.

The neoliberal local development agenda had at least one positive advantage. It forced us to recognize the limitations of the state and to pay attention to other factors affecting the capacity of localities to influence and control their own development. Now, having recognized the role and significance of these other factors, we are better able to write a new local development agenda for the post-liberal world.

The project of local development may be seen from two standpoints: 'alternative' development or 'radical practice' aiming at political change; and official 'development policy' based on contradictory processes of centralization and decentralization that emphasize administrative and bureaucratic procedures and relations. The economic crisis of 2008–9 will probably strengthen social and political movements reflecting both standpoints in a struggle played out especially at the margins of society or 'peripheries'. A 'market'-led ideology, espousing decentralization, subsidiarity and self-reliance as means of reducing national commitment to 'equity' or 'equivalence' between regions, transferred responsibility without real power or public funds in order to reduce budgets. This will now increasingly be faced with the contradictions inherent in the development of social and territorial inequality and in particular in the waste of human capacities and place-based assets. 'Market forces' *cannot* be effective in delivering the benefits derived from public goods: equivalence policies are essential, in other words, for the effective functioning – and regulation – of the market.

Dissatisfaction with those same market-based ideologies and policies, as well as a lack of trust in central states and their combined impact on society, environment and economy will at the same time lead to a resurgence of 'alternative development' ideologies and practices, with significant political ramifications.

Local development in a post-liberal world

The following policies combine a radical practice of local development with some elements of the new public management:

Economize in the use of critical resources, including water, nutrients, energy and space. This means switching to ecological sanitation, renewable energy, waste control and recycling and efficient irrigation systems, as well as living in smaller settlements with local government, green space and means of livelihood within bicycle distance from habitation. (See *Ecological Economics* and *Mobility*)

Encourage community ownership and control of critical resources as a way of democratizing capital and ensuring local benefits, for example through community land trusts and community enterprises, including some dealing with renewable energy and waste management.

Align economic and political democracy by limiting the power of monopolies, oligopolies and large corporations and making them locally accountable. Tackle issues of poverty through minimum wages and pensions, and providing adequate welfare safety nets.

Transfer land ownership to communities and individuals, while imposing residence and use requirements.

Create socially useful roles and occupations for segments of the population that the dominant society has marginalized, including the young and elderly, handicapped and in some cases women.

Encourage the use of endogenous untapped resources, especially natural and cultural assets, to improve the quality of life and generate opportunities for small enterprises, both individual and co-operative.

Promote local fresh food production, including individual allotments and co-operative gardening.

Stimulate place-based education that retains and promotes local knowledge as well as connection with and understanding of place and environment.

Encourage collective approaches to solving problems of high-speed internet access and to the development of creative local uses and applications of information technology.

Develop 'green money' schemes to exchange skills and labour locally. (See *Community and Complementary Currencies*)

These suggestions are drawn from a number of sources, as well as from my own work on sustainable rural communities, tangible and intangible assets, information technology, the dynamics of rural areas and land reform. They should form at least part of a post-liberal agenda for value-based action aiming at self-reliant local development. They pose a challenge to the state to re-think regulation, modes of investment support and physical planning, as well as to local communities themselves.

Implications for the social sciences

We must be more vigorous in our critique of social science approaches restricted to large data sets and abstract models based on naive behavioural assumptions (see *Ecological Economics*). The current economic crisis has its roots in these methods. Social scientists should work less with governments and more with people, communities and citizen movements in a spirit of equal collaboration. We must write for people and not for each other. Approaches to managing the universities, such as Britain's 'Research Assessment Exercise' are implicated in this. And we must use more mixed methods, tools designed to solve real problems and freed from disciplinary tyranny.

We also need ongoing assessment of the impact of different policies on local people, communities and places. This is too important to be left to government alone. Researchers, somewhat removed from and certainly independent of government, are vital if local development is to have its own valid evidence base and is to be honest and open. At present, the practice of 'policy proofing' has descended from its original high ideals to a 'tick-box' exercise typical of the new managerialism's shallowness.

We must also address concrete areas neglected by social science. One concerns local government, which must surely remain the core of democratic community empowerment and legitimate local action. This is still subject to reforms in many countries employing a primitive rationale focused on economies of scale and critical mass. The field is largely ignored by social scientists despite its critical role in democratic practice, the defence of minorities, the integration and co-ordination of areas of public concern and the prevention of damaging 'grand plans' that ride roughshod over contextual conditions and priorities. The fiscal and decision-making autonomy of local government and its scale of operations are critical for local economic performance. This should be the bedrock of local democracy, a political arena for real places and communities to work out their idiosyncrasies, varied resources and opportunities, challenges and priorities.

An associated concern is the relationship between political and economic democracy, a relationship that was widely denied by neoliberals in acquiescing to growing inequality at home and internationally. People must be able to vote equally with both their pocket and the ballot if democracy is to function. And they must see that their votes have an impact or apathy will set in. We need more critical discussion of and research into the concept and practice of democracy.

We must understand better the differences between a 'development' born of big capital and central government, in which benefits to locals are at best elusive and one created and owned by local people and communities. These differences are social, cultural and political as well as economic. Some Scandinavian governments once understood this point when they attempted to mitigate such differences, for example, in Norway's fresh fish acts and concession laws and in Denmark's regulations for wind farming. But few social scientists have researched and articulated these differences in outcomes over time.

In the end, a self-reliant community in charge of its own development is, as John Friedmann aptly observes, 'an inclusive, non-hierarchical society that stresses co-operation over competition, harmony with nature over exploitation, and social needs over unlimited personal desire. It represents the one best chance for the survival of the human race'. This is not just of interest to local inhabitants, but is consistent with the possibility of international harmony and co-existence. As such, a more effective strategy of local development would take us towards the Kantian ideal of 'perpetual peace' rather than away from it.

Further reading

Alparovitz, G. (with Williamson, T. and Imbroscio, D.) (2002) *Making a Place for Community: Local Democracy in a Global Era*. Routledge, New York.

Bassand, M., Brugger, E., Bryden, J., Friedmann, J. and Stuckey, B. (1986) *Self-Reliant Development in Europe*. Gower.

Brox, O. (2006) *Political Economy of Rural Development*. Eburon.

Bryden, J. and Geisler, C. (2007) Land reform and community: a 'new wave' land reform? *Land Use Policy*.

Bryden, J. and Hart, K. (2004) *A New Approach to Rural Development in Europe: Germany, Greece, Scotland and Sweden*. Edwin Mellen, Lampeter.

Fraser Taylor, R. and Mackenzie, F. (1992) *Development from Within: Survival in Rural Africa*. Routledge.

Friedmann, J. (1992) *Empowerment: The Politics of Alternative Development*. Blackwell.

Galtung, J., O'Brien, P. and Preiswerk, R. (eds) (1980) *Self-Reliance, a Strategy for Development*, London.

Scott, J. (1998) *Seeing like the State: How Certain Schemes to Improve the Human Condition have Failed*. Yale University Press, New Haven.

Seers, D. and Ostrom, S. (1983) *The Crisis of the European Regions*. Macmillan.

Stohr, W. (1992) *Global Challenge and Local Response*. UNU and Mansell Press.

Tilley, C. (1999) Power: Top down and bottom up. *Journal of Political Philosophy* 7, 330–52

24

Non-Governmental Organizations (NGOs)

David Lewis

In the twenty-first century, non-governmental organizations (NGOs) are a taken-for-granted feature of many Western and non-Western countries. They are recognized as important and influential actors in the institutional landscapes of modern capitalist societies. NGOs are found working across most fields of human endeavour, from the arts, leisure and recreation to international solidarity, missionary work, development, human rights, the environment and a host of other fields. Within these areas, NGOs may be active in a range of specialized roles such as democracy-building, conflict-resolution, cultural preservation, policy analysis, research and information provision. In what follows I will refer mainly to NGOs working in the area of international development.

For many people, NGOs have come also to be identified as part of a 'third sector' of organizations that are seen as distinct from the other two sectors of government and business – an institutional area or space sometimes also termed 'civil society' by political scientists (see *Third Sector, Community Participation*). In Britain, for example, NGOs have become high-profile organizations visible in the media in key international roles from the post-2004 *tsunami* reconstruction efforts in Indonesia, India and Sri Lanka, to 2005's *Make Poverty History* campaign for trade reform and debt cancellation. These two examples illustrate the two basic activities associated with NGOs: the delivery of services to people in need; and public campaigning in pursuit of social transformation.

Despite their ubiquity, 'NGO' is a notoriously imprecise acronym that is sometimes used in a very broad sense and at other times more narrowly. At its broadest, it encompasses the diverse range of non-state organizations, from small-scale community-based self-help groups to large-scale professionalized organizations, interest groups and networks. In its narrower sense, the term NGO is often used as shorthand to refer to a particular sub-group of such organizations that work in the broad field of 'development' (see *Development, Local Development*). Many such organizations rely on funds from sources within the international aid industry and may act as subcontractors for mainstream agencies such as bilateral donors or governments. Others raise funds directly from the public and undertake activities that seek to challenge mainstream development and its orthodoxies. I offer here a brief overview of NGO activities and debates within the world of international development.

Origins

The acronym 'NGO' was coined in the years immediately following the Second World War. Its origin lies in the formation of the United Nations in 1945, when the designation 'non-governmental organization' was awarded to certain international non-state organizations that were to be given consultative status in UN activities. But NGOs were not new. They had been active at the international level since the eighteenth century in Western countries, when national level issue-based organizations focused on the abolition of the slave trade and the movement for peace. By the start of the twentieth century, there were associations of NGOs promoting their identities and agendas at national and international levels. For example, at the World Congress of International Associations in 1910, there were 132 international associations represented, dealing with issues as varied as transport, intellectual property rights, narcotics control, public health issues, agriculture and the protection of nature; and NGOs became prominent at the League of Nations after the First World War, being active on issues such as labour rights. Many of the world's well-known NGOs in fact predate the emergence of the development industry. Save the Children Fund (SCF) was founded by Eglantyne Jebb in 1919 after the trauma of the First World War. Oxfam, which was originally known as the Oxford Committee Against the Famine, was established in 1942 in order to provide famine relief to victims of the Greek Civil War. CARE began its life sending US food packages to Europe after the Second World War.

Today, there are few if any countries where NGOs do not exist or operate, yet their local form and values are rooted in specific contexts. As Thomas Carroll has pointed out, 'all NGOs operate within a contextual matrix derived from specific locational and historic circumstances that change over time'. In Latin America, the tradition of peasant movements seeking improved rights to land and the efforts of political radicals working towards more open democratic societies both fed into the emergence of local NGOs. NGOs were also influenced by the rise of 'liberation theology' that signalled a renewed commitment to the poor among some sections of the Catholic Church. The Brazilian educator Paulo Freire's radical ideas about 'education for critical consciousness' inspired many other NGOs in developing countries. Alongside these radical influences, there were also more professionalized and careerist organizations, with close relationships to donors and governments. In Asia, NGOs were in part shaped by Christian missionaries, by the growth of the reformist middle classes and in the Indian subcontinent by the ideas of Mahatma Gandhi, who placed a concept of voluntary action at the centre of his vision of social transformation. In South Asia, NGOs working in the credit and savings field have drawn ideas from local self-help traditions, such as rotating credit groups in which households pool resources into a central fund and then take turns in borrowing and repaying. The global rise of Bangladesh's Grameen Bank seemed to provide a home-grown solution to the problem of poor rural people's lack of access to credit, and helped build a global microfinance movement based on its innovative group-based approach to small-scale lending (see *Microcredit*). Local associational activities underpin many African societies, such as the hometown associations common in Nigeria. These organizations mediate resources and relationships between local communities and global markets for labour and education.

Development NGOs in the modern sense became prominent from the late 1980s onwards, when they came to be regarded – mainly for ideological reasons – as offering potentially new and different solutions to longstanding development challenges. As a consequence, NGO numbers increased dramatically in the decade or more leading up to the millennium. NGOs began to assume far greater roles in development work than previously. They were first discovered and then celebrated by international development donors (see *International Organizations*) as potentially bringing fresh solutions to longstanding development problems in the wave of privatization that came to be known as neoliberalism (see *Alter-Globalization*). Government-to-government aid was thought to be inefficient and public sector development projects ineffective. The not-Government aspect of NGOs found favour as a result.

Solutions involving NGOs included new ideas about local voice and participation, ideas about empowerment, the concept of sustainability, a stronger gender focus and a range of more 'people-centred' approaches to development and poverty-reduction work. Michael Cernea argued that NGOs embodied 'a philosophy that recognizes the centrality of people in development policies' and this, in a context of market liberalization, gave them a 'comparative advantage' over government. At the same time, as one aspect of the effort by mainstream development agencies to 'roll back' the state through the World Bank's and IMF's 'structural adjustment' policies (the radical scaling down of public sector revenues and expenditures), NGOs were also seen as a cost-effective alternative to public-sector service delivery.

The increased profile of NGOs was also driven by two other factors. The first was the rediscovery of ideas about 'civil society', particularly among anti-authoritarian activists in Eastern Europe and Latin America during the 1980s. Many of these activists were drawn to Gramsci's view of civil society as a site of anti-hegemonic resistance. The second was the growth during the 1990s of the so-called 'good governance' agenda of agencies such as the World Bank. This discourse saw development outcomes as emerging from a balanced relationship between governments, the market and the 'third sector'. It also valued NGOs as flexible agents of privatization, with important roles to play in democratization and service delivery. Such an approach was closer to Tocqueville's view of civil society associations as a counter-weight to the state. 'Non-governmentalism' has thus been a dominant strand within ideologies of neoliberalism.

It is hard to know how many NGOs there are today, because few comprehensive or reliable statistics are kept. Some estimates put the figure at a million organizations, if both formal and informal variants are included, while the number of registered NGOs receiving international aid is probably closer to 'a few hundred thousand'. The United Nations estimates that there were about 35,000 large NGOs in 2000. Nor are there any accurate figures available for the quantity of resources that NGOs receive from aid, contracts and private donations. In 2004, it was estimated that NGOs were responsible for about US $23 billions of aid or approximately one third of total Official Development Assistance (ODA). In 2005, *Newsweek* cited figures indicating that ODA provided through NGOs had increased from 4.6 per cent in 1995 to 13 per cent in 2004, and that during the same period total aid volume had increased from $59 billion in to $79 billion.

The new attention given to NGOs from the late 1980s onwards brought large quantities of aid resources and efforts at building capacity to scale up their work. It led ultimately to important changes in mainstream development thinking and practice, including ideas about alternative approaches to development. Before long, however, too much came to be expected of NGOs and they were regarded as a 'quick fix' for development problems in some quarters. A backlash against NGOs took place among many of these donors during the 1990s, when evaluation evidence began to suggest that NGOs had been oversold as a 'magic bullet' for development. A global shift also now took place among international donors towards finding new ways of working with developing country governments, using mechanisms such as 'budget support' and 'sector-wide approaches'. Yet NGOs continue to be prominent in the worlds of welfare, humanitarian relief and emergency work.

Roles

NGOs are a diverse group of organizations that often seem to defy meaningful generalization, ranging from small informal groups to large formal agencies. NGOs play different roles and take different shapes within and across societies. As a result, 'NGO' as an analytical category lacks clarity. For example, despite the fact that NGOs are neither run by government nor driven by the profit motive, there are nevertheless many NGOs that receive high levels of government funding and others that seek to generate profits from market-based activity and then to plough back these into their work. Boundaries are blurred, as one might expect from a classification that emphasizes what they are *not* rather than what they *are* (see *Third Sector*). This has generated complex debates about what is and what is not an NGO. In relation to structure, NGOs may be large or small, formal or informal, bureaucratic or flexible. In terms of finance, many are externally funded, while others depend on locally mobilized resources. Although many NGOs form an integral part of the 'development industry' (the world of bilateral and multilateral aid donors, the United Nations system and the Bretton Woods institutions) and receive funds from it, there are also NGOs which choose to work *outside* the world of aid as far as possible.

One basic distinction common in the literature is that between 'Northern NGO' (NNGO) which refers to organizations whose origins lie in the industrialized countries, while 'Southern NGO' (SNGO) refers to organizations from the less-developed areas of the world. Another key distinction is between forms of NGO membership, such as community-based organizations or people's organizations, and intermediary forms of NGO that work with communities from outside, sometimes termed grassroots support organizations (GSOs). There are also numerous examples of bogus NGOs, such as those established as fronts by government (GONGOs – government-organized NGOs) or 'briefcase' NGOs set up by individuals for purely personal gain.

Some NGOs are well-resourced and affluent, while others lead a fragile 'hand-to-mouth' existence, struggling to survive from one year to the next. There are NGOs with highly professionalized staff, while others rely heavily on volunteers and supporters. NGOs are driven by a range of motivations and values. There are both secular and 'faith-based' organizations. Some NGOs may be charitable and paternalistic, while others seek to pursue radical or 'empowerment'-based approaches. Some NGOs aim to meet only peoples' immediate needs, while others take a longer-term view and seek to develop alternative ideas and approaches to problems. A single NGO might combine several of these different elements at any one time.

The work undertaken by development NGOs can be loosely categorized in terms of three main roles: implementer, catalyst and partner. The *implementer* role is concerned with the mobilization of resources to provide goods and services to people who need them. Service delivery is carried out by NGOs across a wide range of fields such as health care, microfinance, agricultural extension, emergency relief and human rights. This role has increased as a result of governance reform and privatization policies, so that NGOs have been increasingly 'contracted' by governments and donors to carry out specific tasks in return for payment; it has also become more prominent as NGOs respond with humanitarian assistance to man-made emergencies or natural disasters.

The *catalyst* role may be defined as an NGO's ability to inspire, facilitate or contribute to improved thinking and action to promote social transformation. This effort may be directed towards individuals or groups in local communities or among other actors in development such as governments, businesses or donors. It may include grassroots organizing and group formation, gender and empowerment work, lobbying and advocacy work, and attempts to influence wider policy processes through innovation and policy entrepreneurship.

The *partner* role reflects the growing trend for NGOs to work with governments, donors and the private sector on joint activities, such as providing specific inputs within a broader multi-agency programme or project, or undertaking socially responsible business initiatives. It also includes activities that take place among NGOs and with communities, such as 'capacity building' work which seeks to develop and strengthen capabilities. The current policy rhetoric of 'partnership' seeks to bring NGOs into mutually beneficial relationships with these other sectors.

As their name implies, NGOs also need to be viewed in the context of the governments against which they seek to define themselves. As 'non-governmental' organizations, NGOs are conditioned by, and gain much of their legitimacy from, their relationships with government. John Clark suggested that NGOs 'can oppose, complement or reform the state but they cannot ignore it'. NGOs will always remain dependent for 'room for manoeuvre' on the type of government they find themselves dealing with at international, national or local levels. Government attitudes to NGOs vary considerably from place to place and tend to change with successive regimes. They range from active hostility, leading governments to intervene in the affairs of NGOs or even to dissolve them (with and without good reason), to periods of active courtship, 'partnership' and sometimes 'co-optation' as governments and donors seek to incorporate NGOs into policy and intervention processes.

Debates

The world of NGOs contains a bewildering variety of labels. Confusingly, 'non-governmental organization' is often used interchangeably with related overlapping terms such as 'voluntary organization', 'non-profit organization' and 'community-based organization'. Each term possesses a distinctive origin and history, often embedded in different geographical and cultural contexts. Use of these various terms may not reflect much descriptive or analytical rigour, but arises rather from the setting in which thinking about NGOs has emerged. For example, 'non-profit organization' is frequently used in the United States, where the market dominates society and where citizen organizations are rewarded with tax breaks if they can show that they are not commercial or profit-making while working for the public good. In Britain, the terms 'voluntary organization' or 'charity' are commonly used in conformity with a long tradition of voluntary work informed by Christian values and the emergence of charity law in response to it. In the latter case a crucial distinction is that charitable status depends on an NGO being 'non-political', so that while Oxfam has the formal status of a registered charity (with associated tax benefits) because of its humanitarian focus, Amnesty International cannot, because human rights work is seen by the UK Charity Commission as 'political'.

Researchers have struggled with the task of defining, categorizing and understanding these non-governmental actors. The Johns Hopkins Comparative Non-Profit Sector Project (see *Third Sector, Solidarity Economy*) pointed out that 'the non-governmental sector is complex and needs to be understood holistically'. Definitions tend to be either *legal* (focusing on the type of formal registration and status of organizations in different country contexts), *economic* (in terms of the source of the organization's resources) or *functional* (based on the type of activities undertaken). Finding such approaches incomplete and partial, they constructed a 'structural/operational' definition that was derived from a fuller analysis of an organization's observable features. This definition proposed that a non-governmental organization needs to have five basic characteristics: it is *formal*, that is, the organization is institutionalized in that it has regular meetings, office bearers and some organizational permanence; it is *private* in that it is institutionally separate from government, though it may receive some support from government; it is *non-profit distributing*, and if a financial surplus is generated it does not accrue to owners or directors (often termed the 'non-distribution constraint'); it is *self-governing* and therefore able to control and manage its own affairs; and finally it is *voluntary*, and even if it does not use volunteer staff as such, there is at least some degree of voluntary participation in the conduct or management of the organization, such as in the form of a voluntary board of directors.

This approach helps us to clarify what constitutes a development NGO (taking the narrower usage of the term). It can be understood as part of a sub-set of third-sector organizations that are primarily engaged in development or humanitarian action at local, national and international levels. Drawing on elements of the structural-operational definition set out above, Anna Vakil defines NGOs as 'self-governing, private, not-for-profit organizations that are geared to improving the quality of life for disadvantaged people'. We can therefore contrast NGOs with other types of 'third-sector' groups such as trade unions, organizations concerned with arts or sport and professional associations.

Since the 1990s, NGOs have moved away from being seen primarily as 'a force for good' and now receive fierce criticism in some quarters. In 1999, an influential and highly critical article in *The Economist* was entitled 'Sins of the secular missionaries'. One set of critics argue from the left that NGOs have played a role in shifting attention away from state institutions towards more privatized – and potentially less accountable – forms of public-sector reform. For such critics, NGOs helped facilitate neoliberal policy changes either by participating in *de facto* privatization through the contracting-out of public services or by taking responsibility for clearing up the mess that is left by neoliberal policies which have disproportionately disadvantaged poorer or more vulnerable people. Another strong area of criticism has focused on what are seen as the shortcomings of NGO accountability. For example, G. D. Wood raised concerns about the creation of what he termed a 'franchise state' in Bangladesh where key public services were increasingly delegated to foreign-funded local NGOs that were only weakly accountable to local citizens. A third criticism follows from this – that NGOs have a tendency to become self-interested actors which impose their own agendas on the people in whose name they act. For example, some argue that NGOs sap the potential of radical groups, by drawing such activity into the safe professionalized and depoliticized world of development practice. NGOs may thus represent the end points of 'domesticated' social movements that have lost their political edge. In the field of humanitarian action, NGOs are often criticized for providing only patchy and unco-ordinated assistance to people in emergency situations, leading to frequent duplication of effort, limited understanding of local circumstances among international NGOs and a naive approach to the underlying causes of conflict and instability.

Critiques of NGOs are not confined to the 'developing' world nor necessarily to people on the political left. The neoconservatives in the United States argued during the 2000s that the actions of NGOs were potentially harmful to US foreign policy and business interests. The American Enterprise Institute (AEI), a think-tank close to the Bush administration, made headlines in June 2003 when it set up an NGO 'watchdog' website that set out to highlight 'issues of transparency and accountability in the operations of non-governmental organizations' which were seen as organizations who restricted US room for manoeuvre in foreign policy. Such debates have continued to take place between NGO 'supporters' and 'critics' partly because of the diversity of cases and contexts and partly because there is surprisingly little data available relating to the performance and effectiveness of NGOs.

Conclusion

The rise of NGOs was linked to a range of inter-related factors: new interest in the long-dormant concept of 'civil society'; the organizational concept of the 'third sector'; the history of transnational humanitarian action, from missionary activity to movements for labour rights; and the rise of neoliberalism with its emphasis on the private realm of institutional action, cost-effective forms of organizational flexibility and a reduced role for the state. The dominant view of NGOs as heroic organizations seeking to 'do good' in difficult circumstances has rightly become tempered as their novelty has worn off after the millennium. The idea of NGOs as a straightforward 'magic bullet' that would solve longstanding development problems has also now passed. For Anthony Bebbington and his associates, the value of development NGOs is their potential role in constructing and demonstrating 'alternatives' to mainstream development practice:

> In being 'not governmental' they constitute vehicles for people to participate in development and social change in ways that would not be possible through government programmes. In being 'not

governmental' they constitute a 'space' in which it is possible to think about development and social change in ways that would not be likely through government programmes . . .

For some, NGOs are useful actors in development because they can provide cost-effective services in flexible ways, while for others NGOs are campaigners fighting for change or generating new ideas and approaches to development problems.

The large volume of resources that NGOs receive, combined with the fact that they are given a higher level of public exposure and scrutiny than ever before, speaks to their continuing importance. In a sense, NGOs benefit from 'meaning all things to all people'. Tessa Morris-Suzuki writes that 'NGOs may pursue change, but they can equally work to maintain existing social and political systems'. For example, for radicals who seek to explore alternative visions of development and change, NGOs may be seen as progressive vehicles for change. For conservative thinkers seeking private alternatives to the state, NGOs may be regarded as part of market-based solutions to policy problems. All this means that NGOs have come to be seen as a kind of *tabula rasa*, onto which a range of current ideas, expectations and anxieties about social transformation and development have been projected. The fact that NGOs have now become the focus of criticism from many different political perspectives is both a reflection of the wide diversity of NGO types and roles that exist and of their increasing power and importance in the twenty-first century. Perhaps policy-makers and the general public will now take a more realistic view of what NGOs can and cannot achieve.

Further reading

Bebbington, A., Hickey, S. and Mitlin, D. (2008) Introduction: can NGOs make a difference? The challenge of development alternatives. In Bebbington, A., Hickey, S. and Mitlin, D. (eds) *Can NGOs Make a Difference? The Challenge of Development Alternatives*. Zed Books, London, pp. 3–37.

Cernea, M. M. (1988) Non-governmental organisations and local development. *World Bank Discussion Papers*. The World Bank, Washington, DC.

Charnovitz, S. (1997) Two centuries of participation: NGOs and international governance. *Michigan Journal of International Law* 18 (2), 183–286.

Clark, J. (1991) *Democratizing Development: The Role of Voluntary Organizations*. Earthscan, London.

Fisher, W. F. (1997) Doing good? The politics and anti-politics of NGO practices. *Annual Review of Anthropology* 26, 439–64.

Howell, J. and Pearce, J. (2001) *Civil Society and Development: A Critical Exploration*. Lynne Rienner Publishers, Boulder, CO.

Kaldor, M. (2003) *Global Civil Society: An Answer to War*. Polity, Cambridge.

Korten, D. (1990) *Getting to the 21st Century: Voluntary Action and the Global Agenda*. Kumarian Press, West Hartford.

Lewis, D. (2005) Individuals, organisations and public action: trajectories of the 'non-governmental' in development studies. In Kothari, U. (ed.) *A Radical History of Development Studies*. Zed Books, London.

Lewis, D. and Kanji, N. (2009) *Non-Governmental Organizations and Development*. Routledge, London.

Morris-Suzuki, T. (2000) For and against NGOs. *New Left Review*, March/April, 63–84.

Riddell, R. (2007) *Does Foreign Aid Really Work?* Oxford University Press, Oxford.

Tvedt, T. (1998) *Angels of Mercy or Development Diplomats? NGOs and Foreign Aid*. James Currey, Oxford.

25

Social Capital

Desmond McNeill

The last decade has witnessed a rapidly growing literature on social capital. Although he did not invent the term, it was the political scientist Robert Putnam, with his book *Making Democracy Work*, who caused it to 'take off' so dramatically in the mid 1990s – in the media as well as the academy.

Social capital, says Putnam, 'refers to features of social organization, such as trust, norms and networks, that can improve the efficiency of society by facilitating co-ordinated action'. What he sought to show in the book, through a comparative analysis of the economic development of Northern and Southern Italy, was that social capital played a central part in the relative economic success of the former.

The concept of social capital was popular for several reasons, in addition to Putnam's own skills in promoting it. One reason, which many have noted, is that the idea – and the main thesis of Putnam's book – appeals perhaps to a nostalgic view of values which are in danger of being lost in the modern world. It clearly fitted the prevalent concern, especially in USA, with a 'loss of community'. Francis Fukuyama's book *Trust* came out at much the same time. Indeed, another article by Putnam, 'Bowling alone' (later a book), hit the headlines in Washington. President Clinton even used the term social capital in a State of the Union address.

Putnam also offers a hard-headed argument in favour of such

values; that they actually encourage economic growth. The concept of social capital helps one to believe that community, trust and shared values are 'a good thing', as demonstrated by Putnam's comparison between the very different economic fortunes of Northern and Southern Italy. His book, he says, 'helps explain why social capital, as embodied in horizontal networks of civic engagement, bolsters the performance of state and economy'. Encapsulated in a single sentence, Putnam's thesis is: 'strong society, strong economy; strong society, strong state'. He contrasts this position with two others that have recently had some impact on the state–society–market debate: Mancur Olson's 'strong society, weak economy' and Joel Migdal's 'strong society, weak state'.

Alejandro Portes describes the development of the term: 'The journey was fast, explaining major social outcomes by relabeling them with a novel term, and then employing the same term to formulate sweeping policy prescriptions.' In academia, scholars with widely differing perspectives found the concept attractive. As one critical reviewer put it, 'Putnam has interpreted his results in such catholic terms that students of cultural interpretation and public choice – who differ in so many ways – can find common ground in the outcome.'

To economists, social capital supplied a new explanatory variable which could be used in the analysis of economic performance; and it appealed also in other fields such as organization studies and social work. It is claimed, for example, that social capital influences career success, helps workers find jobs, facilitates inter-unit resource exchange and product innovation, reduces turnover rates, and strengthens supplier relations, regional production networks and inter-firm learning. In the field of development policy, where the World Bank was a powerful advocate, it promised a new opportunity for development planners not merely to measure social capital, but even to build it. The potential for social engineering was thus still further enhanced.

The term had been used earlier by the sociologist Pierre Bourdieu, though in a rather different sense. A measure of the success of Putnam's version is provided by a bibliometric analysis which shows that, in *Sociological Abstracts*, the term 'social capital' was, by the end of the century, as common as the term 'social relations'. But it has been largely ignored by anthropologists and has met with some criticism from other social scientists.

The origins and meanings of the term

Putnam says that he took the term from the sociologist James Coleman, who, in his seminal 1988 paper, expressly adopted a perspective from methodological individualism. Coleman himself states that he adopted the term from an economist, Glenn Loury, who in turn drew on the sociological literature. One of the first known references to social capital was in a 1916 article on support for rural schools.

Although Bourdieu coined the term independently, his usage is rather different, being less individualistic. It is Coleman and Putnam, not Bourdieu, who shaped the subsequent debate. Of academic articles using the term 'social capital' in the period 1972–2002, 320 cite Putnam and only eighteen cite Bourdieu. For newspapers, the figures are even more stark: in articles concerning social capital, 260 refer to Putnam and only four to Bourdieu. Clearly it was Putnam who hit the headlines.

Coleman saw his task as to make a revisionist analysis of the functioning of economic systems: 'to maintain the conception of rational action, but to superimpose on it social and institutional organization – either endogenously generated, as in the functionalist explanations of some of the new institutional economics, or as exogenous factors, as in the more proximate-causally oriented work of some sociologists'.

To assist in this task, he adopts the concept of social capital, which, unlike other forms of capital, 'inheres in the structure of relations between actors and among actors'. 'The value of the concept of social capital lies first in the fact that it identifies certain aspects of social structure by their functions . . . (namely) the value to actors of resources that they can use to achieve their interest.' 'Actors establish relations purposefully and continue them when they continue to provide benefits . . . Norms arise as attempts to limit negative external effects or encourage positive ones.'

From these few quotations it can be seen that Coleman adopts a perspective close to that of economics. Indeed, he concludes as follows: 'This (paper) is part of a theoretical strategy that involves the use of the paradigm of rational action but without the assumption of atomistic elements stripped of social relations.' In other words, he sought to retain the rationality paradigm without the assumption of autonomy. And he asserts the importance of relations. Yet his notion of social relations and norms clearly derives from an individualistic and self-interested perspective.

There are other definitions of social capital, both broader and narrower. According to the World Bank, 'The most encompassing view of social capital includes the social and political environment that shapes social structure and enables norms to develop.' This definition is so broad that it includes almost anything in the social and even political arena.

Putnam's definition is somewhat narrower. As noted above, he says it 'refers to features of social organization, such as trust, norms and networks . . .' He also refers to these 'features' as 'forms', 'stocks' or 'components' of social capital. Trust, he says, is an essential component of social capital. And he further distinguishes between thick trust and thin trust, by which he means personal trust, based on individual relations, and social trust, where individuals do not necessarily know each other. The second of these is especially important because he sees it as a key to 'community' (see *Community Participation*). It is also, of course, more difficult to explain from an individualistic standpoint. How does such trust come about and how can it persist over time? To explain this, he turns to the other two forms of social capital: 'Social trust in complex modern settings can arise from norms of reciprocity and networks of civic engagement.'

Norms, in his words, undergird social trust; and the most important norm is reciprocity which may be specific or generalized. Such norms are closely linked to networks of civic engagement or of commerce and exchange: 'An effective norm of generalized reciprocity is likely to be associated with dense networks of social exchange . . . Conversely, repeated exchange over a period of time tends to encourage the development of a norm of generalized reciprocity.' And networks are also of two kinds – horizontal or vertical ('weblike' or 'maypolelike'): 'bringing together agents of equivalent status and power, or unequal agents in asymmetric relations of hierarchy and dependence'.

Putnam distinguishes between bonding and bridging social capital. The former applies to links between socially homogeneous groups of people, the latter to heterogeneous groups. Though both are, it is claimed, positive for those involved, bonding social capital may have negative consequences for outsiders, as in the case of criminal gangs.

Promotion by the World Bank

Part of social capital's success as a concept may be attributed to its having been promoted by the World Bank – or at least by some members of that powerful organization. In recent years, there has been increasing recognition by the World Bank – and more generally among development assistance agencies – of the importance of community participation. This is manifested in, or at least related to, an increasing involvement of 'civil society' – often, in practice, taken as being synonymous with non-governmental organizations (see *NGOs*) – both in the planning and implementation of projects in the field, and in consultation processes at headquarters. A related factor is the growing number of anthropologists and sociologists working for the Bank and organizational changes that have given greater prominence to social issues. There has been a significant shift within the Bank towards the inclusion of political issues, notably through its work on 'governance'. These changes have given greater recognition to the need for insights from disciplines such as sociology and political science.

The World Bank has always had an ambition – one that it has been rather successful in achieving – to be at the forefront of ideas in the realm of development policy; if not initiating them, then at least rapidly taking them over (see *Informal Economy*). The discipline and language of economics has for many years been dominant within the World Bank, and especially in its Research Department. In order to be accepted, therefore, new ideas must survive criticism by this particular discipline. The reason why the concept of social capital is so attractive to the World Bank is that it allows the dominant economic perspective to take account of sociological and political considerations which have increasingly been recognized as important. The concept fits well at the interface between economics and sociology – in the so-called 'new institutional economics'. (This approach is closely linked to rational choice theory in sociology, such as that favoured by Coleman. It stands in contrast to the 'old' institutional economics of Polanyi and Veblen. The difference between the two is, in a nutshell, that the former treats institutions as if they were markets, while the latter treats markets as if they were institutions.)

Thanks to the work of Putnam, Coleman and others, staff in the World Bank could thus adopt a new term which was at the forefront of both academic and popular debate, not only within the disciplines of sociology and political science but – most important (for the Bank) – perhaps also in economics. It is therefore understandable that research-minded Bank staff had an *a priori* interest in the idea. This was a necessary condition for its success, but hardly sufficient. The rapid progress of the idea required its being actively taken up by those that count.

As in any organization, certain key individuals played an important role, and in this case several contributed to giving the idea of social capital prominence in the Bank. The President himself, James Wolfensohn, showed a special interest in the participation and involvement of NGOs, which created a supportive context. The Chief Economist at this time, Joseph Stiglitz, who enjoyed a very high reputation for his work on the economics of information and institutions, played an important part. 'Together, the theoretical and political advances secured by this unlikely duo (Wolfensohn and Stiglitz) have pushed the Bank into the mainstream of social development thinking.' But a very important role was also played by Ismail Serageldin, formerly Vice-President for Sustainable Development, who had a keen interest not only in the environment, but also in social dimensions of development.

External actors made a significant contribution too. On the invitation of key individuals within the Bank, Mancur Olson was actively involved at an early stage, before his untimely death. Others participated in workshops and other events where World Bank staff and academia were in dialogue. Putnam was brought in and participated in the Bank's Social Capital Initiative (SCI), and he gave a high-profile public lecture at a 1999 conference. 'Putnam was the most important. . . You can get any old fad going, but to be sustainable it must have a core of rigour to it. That comes from the academic side.' (Paul Collier, personal communication). Neither Olson nor Putnam was an economist, but – in what may be seen as an important tactical move – a number of very prestigious economists were invited to informal meetings at the World Bank to discuss the concept. This led to the publication of a book, by Dasgupta and Serageldin, with contributions by many of those mentioned above, as well as by Nobel Prize-winning economists Kenneth Arrow and Robert Solow.

It was of crucial importance that senior economists within or close to the World Bank should take social capital seriously. In addition to enlisting the interest, and in some cases support, of prestigious economists, Serageldin was also active in obtaining external funding for two research programmes on social capital. But opinions among influential figures in the Bank apparently differed. At a major conference organized to discuss the research at the World Bank, one staff member regarded the empirical results claimed as 'terribly contrived'; but another felt that there was a 'pot of gold' here.

Serageldin's definition of social capital is broad: 'the institutional and cultural basis for a society to function'. 'Without a degree of common identification with the forms of governance and of cultural expression and social behavior that make a society more than the sum of collection of individuals it is impossible to imagine a functioning social order.' Like others, he saw it as a natural addition to earlier types of capital, but in his case linked expressly to the concept of sustainable development.

In brief, a conjuncture of key individuals and structural factors may be said to have played their part in causing the concept of social capital to achieve such rapid prominence in the Bank. But the most crucial issue was that it seemed to allow economists to categorize sociological and political factors in terms amenable to their own discipline and perspective. It even seemed to promise that this new phenomenon could be quantified, and that social capital could actually be 'built' through appropriate development programmes and projects.

A former Director of Research, Paul Collier, had this to say about how economists may collaborate with other social scientists:

> Economists are trained to high standards of precision in thought, especially causal arguments. The mindset which gives you econometrics is the mental hygiene of disentangling causation. Putnam's work was interesting, but there was not absolute clarity on the causal structure. I felt it was right (but) what was missing was the analytical microfoundations, the part economists are best able to get into is the notion of networks. That nests in neatly with costly information. This notion is the single most important revelation of economics in our lifetime.

As indicated at the outset, the attraction of Putnam's social capital is that it appears to promote both economic growth and community; giving the development policymaker the best of both worlds. The gap between competing policies is thus apparently bridged.

Samuel Bowles sees social capital as the bridge between what may be an even broader ideological divide – state vs. market: 'The demise of the twin illusions of our century – laissez-faire and statism – (thus) cleared the intellectual and rhetorical stage for social capital's entry' and 'Once everyone realized that market failures are the rule rather than the exception and that governments are neither smart enough nor good enough to make things entirely right, the social capital rage was bound to happen. Conservatives love it . . . Those to the left of centre are no less enchanted.'

When considering alternative policies at this level of generality, ends and means start to become entangled. Certainly social capital relates to means as well as ends. Thus it appears also to provide a bridge between two approaches to development intervention that usually contrasted: the participatory, bottom-up approach and the more technocratic, top-down approach.

Criticisms

While social capital was much used in the World Bank, it is almost entirely absent in publications by its 'competitor', the United Nations Development Programme (UNDP). In academia, it has been very widely used in political science and sociology. (In social science dissertations, it appears twice in the 1970s and nineteen times in the 1980s, taking off in the early 1990s and increasing rapidly thereafter: 275 dissertations used 'social capital' as compared to 636 for 'social relations' in the period 1996–2000). But the term is hardly used at all in anthropology and has had a mixed reception in economics. Of course some of those who use the term are critical of it; but it cannot, apparently, be ignored.

Among economists, criticism comes even from some of those invited by the World Bank to contribute to their book. These authors note that 'it is difficult to think of an academic notion that has entered the common vocabulary of social discourse more quickly than the idea of social capital'. But they add that 'while the term has gained wide currency, it has not found favour among economists'. In his chapter, Arrow recognizes the importance of social networks, but rejects the term 'social capital', mainly because it fails to satisfy the requirement of capital of 'deliberate sacrifice in the present for future benefit'. The other Nobel prize-winner, Solow, also doubts that social capital is the right term to describe the important phenomenon under discussion, namely 'behaviour patterns' such as 'trust, the willingness and capacity to co-operate and co-ordinate, the habit of contributing to a common effort even if no one else is watching

. . .' He notes that economists try but often fail to analyse everything in terms of rationality and individual greed and adds, 'Patterns of behaviour, of acceptable and expectable behaviour, start off as social norms, enforced by parental pressure or peer pressure or religious instruction, or in some other way, and are eventually internalized.'

The (then) Chief Economist of the World Bank, Stiglitz, is rather more positive about the concept, and relates it to a hypothetical evolution inspired in part by Karl Polanyi, but with a rather different conclusion: 'a change from a situation in which economic activity is embedded in social relations to one in which social relations are embedded in the economic system'.

In the concluding chapter of the book (which contains contributions also from sociologists and political scientists), another reputed economist and co-editor, Partha Dasgupta, seeks to give a provisional verdict on the merits of the term. He concludes that Putnam's characterization of social capital suffers from a weakness: 'it encourages us to amalgamate incommensurable objects, namely (and in that order), beliefs, behavioural rules and such forms of capital assets as interpersonal networks'.

In summary, the weakness of the concept of social capital, as judged by mainstream economists, seems to lie not so much in the 'social' as in the 'capital'. Commentators recognize that the phenomenon in question ('norms and networks') is important, not least because it has an impact on economic phenomena, such as an individual's or group's material well-being. But they doubt whether our understanding of the phenomenon is enhanced by regarding it as capital.

Ben Fine is much more critical in his scathing study of the concept of social capital, where he deals at some length with economists' usage of the term. Before social capital was invented, he asserts, 'it was necessary to take the social, institutions and customary behaviour as given, with the latter taken to be irrational. Now, even on the continuing basis of methodological individualism, this need no longer be the case.' He sees the adoption of the term by economists as yet another example of its colonization of the social sciences and draws some 'harsh and general' conclusions about how economics proceeds in such circumstances:

> First, it tends to be parasitical on the other social sciences, picking up
> ideas that have originated there and reworking them through the new

economic principles . . . Second, contributions are often profoundly
ignorant of existing literature . . . From an analytical perspective, however, the most important feature of economics' incursion into other
social sciences is its reductionism.

Certainly one can find evidence for Fine's claim that economists
writing about social capital have tended to ignore the existing literature from other disciplines. In the World Bank publications, there
are very few references to anthropology, most are to sociology and
political science, this despite a massive empirical literature in anthropology concerned with communities; and a significant theoretical
literature concerning social networks dating back to the 1970s.

Conclusion

Many have been surprised, and some outraged, at the remarkable
success of the concept of social capital. One of its attractions lies in
its apparent potential for linking research and policy, drawing on the
insights of social scientists to design a better world. But within the
social sciences, the two disciplines that represent the methodological
extremes – anthropology and economics – are both rather critical
of the concept, for very different reasons. Many contend that the
weakness of social capital is that it can mean all things to all people.
Perhaps this is precisely its appeal.

Further reading

Adler, P. and Kwon, S. (2002). Social capital: prospects for a new concept.
    The Academy of Management Review 27 (1), 17–40.
Bourdieu, P. (1986) The forms of capital. In Richardson, J. (ed.) *Handbook of
    Theory and Research for the Sociology of Education*. Greenwood Press, Westport,
    CT.
Bowles, S. (1999) Social capital and community governance. *Focus* 20 (3),
    6–10.
Coleman, J. (1988) Social capital in the creation of human capital. *American
    Journal of Sociology* 94 (Supplement), 95–120.
Dasgupta, P. and Serageldin, I. (eds) (2000) *Social Capital: A Multifaceted
    Perspective*. World Bank, Washington, DC.
Fine, B. (2000) *Social Capital versus Social Theory: Political Economy and Social
    Science at the Turn of the Millennium*. Routledge, London and New York.
Harriss, J. (2001) *Depoliticizing Development: The World Bank and Social Capital*.
    Leftword, New Delhi.

McNeill, D. (2004) Social capital and the World Bank. In Bøås, M. (ed.) *Global Institutions and Development: Framing the World?* Routledge, London.

McNeill, D. (2006) The spread of ideas in development theory and policy: a bibliometric analysis. *Global Social Policy* 6 (3), 334–54

McNeill, D. (2007) Social capital or sociality? Methodological contrasts between economics and other social sciences. In Ioannides, S. and Nielsen, K. (eds) *Economics and Social Sciences: Complements, Competitors, Accomplices?* Edward Elgar Press, Cheltenham.

Putnam, R. (2000) *Bowling Alone: The Collapse and Revival of American Community.* Simon and Schuster, New York.

Putnam, R., Leonardi, R. and Nanetti, R. (1993) *Making Democracy Work: Civic Traditions in Modern Italy.* Princeton University Press, Princeton, NJ.

26

Social Enterprise

Jacques Defourny and Marthe Nyssens

Historical background

Field organizations, corresponding to what are now called 'social enterprises', have existed well before the mid 1990s when the term began to be used in Western Europe and the United States. Indeed, the third sector, whether it is called non-profit, voluntary or the social economy (which includes co-operatives in the European tradition), has long witnessed entrepreneurial dynamics. These resulted in innovative solutions for providing goods and services to persons or communities whose needs were met neither by private companies nor by public providers. But for reasons that vary according to national or regional context, the concept of social enterprise is now fast becoming popular across the world, along with two closely related terms, namely 'social entrepreneur' and 'social entrepreneurship'.

1. *Western Europe*

In Europe, the concept of social enterprise as such seems to have first appeared in Italy, where it was promoted through a journal launched in 1990 and entitled *Impresa sociale*. In the late 1980s indeed, new co-operative-like initiatives emerged in that country to respond to unmet needs, especially in the field of work integration as well as personal services. As the existing legislation did not allow associations to develop economic activities, the Italian Parliament passed a law in 1991 creating a new legal form of 'social co-operative' which proved to be very well-adapted to those pioneering social enterprises.

The remarkable development of the latter also inspired various other countries during the following two decades, across Europe and outside (for instance in South Korea). Indeed, several other European countries introduced new legal forms reflecting the entrepreneurial approach adopted by this increasing number of 'not-for-profit' organizations, even though the term social enterprise was not always used as such in the legislation.

In many European countries, besides the creation of new legal forms or frameworks, the 1990s saw the development of specific public programmes targeting the field of work integration. Social enterprises may be active in a wide spectrum of activities, as the social purpose they pursue may refer to many different fields. However, since the mid-1990s, one major type of social enterprise has been dominant across Europe, namely 'work integration social enterprises' (WISEs). The main objective of work integration social enterprises is to help low-qualified unemployed people who are at risk of permanent exclusion from the labour market and to integrate these people into work and society through a productive activity. This has even led, in several cases, to the concept of social enterprise being systematically associated with such employment-creation initiatives.

2. United States

In the US, the first strand of the debate on social entrepreneurship and social enterprises referred to the use of commercial activities by non-profit organizations in support of their mission. Although such behaviour may be traced back to the very foundation of the US, when community or religious groups were selling homemade goods or holding bazaars to supplement voluntary donations, it gained a particular importance in the specific context of the late 1970s and 1980s. The downturn in the economy in the late 1970s led to welfare retrenchment and to important cutbacks in federal funding. Non-profits then began to expand their commercial activities to fill the gap in their budget through the sale of goods or services not directly related to their mission.

Based on a broader vision of entrepreneurship, the second strand of this debate can be traced back to B. Drayton and Ashoka, the organization he founded in 1980, as its primary driving forces. The mission of Ashoka was (and still is) to identify and support outstanding individuals with pattern-setting ideas for social change. Ashoka focuses on the profiles of very specific individuals, first referred to as public entrepreneurs, able to bring about social innovation in various fields, rather than on the forms of organization they might set up. Various foundations involved in 'venture philanthropy', such as the Schwab Foundation and the Skoll Foundation, have embraced the idea that innovation is central to social entrepreneurship and provide support to social entrepreneurs.

Major conceptualizations

When looking at the US landscape, what is striking is the diversity of concepts which have been used since the early 1980s to describe entrepreneurial behaviour with social aims that developed in the country, mainly although not exclusively within the non-profit sector: 'non-profit venture', 'non-profit entrepreneurship', 'social-purpose endeavour', 'social innovation', 'social-purpose business', 'community wealth enterprise', 'public entrepreneurship', 'social enterprise'. . . Although the community of non-profit studies early identified trends towards commercialization, the bulk of this conceptual debate has been shaped by scholars belonging to business schools. To classify the different conceptions, Dees and Anderson have proposed to distinguish two major schools of thought. The first school of thought on social entrepreneurship refers to the use of commercial activities by non-profit organizations in support of their mission. Organizations like Ashoka fed a second major school, named the 'social innovation' school of thought.

Although field initiatives blossomed across Europe, the concept of social enterprise as such did not really spread until the late 1990s. In the academic sphere however, major analytical efforts were undertaken from the second part of the 1990s, both at the conceptual and empirical levels, especially by the EMES European Research Network, bringing together mainly social science scholars, especially economists and sociologists.

We now focus on these three conceptual approaches while testifying to the growing mutual influence of each side of the Atlantic upon the other, probably with a stronger influence of the US on Europe than the other way round. More precisely, various authors from European business schools, such as Nicholls and Mair, Robinson, Hockerts, among others, contributed to the debate, relying on the concept of social entrepreneurship as it took root in the US context, although of course they brought in their own backgrounds as Europeans.

1. The 'earned income' school of thought

The first school of thought set the grounds for conceptions of social enterprise mainly defined by earned-income strategies. The bulk of its publications were based on non-profits' interest in becoming more commercial and could be described as prescriptive: many of them came from consultancy firms and they focused on strategies for starting a business that would earn income in support of a non-profit organization's social mission and that could help diversify its funding base.

In the late 1990s, the Social Enterprise Alliance, a central player in the field, defined social enterprise as 'any earned-income business or strategy undertaken by a non-profit to generate revenue in support of its charitable mission'. Such a market-oriented conception of social enterprise crossed the ocean when a 'Social Enterprise Unit' was created by the British government to promote social enterprise across the country. Although no reference was made to the percentage of market resources in the definition adopted by the Social Enterprise Unit or in the Community Interest Company (CIC) law, it is widely accepted that a significant part (usually 50 per cent or more) of the total income must be market-based for an organization to qualify as a social enterprise.

From such a perspective, it is straightforward to name that first school the 'earned income' school of thought. Within this, however, we suggest a distinction between an earlier version, focusing on non-profits, that we call the *commercial non-profit approach*, and a broader version, embracing all forms of business initiatives, that may be named the *mission-driven business approach*. This latter approach also refers to the field of social purpose venture as encompassing all organizations that trade for a social purpose, including for-profit companies.

2. The 'social innovation' school of thought

This second school puts the emphasis on social entrepreneurs in the Schumpeterian meaning of the term, in a perspective similar to that adopted earlier by the pioneering work of Young. Along such lines, entrepreneurs in the non-profit sector are change-makers as they carry out new combinations in at least one the following areas: new services, new quality of services, new methods of production, new production factors, new forms of organizations or new markets. Social entrepreneurship may therefore be a question of outcomes and social impact rather than a question of income. Moreover, the systemic nature of innovation brought about and its impact at a broad societal level are often underlined.

Dees has proposed the best-known definition of social entrepreneurs. He sees the latter as 'playing the role of change agents in the social sector by adopting a mission to create and sustain social value, recognizing and relentlessly pursuing new opportunities to serve that mission, engaging in a process of continuous innovation, adaptation and learning, acting boldly without being limited by resources currently in hand, and finally exhibiting a heightened sense of accountability to the constituencies served and for the outcomes created'.

Although many initiatives of social entrepreneurs result in setting up non-profit organizations, most recent works of this school tend to underline blurred frontiers and opportunities for entrepreneurial social innovation within the private for-profit sector and the public sphere as well. By the way, the concept of social entrepreneurship is increasingly described as a very wide spectrum and often appears as the broadest of the three 'SE concepts'.

The divergence between the 'social innovation' and 'earned income' schools should not be overstated, though. Viewing social entrepreneurship as a mission-driven business is increasingly common in business schools and foundations that foster business methods more broadly, not just earned-income strategies, as a path towards social innovation. Recent work stresses a 'double bottom line' vision as well as the creation of 'blended value' in an effort to balance and better integrate economic and social purposes and strategies.

3. The EMES European approach to social enterprise

As early as 1996, that is before most European public policies were launched, a major research programme funded by the European Commission was undertaken by a group of scholars coming from all EU member states. Named the EMES European Research

Network,[1] that group first devoted itself to the definition of a set of criteria to identify organizations likely to be called social enterprises in each of the fifteen countries forming the EU by that time.

The EMES approach derives from extensive dialogue among several disciplines (economics, sociology, political science and management) as well as among the various national traditions and sensitivities present in the European Union. Moreover, guided by a project that was both theoretical and empirical, it preferred from the outset identification and clarification of indicators over a concise and elegant definition.

Four criteria reflect the economic and entrepreneurial dimensions of social enterprises:

- a continuous activity producing goods and/or selling services;
- a high degree of autonomy;
- a significant level of economic risk;
- a minimum amount of paid work.

Five other indicators encapsulate the social dimensions of such enterprises:

- an explicit aim to benefit the community;
- an initiative launched by a group of citizens;
- decision-making power not based on capital ownership;
- a participatory nature, which involves various parties affected by the activity;
- limited profit distribution.

Such indicators were never intended to represent the set of conditions that an organization should meet to qualify as a social enterprise. Rather than constituting prescriptive criteria, they describe an ideal-type in Weber's terms, i.e. an abstract construction that enables researchers to position themselves within the 'galaxy' of social enterprises. In other words, they constitute a tool, somewhat analogous to a compass, which helps the researchers locate the position of

---

[1]   The letters EMES stand for *'EMergence des Enterprises Sociales en Europe'* – i.e. the title in French of the vast research project carried out from 1996 through 2000 by the network. The acronym EMES was subsequently retained when the network decided to become a formal international association. See www.emes.net.

the observed entities relative to one another and eventually identify subsets of social enterprises they want to study more deeply. These economic and social indicators allow the identification of brand-new social enterprises, but they can also lead to older organizations being designated as social enterprises when they are reshaped by new internal dynamics.

While stressing a social aim embedded in an economic activity, as in the two previous schools, the EMES approach differs from them mainly by stressing specific governance models (rather than the profile of social entrepreneurs) which are often found in European social enterprises and may be analysed in a twofold perspective. First, democratic control and/or participatory involvement of stakeholders reflect a quest for more economic democracy inside the enterprise, in line with the tradition of co-operatives which represent a major component of the third sector/social economy in most European societies. Combined with constraints on the distribution of profits, it can be viewed as a way to protect and strengthen the primacy of the social mission in the organization. Secondly, those two combined guarantees also act as a signal allowing public authorities to support social enterprises and scaling up social innovation in various ways (legal frameworks, public subsidies, fiscal exemptions etc.). Without such guarantees (often involving a strict non-distribution constraint), the risk would be greater that public subsidies just induce more profits to be distributed among owners or managers. In turn, such public support often allows social enterprises to avoid purely market-oriented strategies, which, in many cases, would lead them away from clients who cannot afford market prices and nevertheless constitute a target group according to their social mission.

The first research carried out by the EMES network also presented an initial attempt to outline a theory of social enterprise: an ideal-typical social enterprise could be seen as a 'multiple-goal, multi-stakeholder and multiple-resource enterprise'. These theorized features paved the way for another major research programme. Although social enterprises are active in a wide variety of fields, including personal social services, urban regeneration, environmental services and the provision of other public goods or services, EMES researchers decided to focus on work integration social enterprises (WISEs), with a view to allowing meaningful international comparisons. On this basis, they made an inventory of the different types of social enterprise in the field of on-the-job training and work integration of low-qualified persons in order to test empirically the ideal-typical social enterprise.

To conclude, it clearly appears that distinctive conceptions and concrete expressions of social enterprise and social entrepreneurship are deeply rooted in the social, economic, political and cultural contexts where they emerge. Each context produces specific debates. In the US, strong reliance on private actors could result from a kind of implicitly shared confidence in market forces to solve an increasing part of social issues in modern societies. Even if various scholars stress the need to mobilize different types of resources, it is not impossible that the current wave of social entrepreneurship may act as a priority-setting process and a selection process for social challenges that deserve to be addressed because of their potential in terms of earned income. In Europe, the key role of public bodies in the field of social enterprises may reduce them to instruments to achieve specific goals that are given priority in a political agenda, with the risk of curbing the dynamics of social innovation.

All this means that supporting the development of social enterprise cannot be done by relying only on US or European approaches. Unless they are embedded in local contexts, social enterprises will just be replications of formulas that last only as long as they are fashionable.

Further reading

Austin, J. E., Leonard, B., Reficco, E. and Wei-Skillern, J. (2006) Social entrepreneurship: it's for corporations too. In Nicholls, A. (ed.) *Social Entrepreneurship: New Models of Sustainable Social Change.* Oxford University Press, pp. 169–80.

Borzaga, C. and Defourny, J. (eds) (2001) *The Emergence of Social Enterprise.* Routledge, London and New York.

Dees, J. G. (1998) The meaning of social entrepreneurship. *The Kauffman Center for Entrepreneurial Leadership Working Paper.*

Dees, J. G. and Anderson, B. B. (2006) Framing a theory of social entrepreneurship: building on two schools of practice and thought. *ARNOVA Occasional Paper Series: Research on Social Entrerpreneurship* 1 (3), 39–66.

Defourny, J. and Nyssens, M. (2010) Conceptions of social enterprise and social entrepreneurship in Europe and the United States: convergences and divergences. *Journal of Social Entrepreneurship* 1 (1).

Emerson, J. (2006) Moving ahead together: implications of a blended value framework for the future of social entrepreneurship. In Nicholls, A.

(ed.) *Social Entrepreneurship: New Models of Sustainable Social Change*. Oxford University Press, pp. 391–406.

Kerlin, J. A. (ed.) (2009) *Social Enterprise: A Global Perspective*. University Press of New England, Lebanon, NH.

Mair, J., Robinson, J. and Hockerts, K. (eds) (2006), *Social Entrepreneurship*. Palgrave Macmillan, New York.

Nicholls, A. (ed.) (2006) *Social Entrepreneurship: New Models of Sustainable Social Change*. Oxford University Press.

Nyssens, M. (ed.) (2006) *Social Enterprise: At the Crossroads of Market, Public Policies and Civil Society*. Routledge, London and New York.

Young, D. (1986) Entrepreneurship and the behavior of non-profit organizations: elements of a theory. In Rose-Ackerman, S. (ed.) *The Economics of Non-Profit Institutions*. Oxford University Press, New York, pp. 161–84.

27

Social Entrepreneurship

Lars Hulgård

Public and social entrepreneurs work in the inter-related areas of public and social policy. They are to be found among entrepreneurial citizens who, either for limited periods or for a lifetime, commit themselves to the development of local communities and governance networks. And they are to be found in projects and organizations aiming to cross the borders of well-known professions and sectors. Public and social entrepreneurship also applies to professionals in public administration who take chances and risks by their direct involvement in innovations affecting public institutions.

Who are they? What motivates them? What is the role of entrepreneurs in public policy innovation and community development? Such entrepreneurs are driven by two opposing types of motives: free enterprise and community. Both types of entrepreneurs can be identified by their endeavours in producing and sustaining collective goods by innovative and collaborative means.

Public entrepreneurship

In her 1965 dissertation, Elinor Ostrom defined a public entrepreneur as someone who 'has to envision the possibilities of joint action and bring together the necessary factors of production into one unit'. For this approach to entrepreneurship Ostrom was awarded the Nobel Prize in Economics in 2009: 'Elinor Ostrom has demonstrated how common property can be successfully managed by user associations . . . [She] has challenged the conventional wisdom that common property is poorly managed and should be either regulated by central authorities or privatized'. The Academy further argued that users organized for the sake of managing common goods or interests often produce much better outcomes than predicted by conventional economic theory.

Ostrom represents an alternative to reductionist versions claiming that human beings always seek to maximize their individual benefits, that they are 'interested in fairly narrow selfish goals' (Tullock). According to this approach, public entrepreneurs engage in innovative actions only to earn an individual entrepreneurial profit. Ostrom's approach to public entrepreneurship and self-organization, however, shows that in situations where there is a social dilemma conventional wisdom concerning individual behaviour cannot explain why people choose to pool their resources for the benefit of joint action and governance.

Whereas rational choice theorists from James M. Buchanan to Mark Schneider *et al.*'s theory of public entrepreneurship assume that individuals seek to maximize their individual benefits in all situations because they are motivated by a desire for personal gain, Ostrom argues that public entrepreneurship can as well be joint action aimed at bringing 'together the necessary factors of production into one unit'. To over-emphasize the individual entrepreneur's rational choices is to ignore the fact that innovative actions are often embedded in forms of community and co-production.

Although community, collectivity and solidarity are important aspects of public and social innovation, rational choice approaches have little to say about the embedded character, forms of solidarity and institutional configurations of social entrepreneurship. Simple cost-benefit analysis does not work as a framework for understanding the actions of public and social entrepreneurs engaged in community development, solidarity economy and local governance. As Jürgen Habermas has pointed out, rational choice theory cannot explain how society can possibly exist if all persons exclusively make decisions based on their own individual preferences and benefits. He asks the apparently trivial, but important question: If nobody has the collective or community as a guiding principle for their actions, how can these entities provide binding and guiding principles for regulation? Habermas further argued that 'the empirical evidence spoke against all models that were premised on egocentric decisionmaking' because they fail to explain how individuals are embedded in social structures and thereby disregard 'how changes in interests and value-orientations relate to social context'.

Arenas of social entrepreneurship often include examples of deliberative democracy and public inputs to the policy process (Habermas). They are, in John Keane's terms, 'micro-public spheres'. Keane suggests that various local spaces today provide a counterpart the coffeehouses, town meetings and literary circles where early modern public spheres developed. Micro-public spheres are *'local spaces in which citizens enter into disputes about who does and who ought to get what, when and how'* and they are a vital feature of social movements see *Local Development*).

Social entrepreneurship

Until the late 1990s social entrepreneurship (SE) was first of all a field of interest for practitioners who saw themselves as civic entrepreneurs working in collaborative arenas to improve the resilience of specific communities or social entrepreneurs seeking to effect systemic change within a wide range of social and financial services. Since the millennium this picture has changed. Social entrepreneurship has come to occupy the centre stage of general entrepreneurship theory. It has been estimated that three-quarters of all academic articles on social enterprise and social entrepreneurship were published in the first years of the 2000s, illustrating the novelty of and surge of interest in issues related to SE. The origin of the expression 'social entrepreneurship' is vague, and yet the idea has proven to be a powerful vehicle for social change. Three people have especially influenced the initial interest in SE: Charles Leadbeater as a consultant and policymaker, Gregory Dees as a scholar, and Bill Drayton as the social entrepreneur and lobbyist who founded the social entrepreneurship organization Ashoka.

Charles Leadbeater predicted the rise of social entrepreneurs in 1996. He based his prediction on a case study of five projects: 'which exemplify the potential of social entrepreneurs to create forms of active welfare which are both cheaper and more effective than the traditional services offered by the welfare state'. Leadbeater connected his prediction to a critique of the welfare state. He argued that the social entrepreneur would become an effective and cheap alternative to the welfare state (see *Welfare*). His argument was not supported by research or evidence.

Current theories of SE do not constitute a single body of ideas, but rather form a cluster of theories and approaches sharing a few basic viewpoints:

1. Social entrepreneurs are one way or another equivalent to business entrepreneurs, but work within the social sector, whatever that means.
2. Social entrepreneurs, whether as social groups and movements or as spirited individuals, are guided by the idea of producing a social value or work for a social purpose.
3. Successful social entrepreneurs are able to mediate actively between different interests and connect partners from several spheres and sectors.

Several early writers on social entrepreneurship shared Leadbeater's view that the welfare state was more of a barrier to than a source of sustainable solutions to social problems. Scholars and experts working within the field of SE tend to claim that 'The megastate in which the twentieth century indulged has not performed, either in its totalitarian or in its democratic version. It has not delivered on a single one of its promises' (Peter Drucker) and 'We have a welfare state system which we know is ill-equipped to deal with many of the modern social problems it has to confront.' (Charles Leadbeater). According to the SE perspective, the modern state was devised to respond to the social problems that developed throughout the twentieth century and continues to do so. The welfare state has failed not only because of its bureaucratic and inflexible structure, but too so have state-based solutions in general failed to address modern social problems effectively. According to this perspective, social entrepreneurs correct what states have either done wrong or failed to do. As such the state, one of the three spheres that constitute modern society in its huge diversity of national and regional forms, has failed. It is argued therefore that a new type of leadership is needed for alliances that can combine the social purposes and activities of poor constituencies with the capital, know-how and managerial structures developed in the for-profit or market sphere.

Definition

A review of the literature on social entrepreneurship reveals 'social value' as the core of any definition; and the most commonly accepted definition is: social entrepreneurship is about creating social value through innovations. One of the shortest draws the line with commercial entrepreneurship as follows: 'Social entrepreneurship is not about starting a business or becoming more commercial. It is about finding new and better ways to create social value' (Dees *et al.*). The type of organization or tools the entrepreneur uses is not considered to be decisive, since SE may be materialized in many institutional configurations. Some social entrepreneurs create enterprises, some build other types of organizations: 'As it is generally defined, any innovative initiative to help people may be described as social entrepreneurship . . . All those who run social businesses are social entrepreneurs. But not all social entrepreneurs are engaged in social business' (Yunus). Nor is it decisive whether social value is created through commercial means. What matters is whether the individual or collective entrepreneur is producing social value.

A more complex definition was produced by a survey of 500 publications: SE is 'an effort by an individual, group, network, organization, or alliance of organizations that seeks sustainable, large-scale change through pattern-breaking ideas in what governments, non-profits, and businesses do to address significant social problems' (Light). This definition is important because it emphasizes innovation, so that only pattern-breaking contributions to systemic change count as examples of social entrepreneurship.

The following definition of SE is based on information provided by networks such as EMES European Research Network, the Skoll Centre and Ashoka: 'the creation of a social value that is usually produced in collaboration with people and organizations from civil society who are engaged in social innovations that often implies an economic activity'. This definition is based on four criteria: social value, civil society, innovation and economic activity. Whereas social value is present in most approaches to SE, the remaining three elements (civil society, innovation and economic activity) may be more contested. Civil society allows us to distinguish social entrepreneurship from CSR in the private commercial sector (see *Corporate Social Responsibility*) and from innovations in public policy. Innovation is included in the definition to highlight the fact that SE is about developing a *new* approach to a social problem and not just the ambition to form an enterprise. SE activities often have an economic impact either on the communities that are involved in them or on the enterprise itself.

Two scenarios

The 1990s and 2000s saw a high degree of enthusiasm for all issues that link 'social' to 'economy'. Ordinary citizens became committed social entrepreneurs, determined to make a difference. This enthusiasm was comparable to that which marked other historic periods of dramatic change driven by major social movements and religious revivals. Social entrepreneurship is rooted in two major trends that have had a tremendous impact on policy-making around the world since the mid 1980s. The first is marketization and the privatization of responsibility for public welfare. The second is experimentation with new forms of solidarity, collectivism and social activism by civil society groups and social movements entering the sphere of high politics. Social entrepreneurship reflects both the Marketization and Civil Society trends as a relevant response to social challenges in contemporary society. But two very different scenarios illustrate how the potential of social entrepreneurship might be realized in very different ways.

Scenario 1: SE as a replacement for public welfare

'The Silent Surrender of Public Responsibility' (Gilbert) refers to a fundamental shift in the institutional framework for social protection that is taking place in all advanced countries. This consists of fundamental alteration of the existing framework for social policies. Indeed, policies firmly held as social rights that were previously framed by a universal approach to publicly delivered benefits and designed to protect labour against the vicissitudes of the market are currently evolving into policies framed by a selective approach to private delivery of provisions designed to promote labour force participation and individual responsibility. More specifically, a shift is occurring towards work-oriented policies, with privatization of the responsibility for social welfare and an increase in targeting benefits. This is a shift from an emphasis on the social rights of citizens (see *Citizenship*) to the civic duties linked to being a member of a

community, providing space for active citizens to become successful social or public entrepreneurs. These changes are taking place
in basic welfare areas such as benefit policies and pension systems
and are sustained by growth in social inequality as a result of recent
increases in the number of shareholders.

Victor Pestoff sees three possible ways of facing this new reality:
drastic cut-backs in public spending for welfare services; massive
privatization of welfare services; or a greater role for the third sector
(see *Third Sector*). If this scenario comes to shape social reality, then
we must ask to what extent *social entrepreneurship* and *social enterprise* are
implicated in a serious and comprehensive attack on the post-war
welfare-state consensus (see *Welfare*) in the advanced nations. In this
scenario social entrepreneurs will find it hard to balance advocacy,
active citizenship, empowerment and deliberation on the one hand
and social service delivery on the other. Many social enterprises and
social entrepreneurs are already experiencing this as a reality in their
daily life.

Scenario 2: SE as a new terrain for civil society

Even though the vocabulary of social entrepreneurship matches
perfectly prevailing trends of privatization and marketization, this
'tragic vision' is only one side of the coin. A re-orientation of welfare
states in the direction of privatization and community membership
does not only favour individual responsibility; it also generates a
new platform for civil society and creates more room for collectives
and solidarity movements to influence welfare society's evolution in
future. Thus SE may be seen as being simultaneously an aspect of
privatization and a manifestation of the power of civil society.

In this second scenario the emergence of new forms of solidarity
and collectivism is as fundamental as the first trend if we wish to
understand the current enthusiasm for SE. Some even claim that the
financial crisis of September 2008 could very well have paved the way
for further development of the 'solidarity economy' as an alternative
to the shareholder-based private economy (see *Solidarity Economy*).
Already in 2000 World Bank researcher, Michael Woolcock welcomed the current interest in social capital and civil society because it
facilitated the re-entry of sociology into high-level policy discussions
concerning the impact of local civic engagement on the efficiency
of state institutions. Marilyn Taylor referred to this as a turn from

pure market supremacy to a readiness to invest in social enterprise and civil society as a crucial part of informal and reciprocity-based economies.

How are we to understand this increase in expectations for the policy relevance of solidarity-based SE? Is it a sign of a real increase in the impact of civil society as a sphere where social solidarity is commonly expressed? Or is it a sign that private commercial actors are becoming more interested in the third sector as a way of enhancing market penetration at the bottom of the pyramid? As Habermas might put it, is it a simple question of colonization or a new ground for civil society to influence policy where it is made?

Further reading

Dees, J. G., Emerson, J. and Economy, P. (2002) *Strategic Tools for Social Entrepreneurs: More Tools for Enterprising Nonprofits*. Chichester, New York.

Gilbert, N. (2002) *Transformation of the Welfare State: The Silent Surrender of Public Responsibility*. Oxford University Press, Oxford.

Habermas, J. (1996) *Between Facts and Norms*. Polity, Cambridge.

Henton, D., Melville, J. and Walesh, K. (1997) *Grassroots Leaders for a New Economy: How Civic Entrepreneurs are Building Prosperous Communities*. Jossey Bass Publishers, San Francisco.

Hulgård, L. 2004. Entrepreneurship in community development and local governance. In Bogason, P., Kensen, S. and Miller, H. (eds) *Tampering with Tradition: The Unrealized Authority of Democratic Agency*. Lexington Books, Lanham, MD.

Keane, J. (1998) *Civil Society: Old Images, New Visions*. Polity, London.

Mawson, A. (2008) *The Social Entrepreneur: Making Communities Work*. Atlantic Books, London.

Nicholls, A. (ed.) (2008) *Social Entrepreneurship: New Models of Sustainable Social Change*. Oxford University Press, Oxford.

Pestoff, V. (2009) *A Democratic Architecture for the Welfare State*. Routledge, London.

Schneider, M., Teske, P. and Mintrom, M. (1995) *Public Entrepreneurs*. Princeton University Press, Princeton, NJ.

Taylor, M. (2003) *Public Policy in the Community*. Palgrave Macmillan, Houndsmills.

Tullock, G. (1970) *Private Wants, Public Means*. Basic Books, New York.

Part V

New Directions

28

Community and Complementary Currencies

Jérôme Blanc

What are we talking about?

The expressions 'community currency' and 'complementary currency' refer to a variety of schemes for exchanging goods, services or knowledge organized by and for small groups using *ad hoc* forms of currency. The groups in question take the form of associations organized on a formal or informal basis. The currency usually takes one of two forms: either accounts are opened for members and internal units of currency are used to record debits and credits for the goods or services exchanged, or a paper currency circulates between members and sometimes outside the circle of members.

The expression 'community currencies' places the emphasis on the group that creates and uses the currency. Hence the title of the on-line journal *International Journal of Community Currency Research* founded by Colin Williams (University of Leicester) and now edited by Gill Seyfang (University of East Anglia). The reference to 'community' indicates that the schemes involved are small-scale, closed organizations (in the sense that use of the currency implies formal membership). The expression 'complementary currencies' places the emphasis on the articulation between such currencies and the existing monetary system and stresses that they complement one another. The idea of complementarity indicates that the currencies circulate within relatively large structures based on a neighbourhood, town or region rather than communities; they are therefore open to non-members. It also underlines the fact that the existing monetary system appears to be inadequate and that regional or local equivalents are required to complement it. The use of the acronym 'CC' is a way of avoiding debates over terminology. In other languages, the emphasis is placed on the idea of 'complementary currencies' rather than 'community currencies', but equivalents to 'social currencies' are increasingly used in French, Spanish and Portuguese.

Whatever the terms used, they point to the great differences between CCs and normal currencies. For a long time, this suggested to many activists and users, as well as some observers, that such systems involved a form of barter rather than actual currencies. Fears of infringing the law on issuing money helped to foster the same impression. That confusion was gradually dispelled as the founders and users of these schemes developed a better understanding of what they had created and as the authorities made it clear that they would tolerate their existence.

Community or complementary currencies are not just local currencies, as their three main objectives indicate how they differ from standard currency systems.

- The first objective is to promote trade within community or local spaces in an attempt to resist the deterritorialization of economic activity: the local currency is designed, that is, to encourage local use of income generated by local production.
- The second objective is to give a new dynamism to exchanges taking place within these spaces. They work to the benefit of local populations, either because they provide access to some form of credit or because they speed up the currency's circulation by levying regular taxes on assets ('demurrage') in order to discourage hoarding. CC systems are opposed to the accumulation, conservation and concentration of wealth: they are designed to achieve a fairer distribution of wealth.
- The third objective is to transform the nature of trade; hence the use of the expression 'social currencies' in some languages. Such schemes are designed to transform three key elements in how they operate and how they are seen. They may transform the status of traders by valorizing the productive capacities of individuals who are not regarded as productive in that they are neither wage-earners nor members of the independent

professions (the individual becomes a 'prosumer', or in other words both a 'producer' and a 'consumer). They can also transform the existing relationship between traders by promoting the development of trust-based interpersonal relationships ranging from conviviality to friendship. They may, finally, exempt trade from the laws of the market by establishing different rules for fixing prices, by defining what can and what cannot be exchanged, and so on.

The current fashion for community and complementary currency systems developed in the early 1980s; and such systems have now expanded all over the world, with one million members in over 4,000 associations in over forty countries, most of them in the West, Latin America and Japan. With the notable exception of Argentina, CC systems have never developed on a significant scale compared with economic and social activity at the national level: as a rule, they concern less than one per cent of the population, though the figure rises to three per cent in some small countries such as New Zealand. In Argentina, CC systems involved over ten per cent of the population in 2002, following the spectacular collapse of the country's economy and prior to their own equally spectacular collapse, due this time to a growing distrust of the *trueque* (barter) system itself.

Historical background and context

When we speak of the current fashion for community and complementary currency systems, we imply that there is nothing new about it. Earlier attempts to create such systems did not get very far, but include Robert Owen's Equitable Labour Exchange in England (1832–4), local currencies, often in the form of 'free money' in Europe and North America in the 1930s, when money was scarce during the great depression, and local 'free money' schemes in France and Brazil in the late 1950s. The list is not exhaustive, but it does indicate what is new about the new systems: they involve many countries, thousands of 'communities', and hundreds of thousands of people, and are obviously sustainable, even though they can undergo rapid transformation. There is still some interest in the earlier approach advocated by Proudhon's disciple Silvio Gesell, and 'free money' and 'demurrage' systems have been adopted by a number of modern schemes, especially in Argentina and the German-speaking countries.

There is also an interest in the 'social economy' (*économie solidaire*) and the third sector, a widespread disenchantment with market mechanisms (to say nothing of capitalism), and a distrust of public institutions, which are often seen as subordinate to or associated with private banking interests that restrict the amount of money in circulation and therefore increase social inequality. Taken as a whole, these approaches allow a certain reading of contemporary theoretical and activist attitudes towards community and complementary currencies.

Although Robert Owen's experiment seems similar, in spirit, to many contemporary schemes, the precedent that is cited most often is that of the small Austrian village of Wörgl in 1932–3. This was one of the very first attempts to implement Silvio Gesell's proposals for a local currency. Local notes were issued, but were valid only if they carried stamps purchased on a regular basis ('demurrage'). Anyone who wished to avoid buying a stamp had to spend money, and this game of pass the parcel helped to accelerate the circulation of the notes. It is usually said that the village experienced a miracle in the space of a few months. The Wörgl experiment was halted at the request of the National Bank of Austria, which feared that it was beginning to be imitated throughout Austria. The experiment lasted for less than two months and concerned at the very most a few thousand people.

The rapid development of community and complementary currency systems since the 1980s went hand in hand with the emergence of the 'social economy' or the 'new social economy'. Despite differences between them, it is undeniable that CC systems have something in common with the much broader notion of a social economy. Both the political and economic dimensions are there, albeit to differing degrees. In political terms, the community is constructed as a space for conviviality, openness and debate, and lays the foundations for a local participatory space. Constant debates, often within structures that have no formal constitutional basis, are a prominent feature of many LETS models in particular. The economic dimension of the social economy is less obvious in that some CC systems tend to trade commodities at the local level, while others are based on the logic of reciprocity. Most CC schemes are, however, consensus-based, and the consensus can change as a result of internal tensions. Similar tensions can also lead to disagreements, splits and even the collapse of the scheme. The short history of community and complementary currency systems in the last quarter of the twentieth century is full of similar difficulties.

The contemporary fashion for community and complementary currency systems

The contemporary fashion for community and complementary currency systems began with the establishment of the LETS system in Comox Valley, Vancouver (Canada) in 1983. The context was one of massive unemployment resulting from the closure of a local industry. The acronym LETS is now widely used and is usually understood to mean 'Local Exchange Trading System'. The real novelty is that these systems use what Rizzo calls 'personal currencies', as opposed to 'complementary currencies': these are purely scriptural mutual credit systems in which the total balance of members' accounts is always zero. Every individual account, in contrast, goes up and down: it is credited when the individual 'gives', and debited when he or she 'receives'. The currency does not exist before trading begins: the two are consubstantial. Trading is in itself, and by definition, an act of trust: trust in one's partner and, of course, in the community that supports the traders. The model spread, first to English-speaking countries (in America, Oceania and Europe) and then, in the 1990s to other European countries including Germany (Tauschring), France (SEL systèmes d'échange local), Italy (Banco del Tempo), Belgium (LETS: Libres échanges de talents et de services), and the Netherlands (Noppels). Similar experiments began in Eastern Europe in about 2000.

When they are launched in any given country, these schemes spread at what appears to be an exponential rate for four or five years, because they benefit from the attention they receive in the media, and because they activate the alternative networks that support them. This period of growth soon slows down and the schemes may even disintegrate rapidly, as a public that was *a priori* well disposed towards them becomes disappointed and disillusioned. That is one explanation for the downturn experienced in most European countries since the end of the 1990s. The other interpretation, which is often put forward by activists, is that such schemes have a rapid turnover and that non-active members vanish from their lists. Because of this rapid turnover, community and complementary currency systems appear to have a limited impact on society as a whole. The way they change over time is also related to external factors. The violent crisis triggered in 2007–2008 had, for instance, the effect of reviving interest in older schemes such as LETS.

The number of community and complementary currency systems is increasing as they spread to more and more countries. But as they spread, they take different forms. They obviously have to adapt to local conditions, but they also take different forms because they activate a culture of experimentation and because they lead to a growing awareness that a currency is a flexible instrument that can be adapted to ends that can also be defined by civil society. This process of differentiation has, since the 1990s, resulted in the emergence of a broad range of schemes that cooexist alongside LETS-style systems:

- The Time Dollar systems developed in the US in 1991 (earlier and more dynamic forms known as Fureai Kippu exist in Japan) are designed, among other things, to encourage intergenerational mutual aid by paying people for the time they spend helping the sick, old people or anyone else requesting help, in the form of 'hours'.
- Local currency systems such as the Ithaca Hour system developed in the US in 1991. Notes circulate with a community-based territorial space to stimulate a local and ecological economy.
- Systems of the *trueque* type, as developed in Argentina in 1995. Paper currencies circulate within small-scale communities organized into hierarchical networks; they currencies are convertible inside those communities and networks. Such systems are designed to fight poverty rather than to raise local revenues.
- Local currencies of the Palmas type. The name derives from the currency introduced by the founders of the Banco Palmas community bank, which was founded in 1992 in a *favela* in Fortalzeza (Brazil). The combination of microcredit and a local currency is, to date, highly unusual.
- Currencies designed to stimulate specific types of socio-economic activity by using a broad range of tools (vouchers, mutual credit systems, loyalty cards . . .). The SOL currency created in France in 2007 is one example.
- On the fringes of a movement that has grown out of civil society and social economy associations, there are also firms that use in-house barter-systems based on internal accounting systems. Most are inspired by the Swiss bank WIR, which was established in 1934.

The community and complementary currencies movement initially concerned Western countries, and it was only in the second half of the 1990s that it spread to the countries of the South, where it was much stronger in Latin American countries than in Africa or Asia. Such currencies therefore cannot be seen just as a corollary of underdevelopment, as they first appeared alongside existing forms of economic, social and political organization in Western countries. Several factors explain why the South is so out of step with the North. The first and more general explanation relates to the weakness of civil society and intermediary social organizations, as opposed to traditional societies that are independent of the state, in the South, where democracy is weak. In Argentina and Brazil, where the 'social currencies' movement is, in contrast, very strong, there has been a successful return to democracy, and civil society is both powerful and structured. The second explanation has to do with problems relating to transport and communications, which are essential if these experiments are to be expanded. The development of the internet and of active 'alter-globalization' movements has done something to alleviate those difficulties. A third explanation is that the countries of the South have a different relationship with money and solidarity. In the West, money is primarily a vector for the market and individualism, and traditional community-based social relations have largely disappeared. Except in a few isolated cases (Argentina, Mexico and Brazil), the initiative behind community and complementary currency systems in the South therefore comes from outside rather than inside the communities concerned.

The development of the internet has done more than any other factor to encourage the rapid spread, and often the 'viral' nature, of community and complementary currency systems since the 1990s. The increasingly widespread use of English, the development of web sites and subscriber lists, and the organization of conferences with a dedicated international audience, their inclusion in broader agendas (such as World or Regional Social Forums), and the support lent them by what can be very active NGOs (Alliance for a Responsible, Plural and United World, Aktien Strohalm, New Economics Foundation, Schumacher Society . . .) have all helped to structure the movement at the international level and to lend it credibility, especially in the eyes of what are now described as 'alter-globalization' networks (see *Alter-Globalization*). This had led to the rationalization of their systems and encouraged clearer presentations of the advantages that will accrue from establishing them in the South. The NGOs concerned are aware of the need to persuade the target populations to appropriate the idea, and have therefore avoided falling back upon types of organization that have proved successful elsewhere, and are constantly trying to find new solutions. Expertise, action-based research and studies of the systems' impact are becoming more widespread. Because they have been able to activate international networks and debates, community and complementary currency systems have gradually ceased to be amateurish, and are becoming more systematic and professional.

The spread of these schemes and their continued dynamism has led to the emergence of emblematic theoreticians at the international level. Thomas Greco adopts a libertarian approach in an attempt to break the monetary stranglehold of the state and the banks. Bernard Lietaer emphasizes the need to free people from existing monetary organizations by encouraging the growth of complementary currencies. Margrit Kennedy is recycling Gesell's ideas, and so on. Other emblematic figures gained their early experience in this field. Michael Linton was behind the first LETS scheme in history and is still actively promoting the idea. Héloisa Primavera is one of the central figures in Argentina's *truecque* scheme, and the only one to have gained a truly international reputation. Having begun a novel experiment in Puglia (Italy), Panteleo Rizzo is now both a theoretician and the designer of co-operative schemes in Africa. Stephen de Meneulaere has developed initiatives in rural communities in Asia and elsewhere, while the indefatigable traveller Miguel Yasuyukie Hirota has been able to establish links between a great variety of experiments.

A modest innovation or a new paradigm for society?

Community and complementary currency systems have now been in existence for twenty-five years, but they still face the major challenge of establishing their legitimacy on a permanent basis. The general public has to be convinced that they are not just alternative trade circles or the preserve of activists or of those who sympathize with some cause or other. The monetary authorities have to be convinced that they are not in competition with national currencies and that they complement them because they make possible developments that cannot be facilitated by national currencies alone. Welfare systems have to be convinced that these trading schemes are not a substitute for the primary or secondary incomes that are paid in national currencies, but that they do a great deal to promote social inclusion, either directly (formal wage-earning activity or micro-businesses) or indirectly (inclusion in social networks, the development of new skills). Local authorities must be convinced that such schemes can make a contribution to local development and can enter into partnerships without coming under any central-ized control – and this is a problem that applies to every aspect of the social economy.

This raises the question of organization and of how choices are to determined on the basis of clearly identified objectives. Reconciling these organizational issues with such objectives will be a major issue for CC systems in future. It is also an essential precondition if gov-ernment and parliamentarians are to change existing legislation or, if need be, introduce new legislation. Professionalization of community and complementary currency systems is essential if they are to make a useful contribution to combating social exclusion or to stimulate local economies by facilitating access to goods and services and to credit in local currencies.

One factor that may work in favour of local currency systems is that human societies will have to re-organize economic activities on a local basis in view of both climate change and the economic crisis (see *Mobility*). A currency circulating on a local basis and with limited convertibility can be a powerful stimulus to local economic activity because it can stimulate the local production of goods and services for local needs.

The entire history of community and complementary currency systems since the building of nation-states suggests, however, that they should set themselves more modest goals, though they may be surprised by their own success. To suggest that the whole of society can be transformed by community and complementary cur-rency systems is to over-estimate the role of currency and its ability to overthrow the existing monetary order. Currency is not the key: it is not as though we could lock out the failings of today's human sciences by finding the key that opens the door leading to a radiant future of endless possibilities. It can, on the other hand, be seen as a lever in the sense that new forms of currency may prove to be a way of influencing economic activities, their territorial basis and the social relations they generate.

If they are to have any chance of success, we therefore need to discuss innovative schemes without ignoring the need to put them on a solid economic and political footing.

Further reading

Blanc, J. (ed.) (2006) *Exclusion et liens financiers: monnaies sociales: Rapport 2005–2006*. Economica, Paris.

Gesell, S. (1958 [1916]) *The Natural Economic Order* (trans. Pye, P.). Peter Owen, London.

Gomez, G. (2009) *Argentina's Parallel Currency: The Economy of the Poor*. Pickering and Chatto, London.

Greco, T. (2009) *The End of Money and the Future of Civilization*. Chelsea Green, White River Junction, VT.

Kennedy, M. (1995 [1987]) *Interest and Inflation Free Money: Creating an Exchange Mechanism that Works for Everyone and Protects the Earth*. Seva International, Lansing, MI.

Lietaer, B. (2001) *The Future of Money: Creating New Wealth, Work and a Wiser World*. Century, London.

Rizzo, P. (2003) *L'Économie sociale et solidaire face aux expérimentations monétaires: Monnaies sociales et monnaies multilaterales*. L'Harmattan, Paris.

Servet, J.-M. (ed.) (1999) *Une économie sans argent. Les systèmes d'échange local*. Seuil, Paris.

Seyfang, G. (2009) *The New Economics of Sustainable Consumption: Seeds of Change*. Palgrave Macmillan, Basingstoke and New York.

29

Digital Commons

Felix Stalder

Definition

The digital commons comprises informational resources created and shared within voluntary communities of varying size and interests. These resources are typically held *de facto* as communal, rather than private or public (i.e. state) property. Management of the resource is characteristically oriented towards use within the community, rather than exchange in the market. As a result, separation between producers and consumers is minimal in the digital commons.

The digital commons has generated new paradigms for the production and dissemination of cultural works and knowledge goods, based on the right of users to access, distribute and transform them. These new paradigms are articulated by three loosely aligned, networked social movements, each committed to large-scale, collective action aiming to transform social reality. The oldest and most advanced is the *Free Software Movement* which focuses on software code. The *Free Culture Movement*, which focuses on cultural goods, is younger and still in a formative phase. The *Access to Knowledge (A2K) movement* focuses on knowledge-intensive goods, such as scholarly publications or medicines. All three share an understanding that in a digital context cultural works and knowledge goods are fundamentally different from physical goods, since they can be easily and cheaply copied, shared and transformed. Because sharing means multiplying rather than dividing, they are naturally abundant. Thus, there is no ethical justification to prevent anyone from enjoying the benefits of using them. Scarcity exists only when it is artificially introduced after production.

At the political level, the Free Software Movement aims to empower communities of users to use freely, examine and change what is arguably the most critical layer of the infrastructure of the network society, computer software. The Free Culture Movement aims to increase *semiotic democracy*, that is, the ability of all people to take active part in the production of culture and to contribute freely to the exchanges that constitute public life. The Access to Knowledge movement aims at improving social equity, particularly in the North/South context, by removing barriers to access to knowledge goods, increase social welfare and broaden the range of actors who can contribute to their further development, particularly scientists in developing countries.

The emergence of the digital commons is one expression of a historical shift from the industrial economy (Fordism) to the networked economy. Firms and markets are reorganizing – away from large hierarchical firms producing for mass markets towards flexibly networked, smaller units producing highly targeted goods and services. Moreover, the scope for value creation expands from the economy proper into society at large, at least partially escaping from property regimes and the need for market exchange. The social reality produced by this structural transformation is variable and contradictory. The digital commons represents a cluster of practical visions to steer it in a more democratic and equitable direction by advancing processes of decentralization, lowering obstacles to participation and reducing positions of power created by monopolies over intellectual property. This commons represents a third model of social production, neither dependent on the state nor oriented towards the market, even though it may partially overlap with both.

Free software

The new paradigm of producing in the digital commons emerged first in software development during the late 1980s. At that time, the notion of software as a standardized product for mass markets was still relatively new, established only in the mid-1970s by a new generation of companies such as Microsoft (founded in 1975). Before that, the computer industry regarded software as an add-on to the actual product, hardware. Improving software through mutual help among programmers was part of the original software culture, later reactivated as a strategy to fight the new, artificial separation between producers and users. To organize an alternative, Richard M. Stallman founded the Free Software Movement to realize four essential freedoms in relation to software: the freedom to run the software for any purpose; the freedom to change the programme without restrictions; the freedom to distribute copies of the programme to help others; and the freedom to distribute changes of the programme so that others might benefit from your work. To make these freedoms dependable, he drafted a licence (the GNU General Public Licence or GPL), under which most free software is released today. The licence includes the clause that whoever distributes the software – exact copies or improvements – must do so under the same licence. Those who do not agree with this condition have no right to use the software in the first place. Over time, the pool of free software grew considerably; and, when Linus Thorvalds contributed the last major missing piece (the kernel, Linux) in the early 1990s, an entire free operating system became available. At the end of the decade, free software (or Open Source Software, a term coined in 1998 to make it sound more business-friendly) began to reach the mainstream: first on the back-end (server software) and also in the last few years on desktop and mobile devices.

The success of free software showed that under the conditions of the internet – cheap, mass self-communication, decentralized distribution and sophisticated tools to organize information – open, self-directed co-operation was not only ethical, but at least in this case also very efficient in terms of quality, price and innovation. In competition with the Fordist model of production, a new institutional ecology emerged, characterized by open, yet highly structured volunteer communities, non-profit foundations serving these communities and commercial and non-commercial actors using and contributing to the common resource (the code basis) in the pursuit of their individual goals and strategies. A new business model was established that focused on solving unique problems rather than selling identical copies; and new social norms took hold that combined competition for personal recognition among peers with collaboration in solving shared problems. Copyright, while not altered at the level of formal law, was turned upside down in practice through free licences that guaranteed user freedom instead of producer control. The Free Software Movement has also become a powerful political force, supported by a growing segment of the information technology industry. In 2007, a co-ordinated political campaign at the level of the EU parliament succeeded in preventing a change in patent law that would have allowed businesses to patent 'computer-implemented innovation' (software patents). This was a historic achievement. For the first time ever, the expansion of intellectual property protections was halted with the help of an explicit argument drawn from the practice and vision of a digital commons and the production model of free software it enables.

Much of the internet runs on free software and, without its availability and the strength of its diverse communities, the democratic potential of new technologies would be significantly smaller: more people would be excluded because software would be expensive rather than free of charge; media literacy would be lower because there would be fewer communities educating their members in how to use the software; the range of functionality and language versions would be narrower, because there would be much less software for which there is social but not financial motivation; power would be more unbalanced because software would be more geared towards the interests of those who sell it, rather than those who use it; and the obstacles to innovation would be greater because lack of access to the source code of existing software would make it much more difficult to develop new software and services. Given software's ability to enable and shape a vast range of social activities, the success of the Free Software Movement has been very significant.

Free culture

By the early 1990s, the internet turned into a mass-medium for programmers, thereby setting the stage for the rapid development of the free software model. At the millennium, affordable computers had become powerful enough to support a broad range of (semi)professional cultural production, significantly lowering the barriers to many aspects of cultural production. Moreover, the internet had spread widely throughout society (although unevenly in respect to region and class). Core sectors of the economy at large were changing from the logic of mass production to an 'informational paradigm' which demands communicative and creative skills from its workforce and vastly expands the field of cultural production (in the *creative indus-tries*). Thus more people than ever before had the skills and the means to produce and distribute their own cultural works.

Cultural production has been deeply affected by the effects of cheap mass (self-)communication, easy conversion between media and decentralized distribution. First, remixing – using existing works to create new ones – has become central to cultural production. Second, subcultures of small or non-commercial cultural produc-ers, long excluded by the efficient distribution mechanisms of the cultural industries, found themselves on the same technological foot-ing with established players and able to connect to audiences of any size. This helped them to increase and improve their cultural output. Third, many of the actions that copyright law granted exclusively to rights-holders – making and distributing exact copies or trans-formed works – were now being done by masses of people without authorization, not in the privacy of their homes but online (that is, in public). Copyright fell into a deep crisis. Much of what constituted the new digital mass culture was a violation of copyright law and rights owners – fearing loss of control over cultural works which they regard as their exclusive property – organized to reassert that con-trol. In a series of international agreements (most importantly, the World Intellectual Property Organization Copyright Treaty, 1996) and national legislations (for example, the US Digital Millennium Copyright Act, 1998 and the EU Copyright Directive, 2001) the rights of owners were strengthened. At the same time, litigation against copyright infringement escalated.

By the end of the 1990s, the tension between the enforcement of increasingly restrictive laws and the growing popularity of permissive cultural practices rose to the surface and spilled into the mainstream. In part as a response to the aggressiveness of the cultural industries, in part drawing inspiration from the Free Software Movement, large numbers of users and producers recognized the need to defend their culture. Their goal has been to protect and advance the freedoms that had come to define the digital commons. In a series of influ-ential books, Lawrence Lessig, a law professor and leading figure of the Free Culture Movement, argued that recent changes in law and technology could easily restrict freedoms and create what he called a *permission culture*. This would allow owners of past cultural works to grant or withhold permission, at their discretion, to those seeking to create the culture of the present. The effect would be a vast increase in the control exercised by a few over the many, implemented through Digital Rights Management (DRM) technologies and ubiquitous surveillance of social communication. This would cripple the potential for the emergence of a *read/write culture* in which the ability to consume cultural works (read) would be matched by that to produce them (write). For such a culture to flourish, he argued, people need to be able – technically, legally, and socially – to build on and transform the culture in which they live.

The Free Culture Movement began to take shape. One focus was to develop tools allowing copyright law, as it exists, to support rather than restrict the sharing and transformation of cultural works. Following the lead of free software, a series of licences was developed to enable creators to make their works available freely. Among the first were the Open Content Licence (1998) and the Free Art Licence (2000), both based closely on the GNU GPL licence. In 2001, Creative Commons (CC) established itself as one of the central hubs of Free Culture, by offering easy-to-use, customizable licences granting some rights to the public. Works published under a Creative Commons licence are always freely usable for non-commercial purposes. Some versions of the licence also allow free transformation of the works and others allow commercial use. A combination of good timing, solid and user-friendly implementation and significant support from leading American universities made CC licences the *de facto* standard legal foundation of free culture. By mid-2009, it was estimated that some 250 million works had been published under one or other of the CC licences. This mass adoption of CC licences shows the breadth of the Free Culture Movement.

In its wake, new models for production and distribution are emerging. The most widely successful Free Culture project is Wikipedia, an encyclopaedia that is co-operatively written (by ten million registered users and countless anonymous ones in English language version alone) and financed by donations from the community. Since the project was started in 2001 it has become the most popular and comprehensive reference source online, used by about 330 million people every month (in mid 2009). While Wikipedia is the best-known example, in all fields of cultural production there are successful experiments to develop an ecology to support free culture. The tools, practices and business models vary widely across domains. After all, writing an encyclopaedia is very different from shooting a film, and some cultural works can be produced co-operatively, while others are most interesting if they reflect the unique experience of an individual. Yet, across the whole range of these initiatives, there is a renewed understanding that the primary relation between author and audience, or more accurately, between producers and users, is not best expressed within a market, where commodities are exchanged, but within a community producing collectively the cultural landscape within which individual works become meaningful. From this recognition, new patterns are emerging: of competition (for scarce resources such as recognition) and co-operation (in preserving, modifying and expanding a particular set of cultural practices). These comprise volunteer networks, non-profit and for-profit organizations, as well as a new mix of market- and community-oriented activities.

Despite the importance of CC for the Free Culture Movement, the project has not been immune to criticism from within. The most pertinent issue raised has focused on the CC project's failure to define freedom. It offers a series of licences that are not only incompatible with each other (for example, works that allow commercial use cannot be remixed with those prohibiting it), but that also restrict users far more than do the free software licences, after which CC was modelled. The most commonly used CC licence does not allow commercial use and about a quarter of all CC-licensed works do not allow modifications. While some criticism has since been addressed by the CC project, this issue has revealed fundamental cleavages in the Free Culture Movement. One side, grounded in the liberal philosophy of individual rights, takes as its starting point the affirmation of the right of creators to control how their works are being used. What is needed, in this view, are licences to make it convenient to grant certain uses to the public, thus making copyright more workable in the digital domain. The other side, which is more influenced by the Free Software Movement's communitarian ethos, takes the separation of producers and users to be artificial and thus starts from the need of the community to access and build upon works with the aim of expanding the common pool of resources over time. Thus, the fact that a work (or part thereof) has been created by an individual person should give them the right of attribution (to gain recognition) but not the right to exclude others from using or building on it. For one side, such a communitarian orientation is one of several options (the most liberal CC licence is, in practice, about the same as a free software licence), for the other, it is the baseline of what Free Culture is about. While these philosophical differences are unlikely to be overcome any time soon, work is being done to reduce the friction in practice, for example, by reducing the incompatibility of the various free culture licences, thereby increasing the flow of works across different domains.

Access to knowledge (a2k)

An original stimulus for the a2k movement was the fight over access to anti-retroviral drugs in South Africa. During the 1990s, a new class of drugs had become available to combat the outbreak of HIV/ AIDS, greatly improving the life-expectancy of people with the disease. These drugs, however, were sold in developing countries at prohibitively high prices, making them effectively unavailable to most people who needed them. To address this situation, the South African government amended its laws to facilitate 'parallel imports', that is, buying not from official, but third-party vendors, particularly Indian and Brazilian manufacturers of generic versions of the drugs. In response, 39 of the largest pharmaceutical manufacturers sued the South African government in 1998 as part of an effort, co-ordinated with US and EU governments, to prevent South Africa importing such products. This prompted an international campaign, led by groups such as *Médecins sans frontières,* to support the South African government's right to make these essential drugs accessible to its people. In 2001, this campaign succeeded when the law suit was withdrawn. This led other developing countries, despite ongoing pressures from the pharmaceuticals companies and Western governments, to issue similar legislation, enabling parallel import and compulsory licences. In the course of such disputes, developing countries became increasingly vocal in asserting their interests in intellectual property policy and demanded that their needs, which were different from those of the IP industries, be recognized at the highest level of policy-making, namely by the World Intellectual Property Organization (WIPO), a sub-organization of the United Nations. The result of this was the formulation of a *development agenda*, which stated the need for access to intellectual property to meet development goals and for recognition of the 'benefits of a rich public domain' and called for the 'protection of traditional knowledge' as explicit goals of further policy development. After years of campaigning and lobbying governments, the development agenda was formally adopted in 2007. Like the defeat of software patents in the European parliament, the adoption of the development agenda represents a major political victory. For the first time, the value of knowledge regimes other than personal and corporate IP was recognized and it was stated that concern for such forms of property needs to be balanced with concern for social development.

The second major focus of the a2k movement is transformation of scientific publishing through open access. There is a well-established tradition that scientists publish their papers to their communities freely and receive no direct compensation for it. Over the last decade, however, the prices for commercial scientific journals, particularly in the natural and life sciences, have risen enormously, putting considerable strain on library budgets and reducing the range of scientists who have access to them. One of the answers to this problem is the creation of open-access journals. In these journals, the scientific review process (peer review) is just as rigorous as in traditional ones, the main difference being that the final results, accepted papers, are made available free of charge to everyone, often under a CC licence. In many ways, this is simply updating one of the central practices of modern science – submitting research results to the widest possible scrutiny through publication – by taking advantage of the possibilities afforded by the internet. Since the beginning, with the *Budapest Open Access Initiative* in 2002, a large number of new open-access journals have been created and many public funding bodies are now requiring that research funded by their grants be made freely accessible within a reasonable time span.

Like the Free Software and Free Culture Movements, the a2k movement recognizes that, in order to enable free access, new models of production are necessary. How to finance the creation of the first copy? The model that requires the initial development costs to be offset by controlling access to subsequent copies is clearly broken. In the case of open access journals, this is relatively straightforward. Since the costs of running such a journal are comparatively low – after all writing and reviewing the papers is done by the scientists themselves and there are free software solutions to manage the work flow – the money can be raised either through contributions from by the scientists themselves (as part of general research funding) or through endowments and other community-based means. The case for drugs research is much more complex. One approach is to focus on large cash prizes, that is, to reward researchers directly for their work, which can then be made available to all, rather than by granting them patent rights to exploit monopolies. The advantage of a prize system to finance research would be not only that once the drugs have been approved there could be competition between generic manufacturers for production quality and price, but also that research could be more likely be directed towards areas where there is a social need, but no market because the illnesses mainly affect poor people (for example, tuberculosis). In addition, free access to knowledge financed through prizes would facilitate innovative follow-up and lower prices across the board. Such a system can be justified on ethical as well as on economic grounds. In 2007 this idea was taken up by the World Health Organization which passed a resolution calling for proposals on 'a range of incentive mechanisms . . . addressing the linkage between the cost of research and development and the price of medicines . . . with the objective of addressing diseases that disproportionately affect developing countries'.

Outlook

Within a relatively short period, moves towards the formation of a digital commons have been extremely successful in providing practical answers to urgent problems. These answers take full advantage of the new possibilities of a networked world where an unprecedented number of people have the skills and tools to contribute to the creation of value, while pursuing diverging economic, social, cultural or research interests. Although many political, legal and economic questions remain to be solved, the digital commons represents a paradigm change, whereby new technological, social and economic frameworks have already generated an informational order in outline that is socially more just, economically more productive and politically more democratic than the current regime of informational monopolies. This movement could unleash the empowering, rather than the controlling, potential of our new digital infrastructures. Yet, gains made so far are not yet sufficient, nor are they certain to endure.

Free software is threatened by a commercial move towards 'software as service', where users no longer gain access to the software itself, but are allowed to use its front-end under ever-changing terms-of-service. When the software itself no longer needs to be distributed, the force of the free software licence does not apply. Users could again become dependent on tools that are shielded from public scrutiny and developed to advance their owners' rather than their users' interests. The digital commons is threatened by the entertainment industry's unrelenting drive to protect its outmoded business models through ever more draconian IP legislation. Yet, it is also threatened, perhaps more surprisingly, by the emergence of the social networking platforms of Web 2.0. Even as they enable many co-operative practices, they also create new centres of power based on informational monopolies – this time not at the level of content, but through the user data amassed in the back-ends of centralized platforms. Here then, is the paradoxical situation of an infrastructure that realizes both the empowering and controlling potential of the new technologies, leaving users at the mercy of powerful corporations, which can, more or less subtly, shape experience in a way that is beneficial to their commercial interests. The policy gains of the a2k movement are threatened by shifts in the institutional setting for international policy-making, which might move away from formally representative, public bodies such as WIPO, if they are perceived as being hostile to the interests of power centres. Such a shift may occur either through secret negotiations between a few states or by placing more emphasis on bilateral agreements between parties who bring very unequal power to the negotiating table.

In the information age, the way we access, use and distribute information, culture and knowledge goods goes to the heart of what kind of society we live in. The ethics and practices that constitute the digital commons are essential to realizing our human aspirations for meaningful democracy, social justice and a renewed experience of lived community and solidarity. The pieces are all there, but it will require a lot of creativity and determination to put them together into a picture that most of us will like.

Further reading

Benkler, Y. (2006) *The Wealth of Networks: How Social Production Transforms Markets and Freedom.* Yale University Press.

Bollier, D. (2008) *Viral Spiral: How the Commoners Built a Digital Republic of Their Own.* New Press, New York and London. Also available at: http://www.learcenter.org/pdf/ViralSpiral.pdf.

Ghosh, R. A. (ed.) (2006) *CODE: Collaborative Ownership and the Digital Economy.* MIT Press, Cambridge, MA.

Castells, M. (2000) *The Rise of the Network Society: The Information Age: Economy, Society and Culture* Vol. I, 2 edn. Blackwell, Oxford.

Foti, A. (2009) The precariat and climate justice in the great recession. *Great Recession* Nov. 3 [online]. Available at: http://www.greatrecession. info/2009/11/03/the-precarious-question-and-the-climate-struggle.

Hardt, M. and Negri, A. (2009) *Commonwealth*. Belknap Press of Harvard University Press. Cambridge, MA

Hess, C. and Ostrom, E. (eds) (2007) *Understanding Knowledge as a Commons*. MIT Press, Cambridge, MA.

Lessig, L. (1999) *Code and Other Laws of Cyberspace*. Basic Books, New York.

Lessig, L. (2004) *Free Culture: How Big Media Uses Technology and the Law to Lock Down Culture and Control Creativity*. Penguin Press, New York. Also available at: http://www.free-culture.cc/freecontent.

Love, J. and Hubbard, T. (2007) The big idea: prizes to stimulate R&D for new medicines. *Chicago–Kent Law Review* 82 (3) [online]. Available at: http://www.keionline.org/misc-docs/bigidea-prizes.pdf.

Stalder, F. (2005) *Open Cultures and the Nature of Networks*, [online]. Available at: http://felix.openflows.com/pdf/Notebook_eng.pdf.

Stallman, R. M. (1996) *The Free Software Definition*. [online] Available at: http://www.gnu.org/philosophy/free-sw.html.

30

Mobility

John Urry

On the move

Sometimes it seems as if the whole world is on the move. The early retired, international students, terrorists, members of diasporas, holidaymakers, business people, slaves, sports stars, asylum seekers, refugees, backpackers, commuters, young mobile professionals, prostitutes – these and many others seem to find the contemporary world is their oyster or at least their destiny. Criss-crossing the globe are the routes of these many groups intermittently encountering one another in transportation and communication hubs, searching out in real and electronic databases the next coach, message, plane, back of lorry, text, bus, lift, ferry, train, car, web site, wifi hot spot and so on.

The scale of this travelling is immense. There are one billion legal international arrivals each year (compared with 25 million in 1950); there are four million air passengers each day; at any one time 360,000 passengers are in flight *above* the US, equivalent to a substantial city; 31 million refugees roam the globe; and there are over 650m cars. In 1800 people in the US travelled on average 50 metres a day – they now travel 50 kilometres a day. Today world citizens move 23 billion kilometres; by 2050 it is predicted that that figure will have increased fourfold to 106 billion.

People do not spend more time travelling, however, since this appears to have remained more or less constant at just over one hour or so per day. People also do not necessarily make more journeys. But what is crucial is that people are travelling further and faster. Globally, travel and tourism constitute the largest industry in the world, worth $6.5 trillion directly and indirectly, and accounting for 8.7 per cent of world employment and 10.3 per cent of world GDP. This mobility affects almost all places: the World Tourism Organization publishes travel statistics for over 200 countries and most countries send and receive significant numbers of visitors.

Wolfgang Schivelbusch concludes that overall for 'the twentieth-century tourist, the world has become one large department store of countrysides and cities', although of course most people in the world can only dream of voluntarily sampling that department store on a regular basis. This pattern of mainly but not entirely voluntary travelling is the largest ever peaceful movement of people across borders. Until 2008 such movement has shown little sign of *substantially* abating in the longer term even with September 11, the Bali, Madrid and London bombings, pandemics and other global catastrophes. Being physically mobile has become for the rich and even for some poor a 'way of life' across the globe. And materials too are on the move, often carried by these moving bodies whether openly, clandestinely or inadvertently. The multinational sourcing of different components of manufactured products also involves just-in-time delivery from around the world. The internet has simultaneously grown with incredible speed, faster than any previous technology and with a huge impact throughout much of the world. Worldwide there are 2–3 billion mobile phones and related devices whose use occurs in part on the move.

These converging mobile technologies appear to be transforming many aspects of economic and social life which share in some sense being on the 'move' or away from 'home'. In a mobile world there are extensive and intricate connections between physical travel and modes of communication; and these form new fluidities which are often difficult to stabilize. Physical changes appear to be 'de-materializing' connections, as people, machines, images, information, power, money, ideas and dangers are 'on the move', making and remaking rapid connections around the world.

Issues of movement, of too little movement for some or too much for others or of the wrong sort and at the wrong time, are central to many people's lives and to the operations of many small and large public, private and non-governmental organizations. From swine flu to plane crashes, from airport expansion controversies to global terrorism, from obesity caused by the 'school run' to oil wars in the Middle East, from global warming to slave trading, issues of 'mobility' are centre-stage on many policy and academic agendas.

Mobilities

There are four main senses of the term 'mobile' or 'mobility'. First, there is the sense of mobility deployed in mainstream sociology/ social science. This is upward or downward *social* mobility. Second, mobile means something that moves or is *capable* of movement, as with the mobile (portable) phone but also with the mobile person, home, hospital, kitchen, and so on. Third, there is the sense of mobile as a *mob*, a rabble or an unruly crowd. The mob is seen as disorderly precisely because it is mobile, not fully fixed within boundaries. Finally, there is mobility in the longer-term sense of migration or other kinds of semi-permanent geographical movement. This is a horizontal sense of being 'on the move', and refers especially to moving country or continent often in search of a 'better life' or to escape from drought, persecution, war, starvation and so on. I use mobility to cover all these senses.

And indeed in the contemporary world twelve main mobility forms are now significant, each of which has generated a whole body of research and debate. These overlapping forms of mobility are: asylum, refugee and homeless travel and migration; business and professional travel; discovery travel of students, au pairs and other young people on their 'overseas experience'; medical travel to spas, hospitals, dentists, opticians and so on; military mobility of armies, tanks, helicopters, aircraft, satellites and so on which have many spinoffs into civilian uses; post-employment travel and the forming of transnational lifestyles within retirement; 'trailing travel' of children, partners, other relatives and domestic servants; travel and migration across the key nodes within a given diaspora such as the overseas Chinese; travel of service workers around the world and especially to global cities; tourist travel to visit places and events; visiting friends and relatives where those friendship networks may also be on the move; and last but not least work-related travel including commuting.

Partly in response to such developments theorists as well as more empirical analysts are now launching a 'mobility turn', a different way of thinking through the character of economic, social and political relationships in the contemporary world. Such a turn is spreading in and through the social sciences, mobilizing analyses that have been historically static, fixed and concerned with predominantly a-spatial 'social structures'. The mobility turn is post-disciplinary, concerned with the multiple ways in which economic and social life is performed and organized through time and across various spaces. Analyses of the complex ways that social relations are 'stretched' across the globe are generating theories, research findings and methods that 'mobilize' or assemble analyses of social ordering that are achieved in part on the move and contingently as processes of flow. There is a new journal called *Mobilities*.

Overall, mobilities have been a black box for the social sciences, generally regarded as a neutral set of processes permitting forms of economic, social and political life that are explicable by other more causally powerful processes. To the extent that transport and communications have been studied, they are placed in separate categories that allow for little interchange with the rest of social science. Holidaymaking, walking, car driving, phoning, flying and so on are mainly ignored by the social sciences, although they are manifestly significant within people's everyday lives. Further the significance of such movement *for* the nature of work relations, family life, leisure, politics and protest is minimized. These all involve movement or potential movement and affect the form taken by such social relations.

Moreover, the social sciences concentrate too much on human subjects interacting together and ignore the enduring *systems* that provide what we might call the infrastructures of social life. Such systems enable the movement of people, ideas and information from place to place, person-to-person, event to event, and yet their economic, political and social implications are mostly unexamined in social science.

Each intersecting 'mobility' presupposes a 'system' (in fact many such systems). These systems make possible movement: they provide 'spaces of anticipation' that the journey can be made, that the message will get through, that the parcel will arrive, that the family group can meet up. Systems permit predictable and relatively risk-free repetition of the movement in question. In the contemporary world these systems include ticketing, oil supply, addresses, safety, protocols, station interchanges, web sites, docks, money transfer, inclusive tours, luggage storage, air traffic control, barcodes, bridges, timetables, surveillance and so on. The history of these repetitive systems is in effect a history of those processes by which the natural world has been 'mastered' and made secure, regulated and relatively risk-free. For people to be able to 'move' and for them in turn to move objects, texts, money, water, images, is to establish how nature has been subdued.

The origins of modern movement

The significance attached to ideas of movement and especially of circulation followed Harvey's discovery of how blood circulates within the human body and Galileo's notion that a natural state is to be in motion and not at rest. Circulation is a powerful notion that had many impacts upon the social world, especially in the development of political philosophy following Hobbes. With regard to the city more precisely, planners wanted its very design to function like a healthy body, freely flowing. Systems were increasingly developed where there is an obligation to be circulating; and this is true of water, sewage, people, money, ideas. In the modern world there is an accumulation of movement analogous to the accumulation of capital – repetitive movement or circulation made possible by diverse, interdependent mobility-systems.

Some pre-industrial mobility-systems included walking, horse-riding, sedan chairs, coach travel, inland waterways, sailing ships and so on. But many of the mobility-systems that are significant now date from England and France in an extraordinary period around 1840 when the modern world can be said to have been mobilized. Their interdependent development defines the contours of the modern mobilized world, bringing about an awesome 'mastery' of the physical world. Nature gets dramatically and systematically 'mobilized' in mid-nineteenth-century Europe.

Systems dating from that exceptional moment include a national post system in 1840 (Rowland Hill's Penny Post in Britain based on the simple invention of the prepaid stamp), the first commercial electrical telegram in 1839 (constructed by Sir Charles Wheatstone and Sir William Fothergill Cooke for use on the Great Western Railway), the invention of photography and its use in guide books and advertising more generally (Daguerre in France in 1839, Fox Talbot in England in 1840), the first Baedeker guide in 1839 (for the Rhine), the first railway age and the first ever national railway timetable in 1839 (Bradshaw), the first city built for the tourist gaze (Paris), the first inclusive or 'package' tour in 1841 (organized by Thomas Cook between Leicester and Loughborough in Britain), the first scheduled ocean steamship service (Cunard), the first railway hotel (York), the early department stores (first in Paris in 1843), and the first system for the separate circulation of water and sewage (Chadwick in Britain).

In 1854 Thomas Cook declared as the slogan for such a mobile middle of the nineteenth century: 'To remain stationary in these times of change, when all the world is on the move, would be a crime. Hurrah for the Trip – the cheap, cheap Trip.'

Mobility systems

The twentieth century then saw a huge array of other 'mobility-systems' develop, including the car, national telephones, air power, high-speed trains, modern urban systems, budget air travel, mobile phones, networked computers. And as we move into the twenty-first century, these 'mobility systems' are developing some further characteristics. First, they are becoming even more complicated, being made up of many elements and based on an array of specialized and arcane forms of expertise. Mobilities have always involved expert systems but these are now highly specific, many being served by entire university degree programmes; and there is the development of highly specialized companies too. Second, such systems are much more interdependent, so that individual journeys or pieces of communication depend on multiple systems, all needing to function and interface effectively with each other. Third, from the 1970s onwards, systems depend much more on computers and software. Specific software systems have been generated that need to 'speak' to each other in order for particular mobilities to take place. Fourth, these systems have become especially vulnerable to 'normal accidents', accidents that are almost certain to occur from time to time, given the tightly locked-in and mobile nature of many such interdependent systems .

As daily and weekly time–space patterns in the richer parts of the world are desynchronized from historical communities and places, so these multiple systems provide the means for work and social life to be scheduled and rescheduled. Organizing 'co-presence' with key others (workmates, family, significant others, friends) each day, week, month and year becomes more demanding with this loss of collective 'localized' co-ordination. The greater the personalization of networks, the more important are systems to enable the array of meetings and intermittent co-presence that are necessary for family, friendship and professional life to be lived at a distance.

Moreover, these systems entail changes in the nature of human beings who are being reconfigured as bits of scattered information distributed across various 'systems' of which most of them are unaware. Individuals thus exist beyond their private bodies, leaving traces of themselves in space. In particular, as vast numbers of people are on the move, so too these traces enable them to be subject to systems of intrusive digital regulation. In what some call the 'frisk society', places like airports are increasingly using novel systems of monitoring, surveillance and regulation to control those mobile bodies.

Cheap oil and after

The 'social practices' of modern life have thus come to involve regular and predictable long-distance movement of people (including commuters, holidaymakers and those making family and friendship visits) and objects (including water and food). This long-distance mobile world moreover is deeply dependent on and embedded in abundant cheap oil. Most industrial, agricultural, commercial, domestic, and mobility systems are built around the plentiful supply of 'black gold'. As Thomas Homer-Dixon notes, oil powers virtually all movement of people, materials, foodstuffs, and manufactured goods around the world. Oil provides 95 per cent of transport energy. It is remarkably versatile, convenient and during the twentieth century relatively cheap. Oil became vital to virtually everything done and especially to everything that moves on the planet. This oil-based infrastructure was a twentieth-century phenomenon, with the US as a disproportionately high energy-producing and -consuming society.

Moreover, during the last century it seemed that this modern mobile civilization would continue into the foreseeable future, with 'mobile lives' spreading to all continents and most peoples, albeit with a hugely unequal distribution. But for three main reasons this no longer seems to be the case. First, oil is simply not plentiful nor is it growing in supply: three to four barrels of oil today are consumed for every one discovered. Worldwide the largest oilfields were discovered half a century ago, with the peak of oil discovery being in the mid-1960s. Over the longer term energy will become increasingly expensive and there will be frequent shortages because of the fall in *per capita* availability. With 'business as usual' needing supplies to double by 2050, many analysts consider that there is not enough oil to fuel such systems of global consumption.

Second, such an energy descent would be especially troublesome since the world's population is continuing to increase in size and in its degree of urbanization. It is growing by about 900 million people per decade, the largest absolute increases ever recorded, and is expected to reach nine billion by 2050. City-based populations use much more oil and other expensive energy sources than do rural populations.

Third, global temperatures have risen by at least three-quarters of a degree Celsius as a consequence of higher levels of greenhouse gases in the earth's atmosphere. Climate change brought about by exceptional human use of fossil fuels is now held to be 'unequivocal' by the International Plant Protection Convention (IPPC). Indeed, the IPPC has enabled the organized actions of many scientists around the globe to transform public debate. Moreover, these greenhouse gas levels and world temperatures will significantly increase *further* over the next few decades through multiple positive feedback effects.

Thus twentieth-century capitalism generated the most striking of contradictions. Its pervasive, mobile and promiscuous commodification involved utterly unprecedented levels of energy production and consumption, a high-carbon society whose legacy we are beginning to reap. This contradiction could result in a widespread reversal of many of the systems that constitute capitalism as it turns into its own gravedigger. A 'carbon shift' is inevitable. In the twenty-first century capitalism seems to be unable to control those powers that it called up by the spells set in motion during the unprecedented high-carbon twentieth century which reached its peak of global wastefulness within the neoliberal period from the 1980s onwards.

Four scenarios

There are four possible scenarios for 2050. The first is '*hypermobility*'. The current pattern of mobile lives based on new communications and transportation continue to develop to an extreme level. The resource shortages and effects of climate change turn out to be less significant at least for those in the rich North of the globe. Peoples' movement becomes more extensive and frequent with new kinds of fuel and vehicles that overcome limits of space and time. Personalized air travel, São Paulo writ large, would be common through the use of second- (or third-) generation bio-fuels. Cars would be unfashionably stuck on the ground as a Corbusier-inspired future beckons us all to the skies, including regular flights into space with Virgin Galactica! The final frontier is indeed overcome.

In the second, the effects especially of the politics of climate change, the peaking of oil supplies and periodic economic crises could reinforce '*local sustainability*'. Travel is substantially reduced and far more local. There may be some 'cars' around, but their monopoly of roads will have long since passed. Global population will be smaller as a result of worsening health care and reduced food supplies; and urban centres will have decayed. There will be a global shift towards lifestyles and forms of movement that are more local and smaller in scale. Friends would be chosen from neighbouring streets, families would not move away when forming new households, work would be found nearby, education would be sought only in local schools and colleges, the seasons would determine which foodstuffs were consumed, and most goods and services would be simpler and produced nearby. Global GDP will be smaller, but well-being may be higher for those who are part of this 'small is beautiful' future (see *Ecological Economics*).

A third alternative, a bleaker version of the second, may be termed '*regional warlordism*'. In this 'barbaric' future there are oil, gas and water shortages and intermittent wars. Many of the mobility, energy and communication connections that now straddle the world break down. The standard of living will plummet, movement will be restricted to the local level, governments will be relatively weak and local 'warlords' control recycled forms of mobility and weaponry. Infrastructures collapse and there is increasing separation between different regions. Cars and trucks, buses and trains, would rust away in the deserts or be washed away in floods. Often regions would be at war with their neighbours, especially for control of water, oil and gas. All of this was prefigured of course in *Mad Max 2*.

Finally, there is a post-car future where digital and transport technologies are combined and integrated together. This may be called the '*digital nexus*' future. Here new software 'intelligently' works out the best means of doing tasks, whether this involves meeting up or getting to some place or event. Some effects of meeting up would be effectively simulated through radically improved virtual communications. There would be small, ultra-light, smart, probably battery-based 'vehicles' for hire, a bit like the bikes available for hire now in Paris or Barcelona. Streets will be full of speed-controlled micro-cars, demand-responsive mini-buses, bikes, hybrid vehicles and pedestrians seamlessly integrated together with larger-scale public transport. 'Smart cards' would control access and payment for all forms of transport. Some vehicles would be driverless. Neighbourhoods would be redesigned so as to constrain sprawl. The currency would be carbon allowances allocated, monitored and individually measured. Much physical movement would be effectively rationed. There would be less 'freedom' to walk, drive or move without traces being left. The digital nexus system is a bit like living in an airport and such a world would need to be subject to energetic democratic impulses in order to make it less obviously Orwellian.

So the mobile twentieth century has left some constrained opportunities for mobility in this century. The future of 'mobility' is central to deciphering the future of life itself which could develop in one of a number of directions. What we should not assume is that the twentieth-century mobile world, building on innovations from around 1840, will continue to supply the principles by which this one will be organized. Some now argue that in the twenty-first century climate change, the build-up of toxic chemicals in the environment, energy shortages and similar internal contradictions will hugely constrain the possibilities for reengineering future mobility and energy uses. It will be hard to avoid a 'societal collapse' of the sort that happened to the Roman Empire or Mayan civilization. Mobility for the masses may turn out to have been short-lived. For a century or so the rich world went mad before its contradictions kicked in, so that twenty-first-century populations will have to deal with much slower conditions as societies go into reverse. Mobile lives may thus be a short if remarkable interlude in the history of humanity and their surprising mobile machines.

Further reading

Bauman, Z. (2000) *Liquid Modernity*. Polity, Cambridge.
Buzard, J. (1993) *The Beaten Track*. Clarendon Press, Oxford.
Cresswell, T. (2006) *On the Move*. Routledge, London.

Graham, S. and Marvin, S. (2001) *Splintering Urbanism: Network Infrastructures, Technological Mobilities and the Urban Condition*. Routledge, London.

Homer-Dixon, T. (2006) *The Upside of Down*. Souvenir, London.

Kellerman, A. (2006) *Personal Mobilities*. Routledge, London.

Larsen, J., Urry, J. and Axhausen, K. (2006) *Mobilities, Networks, Geographies*. Ashgate, Aldershot.

Perrow, C. (1999) *Normal Accidents*. Princeton University Press, Princeton, NJ.

Schivelbusch, W. (1986) *The Railway Journey. Trains and Travel in the Nineteenth Century*. Blackwell, Oxford.

Urry, J. (2002) *The Tourist Gaze*, 2nd edn. Sage, London.

Urry, J. (2007) *Mobilities*. Polity, Cambridge.

Virilio, P. (1986) *Speed and Politics*. Semiotext(e), New York.

31

Alternative Energy

Arnaud Sales and Leandro Raizer

The challenge

Global warming means that we must seriously question the use of fossil fuels. Yet they are still the most common source of energy. They are typical of industrial society, but they exacerbate the global environmental crisis by the day. Because they emit few greenhouse gases and are potentially renewable, alternative energy forms can be part of a multiple strategy for stabilizing and then reducing CO_2 emissions into the atmosphere. While they arc not necessarily new, these technologies can gradually free us from the dominance of industrial society's traditional ways of producing energy, even though the latter will remain important for decades to come. We attempt here to place renewable energy in the context of the challenges posed by the global warming crisis.

Forms of energy offering an alternative to fossil fuels typically leave a small footprint on the ecosystem and use renewable resources. They use technologies that transform renewable forms of primary energy (hydro, wind, geothermal, solar, tidal, purified coal, hydrogen . . . biomass) into different forms of secondary energy (mechanical, electrical, electromagnetic, thermal, combustible etc.) for use in lighting, heating, domestic appliances, productive activities and vehicle-propulsion. They include efficient technologies (cogeneration, energy recovery) that make it possible to save energy. They represent an alternative to energy using non-renewable resources with negative environmental effects – either direct or indirect – because they emit carbon dioxide or other gases (combustible fossils) that pose the threat of catastrophic effects on a grand scale or produce radioactive waste that is very difficult to eliminate (nuclear energy). Alternative energy may be produced in decentralized ways and can easily be exploited in the developing countries. With the exception of hydroelectricity, the most advanced renewable forms have yet to make their mark in either technological or economic terms. Innovation is a basic key to the long-term success of alternative energy, as some of the technologies involved are still in their infancy.

According to *International Energy Outlook 2009*, renewable forms of energy accounted for only 8.4 per cent of world consumption in 2008; this figure is low if we consider that it includes hydroelectricity. If, however, we take into account the use of renewable combustibles and their waste products, the figure is probably higher, since statistics for the non-commercial use of biomass in the developing countries are inaccurate. According to the US Energy Information Administration, bioenergy alone supplied 14 per cent of primary energy. Oil, in contrast, represented 35 per cent of world energy consumption in 2008, with coal supplying 26 per cent, natural gas 23 per cent and nuclear energy six per cent. Despite all the international measures, debates, agreements and protocols, the use of fossil fuels is still growing, as though all were well with the world. The US Energy Information Administration's projections estimate that, given world average growth of 44 per cent in 2030 (73 per cent for non-OECD countries), coal, natural gas and liquids (including biofuel) will still play a major role, despite continuous growth of renewable energies. Carbon dioxide (CO_2) emissions will go on rising from 29 billion metric tons in 2006 to 40 billion in 2030 – an increase of 39 per cent over the projection period.

The production of electricity alone generates 300–800g of CO_2 per Kwh when fossil combustibles are used, as against 130g for photovoltaic energy, 5–30g for wind energy and 4–20g for hydroelectric energy. This last, together with nuclear energy when it comes on stream, is the most efficient source in terms of emissions of greenhouse gases. These figures give some idea of the challenges involved if we wish to transform a structure as sophisticated as the fossil-energy industry where so many economic interests are at stake.

Moving beyond industrial society

Relations between human beings and between us and nature may be characterized by how energy is produced, allocated and distributed. Exploitation of available energy allowed new forces to be deployed that are much more powerful than human capacities. These facilitated the development of new agricultural, craft-based, industrial or software techniques. They also encouraged the development of exchange of commodities and knowledge, long-distance and rapid transport (see *Mobility*), new cultures and practices and of course new relations of power and domination. When a society commits itself, consciously or otherwise, to choosing appropriate energy and technology, it effectively chooses a new kind of 'development' and to define a specific relationship with nature. And, as we now know, such choices can have unexpected and risky, even dangerous consequences.

The main motor forces were once provided by human beings, animals, water and wind; and most combustibles came from the biomass. But with the industrial revolution came the massive use of coal and the emergence of new kind of society. Industrial society developed thanks to modes of production and consumption that were from the outset based on the expected accumulation of profits and on the exploitation of labour tending machines. We tend to forget that this machinery depended on technologies that were invented, perfected and built by engineers and scientists to harness the movement of water, the combustion of coal, oil and natural gas and ultimately nuclear fission. Technological advances that themselves were inseparable from economic choices and the political balance of power had a major impact on the organization of production, labour, transport, communications and the dynamics of economic development, not to mention many spheres of social life more generally. Although this mastery of technology bound together the human and physical worlds, it often reinforced the impression of a divorce between man and nature, which was often seen as something that could simply be instrumentalized or, as Beck puts it, integrated into and contaminated by industry. Environmental and climatic problems are a reminder that the relationship should be described as symbiotic and not parasitic.

We have seen dazzling developments in scientific knowledge, in information and communications technology, in globalized forms of production and circulation and in the institutional reorganization of power at every level. The consequent rearrangement of influence and many transformations of social life have led some to argue that we now live in a post-industrial society. But we have not really left the industrial society behind, when we recall that ± 90 per cent of all the energy we use still comes from fossil fuels. The interests of actors at the centre of the industrial energy system still shape contemporary models of production and consumption. The markets that result do not take into account major negative externalities affecting the environment, so that we continue to abuse fossil fuels. Although it is still dominant, and is now being globalized, the prevailing model is nonetheless obsolete because it underpins the current environmental crisis. We cannot begin to cut our use of fossil fuels without at the same time redefining our version of 'material civilization' (in Fernand Braudel's sense) and our intimate relationship with nature.

Renewable energy technologies today

What renewable energy technologies are available to us today? What is their role in the production of energy, and what are their potential drawbacks?

1. Hydraulic energy

Water was the first source of energy to be harnessed in the early stages of the industrial revolution during the 1780s, when it was used to power the cotton industry's machines for cleaning, carding and spinning; but the production of electricity proved to be hydraulic energy's most productive use. Electricity was produced by waterwheels in the nineteenth century, but the twentieth century saw the development of increasingly powerful turbines such as those used in the La Grande complex in Canada (1,700 MW), Itaipu in Brazil (1,400 MW) and the Three Gorges in China (1,800 MW). These three countries are the biggest producers of hydroelectricity in the world. Huge turbines coupled with the alternators in hydroelectric dams mean that hydraulic energy is now one of the most powerful and least expensive sources of renewable energy. In 2008 it accounted for 2.2 per cent of world energy output and 16 per cent of all the electricity produced. 86 per cent of that output came from renewable sources, which accounted for 19 per cent of all electricity. The potential is enormous, especially in Latin America and Africa.

Hydroelectricity produces very few greenhouse gases and is, in economic terms, very viable because of its low maintenance costs. This does not mean it has no drawbacks, which explains why very big dams are not regarded as alternative energy. The flooding of land around the dams – for a period of at least twenty years – results in intense bacterial activity that converts the mercury found in the earth and plants into methyl mercury, a neurotoxic substance that builds up in the aquatic food chain. And, as we have recently seen with the Three Gorges dam, which many experts regard as dangerous, the flooding of large areas and building of huge supply lines can affect vast human communities (well over one million people have been displaced), damage the diversity of local fauna and destroy the primal beauty of the landscape. Hence the debates over whether water-courses with a hydroelectric potential must be protected so as to keep them in their natural state (in Sweden and Canada that position has been adopted in response to the demands of native populations) or whether cutting emissions of greenhouse gas is more important as we enter the twenty-first century.

2. Biomass

Defined in the broadest sense, the 'biomass' is made up of all the organisms that live on our planet. In terms of the production of renewable energy, usually trees and other plants arc uscd in a wide variety of ways. The use of trees ranges from direct combustion for domestic purposes, as in developing countries (where it is the source of 2Gt of CO_2 in the absence of reforestation), to sophisticated combustion technologies. Six per cent of electricity from renewable sources comes from the biomass. This also includes biofuels (ethanol, biodiesel) produced by the fermentation of plants such as sugar cane, maize, *miscanthus* and switchgrass, which have to compete with more productive forms of food production. There are doubts about the ecological qualities of bio-fuels and especially of ethanol corn which emits, it has been claimed, more gas than oil. Technologies that can transform organic raw materials (waste, animal droppings) into methane for the production of biogases are also being developed.

The biomass may be defined as a renewable combustible with regard to the greenhouse effect because, unlike coal, oil or natural gas which are also products of the biomass that were formed hundred of millions of years ago, today's plants and trees capture CO_2 as they grow. The plants that are used have already absorbed CO_2 and the CO_2 that is produced when they are burned will be reabsorbed by plants and algae during the next cycle of photosynthesis. This process is referred to as *carbon sequestration*. Some researchers estimate that if farmland and grasslands are managed ecologically, we will be able to 'sequester up to 15 per cent of the world's annual fossil fuel emissions in soils' (Al Gore).

Forests make up the greater part of the earth's biomass and the rate at which they are used must not be allowed to outstrip their natural rate of regeneration. So-called 'wild' biomass consumption – both non-commercial and commercial – is leading to deforestation and therefore large carbon emissions (2Gt) in developing countries and we must succeed in replacing it with more rational ways of using these resources.

3. Wind energy

Wind turbines were developed in the late nineteenth century, when they were used to bring electricity to rural areas. Now that costs have fallen, world production of electricity from wind energy, along with solar energy, had the most rapid rate of growth in the last decade (30 per cent each). With an output of 215 TWh, wind energy accounted for only one per cent of world energy output and six per cent of renewable energy, which compares favourably with solar energy (0.3 per cent), even though the latter has received so much media attention. The most powerful wind turbines are in the US (25,000 MW), Germany (24,000 MW), Spain (17,000 MW), China (12,000 MW) and India (10,000 MW). In Denmark, which is regarded as one of the leaders in this field, wind energy accounts for 19 per cent (3,000 MW) of all electricity produced.

Three-bladed wind turbines perched on masts 40 to 135 metres tall and with rotors up to 126 metres in diameter are the 'biggest rotary machines man has ever built on an industrial scale' (Chabot). They are now manufactured by companies in Denmark, the USA, Spain, Germany, India and China. Wind turbines can supply small networks and are suitable for use in small communities, especially in developing countries. They can also be concentrated in huge wind farms capable of supplying over 200,000 homes: the biggest in the world is the Roscoe Wind Farm in Texas, with 627 turbines. The debate over such high-power installations now centres on their role in energy production and on how they can be connected to high-voltage supply lines supplying large urban areas. United States estimates claim that grid-connected renewable energy projects could replace 300 coal-fired power plants there. This solution thus has major advantages in terms of respect for the environment since, as mentioned above, US electricity production is still heavily dependent on coal (50 per cent).

Wind systems appear to have few ecological drawbacks, but they cannot be used everywhere. They depend upon their site's wind resources and the annual average wind speed is the major factor. Large wind farms also take up an immense amount of space: the Roscoe Wind Farm covers 100,000 acres. Their visual impact and the (fairly limited) noise they cause mean that they cannot be built close to urban and residential areas. They may also cause radar interference and pose a threat to air traffic control.

4. Geothermal Energy

Thermal sources have been in use since ancient times. They exploit both the immense heat of the globe's central core and flows of heat on its crust (which is on average 35 kilometres thick). The earth's crust itself generates part of its own heat from radioactive bodies. Geothermal electricity is now used in Iceland, California, Mexico, Italy and Japan. Low- or very low-temperature geothermal energy (which involves the use of heat pumps) is used mainly to heat houses or for air-conditioning, while high-temperature geothermals produce electricity. In 2008, geothermal sources produced 63 TWh world-wide, in other words less than two per cent of renewable sources. This energy source is making slow progress. It is defined as renewable only if it is not overexploited.

5. Solar Energy

Despite its extraordinary availability, solar energy currently accounts for only 0.06 per cent of the world's energy production. Its rate of growth, on the other hand, is comparable with that of wind energy. It is used mainly to generate electricity (0.3 per cent of renewables) and to heat suitably designed buildings. Its uses vary greatly, depending on the climate zone. Several technologies are now being used to harness solar energy. A distinction is made between thermodynamic power plants on the one hand and photovoltaic systems on the other. Thermodynamic plants or power tower systems use a large number of tower-mounted heliostats to concentrate the sun's rays. One near Seville (Spain) uses 1,250 heliostats. For its part, Kramer Junction, the biggest thermodynamic plant in the world, heats synthetic oil to a temperature of 750C; the steam produced by large quantities of water causes the turbine to turn and drive the generator that produces the electricity.

Quite apart from the fact that these plants take up vast amounts of room (as do wind farms), ecologists, farmers and residents are all critical of this technology because the phenomenal amounts of water it consumes make unsustainable demands on aquifers (the two plants used in Nevada's Amargosa Valley consume almost five billion litres of water a year). It is now being abandoned in favour of dry-cooled solar thermal technology. Cleaning the mirrors used in solar plants also consumes millions of litres of water, often in desert areas where water is a vital resource.

The use of photovoltaic systems in space is well-known. Thousands of satellites are fuelled by electricity, as was the 'pathfinder' vehicle sent to Mars. Photovoltaic technology has many applications and its modular construction means that it is well-adapted to decentralized production of electricity. It can meet the electricity needs of houses fitted with photovoltaic roofs in southern regions. The excess electricity produced can be fed into the grid, used in water pumps or to power traffic signals. These systems are particularly well-suited to remote regions where the electricity and telecommunications infrastructure is inadequate, especially in developing countries. Photovoltaic cell technology uses one of the properties of photosensitive semi-conductors (usually solar-grade silicon) which, when they come into contact with light photons, bind their electrons and generate electric current. The cells are grouped into modules and, in the case of more powerful plants, arrays of modules, to form PV solar generators. Technological advances and the ready availability of the equipment, which is easily installed, go hand in hand with falling costs. Japan is currently the leader in terms of the production (40 per cent of world output) and use (30 per cent of world sales) of photovoltaic systems. Over 200,000 homes there are now fitted with solar panels and most are grid-connected. Sharp and Kyocera are the world's biggest producers of photovoltaic modules. Japan aims to generate ten per cent of all its electricity from solar energy by 2030.

The role of alternative energy in climate stabilization

To what extent may alternative energies free us from the dominance of industrial society's traditional ways of generating energy, and stabilize and then reduce global warming which results from CO_2 emissions? Advocates of 'ecological modernization' take an optimistic view. They argue, against much criticism, that environmental problems can best be solved through further advancement of technology and industrialization. The resolution of environmental problems is also economically profitable and the dynamism of the market can make environmental protection politically feasible. This requires certain changes: cleaner, more efficient technologies and production practices; social and ecological planning; new accounting methods that encourage the internalization of the ecological costs of their production; and government regulations that make these changes more attractive, such as ecological tax reform.

The 'human ecologists' take a pessimistic view and are highly critical of the above theory. They claim that the ecological sustainability of human societies is now in serious question and that nothing can be expected from continued economic growth and institutional change in the present context. Measuring environmental impact in terms of the 'ecological footprint', they argue that we simply cannot seek greater efficiency by, for example, reducing the amount of raw materials and energy consumed by units of production. If we are to achieve sustainable development, we require drastic reductions in terms of both resources and energy. They do accept, on the other hand, the importance of the search for new technological (and institutional) forms that can reduce the environmental impact of population growth and economic development.

Whether these analysts are optimistic or pessimistic concerning the future of industrial capitalism and whether they put their trust in science and technology to resolve a problem as complex as global warming or harbour doubts about their value, they cannot deny that renewable energy does have the potential to combat it.

Our energy systems are responsible for 70 per cent of greenhouse gases and 'tackling climate change means, to a large extent, tackling our energy-related emissions' (Coley). The first way to do so, as the human ecologists would agree, is to reduce our consumption of energy. This implies changing the practices of individuals and organizations, but it also means that lifestyles have to change and that our material civilization has to be reconstructed. Some, such as Coley, find it difficult to imagine that efforts to conserve energy will be enough to meet the demand for that 60 per cent cut in current levels of emissions which is needed if we are to stabilize and then reduce levels of atmospheric carbon dioxide, especially as the demand for energy on the part of the 'emerging' countries is rising. It follows that we must succeed in promoting alternative energy forms if we are to restrict the use of fossil fuels drastically. The two solutions are not mutually exclusive.

Will this succeed in stabilizing the production of CO_2 over the next fifty years? No, because the fight against climate change is multi-dimensional, especially in technological terms. Pacala and Socolow argue that we must implement at least five strategies that they describe as 'stabilization wedges'; and the appropriate technology is already available. These are: (1) energy efficiency and conservation; (2) fossil fuels shift; (3) nuclear fission (4) renewable electricity and fuels; and (5) management of forests and agricultural soils.

The International Energy Agency's *450 Scenario* proposes that, in the long term, the concentration of greenhouse gases in the atmosphere should be stabilized at 450 parts per million of CO_2. They recommend that four of the above strategies should be implemented by 2030. Most reductions in CO_2 emissions will come from efficiency measures. Using renewables would also cut emissions, but this would account for only 20 per cent of the total (a bit more if bio-fuels are included). These strategies, demanding as they are if implemented, do not rule out fossil fuels, providing that their carbon emissions are cut, the efficiency of power plants and carbon capture and storage are improved and nuclear capacity is doubled, even though the last option is not always viable, given the political threat of nuclear proliferation and terrorism and problems of waste management.

The surprising thing is that all such scenarios are based on existing technologies. But the next fifty to sixty years should see significant discoveries and innovations in the field of energy that are both practical and economically viable. During the Second World War, the United States demonstrated with the Manhattan Project that it was possible to harness nuclear fission *in a very short period of time*. It was of course first used for military purposes, but it paved the way for civilian use of that type of energy. Isn't it time to launch a global project for the development of low-carbon energy science and technology and to mobilize very high-level scientists and engineers on a general and sectoral basis, but this time for peaceful purposes and without the red tape of international organizations?

Implementing the *450 Scenario* for climate stabilization requires much more than a technological and economic *tour de force*. It needs a huge proactive effort consolidated in economic and political agreements involving states, public and private international organizations, corporations, farmers and citizens worldwide. Such agreements are essential, especially as a material civilization that has gone global is complex and less malleable than the above scenarios might suggest: there is no hierarchy of supranational, national and local levels. Conflicts and trials of strength over the environment take place at all levels and the local efforts made by citizens are just as important as inter-state negotiations, if we wish to create a low-carbon world.

Further reading

Beck, U. (1992) *Risk Society: Towards a New Modernity*. Sage, London.

Bradford, T. (2006) *Solar Revolution: The Economic Transformation of the Global Energy Industry*. MIT Press, Cambridge, MA.

Coley, D. (2009) *Energy and Climate Change: Creating a Sustainable Planet*. Wiley, Chichester.

Gore, A. (2009) *Our Choice: A Plan to Solve the Climate Crisis*. Rodale, Emmaus.

Humphrey, C., Lewis, T. and Buttel, F. (2001) *Environment, Energy and Society: A New Synthesis*. Wadsworth, Belmont, CA.

International Energy Agency (2009) *World Energy Outlook 2009*.

Landes, D. (1969) *Prometheus Unbound: Technical Change and Industrial Development in Western Europe from 1750 to the Present*. Cambridge University Press, Cambridge.

Murphy, R. (1994) *Rationality and Nature: A Sociological Inquiry into a Changing Relationship*. Westview, Boulder.

Pacala, S. and Socolow, R. (2004) Stabilization wedges: solving the climate problem for the next 50 years with current technologies. *Science* 305 (5686), 968–72.

Pretty, J. et al. (2007) *The Sage Handbook of Environment and Society*. Sage, London.

Spaargaren, G. and Mol, A. (eds) (2000) *Environment and Global Modernity*. Sage, London.

Spaargaren, G., Mol, A. and Buttel, F. (2006) *Governing Environmental Flows: Global Challenges to Social Theory*. MIT Press, Cambridge, MA.

York, R., Rosa, E. and Dietz, T. (2003) Footprints on the Earth: The environmental consequences of modernity. *American Sociological Review* 68 April, 279–300.

32

Worlds of Emancipation

Antonio David Cattani

The idea

The notion of emancipation encompasses a wide range of values and experiences based essentially on the principle of self-determination – of individuals, specific groups or larger social collectivities. Emancipation involves the utopian desire for things to be different and is thus a call for a transformation that will build something new, expanding the sphere of freedom and asserting the perfectibility of human beings and human activities. Emancipation is not a theoretical concept but a constellation of meanings and projects that are critical of the limitations of the present; it envisages possibilities, revolts and ruptures: it means exploring possibilities, overcoming imposed social and economic limits and daring to build a better world.

Emancipation is linked to the concept of autonomy. In a Kantian philosophy harking back to this term's etymology, autonomy means the self-determination of subjects according to their own laws or those they consider legitimate, not through familiarity or custom but in the full light of consciousness. In order for law and liberty to be linked, we need to be able to distinguish good laws from bad. Good laws are established by free citizens for their own benefit; the latter are imposed by the strong on the weak. Hence autonomy does not mean the capacity of human beings to act in accordance with the law, but the ability to define their own law.

The discourse and reality of autonomy only make sense in collective terms, that is, through living in society; and for this reason the concepts of social emancipation and autonomy will be treated as synonymous here. The general principle of social emancipation may be counter-posed to authoritarian logic and to the discretionary power in decision-making wielded by corporate and state bureaucracies. It may indeed be opposed to any form of collaboration or participation promoted and controlled by elites. Autonomy fuels the libertarian imagination and, both of its own accord and under encouragement, promotes those practices which challenge arbitrary norms, oppressive hierarchies and the rational dictates of private production. Its corollary is collective appropriation, decentralization and conscious participation in the productive process, social life and cultural creation. Social organization according to principles of popular emancipation implies the free association of equal individuals whose participation is voluntary, conscious and contractual. It implies equal responsibilities and opportunities for attaining communal goals, a freely established allocation of work tasks and rationales, and management according to ability and subject to review and recall. The *Solidarity Economy* in its many manifestations currently puts these principles into practice through direct democracy.

In sum, a community is emancipated or free when its laws are not imposed through repressive, tutelary or paternalistic processes; it is autonomous when it does not submit to subjective, extraneous or arbitrary rules; it is truly emancipated when the highest law is the objective and universal common good. In an emancipated society, individuals have maximum freedom, but this is based on equality, reciprocity of rights and duties and ultimately on a civilizing process that guarantees free expression while respecting other people's differences and freedom.

The project

The verb *emancipate* comes from the Latin *emancipare*, from *ex* (out from, no longer) and *mancipium* (slave or dependent person). It refers to the judicial procedure of Roman law concerning legal release, enfranchisement, the removal of guardianship or of one person's power over another. Individuals who have managed to make their own way in the world are emancipated. For centuries the term was used to refer to individuals or small groups; and it was only with the Enlightenment and the French Revolution that it acquired the broad, dynamic meaning it retained until the twentieth century. Ideas of popular sovereignty, free will and social emancipation do not arise in pre-modern societies dominated by religious dogmas and by legitimacy inhering in particular persons or groups. Traditional societies, for a variety of religious, ideological, cultural and political reasons, saw order and a sense of community as arising from and being dependent on forces external and superior to human beings.

Yet the desire for freedom and self-realization has always existed. Popular revolts broke out throughout the ages, but these were usually driven by varieties of messianism and had no lasting consequences (see *Communism*). Moreover, they were not conceived or conducted as emancipatory and universalistic enterprises resulting from human free will. With the advent of modernity, individuals began to confront the reality of their own actions: society was no longer defined in terms of transcendent forces but by human processes of material reproduction and historical creation, in interaction with nature. Modernity saw the emergence of societies endowed with human agency rather than external determinants and the endless repetition of cyclical time.

Ideas of progress, modernization and development stimulated the development of 'societies mobilized and activated by projects' (Boudinet), that is, societies that reproduce themselves through their ability to control social and economic logics. The capacity to see ahead goes further than simple prediction; it is a decisive factor in breaking with inertia and galvanizing forces around projects to reconstruct the present. In the early stages of modernity and capitalist development, the new elites led the process: enterprising or conquering bourgeoisies, enlightened despots and voluntaristic Jacobins. Alongside these innovative political and economic processes, other social forces began to emerge that drew strength and legitimacy from new theoretical frameworks. Theory and practice in combination pronounced universal human rights and the dignity of the masses. There emerged a multitude of movements aimed at bringing about a truly communist society – that is, a society no longer deformed by class struggle or dictatorship exercised through bureaucracy (see *Communism*). These movements ensured that terms like popular sovereignty, liberty, equality and fraternity for all did not remain mere daydreams or rhetorical figures, but became the underlying principles of a project hitherto unknown in human history.

Its negation

We can formulate a better and clearer definition of what social emancipation is by presenting ideas and situations that are its opposite. There has never been a shortage of candidates willing to direct the course of history and bring order to society. Linking up with the most ancient and conservative traditions of political thought, contemporary manifestations of elitism endlessly reaffirm the congenital incapacity of the people to take initiatives on their own and to express and defend their own interests. Starting with the observation that there are real inequalities between individuals in physical constitution, intellectual qualities and talent, elitist thought justifies concentrations of power and wealth in the hands of the most 'capable', considering the mass of the population so mediocre, lacking in will and sheep-like that all they are fit for is to lie down and submit to being led.

The most radical forms of elitist thought, however, are rarely expressed overtly. Softened and disguised versions proliferate, in two or more basic forms. The first presents itself as belonging to the progressive camp, imbued with the best of intentions and desirous of the common good. This form is found in those variants of vanguardism found in Jacobinism and opportunistic adaptations of Leninism. These altruistic vanguards consider that the masses, brutalized by their working conditions, are incapable of developing any concept of the concrete totality, of themselves or of their true interests. What is necessary, according to Lenin, are irreproachable cadres 'capable of assuming power and leading the whole people to socialism, of directing and organizing the new system, of being the teacher, the guide, the leader of all the working and exploited people'. The Jacobin tradition finds expression in Keynesian or Social Democratic policies that seek to promote the common good from on high – without the participation of the interested parties – and, in modern versions of 'Social Caesarism', a political regime that dispenses with intermediate institutions and concentrates power in the hands of charismatic personalities seen as defenders of the people.

The second variant of elitist thought is represented by concepts of a decidedly tutelary nature. In this case, the autonomous participation of the masses is not tolerated since they are considered incapable without the protection of elites claiming to rationalize political action and public life: *Caudillos*, latter-day enlightened despots, populist governors and all those who, with the state as their arena, operate from the top down to integrate the people into the political projects they control. The tutelary approach, seeking the common good at all costs, develops welfarist and charitable practices that reinforce individual and institutional relations of subservience. Repression is adopted, when necessary, if subjects, assumed to be unaware of their true interests, venture on the uncertain path of freedom.

These non-emancipatory forms are conventional, having been present throughout history in relations between sovereigns and vassals, leaders and led, and in varieties of social contract, both spurious and legitimate. The modern form of social control is far more complex, portraying our domination by capitalist relations as natural. These relations take the form of a self-referential, self-institutionalizing market, the supreme controller of all relations between individuals. Classic images of power – the state, tyrant or leader – and their activities are easy to identify, whereas the figure of the market is diluted and vague, resting as it does on the cloudy fiction of a 'sovereign individual'.

According to neoliberal theory, individuals are free and self-aware. They construct a 'possible world' by mobilizing resources in pursuit of their own self-interest according to a rational cost-benefit analysis. The invisible hand of the market is held to ensure the congruence of individuals' expectations, control their preferences and, above all, define each person's place within the social formation. The form of production ruled by capitalist rationality (produce in order to accumulate, accumulate in order to dominate) is the mother cell or the nuclear engine of social reproduction. The domestication of primary producers is given concrete form in the work process. Since their labour power is alienated and taken from them, workers themselves become alienated and submit to the discretionary power of others, losing the capacity to organize their own lives and to fulfil themselves as creative human actors (see *Labour Economy*).

During the twentieth century, the work process was organized by Taylorist and Fordist principles through time management strategies involving task specialization and separation of the functions of conception, planning and execution, ensuring strict control over human labour. Workers were not only exploited but placed in a situation of vulnerability and dependence, leading them to believe that work was inevitably fragmented, repetitive, monotonous and meaningless. A new paradigm, emerging in the 1980s, changed this framework.

Domination was no longer exercised primarily through stable relations, but through sporadic, precarious and uncertain entry into the labour market. A consequence of this form of production and service delivery, or 'flexible specialization', is that it makes workers themselves responsible for their own 'employability' and for entering the labour market as entrepreneurs or freelance professionals. Yet the dominant ideology reaffirmed by these new relations of production again assures us that 'everyone has what they deserve and is in the most suitable place'.

The most recent version of economic liberalism exemplifies this impoverished and short-term vision: the horizon of human self-realization is reduced to a fragmented and mediocre existence. Worship of the self-regulating market as a fetish defines our narcissistic routine of consumption and listless individualism. Current reality is seen as being natural and its limits unchallengeable by individuals or institutions. It may be contemplated or enjoyed, but not changed. Liberalism, given a post-modern twist as neoliberalism, states that our twenty-first century situation is the only one possible and there can be no going beyond it: as such, it is the acme of anti-utopia.

Utopia

There are countless theoretical references to social emancipation. The spirit of the Enlightenment or *Aufklärung*, the 'associative sociability' inspired by Gracchus Babeuf, utopian socialism, anarchism and the philosophy of praxis, all of these run counter to anti-utopias. The Enlightenment challenge, dare to know (*sapere aude*), very soon developed into dare to *imagine* something different, dare to *change*, dare to *create*. Categories of understanding such as dialectic, praxis, contradiction, contingency, consciousness and action were not merely contemplative, nor were processes like power, conflict, class struggle, social movements and historical creation. Utopian reason is linked to action, to questioning facts and givens. It is not enough for us to understand: we must achieve what we desire. The outcomes of movements for liberty and autonomy have meaning. Any critical and practical action is inspired by truly civilizing values: pacifism, cosmopolitanism respectful of local identities (or the society of nations) and, above all, the goal of a democratic, egalitarian, just and fraternal society.

When we refer to the civilizing process, we need to distinguish between mere changes and real advances for society and humanity. 'Civilization is an act of justice' stated the people's delegate Mirabeau during the French Revolution. A civilized person is 'a citizen of the world'. The term *civilis* expresses the social process of creation, the human aspiration to supersede destiny and cyclical time. Civilization is the negation of violence, of paternalistic or messianic tutelage, of aristocratic or *caudillo* paternalism, of racism, preconceptions and privileges, the whole murky world of exclusive particularism. Civilization is: the universality of procedures and specific rights, without any levelling-down or tyrannical imposition; the substantial broadening of politics to entail conscious participation and increased responsibilities; an international society blending cosmopolitanism with local identities and cultures; and the potential for self-realization and individual emancipation without aspirations to self-sufficiency or predation. Finally, civilization means respect for others, fraternal respect for their freedoms and differences. This of course excludes processes representing themselves falsely as emancipatory. Techno-utopias (the hi-tech gift economy), cyber-communism and managerial benevolence foster change of a sort, but not advances in civilization. We must exclude also totalitarian projects and processes, dogmatic elitism and regressive liberalization.

True utopia is a creative prefiguring that blends 'the cold current of scientific thought with the warm current of hope' (Ernst Bloch). Its reformist projects are not just palliatives and anaesthetics for mechanisms that spawn inequality and injustice. A civilizing utopia is not a spectator of social reality. Aiming at a world founded anew, it rejects theories of natural right (including the right to appropriate socially production privately) and sets itself to overcome limits of space and time. Real, consistent emancipation cannot be restricted to amassing theoretical knowledge that aims at abstract freedom in the political sphere. Its *categorical imperative* is to remain grounded in physical survival.

The working community

In the world of work and production, the general principle of social emancipation described above is expressed in various historical concepts and experiences, such as producer autonomy, works councils, workers' associations, self-determination, self-organization, workers' control and the soviets. The principle of autonomy presupposes that power and authority, with their corollary workplace discipline, are reorganized within the enterprise. Private property, the source of domination, is replaced by social ownership of the means of production. The working community becomes free and responsible for establishing the goals and meaning of production. Social emancipation is here manifested as concrete opposition to the dominant economic and social formations, rather than as self-exclusion (alternative communities isolated from society and the economy), restriction to the system's interstices (employees' co-operatives, the informal economy) and all reforms that fail to challenge the power of employers (joint management schemes).

We have innumerable records of workers' free associations throughout history, as well as fictional accounts of how to organize human society more fairly. Thomas More's *Utopia* (1516) initiated the modern cycle of humanist thought on the ideal city. Other notable works in this cycle include Thomaso Campanella's *City of the Sun* and Francis Bacon's *New Atlantis*. These works notably asserted the possibility of power and social relations being organized differently, at a time when absolute monarchy and rigid social hierarchy held sway. The advent of capitalism inaugurated a second cycle of utopian thought with two main strands. The first was inspired by the idea that we should return to a state of nature, humanity's golden age, authentic, harmonious and stable. This strand is sometimes confused with a nostalgic vision of pre-capitalist society and of the *ancien régime* of pre-revolutionary France. There were diverse experiments: alternative communities of an ecumenical bent, a kind of dirigiste collectivism inspired by religion, such as the Shakers and similar sects in the United States from the beginning.

The second strand was rooted in capitalist reality, but sought an alternative space: the co-operative movement espoused by Robert Owen, the phalansteries set up by Charles Fourier and libertarian or directly oppositional collectives as in revolutionary syndicalism. Throughout the last two centuries in the West, we have seen a proliferation of theoretical formulations, practical experiments and autonomous attempts to confront the capitalist order and the power of the state. Among the most interesting are the shop stewards' committees in England during the 1920s, the workers' councils of Northern Italy after the First World War, the Russian soviets before the Revolution and the *Rätesystem* and *Arbeiterräte* of Weimar Germany. Forms of worker self-organization in this period did not separate trade union activity from political action: their demands transcended issues specific to the workplace; they encompassed urban problems and went so far as to demand a wider form of citizenship.

The soviets, created after the aborted revolution of 1905, emerged initially from spontaneously formed strike committees. Between 1905 and 1917 they were transformed into organizations more representative of the Russian working class and were treated as legitimate interlocutors by employers and the Tsarist state. Lenin ignored these early precursors of the soviets that flourished in 1917 and then proclaimed 'All power to the soviets!' After the Revolution, the organizing capacities of the Bolshevik Party were turned to creating a state apparatus that was independent of the working masses. In his pamphlet *Left-Wing Communism: An Infantile Disorder* (1920) Lenin recommended that the soviets and the trade unions should become transmission belts for the Party. The effect of this directive was to eliminate any possibility of autonomous workers' organizations and to initiate the Revolution's slide into degenerate bureaucracy.

After the First World War, worker and trade union struggles suffered a clear setback, particularly in terms of control over the work process. In addition to political factors, the concentration of technical capacities and particularly the adoption of Taylorist and Fordist principles reduced the scope for workers' action. As industrial plants grew ever larger, more complex and automated, disputes over control were obliged to go beyond the immediate context of the shop floor and to engage with the wider society. Trade union activity after the First World War was basically focused on the same reformist practices that characterized the Welfare State. The Turin Workers' Councils and forms of proletarian self-organization that developed during the Spanish civil War (1936–9) exemplify the double adversity, from within and without, faced by the autonomist movement. The Turin Councils, theorized by Gramsci, aimed to be permanent forms of democratic organization with their roots in the shop floor. These Councils, unlike parties and trade unions ('organisms created on the terrain of bourgeois democracy'), were to be the basis for a new industrial order and popular economy. But technical control of production was not sufficient for a total social transformation. The autonomist project foundered on its inability to take over social production as a whole. The short-lived success of autonomist collectives, such as those developed during the Spanish Civil War, was possible only because the country was in a state of war, with its political and legal institutions ill-defined. Once the forces of the right had won the war, Francoist repression was unleashed on the alternative movement, demonstrating the ferocious opposition of conservative elites to any kind of libertarian experiment.

After the Second World War, there were two noteworthy experiments in the self-managed organization of production, albeit implemented in technocratic form by the state apparatus. These were Yugoslavia from 1946 until the 1970s and Algeria in 1962–5. These experiments could not continue because of interference from the governments themselves and failure to reconcile the interests of a complex network of productive units. Autonomist principles were again revitalized in the wake of the movements of May 1968. In some countries, notably Germany and Italy, autonomism reappeared first in the form of political action, then revolutionary action and finally as terrorism. The failures and mistakes of these experiments did not crush the libertarian spirit. The last two decades of the twentieth century saw a renewal of countless initiatives in all the economically developed countries, under names such as the Social Economy, Workers' Co-ops, Grassroots Economic Organizations, Worker Self-Management and Friendly Societies.

Trade union resistance and many new forms of social mobilization (particularly through NGOs) were joined by attempts to construct non-capitalist ways of organizing production. In little more than a decade there appeared thousands of undertakings inspired by the principles of another kind of economy. What was initially seen as just an attempt to develop a popular economy aiming to ensure the survival of an impoverished population turned out to be a massive and politically surprising phenomenon, where autonomy and social emancipation were no longer utopian ideals, but took concrete form, despite practical obstacles and the ideological and political opposition of dominant economic forces.

The *Solidarity Economy* in its many manifestations has achieved positive results that go far beyond providing jobs and incomes, promoting ecological awareness and responsibility, and above all solidarity, the indispensable core of any advance in civilization. After the first World Social Forum in Porto Alegre in 2001, what had been isolated experiments in different countries now developed international links, opening up the possibility of an alternative economy on a global scale (see *Alter-Globalization*).

Contemporary challenges

In fighting against unjust social orders, the control or paternalism of elites and the naturalization of social control that can be seen as 'voluntary servitude', libertarian movements usually encounter repression, social apathy, isolation and the erosion of militancy. Moreover, the social emancipation agenda is constantly expanding as it responds to new demands. These include discrimination on grounds of gender and against ethnic or cultural minorities. They have been joined in recent decades by movements for environmental sustainability and a new counter-hegemonic internationalism. In the face of a predatory capitalism and globalization that excludes most people, truly international popular initiatives to defend the environment and biodiversity are essential. There are at least two new challenges to this. First, technological advances in capitalist hands reinforce and amplify inequalities. Collective self-emancipation through an attempt to equalize opportunities cannot take a regressive direction by proposing to return to a so-called simpler society, lacking modern comforts and technological resources. On the contrary, our challenge is to manage and put to use what the most advanced products of science. The second challenge relates to work. Many eminent authors, progressive and conservative alike, hold that individuals will only achieve true self-realization when work is abolished. For them truly free time is non-work time, leisure time, engaging in activities not imposed by necessity. This idyllic vision of a Golden Age, where producer-philosopher-poet-fishermen stroll through the land of Cockaigne or Shangri-la, empties human action of its transformational potential. Work is an act of creation, beyond discourse and representation, that enables people to face the world and transform it. The utopia we should be seeking is not the abolition of work, but removal of its oppressive and alienating features. In an emancipated society we produce both our present and a different future.

The historic problems and new challenges facing any process of social emancipation are huge and complex. Yet utopian energies are likewise inexhaustible. New actors continually appear on the scene to prevent life from being domesticated and to revive the civilizing impulse.

Utopia may be realized in a more generic and no less important sphere. Creative freedom aiming at social emancipation manifests itself in the struggle against dogmatism of all kinds, against false messiahs, against structural determinisms, against subservience and violence, and finally against domination by reactionary or controlling minorities. Two of the most important social advances we have made, although they were seen initially as being utopian, are the fights against slave labour and the legal use of torture. Social movements have campaigned over the years against hereditary privilege and for an increasing range of human rights inspired by universalistic ethics, such as votes for all. The working-class movement managed to get some rights for millions enshrined in an inclusive welfare state (see *Welfare*). More recently new standards of tolerance and freedom have been gained as a result of feminism, the struggle against racism and child labour, demands for children's rights, education and leisure, as well as for freedom of sexual choice and the defence of minorities. Finally, representative democracy was also an important achievement, especially when participatory democracy was promoted. All these represent advances over minority privilege and domination by elites.

In the last three decades, this resistance has suffered a number of setbacks. Concretely, there has been an increase in the concentration of wealth and in the manipulation of public opinion by the media, while a selfish and predatory individualism seeks to relegate the idea of a libertarian society to oblivion. Nevertheless, this setback is surely only temporary, because the utopian impulse is not time-bound and the dream of liberty is permanent. Two telling examples illustrate the return of the *principle of hope*: the Global Social Forums held since 2001 and the proliferation of non-capitalist economic initiatives.

A superficial reading of the facts reveals an oppressive world controlled by economic despotisms and powerful minorities, one that promotes apathy, subservience and alienated conformity. But beneath the surface, the will to overcome remains, along with the desire to live in a cosmopolitan, creative and global society whose guiding principles are fraternity and equality. The libertarian spirit and new forms of social mobilization are constantly re-emerging. Another world is possible . . .

Further reading

Amin, A. (2009) *The Social Economy*. Zed Books, London.
Bloch, E. (1986) *The Principle of Hope*. MIT Press, Cambridge, MA.
Boutinet, J-P. (1990) *Anthropologie du projet*. PUF, Paris.

Cattani, A. D. et al. (2009) *Dicionário internacional da outra economia.* Almedina, Coimbra.

Gramsci, A. (1994) Unions and Councils. In Bellamy, R. and Geuss, R. (eds) *Gramsci: Pre-prison Writings,* Cambridge University Press, Cambridge, pp. 115–20.

Lenin, V. I. (1917) The eve of revolution. In *The State and Revolution: Ch. 2 The Experience of 1848–51,* [online]. Available at: http://www.marxists.org/archive/lenin/works/1917/staterev/ch02.htm#s1.

Parker, M. et al. (2007) *The Dictionary of Alternatives.* Zed Books, London.

Riot-Sarcey, M. et al. (2002) *Dictionnaire des Utopies.* Larousse, Paris.

Wainwright, H. (2003) *Reclaim the State: Experiments in Popular Democracy.* Verso, London.

Wallerstein, I. et al. (2008) *El futuro del Foro Social Mundial.* Icaria, Barcelona.

INDEX